USING DSM-IV:
A CLINICIAN'S GUIDE
TO PSYCHIATRIC DIAGNOSIS

USING DSM-IV:
A CLINICIAN'S GUIDE
TO PSYCHIATRIC DIAGNOSIS

by

Anthony L. LaBruzza, M.D.
in collaboration with
José M. Méndez-Villarrubia, M.A.

JASON ARONSON INC.
Northvale, New Jersey
London

Production Editor: Judith D. Cohen

This book was set in 10 point Palacio by TechType of Upper Saddle River, New Jersey, and printed and bound by Haddon Craftsmen of Scranton, Pennsylvania.

Library of Congress Cataloging-in-Publication Data

LaBruzza, Anthony.
   Using DSM-IV : a clinician's guide to psychiatric diagnosis /
Anthony LaBruzza, Jose M. Mendez-Villarrubia
     p. cm.
   Includes bibliographical references and index.
   ISBN: 1-56821-333-6
   1. Mental illness—Diagnosis. 2. Diagnostic and statistical
manual of mental disorders. I. Mendez-Villarrubia, Jose M. II. Title.
   [DNLM: 1. Mental Disorders—diagnosis. 2. Psychiatry—history—
United States. 3. Mental Disorders—classification. WM 141 L127u
1994]
   RC469.L33 1994
   616.89′075—dc20
   DNLM/DLC
   for Library of Congress   94-28534

Manufactured in the United States of America. Jason Aronson Inc. offers books and cassettes. For information and catalog write to Jason Aronson Inc., 230 Livingston Street, Northvale, New Jersey 07647.

Dedication

To my wife Linda and my sons Aaron and David for their enduring love, patience, encouragement, good humor, and support.

—Anthony L. LaBruzza, M.D.

To Msgr. Juan Roldán-Coss for his guidance in my early academic years, Rev. Daniel Kent for his continued support and belief in my potential, and Patrick for his unfailing love and devotion.

—José M. Méndez-Villarrubia, M.A.

CONTENTS

ACKNOWLEDGMENTS

We would like to thank our colleagues and friends who read parts or all of the manuscript and offered valuable suggestions. For their various contributions, our special thanks go to Stephen Atkins, M.D., Andrew Balter, M.D., Howard Benditsky, Ph.D., Linda Liefland, Ph.D., Eric Margolies, Sally Moskowitz, Ph.D., Ellen Nasper, Ph.D., Douglas Nygren, M.S.W., José Raúl Pérez-López, Linda Podd, Ph.D., Boris Rifkin, M.D., Francisco Rodriguez, and José Villa, M.D.

We are grateful to Dr. José Villa for his insights, which contributed much to our understanding of cultural issues in working with Hispanic clients. Psychoanalyst and child psychotherapist Dr. Sally Moskowitz contributed to the section on childhood disorders by reviewing the text and offering many helpful suggestions. Dr. Howard Benditsky was helpful in critically reviewing the chapter on the mental status examination. Our editor at Jason Aronson Inc., Dr. Michael Moskowitz, was a delightful collaborator in the process of writing this book.

We also wish to thank the following people for permission to quote from their work. Dr. Folstein and colleagues allowed us to use the Mini-Mental State Examination. Llewellyn Publications gave permission to adapt sections of an unpublished chapter on human sexuality written by the senior author and scheduled to appear in a book by Llewellyn edited by Noel Tyl in late 1994. Rita Haynes and her colleagues (P. J. Resnick, K. C. Dougherty, and S. E. Althof) allowed us to quote from their article on the use of proverbs in the mental status examination. The editors of *DSM-IV* were kind enough to permit us to reproduce the GAF Scale and to quote various passages from *DSM-IV* throughout this text.

Finally, we thank each other for the mutual support, respect, collaboration, and friendship that made this volume possible.

Anthony L. LaBruzza, M.D.
José M. Méndez-Villarrubia, M.A.

PREFACE

"Must the clinician himself be partitioned into healer *and* scientist; can he not be a whole person who is a scientific healer or a healing scientist?"

Alvan Feinstein (1967), *Clinical Judgment*, p. 293

This book is a survey of the history of American psychiatric diagnosis and is intended for use with the *Diagnostic and Statistical Manual of Mental Disorders, Fourth Edition (DSM-IV)* of the American Psychiatric Association. The authors place *DSM-IV* in the broad historical perspective of Western medicine and diagnosis. *DSM-IV* is empirical and atheoretical; this book tries to show the strengths, weaknesses, and potential abuses of the *DSM-IV* approach to psychiatric diagnosis. *DSM-IV* and its precursors, *DSM-III* and *DSM-III-R*, have eliminated the psychodynamic perspective that had dominated psychiatry until the 1970s. One of the dangers of training new generations of mental health professionals in the *DSM-IV* system is its exclusive focus on clusters of observable signs and symptoms rather than on getting to know the person who suffers the cluster of symptoms. The principal advantage of *DSM-IV* is that it provides a reliable system of diagnosis that had been lacking in American psychiatry for many years.

The goal of the authors in writing this book is to give the reader a balanced point of view from which to make the best use of the *DSM-IV* diagnostic system while retaining the psychodynamic emphasis on getting to know the person who presents with a mental disorder. Our work is also in keeping with the spirit of the *DSM-IV*, which has acknowledged the need to become more culturally relevant than its predecessors. Both authors have extensive experience working with a large Hispanic population in Bridgeport, Connecticut, and have repeatedly been confronted with the problems and dilemmas of making culturally sensitive psychiatric diagnoses. The authors have included a lengthy chapter on assessing Hispanic clients and on the prototypic folk illness category of *ataque de nervios*.

The material in this text is based on *DSM-IV* (1994), on the March 1993 Draft of *DSM-IV* criteria, on the extensive literature about cultural issues and psychiatric diagnosis, and on the many journal articles that have chronicled the development of *DSM-IV*. The fourth edition of the APA's *Diagnostic and Statistical Manual* is a remarkable document, reflecting six years of work by more than a thousand individuals. In its almost 900 pages of text, *DSM-IV* is the largest diagnostic manual in the history of American psychiatry. We hope that our efforts will contribute to the reader's enjoyment and judicious use of this latest development in psychiatric nosology.

1

The Sun, the Moon, and Psychiatric Diagnosis: *DSM-IV* in Mythological Perspective

"If you have a mythology in which the metaphor for the mystery is the father, you are going to have a different set of signals from what you would have if the metaphor for the wisdom and mystery of the world were the mother."

Joseph Campbell, *The Power of Myth* (1988)

The significance of Joseph Campbell's comment hit home one snowy evening at Christmastime in 1976. The senior author of this book was the psychiatric resident on duty at the Yale New Haven Hospital Emergency Department when the police brought in an agitated woman who had been roaming the downtown New Haven area, ranting about religious themes. The woman appeared hyperactive, driven, and disorganized. Her speech was loud, pressured, and slightly hostile. She appeared to be hallucinating. For our purposes, the salient part of the interview went something like this:

Woman: I must do God's will.
Psychiatrist: Are you hearing God's voice?
Woman: God tells me what to do.
Psychiatrist: Is He speaking to you now? What does He tell you to do?
Woman (glaring): God tells me I must do Her will. She wants me to bring about peace on earth.

The psychiatrist stood corrected by this grandiose hypomanic woman for whom God was female. He realized how he had introduced his own bias about the gender of the deity into the psychiatric interview. He understood more clearly how cultural influences can color one's perception of clinical material.

Because diagnosis is always influenced by culture, we begin this chapter by trying to place *DSM-IV* in the broad perspective of Western history and culture. We agree with the philosopher who said that those who do not understand their history are condemned to repeat it. Our discussion of this topic will be selective and necessarily incomplete.

We (*Homo sapiens*) are classifying animals. From the dawn of recorded history, our mythology, folklore, and religious texts have chronicled various typologies of human character and behavior. Every system of classification is, of course, culture-bound and suffused with the zeitgeist of its age. The Fourth Edition of the *Diagnostic and Statistical Manual of Mental Disorders* (*DSM-IV* 1994) is no exception.

Western civilization owes its existence to the discovery of agriculture in the Near East, in the region from Iran to Palestine, around the ninth millennium B.C. So long as early humans were simply nomads who hunted or consumed wild fruits and vegetables, an enduring society was not necessary. The switch to farming and the breeding of livestock produced a paradigm shift in world view.

Farmers needed to predict and control natural forces, and these early agrarian humans found it imperative to study and classify nature. With an eye toward the cultivation of their crops, these settlers began living for future objectives rather than merely existing as nomads in the present moment. The mythology of these civilizations, founded upon agriculture and the breeding of animals, worshiped the fertility goddess who assumed archetypal significance in the life of the spirit.

Mythologist Joseph Campbell (1964) points out that the basic motifs of both Occidental and Oriental mythology derive predominantly from the mythology of the Bronze Age inhabitants of the Near East. Around 3500 B.C., these patient toilers of the earth, farmers and breeders living in self-sustaining villages, invented the refined tools of civilization: the alphabet, writing, recorded history, mathematics, architecture, systematized religion, scientific observation and recording of data, and the art of government. The mythological substrate of this Levantine culture was Mother Nature, the bountiful goddess Earth.

According to Campbell (1964), from 3500 to 2300 B.C., the Sumerian civilization regarded the Great Goddess as "a metaphysical symbol: the arch personification of the power of Space, Time, and Matter, within whose bound all beings arise and die" (p. 7). Two fundamental symbols of the mother goddess were the serpent and the moon: the serpent because it sloughs its skin, and the moon because it waxes and wanes in an endless cycle of death and rebirth. The moon and also the bull, whose horns assume the shape of the crescent moon, are ancient symbols of fecundity. The art of the early mythology of Sumer represents divinity equally and without bias in both masculine and feminine forms.

About 1250 B.C., at the end of the Bronze Age and the dawn of the Iron Age, violent tribes of nomadic warriors burst upon the scene, causing a radical reworking of the prevailing lunar mythology, a paradigm shift in world view. The myths of Greece and the Old and New Testaments of the Bible chronicle the male-dominated mythology of these iron-wielding bellicose patriarchs.

Campbell called this shift from the pre–Iron Age lunar mythology of the goddess to a patriarchal warrior male god mythology *solarization*. Replacing the serpent and the moon, the prevailing mythological symbols became the sun god and the mighty phallus in all its disguised forms. Moral goodness was now defined by the deeds of the solar phallic hero, executed with force of muscle and intellect in the tough objective light of day. At the same time the soft, tender, lunar, feminine forces of night, of the unconscious, of darkness and ambiguity, assumed a sinister dimension of danger and evil. The ruling solar patriarchs needed to revise mythology to secure their power base and to mask their hidden fear of the feminine maternal matrix.

Since the dawn of the Iron Age, there has been a tension between solar and lunar mythologies. This tension between sun and moon, light and dark, objective and subjective, conscious and unconscious, logic and intuition, solarization and lunarization, hard and soft, masculine and feminine, penis and vagina, has pervaded Western culture and plays itself out in the development of *DSM-IV*. Even the symbol of the medical profession, the caduceus, a solar phallic staff around which are entwined two lunar serpents, carries this mythological charge. The symbol of the physician suggests that the power to heal the sick must blend the mysterious internal lunar maternal forces with the objective solar executive function in the outer world.

We owe much of what we value in Western civilization to the nomadic patriarchs who revised the earlier symbolic system of the lunar goddess, replacing it with the mythology of the sun god (Louis 1991). The objective rational study of the world in terms of observable data began with the ancient Greeks, who laid the groundwork for modern science.

The fifth century B.C. witnessed some of the most remarkable advances in rational thinking in recorded history. During this period Hippocrates (460–355 B.C.), the father of medicine, developed a diagnostic system that divided personalities (now coded on Axis II of *DSM-IV*) into four types based on the theory of the four elements: earth, air, fire, and water. The four elements became the theoretical underpinning of the diagnostic system based on the twelve signs of the zodiac. Until the seventeenth century, Western physicians in medical school had learned, in the absence of modern laboratory tests, how to consult the horoscopes of their patients as an aid to diagnosis. Entire volumes were written on how to interpret decumbiture charts—that is, horoscopes cast for the moment the patient fell ill.

Medieval alchemist-physicians, like Paracelsus, modified Hippocrates' typology into a doctrine of four humors to account for differences in human temperament. The four humors originated in the Greek idea of four basic qualities of nature: heat, cold, moisture, and dryness. The doctrine of humors provided an explanation for medical and psychiatric disorders. According to medieval physiology, the human body contains four fluids (humors): red blood, white phlegm, yellow choler, and black bile. The relative proportion of these humors determines a person's constitutional type: sanguine, phlegmatic, choleric, or melancholic. An imbalance of humors causes various disorders or disease states.

For example, an abundance of red blood produces a sanguine, joyful temperament associated with warmth, moisture, a sweet taste, and the element air. An excess of yellow choler gives rise to a choleric, combative, fiery temperament associated with hotness, dryness, and a salty taste. Too much white, watery phlegm results in a phlegmatic temperament characterized by subtle and delicate moods and associated with coldness, moisture, and a bitter taste. Finally, an excess of earth constitutes a dark, melancholic temperament characterized by heaviness and brooding and associated with coolness, dryness, and a sour taste.

The doctrine of the four humors held sway in Western medical practice for centuries and continues to pervade our language. Fifteenth century Englishman Robert Burton, in his *The Anatomy of Melancholy*, suggested that the choleric angry humor derives from the gallbladder, whereas the melancholic (meaning "black choler") humor comes from the spleen. We still speak of melancholic moods, cold-blooded killers, and choleric, splenetic, and galling persons. Even *DSM-III* (1980) and *DSM-IV* include criteria for diagnosing melancholia as part of a major depressive disorder. Other remnants of the theory of humors survive in the modern notion of an imbalance of neurotransmitters as the substrate of certain psychiatric disorders.

Another idea derived from Hippocrates is the concept of mental illness as a disease of the brain. Hippocrates was a citizen of the patriarchal Greek culture of the fifth century B.C. Writing about epilepsy, he introduced the concept of psychiatric illness into medicine by challenging the prevailing belief that epilepsy was a "sacred disease" originating in supernatural forces. Hippocrates wrote that, from the brain, "come joys, delights, laughter, and sports; and sorrows, griefs, despondency, and lamentations. . . . And by the same organ we become mad and delirious, and fears and terrors assail us, some by night and some by day. . . . All these things we endure from the brain when it is not healthy."

Hippocrates is called the "father of medicine." We shall see in the next chapter that, in our solar patriarchal culture, there are many fathers but few mothers in the history of Western medicine and psychiatry. We turn next to the precursors of *DSM-IV* in the diagnostic systems of nineteenth and twentieth century American psychiatry.

2

Precursors of *DSM-IV* in Nineteenth- and Twentieth-Century Psychiatry in the United States

"As a rule we disbelieve all facts and theories for which we have no use."

William James, *The Will to Believe*

This chapter continues our effort to put the development of American psychiatric taxonomy, and especially *DSM-III* and its progeny, *DSM-IV*, in historical perspective. Our focus shifts from issues of mythology in Western culture to the psychiatric climate in Europe and the United States that influenced diagnostic thinking in the United States.

During the American Colonial period, there were few resources available for the treatment of mentally ill citizens. Some of those suffering from mental disorders were fortunate enough to receive care from their families; others were neglected, abused, exploited, sold into slavery, or confined to almshouses, workhouses, or prisons.

In reaction to this climate of abuse, neglect, and oppressive confinement of the mentally ill, there arose the movement of asylum psychiatry, spanning roughly the years from 1800 through 1860. Physicians dedicated to the care of the mentally ill began to treat patients in specially designed mental hospitals called insane asylums. The prevailing mode of therapy was the so-called "moral treatment" of the early nineteenth century grounded in a humanistic, humanitarian tradition of respect for those suffering with severe mental disorders. The crusader Dorothea L. Dix (1802–1887) championed the cause of the mentally ill and promoted institutionalization of psychiatric patients for humane treatment.

Benjamin Rush (1745–1813), the father of American psychiatry and one of the signers of the Declaration of Independence, introduced moral treatment at the Pennsylvania Hospital in Philadelphia. Rush recommended both somatic and psychological therapies for his patients. In his *Medical Inquiries and Observations upon the Diseases of the Mind* (1812), Rush located the cause of madness in the blood vessels of the brain. The patients treated in the asylum were those suffering the most severe and disabling forms of mental disorder.

During this era of moral treatment and asylum psychiatry, the 1840 United States census, which sought to gather statistics on the U.S. population, had at its disposal only a single category for mental disorders. The 1840 census classified people as either sane or as suffering from "idiocy/insanity," what we would now call psychotic or major mental disorders. The status of classification of mental disorders in the United States in the mid-nineteenth century was a step backward from even the simple tripartite system of the sixteenth-century Swiss physician Paracelsus, who distinguished three types of mental disorders: those caused by poisoning (vesania), those caused by the phases of the moon (lunacy), and those caused by heredity (insanity).

Henri Ellenberger (1974), a historian of psychiatry, labels the years from 1860 to 1920 the period of the university psychiatric clinic. During these years the focus of psychiatric activity shifted from moral therapy in the asylum to treatment, teaching, and research in university psychiatric clinics. Ongoing psychiatric research and a growing understanding of brain anatomy prompted the development of a more refined diagnostic system.

By the time of the 1880 census, there were seven categories of mental disorder in use in the United States: dementia, dipsomania (alcoholism), epilepsy, mania, melancholia, monomania, and paresis. The 1880 U.S. classification system was not much of an advance over that of ancient Greece and Rome, which differentiated among five phenomenological categories: epilepsy, hysteria, melancholia, mania, and phrenitis.

Many of the pioneers of modern psychiatry flourished in the era of the university psychiatric clinic. Wilhelm Griesinger (1817–1868), the founder of German university psychiatry, took an organic view of mental illness as a disease of the brain. Following the lead of their medical colleagues, who were discovering the origins of medical illness in cell pathology, psychiatrists sought the causes of mental illness in the pathology of the nervous system.

The Greek word *nosos* means disease, and the English word *nosology* means the classification of diseases. Emil Kraepelin (1855–1926), director of the Research Institute of Psychiatry in Munich, introduced a major revision of psychiatric nosology. Well versed in neuroanatomy and experimental psychology, Kraepelin clarified the nosological confusion about insanity. Kraepelin's approach was to statistically record the signs, course, and outcome of clinical syndromes experienced by patients. One of his major goals was to identify the combination of symptoms that would best predict the outcome of an illness. Kraepelin is the spiritual father of the current *DSM-III* and *DSM-IV* classification systems.

Using a careful study of the symptom presentation and life course of psychotic patients, Kraepelin in 1899 divided the endogenous psychotic disorders into two major categories: manic-depressive psychosis (formerly called circular madness) and dementia praecox (now called schizophrenia). He further divided dementia praecox into hebephrenic, catatonic, and paranoid subtypes. Gone was the simple dichotomy of sane versus insane used in the 1840 census. There were now several types of insanity with differing presentations, life courses, and long-term prognoses. Mania and melancholia, which had previously been treated as separate illnesses, were now combined into one disease entity.

True to the spirit of German university psychiatry, Kraepelin believed that mental disorders were rooted in underlying brain pathology. He had trained in the laboratory of German psychologist Wilhelm Wundt and applied Wundt's descriptive behavioral techniques to the objective study of persons with mental illness. Kraepelin's approach is fundamentally behavioral and descriptive—that is, mythologically solar—and Kraepelin became the guiding light of the authors of *DSM-III* and *DSM-IV*.

Kraepelin's approach to nosology, like that of all of modern medicine, has its origins in England in the work of Thomas Sydenham (1624–1689), the father of modern medical nosology. Sydenham applied the burgeoning ideas of modern science and experimental investigation to classifying the illnesses of his medical patients. He contributed the concept of discrete disease entities characterized by clusters of signs and symptoms that follow a natural course and have a particular outcome and prognosis.

Sydenham, an astute clinician, meticulously studied his patients' disorders. He became aware of the frequency of neurotic and hysterical symptoms among his medical patients regardless of their gender. He refuted the popular notion that hysteria (from the Greek *hystera* meaning uterus—hence the disease of the wandering uterus) could only occur in women. Sydenham documented a host of hysterical symptoms in men and children as well as in his female clients.

Another Englishman, the brilliant neurologist Hughlings Jackson (1834–1911), contributed the notion of a hierarchy of functions of the nervous system. Impressed with Darwin's theory of evolution, Jackson theorized that mental structures became increasingly differentiated, reaching higher levels of function through natural selection.

Jackson regarded mental and nervous disorders as dissolutions or regressions to older, more primitive, less sophisticated levels of function. A corollary to Jackson's theory is the idea of positive and negative symptoms of a disorder. Positive symptoms result from the activation of lower-level functions that had previously been inhibited or inactive. Negative symptoms derive from a loss or deficit of higher functioning. For example, Jackson might regard schizophrenic hallucinations as positive symptoms and schizophrenic apathy or withdrawal as negative symptoms of the disorder.

French psychiatrists and neurologists became fascinated with the power of suggestion and hypnosis, thus shifting some of the focus of psychiatry to the often less severe, nonpsychotic disorders. What we now call dissociative disorders used to be termed hysteria.

French neurologist Jean-Martin Charcot (1825–1893) studied hysterical stigmata, hysterogenous zones, and *la belle indifference* of so-called hysterical patients. He hypothesized that often a sexual trauma spawned ideas and feelings that became unconscious (*condition seconde*) and produced the hysterical symptom. Using hypnosis, Charcot was able to reproduce and to cure patients of hysterical symptoms. Charcot believed that hypnosis was an artificially induced morbid condition, a neurosis, occurring only in hysterical persons with an underlying organic diathesis (congenital predisposition).

Disagreeing with Charcot about who might be hypnotizable, French internist Hippolyte Bernheim (1840–1919) of the Nancy school showed that anyone open to suggestion could undergo hypnosis. Bernheim depathologized hypnosis by universalizing the idea of hypnotizability. He refuted Charcot's notion that only hysterical patients, whose disorder lay in some form of brain abnormality, could undergo hypnosis.

Viennese neurologist Sigmund Freud, rooted in the German university psychiatry tradition, studied in France under Charcot in 1886 and under Bernheim in 1889. He struggled in his own mind with the dispute between Charcot and Bernheim over hypnotizability. Freud concluded that a serious study of hypnosis would shed light on the psychological laws governing the normal mental life of healthy individuals (Gay 1988).

In 1896 Freud coined the term *psychoanalysis* to describe his method of treating neurotic disorders. Freud eventually freed himself from the use of hypnosis in therapy and replaced it with the method of free association to enter the lunar world of the dynamic unconscious. Working primarily with nonpsychotic individuals, Freud developed a theory of neuroses and classified them into hysterical, obsessive, and phobic types.

Freud proposed a method to classify mental illness based on his theory of stages of psychosexual development. In this theory, an inner conflict about a drive renders that drive unconscious through the mechanisms of defense. Usually the sexual drives are involved in the conflict because their expression in childhood would produce fear, anxiety, retribution, or guilt. Repression or other defense mechanisms banish the forbidden urge to the unconscious, where, nonetheless, it remains active and seeks expression.

In Freud's theory, neurotic symptoms are the conscious but disguised manifestations of these repressed unconscious drives. What remains in the conscious (solar) mind is a mnemonic symbol of an unconscious (lunar) conflict associatively linked to hidden memories of forbidden wishes or traumatic experiences. A neurosis will develop later in life when an inner conflict reawakens the rudimentary neurosis of childhood.

Freud believed that one particular sexual conflict was universal: the Oedipus complex. According to Freud, all children pass through a stage in which they desire exclusive possession of one parent as a sex object to the exclusion of the other parent. The little boy's desire, for example, to get rid of daddy so that he can have mommy to enjoy all by himself creates a strong conflict in the boy's mind. Eventually the boy may fear daddy as a powerful rival who might even cut off his penis in retaliation. Freud saw such castration anxiety as a powerful factor in male neurosis as well as in cultural stereotypes of masculinity, such as bigger and better weapons, powerful cars, big muscles, erect monuments, and the like. Apparently it is no accident that the Washington Monument is a giant phallic tower, symbolizing the potency of the father of our country.

The authors of *DSM-III* would later reject Freud's classification of neuroses because Freud presupposes an origin (etiology) of the disorders in the dynamic unconscious. In mythological terms, we might say that Freud brought about the lunarization of psychiatry in the first two-thirds of the twentieth century, whereas *DSM-III* represents the solarization of psychiatry in the final three decades of the 1900s.

While Freud was active in Vienna, the Swiss-born Adolf Meyer (1866–1950) became the most influential psychiatrist in the United States. Meyer's approach, termed *psychobiology*, emphasized a holistic view of the patient through a thorough biographical review of the individual's life history and development. Meyer was a pioneer of the modern community mental health movement, advocating the moving of mental patients out of isolated state asylums and back into the community.

Meyer viewed psychiatric disorders as faulty reactions to life's stressors. The first edition of the American Psychiatric Association's (APA) *Diagnostic and Statistical Manual* (*DSM-I* 1952) was a Meyerian document that represented mental disorders as reactions of the person to psychosocial stressors.

Meyer's views gained support from the psychiatric experience of the two World Wars in which even previously mentally healthy individuals appeared to break down under the extreme stress of combat. The idea, derived from wartime psychiatry, that every person has a breaking point became a cornerstone of crisis intervention theory and the community mental health movement.

Strongly influenced by Meyer's ideas, Karl Menninger was another psychiatric leader of this period. Based on his experiences in World War II, Menninger wrote a book, *The Vital Balance* (1963), in which he discussed a unitary concept of mental disorder as the result of a failure to adapt to the environment. Menninger's treatment model emphasized the psychodynamic meaning and understanding of the patient's symptoms. This emphasis on adaptation to the environment and the meaning of symptoms blurred the distinction between psychopathology and mental normality. Menninger also drew attention to the dehumanizing aspects of psychiatric labeling that could be employed impersonally for social control rather than for providing humane treatment to individuals.

Meyer died in 1950. Because prevailing psychiatric opinion moved away from the view of mental disorders as adaptive reactions and toward the concept of discrete psychiatric disease entities, his ideas gradually fell out of vogue. Mainstream psychiatry no longer accepted Meyer's dictum that mental disorders represented reactions of the personality to biopsychosocial factors. *DSM-II* (1968) consciously and deliberately eradicated the Meyerian term *reaction* from the official APA nomenclature. Meyer had had his moment in the sun.

The APA's *Diagnostic and Statistical Manuals* are an outgrowth of a movement that began in the 1920s to standardize American medical terminology and nosology. Until the 1920s various U.S. medical centers and teaching hospitals used their idiosyncratic diagnostic categories based upon the types of patients they treated and the prior training of their medical staff. Even within the same agency, several different classification systems could be in use: one for clinical work, another for disability determinations, and yet a third for statistical purposes. Such a system of local-color nosology made communication across medical centers at times difficult and multi-site standardized research impossible.

In 1928 the New York Academy of Medicine held a National Conference on Nomenclature of Diseases to address the problem of a lack of a standardized diagnostic terminology. A series of conferences and studies ensued and led to the publication, in 1932, of the first edition of *The Standard Classified Nomenclature of Disease (SCND)*, which went through several revisions before being supplanted by the *International Classification of Diseases (ICD)*, now in its tenth revision *(ICD-10)*.

The 1932 document on standardized nomenclature focused on the severe mental disorders demonstrated by patients admitted to public mental hospitals. The occurrence of less severe psychiatric disorders among soldiers in World War II necessitated the development of a broader classification system. Military psychiatrists using the *Standard Classified Nomenclature of Disease* system in World War II had no way to classify 90 percent of the cases they treated!

The U.S. Navy in 1944 and the U.S. Army in 1945 expanded the psychiatric nosology to describe the types of psychiatric disorders occurring among servicemen during the war. In 1946 the Veterans Administration, influenced by the Army's overhaul of the *Standard Nomenclature*, developed a more comprehensive psychiatric nosology. In 1948, *ICD-6*, borrowing from the Veterans Administration nosology and for the first time in an *ICD*, included its own section on mental disorders, encompassing ten types of psychosis, nine psychoneuroses, and seven disorders of character, behavior, and intelligence.

There were now several distinct but related systems of psychiatric nosology in use in the United States. In the late 1940s clinicians continued to find themselves using different diagnostic systems for different purposes. This plethora and diversity of nomenclatures prompted the American Psychiatric Association (APA) to set up a Committee on Nomenclature and Statistics to review the competing taxonomies. This committee contributed the chapter on psychiatric diagnosis for the 1951 edition of the *Standard* and also prepared the first edition of *DSM* (*Diagnostic and Statistical Manual, Mental Disorders*), published by the APA in 1952.

Discrepancies of nomenclature existed between the clinically oriented American *DSM-I* of 1952 and the international statistical classification system, *ICD-6*, of 1948. These incompatibilities persisted in the 1955 revision, *ICD-7*. Between 1960 and 1966 the World Health Organization sponsored a collaborative effort to address cultural disparities in diagnosis and to develop an internationally agreed upon psychiatric nosology. The results of this international collaborative effort became the "Mental Disorders" chapter of the eighth revision of *ICD* (*ICD-8*) in 1968.

The revisions of psychiatric nosology on the international scene also prompted the APA to prepare a revision of *DSM-I*. To this end, in 1965, the APA reconvened its Committee on Nomenclature and Statistics. In spite of the wish to coordinate *DSM-II* with *ICD-8*, some disparities between American and international diagnostic customs remained.

DSM-II represented a significant change in American psychiatric nosology, namely, an effort to revive the predynamic, descriptive Kraepelinian disease model of diagnosis of the turn of the century. The APA committee deliberately tried to expunge any diagnostic terms that implied a particular theory of etiology. Like the Soviets rewriting history, the APA eradicated all mention of Meyerian "reactions" from the manual.

In eliminating Meyer's idea of mental disorder stemming from a person's "reaction sets" to the environment, *DSM-II* rephrased the definition of mental disorders "as if they were tangible and distinct entities" (Millon 1986, p. 36). Mental patients were no longer reacting adaptively to stressors and developmental challenges; now, like their medical patient counterparts, mental patients were suffering from distinct diseases. Some have called this shift in nosology the remedicalization of American psychiatry. More cynical critics have termed the modern changes in psychiatric classification the dehumanization of psychiatry.

Because psychoanalysts in 1968 were still powerful in American psychiatry, the psychoanalytic diagnoses in *DSM-II* (e.g., neuroses, psychobiologic disorders, etc.) survived this first round of expurgation of theory-based nomenclature. The full Kraepelinian solarization of American psychiatric nosology would not occur until the publication of *DSM-III* in 1980.

3

DSM-III and the Remedicalization of American Psychiatry

"Is it possible to develop toward your computer the same attitude of the chieftain who said that all things speak of God?"

Joseph Campbell, *The Power of Myth* (1988)

In this chapter we will look at some of the forces—social, political, economic, cultural, intellectual, religious, and scientific—that led to the development of *DSM-III*, and we will consider some of the consequences of this changing diagnostic paradigm. The third version of the *Diagnostic and Statistical Manual of Mental Disorders* of the American Psychiatric Association represents a return to the medical model and to Kraepelinian descriptive psychiatry. Mitchell Wilson (1993), in a scholarly review of the development of *DSM-III* published in the *American Journal of Psychiatry*, concluded that:

> from the end of World War II until the mid-1970s, a broadly conceived biopsychosocial model, informed by psychoanalysis, sociological thinking, and biological knowledge, was the organizing model for American psychiatry. However, the biopsychosocial model did not clearly demarcate the mentally well from the mentally ill, and this failure led to a crisis in the legitimacy of psychiatry in the 1970s. [p. 399]

The American Psychiatric Association responded to this crisis with the publication of *DSM-III* in 1980. In *DSM-III*, the official psychiatric diagnostic methodology renounced psychodynamic formulations and returned to a pre-dynamic Kraepelinian method of descriptive psychiatry. According to Wilson (1993), *DSM-III* represents a "significant narrowing of psychiatry's clinical gaze" (p. 400). With the official adoption of *DSM-III*, American psychiatry shed the biopsychosocial model of the postwar years and adopted a research-oriented medical model.

The reasons for this paradigm shift are legion. A clinical example may illuminate some of the issues. A group of medical students in 1972 participated in the psychiatric evaluation of a young man in the Bronx. The patient, in his early twenties, was brought to the clinic by his family, who complained that he was doing nothing with his life. The immediate precipitant was that the patient had ordered a coffin delivered to the family home because he was fascinated with all things having to do with death. During the clinical interview, the patient, sporting several tattoos and dressed completely in black, grinned like a Cheshire cat as he denied hallucinations, delusions, depressed mood, and suicidal preoccupation.

The medical students were puzzled about the young man's diagnosis. The patient seemed weird and out of the ordinary, but exhibited no signs of overt psychosis. The students searched *DSM-II* to no avail. Finally, they turned to the attending psychiatrist for help. Like Yoda of the movie *Star Wars*, she nodded knowingly and said, "He's clearly schizophrenic." The medical students had no idea how she reached her diagnosis. What kind of private inferences was she making? How was she able to peer into the secret recesses of this patient's mind? At least one of the students (the senior author) hoped that some day he would develop the same kind of psychiatric x-ray vision that would make the mysterious process of psychiatric diagnosis more accessible to ordinary mortals.

Prior to the *DSM-III*, psychiatric diagnosis was notoriously unreliable, and without reliable diagnoses there could be no meaningful psychiatric research. Psychiatrists who trained in the New York City medical schools tended to label almost any patient who exhibited bizarre behavior as schizophrenic. One of the senior author's teachers quipped that the incidence of schizophrenia in the United States varied inversely with the distance from New York City.

The same psychotic patients who received a schizophrenic diagnosis in New York would receive a manic-depressive or character disorder diagnosis in the United Kingdom. Given the advances in psychopharmacologic therapy of these disorders, the implications for providing proper treatment were profound. Furthermore, New York psychiatrists had a bias toward diagnosing schizophrenia in black patients (Professional Staff of the U.S.-U.K. Cross National Project 1974). Other papers in the psychiatric literature demonstrated that the probability that two psychiatrists would agree on the same diagnosis in the 1950s and 1960s was nearly random.

At the same time dramatic court cases publicly pitted psychiatric experts against one another in blatant disagreement about psychiatric diagnoses. Another jarring embarrassment to official psychiatry was the well-known Rosenhan study (1973) entitled "On Being Sane in Insane Places." Rosenhan sent a group of normal subjects to psychiatric hospitals with instructions to complain of hearing a voice saying "thud." All the subjects were hospitalized and received a discharge diagnosis of "schizophrenia in remission" despite normal behavior while in the hospital. As happens with genuine psychiatric patients, the psychiatric label stuck and the discharged normal subjects ran the risk of being viewed as former mental patients (in remission) in the eyes of society.

There was already a growing anti-psychiatry movement in the United States during the antiauthoritarian 1960s. Ken Kesey's novel *One Flew Over the Cuckoo's Nest* (1962), which later became a popular movie, depicted the horrors of life in a mental institution. Demonstrating how psychiatric labeling could be used for social control, Kesey raised questions about the distinction between sanity and insanity and about issues of freedom versus responsibility. In 1961 Thomas Szasz had already questioned the validity of regarding mental disorders as true illnesses in his book *The Myth of Mental Illness*. Szasz, with other anti-psychiatrists and the labeling theorists, viewed psychiatric diagnosis as serving society's desire to control deviant behavior. In 1963 Menninger in *The Vital Balance* lamented the dehumanizing, stigmatizing aspects of psychiatric labeling.

Perhaps the controversy about the disease status of homosexuality best exemplifies the abuses of psychiatric labeling to ensure social control and doctrinal conformity. By the 1960s many mental health professionals espoused the view that homosexuality was not a valid mental illness. Interestingly, Freud in 1935 had taken a similar position when he wrote to a distraught mother about her homosexual son:

> Homosexuality is assuredly no advantage, but it is nothing to be
> ashamed of, no vice, no degradation, it cannot be classified as an
> illness; we consider it to be a variation of the sexual function, produced
> by a certain arrest of sexual development. [quoted in Jones's biography
> of Freud, 1961, pp. 502 –503]

In the late 1960s and early 1970s, a debate arose in psychiatry about the disease status of homosexuality. Gay rights groups were vocal in their opposition to *DSM-II*'s labeling of homosexuality as a disease and lobbied actively to strike it from the diagnostic manual. They argued that most homosexuals experience discomfort not as a result of their sexual orientation, but rather because of widespread discrimination in a homophobic society. The gay community's complaints echoed the words of Shylock in Shakespeare's plea against discrimination in the *Merchant of Venice:*

> Hath not a Jew eyes? hath not a Jew hands, organs, dimensions, senses,
> affections, passions? fed with the same food, hurt with the same weap-
> ons, subject to the same diseases, healed by the same means, warmed
> and cooled by the same winter and summer, as a Christian is? If you
> prick us do we not bleed? if you tickle us do we not laugh? if you poison
> us do we not die? and if you wrong us, shall we not revenge? If we are
> like you in the rest, we will resemble you in that. [III:1]

Like Shakespeare's Shylock, gay rights proponents objected to the use of diagnosis to codify societal and religious prejudice and stressed the harmful effects of such labeling. They located the cause of the mental anguish of gay men and women in the fabric of society rather than in the neurons of the individual. It was no accident, they argued, that mainstream psychiatry, dominated as it is by affluent white males, was diagnosing the highest rates of psychopathology among blacks, gays, women, and other disadvantaged minorities in American society. As Joseph Campbell (1964) had pointed out, white males have dominated Western society since the dawn of the Iron Age, with its paradigm shift from a matriarchal to a patriarchal mythology.

A web of social, patriarchal, and religious biases had clouded the scientific objectivity of diagnostic nosology. As far back as 1957, research had shown that mental health professionals were unable to differentiate between projective test responses of heterosexuals and homosexuals (Hooker 1957). In 1973 the APA board of trustees voted to strike homosexuality from the *DSM-II*. With a single vote the APA cured millions of gay men and women in America of the "mental illness" of homosexuality. What remained of the disease concept of homosexuality in *DSM-II* was a category of "sexual orientation disturbance," which later became "ego-dystonic homosexuality" in *DSM-III* in 1980 and was finally dropped from *DSM-III-R* in 1987.

The critics of psychiatry saw the homosexuality controversy as further evidence that psychiatric diagnosis was inextricably bound with social needs to regulate perceived deviance. Some likened *DSM* to the *Malleus Maleficarum (The Witches' Hammer)*, a 1486 manual by two Dominicans, Jacob Sprenger and Heinrich Kramer, on how to reliably spot the witches among us. Following the papal bull in 1484 in which Pope Innocent VIII actively encouraged the persecution of witches, the world needed a reliable diagnostic manual on how to spot witches in order to prescribe the correct treatment. This fifteenth-century diagnostic manual for witchery is an early example of a reliable but, by most modern standards, invalid nosological system.

The above examples illustrate some of the problems with the psychiatric diagnoses of *DSM-I* and *DSM-II*. In short, psychiatric nosology of the 1950s, 1960s, and 1970s was unreliable, stigmatizing, and prone to cause adverse social and psychological consequences. In many instances psychiatric diagnosis appeared to be primarily an agent of social control.

Furthermore, the psychosocial model, which lay behind *DSM-I* and *DSM-II*, placed mental illness at the extreme end of a continuum with mental health. The psychosocial model did not clearly demarcate psychopathology from normal mental processes. Meyer regarded mental disorders as failures of adaptation and reactions to life's stressors. Anyone could develop a mental disorder under extreme conditions.

In a similar vein, Harry Stack Sullivan, of the Washington/ Baltimore interpersonal school of psychiatry, placed everyone on a continuum when he stated in a wonderful clinical dictum, "Man is more simply human than otherwise" (quoted in Salzman 1975, p. 45). This blurring of the boundary between mental health and mental illness helped humanize the psychiatric patient, but at the same time posed practical problems from the point of view of economics, hard science, and therapeutics.

In the 1960s most insurance companies covered mental health

services on a par with medical services. As the cost of health care began to rise, the insurance industry sought ways to reduce their expenditures. During the 1970s indemnity insurers began to reduce both the number of psychiatric visits covered and the amount paid for mental health visits to a mere fraction of what they would pay for a medical visit. By 1993 only 2 percent of private insurance plans offered parity with physical health benefits for outpatient care, and only 20 percent offered parity with physical health benefits for inpatient care.

Insurance companies viewed mental health coverage as a bottomless pit and justified their cutbacks by citing the unreliability of psychiatric diagnosis, the lack of clarity about indications of treatment modalities, the absence of outcome studies, and the question of clinical accountability. To reimburse a service, the insurance company wanted a reliable diagnosis, a proven treatment method, and a predictable outcome. As fewer and fewer patients were able to pay out of pocket, psychiatrists realized that they had to do the insurance companies' bidding to stay in business. This economic pressure from the insurance industry is one of the factors that helped shape *DSM-III*.

Not only insurers but also mental health professionals lamented the state of psychiatric diagnosis prior to *DSM-III*. In 1970 Samuel B. Guze, in solar mythological fashion, wrote about the need for "toughmindedness" in psychiatric thinking. In 1973 two other solar warriors, Hagop S. Akiskal and William T. McKinney, also fearing the dark side of the psyche, ridiculed the humanistic psychosocial paradigm of psychiatry as "soft-headed" pseudo-psychiatry. The eternal archetypal struggle between hard and soft, light and dark, masculine and feminine, enlightenment and endarkenment, conscious and unconscious, had now constellated itself in the field of American psychiatry.

By 1977 Alan Stone, president of the APA, warned that the ever-broadening scope of psychiatry to social issues and general concern with human welfare (the realm of the lunar mother goddess) had brought the profession to the edge of extinction. There was a sentiment among psychiatric professionals that mainstream psychiatry had to narrow its focus, realign itself with traditional medicine, and make itself able to receive reimbursement for its services if the profession were to survive.

Part of the problem was the lack of research in psychiatry because of its fuzzy distinction between health and mental illness. An objective Kraepelinian diagnostic system could solve that problem. In fact, a group of neo-Kraepelinian psychiatrists at Washington University had already begun work on such a system. Entitled "Diagnostic Criteria for Use in Psychiatric Research," this 1972 paper by J. P. Feighner, E. Robins, S. B. Guze and colleagues became the most cited article in the psychiatric literature of that decade. The psychiatric community quickly nicknamed these the "Feighner criteria," after the first author.

By being explicit, standardized, descriptive, and rule-driven, the Feighner criteria, for fourteen psychiatric disorders, paved the way for increased reliability and empirical validation of psychiatric diagnoses. Feighner and his colleagues took the guesswork out of the morass of psychiatric diagnosis. They allowed no speculation about unconscious motivations or unseen forces in diagnosis; everything was clean, crisp, objective, and neat. To aid in the statistical manipulation of these descriptive psychiatric labels, Joseph L. Fleiss et al. (1972) developed the kappa technique for "quantification of agreement in multiple psychiatric diagnosis." Spitzer, head of the *DSM-III* task force, applied Fleiss's method to the growing body of data being collected on psychopathology.

During the period when psychoanalysis was the only treatment option for most psychiatric problems, the issue of differential diagnosis was, from a practical point of view, only of intellectual significance. In 1949, however, John Cade, an Australian hospital superintendent, gave lithium to manic patients and discovered its anti-manic properties. In 1952 Jean Delay and Pierre Deniker published the results of successful trials of a new drug called chlorpromazine (Thorazine) in psychotic patients. In 1956 George Crane alleviated severe depressions in a group of patients to whom he administered the drug isoniazid, an inhibitor of the enzyme monoamine oxidase (MAO).

The discovery that specific drugs could treat specific psychiatric disorders made differential diagnosis an important practical concern. Unless the doctor made the correct diagnosis, he or she could not prescribe the correct medication and the patient would not get better. Given the impressive success of specific drugs for specific disorders, scientists and medical researchers joined the bandwagon for a more reliable psychiatric nosology. A new economic pressure for the development of a reliable psychiatric classification scheme arose. The pharmaceutical industry, with its enormous wealth, now supported research on diagnoses that would promote the use of its products.

The 1970s saw an explosion of advances in the basic sciences of medicine. An ever increasing understanding of neurobiology together with the impressive therapeutic efficacy of psychotropic medications brought a number of tough-minded Kraepelinian psychiatrists to power in American psychiatry. Substantial research dollars enabled Kraepelinian psychiatrists to gradually wrest control of medical school departments of psychiatry away from the "soft-headed" psychoanalysts and psychobiologists who had dominated American psychiatry for decades. The psychoanalysts' failure to do significant basic science research contributed to their demise.

In a critique of the politics of *DSM-III*, authors Esther D. Rothblum, Laura J. Solomon, and George W. Albee (1986) pointed out how research funding follows the establishment of diagnostic categories. Increased research leads to more funding for further research on the same categories. In this vicious cycle of funding and research, the group that controls the diagnostic system also controls the pocketbook. A researcher whose career and livelihood depend on the existence of a diagnostic category is not likely to change his or her views too radically about the validity of that diagnosis. As Marx and Engels put it, "The ruling ideas of each age have ever been the ideas of its ruling class." The cynical golden rule of economics—he who has the gold rules—is as true in psychiatry as in the rest of life.

As basic science research becomes the dominant force in American psychiatry, the dynamic view of the mind becomes radically altered. The very existence of the mind is questioned, and psychiatry risks becoming a reductionistic study of pathophysiological mechanisms of mental disorders. Gone are the human elements of the doctor–patient relationship. Doctors become technicians who manipulate the data they collect on their patients. Psychiatric treatment becomes the medical equivalent of taking one's car in for a tune-up.

For example, in a recent issue of *Yale Psychiatry* (Fall 1993), Eric J. Nestler, M.D., Ph.D., introduced Yale's new Division of Molecular Psychiatry with a description of his vision for the future of psychiatry:

> A person faces deteriorating function. Family members grow concerned. The person seeks medical attention. After a complete history

and physical exam, the doctor orders laboratory tests, including blood work and diagnostic imaging. On the basis of this information, the doctor establishes a diagnosis. Implicit in the diagnosis is information concerning etiological factors that led to the disease, the correct course of treatment, the natural history of the disease, and the patient's prognosis. [p. 2]

In this vignette, the doctor examines the patient's body, blood, and diagnostic images to determine the etiology of the disease. The human physician is hardly necessary because such data gathering could be done more efficiently by a computer. The physician has become a technician rather than a healer. Computer-like efficiency has replaced bedside manner.

In fact, no technological advance has more significantly influenced the development of *DSM-III* and the way psychiatrists think about mental illness than the personal computer. With the introduction of the personal computer in the 1980s, every respectable scientist could have a computer in the home or office. Computers rapidly crunch numbers, do statistical analyses, and manipulate large volumes of data. The scientists who run the computers are, as a rule, solar rather than lunar thinkers. They value objective measurement, mathematical precision, and reproducible results. Computers are at a loss with subjective, fuzzy, soft information like feelings, wishes, drives, and inner conflicts.

With their new high-tech toys, research scientists went in search of data to feed to their computers. What better place to look than in the *Diagnostic and Statistical Manual?* Because a computer will only manipulate data in precise quantifiable form, it is necessary to design a diagnostic system that is computer friendly. One needs large sets of data to do multivariate analyses, and one needs quantifiable objective *psychometric instruments* (rating scales that measure the psyche numerically) to provide numbers to feed to the computer. Most psychiatric trainees are familiar with the Beck, the Zung, and the Hamilton rating scales.

In subtle and often unacknowledged ways, modern psychiatry's devotion to the computer has determined its conception of the psyche. Computers deal with data, with numbers, with psychometrics, with Chinese menu checklists from *DSM-III*. Computers do not think, do not feel, do not empathize, do not understand; yet computers are rapidly influencing mental health care in the United States.

For example, William Glazer and Geoffrey Gray (1993) have developed *PsychPro*, a computerized "decision-support tool" designed to help the treating doctor and the physician utilization reviewer to allocate the proper level of care to an acutely ill patient. Using *PsychPro*, managed care companies can punch clinical information into their computers and come up with a recommended treatment plan. According to Glazer, emergency room personnel or hospital admissions staff can enter data into their personal computers and draw upon a database of standardized treatment recommendations. Glazer (1993) describes his computer program as follows:

> *PsychPro* is a decision-assistance software program to objectify, standardize and automate psychiatric decision making. It uses a behaviorally based language that quantifies illness severity and allocates care based upon objective behavioral thresholds. This tool was developed to insure reliable and valid clinical guidelines for the assignment of treatment levels for acutely ill psychiatric patients; to reduce unnecessary and ineffective care; to insure that the appropriate intensity of care is provided; and to provide an objective, verifiable audit and database of the clinical decision making process for quality management and outcome research purposes. [p. 8]

As the above quotation demonstrates, computers, because of their influence on psychiatric diagnosis and the delivery of mental health care, are having a major impact on clinical care. Both *DSM-III* and *DSM-IV* are computer-friendly documents and have a potential for misuse by humans who train mental health professionals. The risk is that, by steeping themselves in computer technology, practitioners will not make use of those qualities in clinical care and assessment that are uniquely human.

Recognizing the potential danger of misuse of *DSM-III*, the eminent nosologist Robert Spitzer, chair of the work group to revise the *DSM-III* manual, warned in the introduction to *DSM-III-R* that "making a *DSM-III-R* diagnosis represents only an initial step in a comprehensive evaluation leading to the formulation of a treatment plan" (p. xxvi). Additional information about the patient "will invariably be necessary," Spitzer cautioned, and proper use of the manual requires "specialized clinical training that provides both a body of knowledge and clinical skills" (p. xxix). Spitzer's advice to clinicians is not to lose sight of the forest as they focus on the computer-enhanced details of the individual trees.

However, many psychiatric educators appear not to have heeded Spitzer's wise and reasoned warnings. Morton Reiser, a seasoned teacher and psychoanalyst, recognized the negative influence wrought by *DSM-III* in the way that psychiatric residents were viewing their patients. In an article entitled "Are Psychiatric Educators 'Losing the Mind'?", Reiser (1988) reported that young psychiatrists in training at a prestigious medical center were able to complete their *DSM-III* checklists, arrive at a correct *DSM-III* diagnosis, and prescribe the proper medication, yet fail to reach a meaningful empathic human understanding of the patient. These robot-like presentations of clinical material by psychiatric residents prompted Reiser to lament:

> . . . often there was no answer to such basic questions as why the patient came for treatment at this time and what seemed to be worrying him or her. Most of these residents could and would have learned more about a stranger who was sitting next to them for an hour on an airplane trip than they had learned in these formal psychiatric interviews. Clearly, this lack of curiosity and wish to *understand* must have adversely affected the patient and his or her ability to form a therapeutic relationship. [p. 151]

Clinicians who immerse themselves solely in the categories of *DSM-III* and its revision *DSM-IV* run the risk of disciplining their minds to act like computers. *DSM-III* has been a great boon to research in psychiatry and to the reliable communication of diagnoses, but its use in training mental health professionals is causing adverse consequences. Our model of reality determines what we see. If our primary interest becomes the completion of computer-friendly checklists to arrive at a *Diagnostic and Statistical Manual* diagnosis, we run the risk of becoming a generation of robotlike clinicians doing cookbook psychiatry. As the introduction to *DSM-IV* states, "it is important that *DSM-IV* not be applied mechanically by untrained individuals" (p. xxiii), yet it seems that its mechanical application is becoming a standard in psychiatric education.

Like Reiser, Wilson (1993), with whose quote we began this chapter, pointed out how the reification (from the Latin *res* meaning "thing": to treat an abstraction as having substantial existence) of *DSM-III* diagnoses has caused a constriction of:

> the range of what we as clinicians take to be clinically relevant, a narrowing of the content of clinical concern. Personality and the ongoing development of character, unconscious conflict, transference, family dynamics, and social factors are aspects of a clinical case that are deemphasized, while the careful description of symptoms is often taken to be an adequate or even proper assessment of the patient. [p. 408]

The dehumanization of clinical care is not limited to the field of mental health. As computers and laboratory tests have gradually dominated the minds of doctors and other clinicians, there has been an erosion of the teaching and learning of the healing aspects of the doctor–patient relationship. Witnessing these changes in medical education, Lewis Thomas, in his book *The Youngest Science* (1983), stated that, if he were beginning his medical career in the 1980s, "I would be apprehensive that my real job, caring for sick people, might soon be taken away, leaving me with the quite different occupation of looking after machines" (p. 60)

Mental health professionals also run the risk of ultimately becoming caretakers of machines. Mental health clinicians should never forget that patients are more than checklists of observable, publicly visible symptoms. *DSM-III* and *DSM-IV* diagnoses are intentionally superficial in that they focus exclusively on the surface manifestations of mental disorder while deliberately eschewing clinical inference and the depth of unconscious process. A computer interacting with a patient can generate a differential *DSM-IV* diagnosis and produce a clinical report on a par with those presented by psychiatric residents to Dr. Reiser. Only a human being can discuss matters in a person-to-person interview with a client in distress, establish a working alliance, look beneath the surface, and provide an empathic understanding of the life course and current predicament of the other person.

Let us see *DSM* for what it is, namely, a diagnostic and statistical manual to be used for providing labels and compiling statistics about disorders. *DSM-III/IV* has finally enabled American psychiatry to produce reliable, consensually agreed upon diagnostic categories that make it possible to do meaningful psychiatric research. *DSM-III/IV* provides a common language with which to describe the surface manifestations of psychiatric disorder. It is an ever-evolving set of guidelines for making psychiatric diagnoses based on the consensus of expert opinion and with a stated purpose of enhancing diagnostic agreement among clinicians and researchers. Because *DSM-III/IV* is intentionally atheoretical and does not look beneath the surface, clinicians need to look elsewhere to learn how to talk with the troubled people who seek their help. Let us not allow the computer to dictate our conception of what it means to be human.

4

The Goals of *DSM-III*

"*DSM-III* and *DSM-III-R* reflect an increased commitment in our field to reliance on data as the basis for understanding mental disorders."
Robert L. Spitzer and Janet B.W. Williams, *Introduction to DSM-III-R*

As mentioned previously, a paradigm shift in American psychiatric diagnostic thinking occurred with *DSM-III*. Although *DSM-III* is an American document, it has had considerable international influence. The subsequent *DSM-III-R* and *DSM-IV* are revisions and refinements of the *DSM-III* system of classification. In this chapter we will review the explicit goals of *DSM-III* and some of the controversies spawned by this new approach to psychiatric thinking.

According to Gerald Klerman (1986), the *DSM-III* of 1980 represents five innovations in psychiatric nosology, namely:

1. Reliance on descriptive rather than etiologic criteria.
2. The concept of multiple and separate disorders.
3. The use of operational criteria to make diagnoses.
4. Field testing of diagnoses for reliability.
5. Multiaxial diagnostic coding.

The Kraepelinian desire of the APA to adopt a classification system that does not imply a particular theoretical framework was first officially seen in the 1968 expulsion of the Meyerian term *reaction* from the DSM-II. Researchers felt that a nosology based on inferences and theories of causation necessarily prejudges the basis of a disorder without sufficient evidence.

There are many schools of psychopathology, each with competing hypotheses about the causation of mental disorders. Rather than adopt the viewpoint of one theoretical school against the others, the APA decided to limit its diagnostic manual to overt descriptive psychopathology. The *DSM-III* task force left it to the researchers to determine the causes (whether biological, psychological, or social) of psychiatric disorders. *DSM-III* could provide a reliable, objective, and atheoretical way to identify groups of patients with psychiatric disorders for further study. The goal was that, with *DSM-III/IV*, mental health professionals could agree on how to identify a mental disorder while possibly disagreeing on how it came about.

In addition to espousing an overt nondoctrinaire approach and avoiding insupportable theoretical assumptions about causation, the *DSM-III* task force committed itself to a goal of syndromal inclusiveness. While trying to maintain compatibility with *ICD-9*, the *DSM-III* committee simultaneously tried to rely on empirical data and to encompass as many clinical syndromes as were relevant in clinical practice. Each new diagnostic category was to be defined by clear, specific, operational criteria that would separate each syndrome with relative distinctness from the other disorders. The goal of diagnostic specificity lends a cookbook quality to the diagnostic manual.

Such clear specific criteria were consonant with the task force's mission of developing a nosology free of misguided and value-laden implications. To this end the *DSM-III* committee struggled, not always successfully, to devise diagnostic labels using plain, everyday English whenever possible. For example, the simple descriptive term *disorganized* replaced *hebephrenic* as a descriptor of schizophrenia, and *histrionic* supplanted the term *hysteria* (of the uterus), to avoid sexist implications.

The labeling theorists who had criticized the stigmatizing effects of psychiatric diagnosis had clearly left their mark. In its effort to be politically correct, *DSM-III* emphasized that diagnostic labels apply to disorders and not to the suffering individuals. Just as the Church had counseled its congregants to "hate the sin but not the sinner," *DSM-III* advised us to treat the disorder of schizophrenia, but never call the person who suffers that disorder a *schizophrenic*. Simply put, *DSM-III* classifies disorders rather than patients. Furthermore, in deference to the growing consumer movement in psychiatry, the very term *patient* was dropped from the *DSM-III* manual and replaced by the words *person* or *individual*. Because of the noble history of the concept of patienthood in Western medicine, we have opted in this text to use the terms *patient* and *client* interchangeably.

The use of operational criteria to define multiple, separate disorders was partly a response to the anti-psychiatry movement that challenged the validity and reliability of psychiatric diagnosis. With the Chinese menu operational method of selecting so many symptoms from column A, so many from column B, and so on, psychiatric diagnosis became almost as easy and reliable as ordering a meal in a restaurant. In addition, *DSM-III* was the first diagnostic system to be tested by practitioners for reliability in the field. Statistical evidence about symptoms and syndromes helped to resolve disputes about *DSM-III* diagnostic categories and to generate new areas of research in preparation for *DSM-IV*.

The use of operational criteria together with the multiaxial system of *DSM-III* constituted two major innovations that had a significant impact on clinical practice. The authors of *DSM-III* realized that a single diagnosis rarely gave sufficient information about a patient's life and experience. To provide a more comprehensive description of the patient's condition, the *DSM-III* offered five axes to record major psychiatric disorders, developmental or personality disorders, medical problems affecting the psychological state, severity of stressors, and level of functioning.

The five *DSM-III* axes are usually listed in order as follows:

Axis I: Clinical syndromes and V codes for conditions not attributable to a mental disorder that are a focus of clinical attention.

Axis II: Developmental disorders, personality disorders, personality traits, and habitually used defense mechanisms. (In *DSM-IV* the developmental disorders, except for mental retardation, have been moved to Axis I.)

Axis III: Current physical disorders relevant to understanding the case and significant associated physical findings.

Axis IV: Nature and severity of psychosocial stressors.

Axis V: Global assessment of functioning, both current and highest level in the past year.

Yet another innovative but controversial feature of *DSM-III* was the inclusion of decision trees for differential diagnosis. Decision trees are flow charts modeled explicitly after computer programming flow charts found in any computer textbook. Just as the programmer's flow chart tells the computer what sequence of steps to follow to execute a program, the *DSM-III* decision chart tells the human clinician exactly what steps to follow to make a diagnosis. The inclusion of diagnostic flowcharts in *DSM-III* and *DSM-IV* is evidence of the pervasive influence that the personal computer has had on American psychiatric thinking.

According to *DSM-III-R*, the avowed purpose of these decision trees is "to aid the clinician in understanding the organization and hierarchic structure of the classification" (p. 377). Each decision tree begins with a set of clinical features, such as psychotic symptoms, mood disturbances, anxiety, physical complaints, or cognitive disturbances. When one of these clinical features is a prominent aspect of the clinical presentation, the clinician can follow the series of questions to climb the tree. Further and further branches along the tree will rule in or out various disorders.

The decision trees unfortunately convey a sense that the human mind is organized like a computer and that human psychopathology is neatly organized like a computer program into a hierarchy of distinct subprograms. *DSM-III-R* instructs the clinician to "proceed down the tree until a leaf (i.e., a point in a tree with no outgoing branches) is found" (p. 377) and, *voilà*, you have made the diagnosis. Would that life in the real world of clinical practice were so simple! A decision tree presumes that each branch point, where the clinician makes a yes or no decision, will lead down a sequential path to a more specific and differentiated disorder. At the same time, the introduction to *DSM-III-R* states, in contradiction to the underlying assumption behind decision trees, that "there is no assumption that each mental disorder is a discrete entity with sharp boundaries (discontinuity) between it and other mental disorders, or between it and no mental disorder" (p. xxii).

DSM-III, according to Theodore Millon (1986), was "an outgrowth of scholarly debate and empirical test" (p. 43), but it was met with a host of criticisms. Some objected to the fact that *DSM-III*'s goal of syndromal inclusiveness had increased its size tenfold over its predecessors. In addition to faulting its enormous size, there were critics who pointed out that *DSM-III* was an American document that could not easily be used in different cultures. Others saw the document as an imperialistic effort by mainstream psychiatry, in a time of decreasing insurance reimbursement, to secure for itself the mental health marketplace. The most heated controversies, however, were with psychologists who objected to the view of mental disorders as a subset of medical diagnoses and with psychoanalysts who objected to the deletion of the concept of neurosis from the official psychiatric nomenclature (Schacht and Nathan 1977).

In 1975 the *DSM-III* task force was trying to invent a suitable definition of mental disorder for use in the manual. Two prominent members of the task force, Robert Spitzer and his research colleague, Jean Endicott, penned a definition expressing their belief that mental disorders are a subset of medical disorders. Although the committee formally rejected this statement for inclusion in the *DSM-III*, Spitzer and Endicott were such influential forces behind the new manual that many psychologists became upset. Some psychologists denounced this mental disorder/medical disorder phrase as psychiatry's attempt to usurp the psychologist's share of the marketplace. Other psychologists demonstrated in a scholarly fashion the absurdity of viewing all behavioral and psychological disturbances as intrinsically organic. The *DSM-III* task force finally settled on the wording that "each of the mental disorders is conceptualized as a clinically significant behavioral or psychological syndrome" (*DSM III-R*, p. xxii).

Even with the publication of *DSM-IV*, the controversy about medical versus psychological disorders has not completely subsided. The official policy of the *DSM-IV* committee was to steer clear of public policy questions by refusing to label certain diagnoses as medical and others as psychological. Dr. Harvey Ruben, consultant to the APA's joint committee on public affairs, however, has criticized *DSM-IV* for using the term *disorder* rather than *disease* or *illness*. According to Ruben (quoted in *Clinical Psychiatry News* May 1994):

> All other physicians talk about diseases, such as liver disease, kidney disease, and heart disease. Our nomenclature continues to perpetuate our separation from the rest of medicine and makes it sound as if psychiatric illnesses are not real diseases. This kind of stigmatizing perspective affects employers, legislators, and insurance companies and, therefore, our patients. [p. 18]

The controversy about neurosis in *DSM-III* was less easily resolved. The *DSM-III* task force took the official position that any diagnosis grounded in a particular theory about etiology without empirical evidence must be expunged from the manual. Just as *DSM-II* had rid American nosology of Meyerian psychobiology, a goal of *DSM-III* was to eradicate any vestige of Freudian psychoanalysis from American psychiatric diagnosis. No doubt the negative transference of some of the authors of *DSM-III* toward the psychoanalysts who had controlled the academic departments of psychiatry in the 1950s and 1960s played a role in this decision.

Like Saturn cutting off the genitals of his father to wrest control of Mount Olympus, the *DSM-III* task force expunged the term *neurosis* from mainstream American psychiatry. Like the newly castrated father Uranus, the psychoanalytic community winced. The analysts as a group threatened to block the acceptance of *DSM-III* at the May 1979 annual APA Board Meeting. What to do? The *DSM-III* task force cleverly finessed the issue by throwing the analysts a bone. The task force agreed to keep the analyst's favorite word *neurotic* in the manual, but to strip it of any substance.

Henceforth, "neurotic" would only imply a Kraepelinian description rather than a dynamic process. The word "neurotic" would no longer refer to a process involving intrapsychic conflict unsatisfactorily resolved in the unconscious through defense mechanisms and expressed overtly through symptoms in symbolic form. The analysts wimpishly accepted this insipid version of their key concept, and the term "neurotic" in *DSM-III* became but a relic of a once vital force in American psychiatry. Even this compromise was too generous for Donald Klein, a staunchly anti-psychoanalytic member of the *DSM-III* task force, who contemptuously chided his colleagues for not ridding the manual of "neurosis" once and for all. Klein wrote that bowing to political pressure from the psychoanalysts to reinsert the term "neurosis" into *DSM-III* was "unworthy of scientists who are attempting to advance our field via clarification and reliable definition" (cited in Millon 1986, p. 47).

5

From *DSM-III* to
DSM-III-R to *DSM-IV*

"The essence of knowledge is, having it, to apply it; not having it, to confess your ignorance."

Confucius, quoted in a Chinese fortune cookie

DSM-III, which was begun in 1974, reached final publication in 1980. It marked the birth of a new era of American psychiatric diagnosis, or, one might say, the rebirth of American psychiatry from a Kraepelinian womb. According to Allen Frances and colleagues (1990), "there was a paradigm shift in *DSM-III* toward descriptive psychiatric diagnosis that was meant to be neutral with regard to etiology and usable across theoretical orientations" (p. 1439).

The diagnoses in *DSM-III* represent the consensus of expert opinions of the APA task force on nomenclature and statistics, of the fourteen advisory committees, and of consultants from allied fields and other professional organizations. The *DSM-III* diagnostic criteria were discussed at conferences and underwent testing in field trials of diagnostic reliability. For the first time a *DSM* presented a working definition of *mental disorder* and listed systematic operational criteria for each disorder. *DSM-III* redefined the major mental disorders and added many new disorders to the classification system. Although not without its critics, *DSM-III* imposed on its diagnostic categories a hierarchical structure that made possible computer-friendly decision trees for differential diagnosis. Another *DSM-III* innovation was the inclusion of a multiaxial evaluation system.

By 1987 over two thousand papers had appeared in the literature addressing aspects of the new *DSM-III* diagnostic system. Many of the articles suggested revisions based on research into the reliability and validity of *DSM-III* categories. In May 1983 the APA initiated a work group to revise *DSM-III*. This group, with its twenty-six advisory committees, brought forth a revised edition of the *Diagnostic and Statistical Manual of Mental Disorders*, *DSM-III-R*, published in 1987.

DSM-III-R was a moderately conservative document. Prompted by the experience gained from using *DSM-III* and supported by research data from empirical studies, *DSM-III-R* added twenty-seven new categories and revised several diagnoses of the original *DSM-III*. Nonetheless, the introduction to *DSM-III-R* cautions that "for most of the categories the diagnostic criteria are based on clinical judgment, and have not yet been fully validated by data about such important correlates as clinical course, outcome, family history, and treatment response" (p. xxiv). The number of diagnostic categories rose to 292 in *DSM-III-R*, an increase from the 265 categories of *DSM-III*, the 182 of *DSM-II*, and the mere 106 of *DSM-I*. *DSM-III-R* also included an appendix of proposed diagnostic categories needing further study.

We wish to stress that the *DSM-III*, *DSM-III-R*, and *DSM-IV* represent diagnosis by consensus. Most of the 292 categories of the *DSM-III-R* are based on the expert opinion and clinical judgment of the members of the committees who developed the diagnostic criteria. Because the *DSM-III* and *DSM-IV* diagnostic sets are largely matters of opinion, they are meant to serve as guides to clinical practice and should never be applied rigidly or taken literally (reified) as some sort of Platonic truth about psychiatric disorders. The authors of *DSM-IV* are aware of the potential danger of reification of the *DSM-IV* diagnoses and have stressed repeatedly, in their writing and teaching about *DSM-IV*, the crucial and essential role that clinical judgment plays in making a psychiatric diagnosis based on the guidelines in the manual.

Notably, the APA work group dropped the political hot potato category of ego-dystonic homosexuality from the 1987 *DSM-III-R* manual. The APA committee noted that to retain this diagnostic label might imply that the APA still considered homosexuality a disorder. Most significant, however, was the fact that the diagnosis of ego-dystonic homosexuality was rarely used in clinical, research, or treatment programs. To the consternation of some feminist groups, however, the politically controversial category premenstrual dysphoric disorder (formerly late luteal phase disorder) was placed in Appendix B for further study.

DSM-III-R also made more use than *DSM-III* of the so-called *polythetic* versus *monothetic* sets of criteria. Many of the criteria sets of *DSM-III-R* and *DSM-IV* combine both the monothetic and polythetic methods in a mixed approach to diagnosis. In polythetic diagnosis, no single feature or group of characteristics defines the disorder; instead, the polythetic disorder may present clinically with a variety of symptom clusters. In monothetic diagnosis, on the other hand, there is a core feature or an essential group of characteristics that always define the disorder. The following examples should help to clarify what these terms mean.

The personality disorders, for example, are all described in polythetic terms—that is, a personality disorder is diagnosed if a certain number of many ("poly" means many) possible signs and symptoms is present. Thus, a schizotypal personality disorder diagnosis requires the presence of any five out of nine possible criteria, including ideas of reference, social anxiety, odd beliefs, unusual perceptions, strange behavior, no close friends, odd speech, inappropriate affect, and paranoid thinking. Thus, two people might receive the diagnosis of schizotypal personality disorder while having only a single criterion of the polythetic diagnostic set in common. Polythetic criteria improve the reliability of diagnoses, but at the same time increase diagnostic complexity and heterogeneity. John Clarkin and colleagues (1983) pointed out that in *DSM-III-R* there are ninety-three ways to display a borderline personality disorder.

In polythetic diagnosis the patient must display several, but not necessarily all, of a list of typical signs and symptoms of a disorder. No single criterion is considered pathognomonic—that is, characteristic or essentially diagnostic of a specific disorder. Polythetic diagnostic sets include symptoms that are often but not invariably present in a disorder. In *DSM-III-R* polythetic diagnostic sets were used extensively in defining the disruptive behavior disorders, the psychoactive substance use disorders, and the personality disorders.

In contrast to polythetic diagnosis, a monothetic classification system requires that each one (*mono* means one) of several diagnostic criteria must be present to make the diagnosis. An example of a monothetic diagnosis from *DSM-IV* is that of depersonalization disorder. To diagnose this disorder, all four of the following criteria must be met:

1. There must be experiences of feeling detached from one's mind or body.
2. During these experiences, reality testing must be intact.
3. The symptom must cause significant distress or impairment.
4. No other disorder can be present that would better account for the symptom.

Just as a chain is as strong as its weakest link, a monothetic diagnosis is as reliable as its least reliable criterion. In addition, monothetic criteria sets must exclude diagnostic features that are useful but not invariably present and in doing so can reduce diagnostic reliability. An underlying assumption of monothetic diagnosis is that certain signs and symptoms may be pathognomonic or essentially characteristic of a disease entity.

In addition to the wider use of polythetic criteria sets, *DSM-III-R* also shifted toward the convention of making multiple diagnoses rather than differential diagnoses. This shift resulted from the removal of many of the diagnostic hierarchies and exclusion criteria of the original *DSM-III*, which implied the existence of a hierarchy of more versus less fundamental psychiatric disorders.

For example, in *DSM-III* a patient suffering from major depression who then develops panic attacks would receive a single diagnosis of major depression, the panic attacks being regarded as a symptom associated with major depression rather than as a separate panic disorder. In *DSM-III-R* the same patient would receive two diagnoses, both major depression and panic disorder. The question is whether panic attacks and major depression are independent but co-occurring disorders or whether they are both part of a more complex overarching clinical syndrome that has been artificially split apart by our arbitrary diagnostic system. Is depression more fundamental than anxiety, or are they both manifestations of an even more fundamental disorder?

Another problem that *DSM-III-R* corrected was that some of the original *DSM-III* codes were not also *International Classification of Diseases (ICD-9)* codes. Because the United States is obliged to use *ICD* codes, the *DSM-III-R* task force made certain that all *DSM-III-R* codes were legitimate *ICD-9* codes. In May 1988, when it became clear that the new version of the *International Classification of Diseases (ICD-10)*, was likely to appear in 1993, the APA appointed a new task force to begin work on *DSM-IV*. A major goal was to publish *DSM-IV* concurrently with *ICD-10* and to eliminate unnecessary differences while increasing the compatibility between the two systems of classification.

In the process of fine tuning *DSM-III*, *DSM-III-R* made many revisions of the original manual. *DSM-IV* attempted to be more conservative than *DSM-III-R* was in making changes in the diagnostic system by remaining as close to *DSM-III-R* as possible. The *DSM-IV* task force felt that *DSM-III-R* had already made substantial revisions and additions to the original *DSM-III* and that any new changes had to be thoroughly grounded in empirical evidence. It was difficult to add new diagnoses to *DSM-IV*.

The preface to the working draft of *DSM-IV* (3/1/93) states that the major goals of the document are "to enhance the clinical utility of *DSM-IV*, to increase its empirical foundation, to maintain full compatibility with the *International Classification of Diseases*, and to be conservative in making any changes." The major innovation of *DSM-IV* lies in the systematic and explicit process by which it was developed and the fact that it is grounded in empirical evidence rather than in any specific changes in its content.

Just how did the *DSM-IV* task force keep its focus on empirical documentation? The APA committee and its work groups established a three-stage process of (1) thorough and systematic literature reviews of the diagnostic categories, (2) reanalysis of previously collected data, and (3) extensive field trials to test diagnostic sets for reliability and to check how changes derived from research applied to clinical settings. A companion to *DSM-IV*, the five-volume *DSM-IV Sourcebook*, documents the empirical basis for changes in the manual from *DSM-III-R*, including 150 literature reviews, data reanalyses, and the results of the field trials.

The criteria for making changes in *DSM-IV* were far more stringent than those used for revising *DSM-III*. The Introduction to *DSM-IV* states that the committee tried to "strike an optimal balance in *DSM-IV* with respect to historical tradition (as embodied in *DSM-III* and *DSM-III-R*), compatibility with *ICD-10*, evidence from reviews of the literature, unpublished data sets, field trials, and consensus of the field" (p. xx). New diagnoses had to be grounded in empirical research rather than being included to stimulate new research. In contrast with *ICD-10*, which contains two sets of criteria—one for clinical work and another for research—*DSM-IV* contains a single set of criteria for use in both clinical and research settings. Although *ICD-10* has been implemented internationally, it probably will not be implemented in the United States until the late 1990s.

Another goal of the *DSM-IV* committee was to make the manual applicable to a variety of settings and useful as a guide to clinical work. One of the criticisms of *DSM-III-R* was that some of the criteria sets, like that for antisocial personality disorder, were too complex and cumbersome for use in the field. In some cases the person who had actually written a particular *DSM-III-R* criteria set (e.g., somatization disorder) could not remember all the items that were included in the criteria. Another criticism was that the 292 categories of *DSM-III-R* already represented too many discrete diagnoses for everyday clinical practice. Rather than add to the existing diagnostic complexity, the APA task force sought to increase the clarity, simplicity, and utility of the *DSM-IV* diagnostic categories.

Like *DSM-III-R*, *DSM-IV* follows a Kraepelinian categorical approach to diagnosis—that is, it divides mental disorders into categories based on criteria sets consisting of defining features of the disorder. The monothetic system of classification is ideal for a categorical approach to diagnosis. The categories provide handy labels that clinicians and researchers can use to discuss various disorders.

A categorical approach avails itself of decision-tree logic in reaching a diagnosis by going down a trail of pathognomonic branch points. The categorical monothetic approach, with its explicit criteria, tends to increase reliability of diagnosis, but may do so at the expense of validity and clinical usefulness. Clinicians and researchers run the risk of reifying diagnostic categories as if they were things in the real world rather than arbitrary mental constructs of expert opinions. By providing symptom checklists, the categorical approach also reduces the need for clinical judgment, for inference about mental processes, and for human contact with the patient.

In an ideal world, all the members of a particular category would be homogeneous and the boundaries between different categories would be sharp, making the categories mutually exclusive. The world of psychiatry, however, is far from ideal. Individuals sharing the same *DSM-IV* diagnostic label may differ from one another in significant ways. Additional clinical information beyond the mere *DSM-IV* diagnosis is almost always required to formulate an adequate treatment plan. In addition, there will always be border cases that do not fit neatly within the confines of a single diagnostic category.

Two other possible diagnostic models include classification by prototype (prototypical) and classification along dimensions (dimensional). In a prototypical model, patients receive a label if they closely resemble someone suffering from a prototypical example of the disorder. If it looks like a duck, waddles like a duck, and quacks like a duck, it's probably a duck. The prototypical model is more compatible than is the categorical model with the polythetic diagnostic sets of *DSM-III-R* and *DSM-IV*. Based on pattern recognition and family resemblance, the prototypical model allows for significant heterogeneity within each diagnostic category. The more one approximates the prototype of the disorder, the more one is likely to receive the diagnostic label. A prototypical approach increases the need for inference and clinical judgment.

Unlike the categorical and prototypical models, a dimensional model completely avoids the use of categories. Instead, this model rates clinical presentations numerically along significant dimensions of pathology. An underlying assumption of a dimensional model is that the clinical attributes forming the dimensions are distributed continuously and that the phenomena being studied do not have distinct boundaries.

A clinical example of a dimensional system is the classification of patients by their two highest abnormal scores on the *MMPI* clinical scales. Thus a patient with a 4–8 *MMPI* profile might meet criteria for such various *DSM-IV* disorders as paranoid schizophrenia, delusional disorder, bipolar disorder, sexual sadism disorder, or a variety of personality disorders. It seems unlikely that clinicians will opt to communicate about patients along numerical dimensions, and there is currently no widely accepted set of dimensions for use in a diagnostic system.

Perhaps we can look forward in the next century to the television announcer saying before the late evening news, "It's 10 o'clock. Do you know where your 4–8s are?"

6

An Overview of *DSM-IV*

'The time has come,' the Walrus said,
'To talk of many things:
Of shoes—and ships—and sealing wax—
Of cabbages—and kings—
And why the sea is boiling hot—
And whether pigs have wings.'

Lewis Carroll (1832–1898)

The time has come to delve into the substance of *DSM-IV*. This chapter paints in broad strokes the structure and organization of the fourth edition of *DSM*. Keeping such an overview in mind will aid the reader in making optimal use of the diagnostic manual.

The major difference between *DSM-IV* and its immediate predecessor is the way in which it was researched and constructed. *DSM-III-R* had been criticized for "over-reliance on the opinions of a small group of experts" (*Mental Health Report*, June 2, 1994, p. 82). The *DSM-IV* task force was committed to producing a document that was as clinically relevant and as evidence based as possible. The evidence gathering was systematic and state of the art. The final product was the labor of about a thousand individuals who participated in thirteen work groups, each chaired by leaders in the field and aided by 50 to 100 advisers.

With such a conservative mission, the *DSM-IV* task force avoided unnecessary or disruptive changes in diagnostic categories from *DSM-III-R*. All changes had to be evidence based, clinically usable, and compatible with *ICD-10*. In addition, the new document was subject to rigorous field trials at multiple sites that were designed to enhance the generalizability of the proposed changes.

One major change was the reconceptualization of the "organic" mental disorders of *DSM-III-R*. *DSM-IV* eliminates the "organic/non-organic" dichotomy. The authors of *DSM-IV* wanted to recognize that many of the so-called "functional" disorders (e.g., mania, schizophrenia, and major depression) do have an "organic" component. To avoid the organic/nonorganic controversy, *DSM-IV* takes a phenomenological approach. Thus, the section on mood disorders in *DSM-IV* now contains criteria for mood disorders due to a general medical condition and for substance-induced mood disorders.

    DSM-IV has added diagrams to provide a longitudinal perspective on the episodic nature and course of the mood disorders. In the field trials clinicians found such diagrams helpful in explaining to clients the nature of their disorders. *DSM-IV* also seeks to be far more specific than *DSM-III-R* in describing the clinical features of many of the other disorders. *DSM-IV* contains more information than its predecessor about the associated features and co-morbidity of disorders. Because of the cultural diversity of the United States, *DSM-IV* also attempts to describe the cross-cultural characteristics of each disorder. References to culture appear in the introduction, in the text about each type of disorder, and in a special appendix on culture-bound syndromes (Appendix I, *DSM-IV*, pp. 843–849) .

    The V codes of *DSM-III-R* have been extended and reconceptualized in the *DSM-IV* section entitled "Other Conditions That May Be a Focus of Clinical Attention." This same section also includes medication-induced movement disorders, which have become a significant concern in psychiatric practice.

    DSM-IV also makes some changes in the multiaxial system. The developmental disorders (including autism and learning disorders) have been moved to Axis I; these had been coded on Axis II in *DSM-III-R*. Mental retardation, however, continues to be coded on Axis II with the personality disorders. The fourth axis of *DSM-III-R* has been revised to serve as a psychosocial and environmental checklist in *DSM-IV*. Finally, the fifth axis GAF Scale has been modified in *DSM-IV* to run from 90 to 100 to take into account superior functioning.

    The issues that remained unresolved in *DSM-IV* have been relegated to the appendix. The *DSM-IV* appendix contains over twenty proposals for new diagnostic categories. The *DSM-IV Draft Criteria* (3/1/93) included some bizarre items such as "telephone scatologia" (talking dirty on the telephone to get sexually aroused), which was eliminated from the final draft. (One critic wondered about including "telephone faxologia"—that is, the mental disorder of sending dirty faxes to get sexually aroused.) Also included in the appendix are a proposed axis for defense mechanisms and two new scales: the *GARF* (Global Assessment of Relational Functioning Scale) and the *SOFAS* (Social and Occupational Functioning Assessment Scale).

DSM-IV stuck closely to the definition of mental disorder given in *DSM-III-R*. The concept of mental disorder is difficult to define. Attempts to delineate mental disorder in terms of other concepts, such as deviation from a norm, disability, loss of control, dysfunction, lack of rationality, symptom presentation, etiology, and so forth, have not been satisfactory. In addition, the notion of a mental, as opposed to a physical, disorder is suggestive of an artificial mind/body dualism. Recognizing the difficulties in adequately defining a mental disorder, the authors of *DSM-IV* agreed upon the idea that a mental disorder is a:

> clinically significant behavioral or psychological syndrome or pattern that occurs in an individual and this is associated with present distress (e.g., a painful symptom) or disability (i.e., impairment in one or more important areas of functioning) or with a significantly increased risk of suffering death, pain, disability, or an important loss of freedom. [*DSM-IV*, p. xxi]

Note that the *DSM-IV* diagnoses disorders that occur only in individuals, rather than in families, groups, or society. Either distress, impaired functioning, or the risk of personal suffering must not only be present, but must also be clinically significant. Expectable distressing responses like normal grief reactions are excluded from the definition, as are conflicts between an individual and society. Furthermore, *DSM-IV* emphasizes that it classifies mental disorders rather than the people who suffer them.

DSM-IV groups mental disorders into sixteen major categories and adds a seventeenth catchall category for "Other Conditions That May Be a Focus of Clinical Attention."

The first section of *DSM-IV* discusses disorders usually first diagnosed in infancy, childhood, or adolescence. Such disorders include mental retardation, attention deficit disorders, pervasive developmental disorders, and so on. Although these disorders usually first appear in childhood, they may come to clinical attention in adulthood. In addition, many "adult" disorders (like major depression, bipolar disorder, and schizophrenia) may have a first onset in childhood or adolescence. The grouping of disorders in this first section according to age of presentation is simply a matter of convenience.

Following this first section of disorders that usually present in childhood or adolescence, there are three sections in *DSM-IV* of disorders that were formerly called *organic mental disorders* in *DSM-III-R*. As mentioned previously, *DSM-IV* has abolished the label *organic mental disorder* because the authors of *DSM-IV* believe that the term *organic* implies that other disorders in the manual do not have a biological basis. The authors of *DSM-IV* would like to make *organic* a four-letter word. In an interview about *DSM-IV*, Harold Alan Pincus, M.D., deputy medical director of the APA and co-chair of the task force on *DSM-IV*, stated that "many 'functional' disorders, such as schizophrenia or mood disorder, have organic components, yet these 'non-organic' diagnoses have been mistakenly considered by the public, insurers and others as not 'true' diseases."

Despite the *DSM-IV's* attempt to eliminate the term *organic* from psychiatric diagnosis, the concept of organicity is so ingrained in the minds of clinicians that it seems unlikely that the term will soon disappear from clinical usage. Just as we speak of the "former Soviet Union," we might say that the "former organic disorders" of *DSM-III-R* are now subsumed under the three *DSM-IV* categories of 1) delirium, dementia, amnestic and other cognitive disorders; 2) mental disorders due to a general medical condition; and 3) substance-related disorders.

The reason that these former "organic" disorders appear in the manual preceding all the remaining mental disorders is that they have first priority in differential diagnosis. Thus, if a patient presents with the symptoms of a disorder appearing later in the manual (e.g., mood, anxiety, or psychotic disorders—formerly called functional disorders) and if there is a causal link between the symptom picture and either brain dysfunction, a medical condition, or substance use, then the more definitively biological disorder takes precedence in diagnosis.

Except for the section on adjustment disorders, the remaining twelve of the sixteen broad categories group disorders according to their shared phenomenology. The twelve remaining categories include schizophrenia and other psychotic disorders, mood disorders, anxiety disorders, somatoform disorders, factitious disorders, dissociative disorders, sexual and gender identity disorders, eating disorders, sleep disorders, impulse control disorders not elsewhere classified, adjustment disorders, and personality disorders. The adjustment disorders may look phenomenologically different from one another, but they are lumped together because they share a common etiology—that is, they are all maladaptive reactions to stressors.

The final section of *DSM-IV* is titled "Other Conditions That May Be a Focus of Clinical Attention." These include medication-induced movement disorders, relational problems, problems related to abuse and neglect, and additional conditions that may be a focus of clinical attention.

For easy reference, here is a list of the seventeen major sections of *DSM-IV* in the order in which they appear in the manual:

1. Disorders Usually First Diagnosed in Infancy, Childhood, or Adolescence. (These are coded on Axis I, except for mental retardation, which is coded on Axis II.)
2. Delirium, Dementia, Amnestic and Other Cognitive Disorders.
3. Mental Disorders Due to a General Medical Condition Not Elsewhere Classified.
4. Substance-Related Disorders.
5. Schizophrenia and Other Psychotic Disorders.
6. Mood Disorders.
7. Anxiety Disorders.
8. Somatoform Disorders.
9. Factitious Disorders.
10. Dissociative Disorders.
11. Sexual and Gender Identity Disorders.
12. Eating Disorders.
13. Sleep Disorders.
14. Impulse Control Disorders Not Elsewhere Classified.
15. Adjustment Disorders.
16. Personality Disorders (coded on Axis II).
17. Other Conditions That May Be a Focus of Clinical Attention.

DSM-IV devotes a chapter to each of the above sixteen classes of disorders and to the seventeenth class of other conditions. Each of these chapters describes the specific disorders in a particular class. For example, the section on mood disorders contains subsections of the depressive disorders, the bipolar disorders, the mood disorders due to a general medical condition, and the mood disorders not otherwise specified. The introductions to these chapters describe the general class of disorders under discussion and review the features they share in common.

We now provide a brief overview of each of the seventeen classes or disorders or conditions described in *DSM-IV*. By definition, all mental disorders are accompanied by clinically significant impairment or distress.

AN OVERVIEW OF DSM-IV DIAGNOSTIC CLASSES

1. *Disorders Usually First Diagnosed in Infancy, Childhood, or Adolescence (DSM-IV*, pp. 37–122): These disorders typically begin before adulthood. Although frequently seen among children and adolescents, syndromes like schizophrenia and mood disorders are classified elsewhere in the manual because they are mainly seen in the adult population. Separation anxiety disorder is an anxiety disorder characteristic of childhood. The eating disorders peculiar to early childhood include pica, rumination, and feeding disorder. Although anorexia nervosa and bulimia nervosa commonly begin in adolescence, they are classified in the eating disorders section of the manual. Some youngsters have difficulty urinating (enuresis) or defecating (encopresis) in socially acceptable ways, as described under the elimination disorders. Children can suffer from a variety of tic disorders, including Tourette's syndrome. The developmental disorders are characterized by absent, inhibited, constrained, suppressed, or distorted emotional, mental, and/or social development. Such disorders include mental retardation (coded on Axis II in *DSM-IV*), pervasive developmental disorders (like autism, Rett's disorder, and Asperger's disorder), communication disorders (including stuttering and problems with expressive or receptive language) and specific learning and motor skills disorders. Among the most common disorders of childhood are the disruptive and attention-deficit disorders, including conduct disorder, attention-deficit/hyperactivity disorder, and oppositional defiant disorder.

2. *Delirium, Dementia, Amnestic, and Other Cognitive Disorders* (DSM-IV, pp. 123–164): The essential feature of delirium is an acute

and fluctuating clouding of consciousness with difficulty sustaining attention. The dementias are characterized by memory impairment and other cognitive deficits that develop gradually and progressively worsen. The amnestic disorders present with the inability to learn new information or to recall previously learned information. These disorders generally have a neurological, substance-related, or medical etiology.

3. *Mental Disorders Due to a General Medical Condition Not Elsewhere Classified* (*DSM-IV*, pp. 165–174): In keeping with *DSM-IV*'s stance of eliminating the "organic/non-organic" distinction in psychiatric nosology, this section contains only three mental disorders due to a general medical condition that are not elsewhere classified, namely: catatonic disorder, personality change, and mental disorder not otherwise specified (NOS) due to a general medical condition. All other mental disorders due to a general medical condition can be found in those sections of the manual with which they share the same clinical phenomenology. *DSM-IV* has eliminated the old *DSM-III-R* category "Organic Mental Disorders associated with Axis III physical disorders." Some medical illnesses can induce catatonia, a syndrome characterized by extreme motor immobility or hyperactivity, negativism, mutism, echolalia, echopraxia, and voluntary movement abnormalities (catatonia due to a general medical condition not elsewhere classified). At times, general medical conditions can cause a persisting personality disturbance (personality change due to a general medical condition not elsewhere classified). At other times, medically ill individuals may experience a variety of psychiatric symptoms that do not meet criteria for any of the specific *DSM-IV* mental disorders (mental disorder due to a general medical condition not elsewhere classified).

The *DSM-IV* criterion for a mental disorder due to a general medical condition reads as follows: "There is evidence from history, physical examination, or laboratory findings that the disturbance is the direct physiological consequence of a general medical condition" (*DSM-IV*, p. 7).

Note: On the phrase *due to*: The very title "Mental Disorders *Due to* a General Medical Condition" implies the concept of a mind/body dualism, which *DSM-IV* has tried to avoid. The use of the phrase *due to* suggests that the *medical* disorder somehow causes the *mental* disorder. It would be preferable to entitle such conditions "Mental Disorders that Are *Part of* a General Medical Condition," so that both the mental and physical symptoms are seen as part of the same underlying condition.

4. *Substance-Related Disorders* (*DSM-IV*, pp. 175–272): These disorders are related to the maladaptive use, abuse, or dependence on certain drugs/substances (legal or illegal). Individuals who use substances, depending on the type of drug and the amount taken, may experience a variety of psychological or psychiatric symptoms, including delusions, hallucinations, depression, irritability, anxiety, euphoria, mania, sexual dysfunction, restlessness, sleep problems, and cognitive disturbances. Such symptoms may be the result of the psychoactive effects of a substance or of acute intoxication, dependence, long-term use, or withdrawal from a substance. The psychiatric literature suggests that substance use is widely underdiagnosed in the evolution of psychopathology, especially in emergency settings.

5. *Schizophrenia and Other Psychotic Disorders* (*DSM-IV*, pp. 273–316): Schizophrenia is characterized by psychotic symptoms and a marked disorganization from previous levels of functioning, usually involving a deterioration in personal care, social relations, and job performance. Common symptoms of schizophrenia include thought disorder, disorganized speech, bizarre delusions, hallucinations, loss of ego boundaries, negative symptoms, and strange behavior. Schizophreniform disorder refers to a disorder that appears to be schizophrenic that lasts more than a month but less than six months. When a full major depressive or manic episode occurs during the course of an apparent schizophrenic disorder, the diagnosis of schizoaffective disorder is made. Delusional disorders are those in which non-bizarre delusions predominate in the clinical picture in an individual who has never met criteria for schizophrenia and whose functioning is not markedly impaired. When individuals in a close relationship share delusions, they are said to suffer from shared psychotic disorder or *folie à deux*. Brief psychotic disorders are those in which psychotic symptoms such as hallucinations, delusions, disorganized speech, or grossly disturbed behavior last more than a day but less than a month. Substance-induced psychotic disorders are those psychotic conditions due to the use of substances.

6. *Mood Disorders* (*DSM-IV*, pp. 317–392): The primary characteristics of these disorders are noticeable disturbances of mood. There are two broad types of affective disorders: depressive and bipolar. Depressive disorders include major depressive episode and dysthymic disorder. Bipolar disorder involves the presence of a manic or hypomanic episode. Bipolar I disorders involve the presence or history of a manic episode. Bipolar II disorders involve recurrent major depressive and hypomanic episodes in patients who have never had a manic episode. In Cyclothymic Disorder there are at least two years of periods of hypomanic symptoms and periods of depressed mood or loss of interest/pleasure that do not meet criteria for a major depressive episode. Substance-induced mood disorders are coded according to the predominant mood disturbance and the specific substance involved. In practice, catatonic symptoms are seen more commonly in affective disorders than in schizophrenia. Psychotic symptoms like hallucinations and delusions also commonly accompany the severe mood disorders.

7. *Anxiety Disorders* (*DSM-IV*, pp. 393–444): These disorders include panic attacks, agoraphobia, social phobia, specific phobias, obsessive-compulsive disorder, posttraumatic stress disorder, generalized anxiety disorder, and acute stress disorder. In *DSM-IV*, generalized anxiety disorder includes the overanxious disorder of childhood of *DSM-III-R*. The acute stress disorder is a new addition to the manual to be used to diagnose individuals suffering from posttraumatic stress symptoms that begin within four weeks of a traumatic event and last between two days and four weeks. Anxiety disorders may also be due to a general medical condition or be substance-induced.

8. *Somatoform Disorders* (*DSM-IV*, pp. 445–470): The main features of these disorders are somatic symptoms, suggesting a physical disorder for which medical assessment and laboratory testing shows insufficient or no organic evidence. These disorders include somatization disorder (Briquet's syndrome of multiple somatic complaints), conversion disorder (symptoms in voluntary sensory or motor functions associated with psychological factors), hypochondriasis (unwarranted preoccupation with serious illness), body dysmorphic disorder (preoccupation with imagined defects in appearance), and pain disorder. Patients with somatoform disorders are not intentionally

pretending to be ill as occurs with factitious disorders and malingering. *DSM-IV* has simplified the definition of somatization disorder to increase its clarity and clinical usefulness.

9. *Factitious Disorders* (*DSM-IV*, pp. 471–476): The main characteristic of these disorders is the intentional feigning or production of physical or psychological symptoms by individuals whose objective is to adopt the sick role. Individuals with factitious disorders often spend much time hospitalized or seeking hospitalization. These individuals are usually noncompliant with hospital rules and treatment. They often have a large fund of knowledge about medical and psychiatric disorders. Factitious disorders are distinguished from malingering by the absence of external incentives, such as economic gain or avoidance of responsibility.

10. *Dissociative Disorders* (*DSM-IV*, pp. 477–492): These disorders are characterized by sudden, temporary disturbances of identity, memory, and consciousness not attributable to a general medical condition. In dissociative amnesia there is an inability to recall important personal information. In dissociative fugue there is sudden, unexpected travel with amnesia for one's past and a complete or partial assumption of a new identity. In dissociative identity disorder (multiple personality disorder) there exist two or more distinct personality states that recurrently take control of the individual's behavior. In depersonalization disorder the individual feels detached from his or her own body or mental processes.

11. *Sexual and Gender Identity Disorders* (*DSM-IV*, pp. 493–538): These disorders are broadly grouped into sexual dysfunctions, paraphilias (sexual deviations), and gender identity disorders. The sexual dysfunctions include sexual desire disorders, sexual arousal disorders, orgasm disorders, sexual pain disorders, and sexual dysfunctions that are either substance-induced or due to a general medical condition. The paraphilias (exhibitionism, fetishism, voyeurism, etc.) include deviant sexual behaviors directed toward objects rather than people, interest in sexual acts not usually associated with coitus, and interest in coitus under bizarre circumstances. Gender identity disorders involve intense and persistent identification with the opposite sex.

12. *Eating Disorders* (*DSM-IV*, pp. 539–550): The *DSM-IV* eating disorders consist of anorexia nervosa and bulimia nervosa. In anorexia nervosa there is an intense irrational fear of gaining weight and

becoming fat, accompanied by a refusal to maintain a minimal normal weight for age and height. Bulimia nervosa consists of recurrent episodes of binge eating, accompanied by a sense of lack of control over eating behavior and inappropriate efforts to prevent weight gain by such measures as laxative abuse, self-induced vomiting, fasting, or excessive physical exercise.

13. *Sleep Disorders* (*DSM-IV*, pp. 551–608): The disorders of sleep are divided into dyssomnias, parasomnias, and another category. The dyssomnias include primary insomnia, primary hypersomnia (excessive sleepiness), narcolepsy (sleep attacks), breathing-related sleep disorder, and circadian rhythm sleep disorder (sleep-wake schedule disorder). The parasomnias include nightmare disorder (dream anxiety disorder), sleep terror disorder, and sleepwalking disorder. There are also categories for sleep disorders (insomnia or hypersomnia) related to another mental disorder, sleep disorder due to a general medical condition, and substance-induced sleep disorder.

14. *Impulse Control Disorders Not Elsewhere Classified* (*DSM-IV*, pp. 609–622): This category concerns disorders of impulse control that are not classified elsewhere in the manual. Included in this section are conditions involving poor impulse control, such as intermittent explosive disorder, kleptomania (impulsive stealing), pyromania (impulsive fire setting), pathological gambling, and trichotillomania (impulsive pulling out of one's hair).

15. *Adjustment Disorders* (*DSM-IV*, pp. 623–628): These disorders are characterized by the individual's short-lived (six months or less) distress or maladaptive reaction to a specific identifiable stressor, such as divorce, job loss, or change of residence. By definition, bereavement is excluded from the category of adjustment disorders. Individuals with adjustment disorders typically experience distress in excess of what would normally be expected following a particular stressor. In addition, social and occupational functioning are often impaired. The criteria for adjustment disorder require that an identifiable stressor must have occurred within three months of the onset of the emotional or behavioral symptoms. The adjustment disorders are further categorized by whether they present with anxiety, with depressed mood, with disturbance of conduct, or with a combination of these symptoms. Commonly, the adjustment disorder subsides when the individual adjusts to the new situation or develops new coping skills. Unlike the *DSM-III-R*, the *DSM-IV* now allows the

adjustment disorder to be coded as chronic if it persists more than six months.

16. *Personality Disorders* (*DSM-IV*, pp. 629–674): These disorders are characterized by deeply ingrained maladaptive patterns of personality responses and by persistent maladaptive ways of viewing one's self and the world. The personality-disordered individual's actions often provoke negative reactions from others and interfere substantially in the areas of love and work. Individuals with personality disorders usually do not perceive themselves as others see them. These disorders are usually recognizable in adolescence and, without treatment, persist throughout adult life. *DSM-IV* groups the personality disorders into three clusters. Cluster A ("eccentric") includes the paranoid, schizoid, and schizotypal personality disorders. Cluster B ("dramatic" or "acting out") consists of the antisocial, borderline, histrionic, and narcissistic personality disorders. Cluster C ("anxious") refers to the avoidant, dependent, and obsessive-compulsive personality disorders. *DSM-IV* has greatly simplified the criteria set for antisocial personality disorder to make it clearer and more clinically useful. Appendix B of *DSM-IV* contains proposed criteria for depressive personality disorder and passive-aggressive (negativistic) personality disorder.

17. *Other Conditions That May Be a Focus of Clinical Attention* (*DSM-IV*, pp. 675–686): These conditions are mainly concerned with problems or presentations that may be a focus of clinical concern but that do not meet criteria for a *DSM-IV* diagnosis. Such problems include psychological factors affecting a medical condition, medication-induced movement disorders, problems with relationships, problems related to abuse or neglect, bereavement, borderline intellectual functioning, malingering, adult antisocial behavior, childhood or adolescent antisocial behavior, noncompliance with treatment for a mental disorder, age-associated memory decline, and problems with the following areas: academics, occupation, phase of life, identity, religion or spirituality, and acculturation.

For each specific disorder, *DSM-IV* provides several types of useful clinical information. As part of a psychoeducational process, many clinicians encourage their patients to read those sections of the manual dealing with their disorder. Patients often feel relieved that their symptoms picture is so well described and, as a result, feel hopeful that treatment is available. The types of information available include (see *DSM-IV*, pp. 8–9):

1. The numerical code and *DSM-IV* name of the disorder, the diagnostic criteria, subtypes and/or specifiers, recording procedures, and illustrative examples of the disorder.

2. Associated features and associated disorders. This section may include clinical features that are common in a disorder but not invariably present. It may include other disorders that precede, co-occur with, or follow the disorder in question. Also included are associated laboratory findings (like EEG patterns of sleep disorders), associated physical exam signs and symptoms, and associated general medical conditions. Only the sections on mental retardation and learning disorders require diagnostic testing (IQ, achievement tests) as part of the diagnostic criteria. Although sleep lab studies may provide a definitive diagnosis, to have included them as part of the sleep disorder diagnostic criteria sets would have necessitated expensive and impractical diagnostic workups to make even the most straightforward sleep disorder diagnosis.

3. Age of onset, cultural, and gender-related information. This section outlines presentations that vary with the developmental stage of the individual, his or her cultural background, and differences between the sexes, including ratios of the prevalence of the disorder in males versus females. *DSM-IV* has made a strong effort to be culturally sensitive.

4. Prevalence, incidence, and risk. This section includes information on point and lifetime prevalence, incidence, and lifetime risk in different settings like inpatient, outpatient, and community patient populations. The point prevalence is the proportion of persons in the population who have the disorder at a specified point in time. The lifetime prevalence is a measure at a given point in time of all the individuals who have ever suffered the disorder. The incidence of a disorder refers to the rate of new cases that have started within a defined time period, usually one year (the annual incidence).

5. Clinical course. This section reviews how a disorder typically presents and evolves over time. The course of a disorder is subdivided into four subsections: (1) What is the typical age and mode of onset? Is it abrupt or slow to develop (insidious)? (2) Is the disorder episodic or continuous? Is there a single episode or are there recurrent

episodes? Is the disorder characterized by distinct periods of illness separated by symptom-free periods? (3) What is the typical length or duration of the illness or of its distinct episodes? (4) Is the disorder progressive? How does it evolve over time? Does it tend to stabilize, worsen, or improve? The "Substance-Related Disorders" section provides diagrams (*DSM-IV*, p. 180) to illustrate patterns of remission. The "Mood Disorders" section also gives diagrams of types of interepisode recovery (*DSM-IV*, p. 388). Many clinicians find such diagrams useful to show to clients.

6. When applicable, *DSM-IV* lists the complications (morbidity) of each disorder. The manual includes the untoward effects of the disorder, such as suicide, violence, homelessness, substance abuse, divorce, financial loss, and illegal activity.

7. When appropriate, *DSM-IV* includes predisposing factors of a disorder, such as characteristics of the person prior to the onset of the disorder that predispose to its development.

8. Familial pattern. This section gives information on the occurrence of the same disorder in first-degree biological relatives (parents and siblings) as compared with the general population and indicates other disorders that are more likely to occur in family members of the person with the disorder.

9. Differential diagnosis. This section outlines other disorders that share similar presentations and tells how to distinguish or differentiate the disorder in question from similar disorders.

Having reviewed in this chapter the general types of clinical information found in *DSM-IV*, we will turn next to the use of diagnostic codes and to multiaxial assessment.

7

Diagnostic Codes in *DSM-IV*

"When I use a word," Humpty Dumpty said in a rather scornful tone,
"it means just what I choose it to mean—neither more nor less."
Lewis Carroll (1832–1898), *Through the Looking Glass*

DSM-IV sought to keep its numerical codes for disorders consistent with the *International Classification of Diseases (ICD)*. The official coding system in use during the development of *DSM-IV* (1988–1994) was the *International Classification of Diseases, Ninth Revision, Clinical Modification (ICD-9-CM)*. The range of numbers that *ICD-9-CM* allocates for mental disorders extends from 290 through 319. Hence, any time a diagnostic code falls between 290 and 319, clinicians can be sure that they are dealing with one of the 30 categories of *ICD-9-CM* mental disorders.

One impetus for revising *DSM-III-R* was to make the American *DSM* consistent with *ICD-10*, which was due for publication in 1993. The *DSM-IV* task force coordinated its efforts with the developers of *ICD-10* to ensure that the *DSM-IV* codes and terms would be fully compatible with both *ICD-9-CM* and with *ICD-10*. While *ICD-10* has been implemented internationally, it will not go into effect in the United States until the late 1990s.

In the United States the Health Care Financing Administration (HCFA) has required that clinicians use numerical *ICD* codes if they wish to be paid for treating Medicare clients. In addition, the World Health Organization, many government agencies, and private insurance companies often require the use of these numerical codes for data collection. While numerical codes are a boon to data processing, they increase the risk of public access to private information.

The numerical codes for disorders are computer friendly and facilitate the collection, rapid retrieval, and easy processing of information about diagnoses. Using these codes, insurance companies can readily discover in a national data bank whether a person carries a diagnosis for a major mental or medical disorder and can use that information to deny life insurance or disability coverage to the individual. Many clients do not realize that, when they sign a standard Health Insurance Claim Form (HCFA-1500), they are signing away their right to privacy about their medical and mental health information. The patient authorization section of the standard HCFA form states, "I authorize the release of any medical or other information necessary to process this claim."

Furthermore, the fine print on the back of the HCFA insurance claim form adds that "the information may also be given to other providers of services, carriers, intermediaries, medical review boards, health plans, and other organizations or Federal agencies, for the effective administration of Federal provisions that require other third party payers to pay primary to Federal program, and as otherwise necessary to administer these programs." Clients rarely realize that, by signing the HCFA form, they are permitting their diagnostic codes to be fed to computers across the nation. The age of Big Brother is here.

Most *DSM-IV* mental disorders receive a four-digit code, often with a fifth and final digit added for greater specificity. The numerical codes, in the form XXX.XX, consist of three whole-number digits followed by a decimal point plus an additional one or two digits after the decimal point. For example, the code for Pedophilia is 302.2 and the code for Voyeurism is 302.82. In the "Mood Disorders" section, the code for Major Depressive Disorder, Single Episode, is 296.2x where the fifth digit "x" identifies the severity or course of the disorder—that is, whether the major depressive episode is mild (296.21), moderate (296.22), severe but without psychotic features (296.23), with psychotic features (296.24), in partial remission (296.25), or in full remission (296.26).

As the above examples illustrate, the fifth digit of the *DSM-IV* code can be used to identify the subtypes, modifiers, severity, or course of a disorder. Many of the modifiers and subtypes of *DSM-IV* diagnoses, however, have no counterpart in the official classification system *ICD-9-CM*. For this reason, the clinician must use names rather than numbers to further specify many *DSM-IV* diagnoses. In fact, the majority of subtypes and specifiers of *DSM-IV* diagnoses require the clinician to write the name of the modifier or subtype after the *DSM-IV* name of the disorder because no fifth digit for that information exists in *ICD-9-CM*.

There are some minor but potentially irritating differences between *DSM-IV* and *ICD-9-CM* codes for mental disorders in the use of the fifth digit. In one case, the Blue Cross Insurance Company of Connecticut refused to pay a psychiatrist for psychotherapy services when he used a five-digit *DSM-IV* code of 300.40 to record his patient's dysthymic disorder (neurotic depression) on the HCFA insurance form. The final zero digit of the *DSM-IV* 300.40 code thoroughly confused the Blue Cross computer, which was trained to accept only the four-digit *ICD-9-CM* code 300.4 for dysthymia and therefore refused to issue payment. After several phone calls to supervisory personnel at Blue Cross, the psychiatrist finally convinced a human at Blue Cross to overrule the refractory computer and pay the bill. A New Haven–based psychologist had a similar experience with a bill submitted with a five- rather than a four-digit code to Traveler's Medicare.

Let us now turn to some of the qualifying phrases, subtypes, and modifiers used in *DSM-IV* to further categorize particular diagnoses.

SUBTYPES: SPECIFY TYPE

(*DSM-IV*, p. 1)

When the diagnostic manual instructs the reader to "specify type," it is referring to what *DSM-IV* calls "mutually exclusive and jointly exhaustive subgroupings" or subtypes within a specific diagnosis. For instance, *DSM-IV* suggests five types of Specific Phobia (300.29, formerly Simple Phobia in *DSM-III-R*): Animal Type; Natural Environment Type; Blood, Injection, Injury Type; Situational Type; and Other Type. If you were morbidly afraid of dogs, you would receive the diagnosis Specific Phobia (300.29), Animal Type, and if you were terrified of thunderstorms, you would be diagnosed as having Specific Phobia (300.29), Natural Environment Type. If diagnostic manuals like *DSM-IV* provoked in you excessive and unreasonable anxiety, your diagnosis would be Specific Phobia (300.29), Other Type. Yet another example is how *DSM-IV* divides delusional disorders (297.1) into seven distinct subtypes according to which theme predominates in the delusion—that is, whether the delusion is erotomanic, grandiose, jealous, persecutory, somatic, mixed, or unspecified.

MODIFIERS: SPECIFY IF

(*DSM-IV*, p. 1)

When *DSM-IV* instructs the reader to "specify if," it is referring to "modifiers" of a disorder rather than to mutually exclusive and jointly exhaustive subtypes of a specific diagnosis. Modifiers allow a clinician or researcher to identify individuals who fall into a more homogeneous group of people with the particular diagnosis. For example, many people with major depression also have melancholia (from the Greek for "black bile" and now meaning significant loss of pleasure or interest and the presence of neurovegetative symptoms) and can be diagnosed as having major depressive disorder, with melancholic features. In another example of the use of modifiers, the clinician can specify whether a person with pedophilia is sexually attracted to males, females, or both.

CURRENT VERSUS PAST PRESENTATIONS: THE PRIOR HISTORY MODIFIER

(*DSM-IV*, p. 2)

By convention, clinicians usually use *DSM-IV* diagnoses to refer to the client's current clinical presentation rather than to past diagnoses from which the person has recovered and that are not a focus of present treatment. A major goal of *DSM-IV* is to enhance its clinical utility, and sometimes it is clinically useful to identify past disorders that are no longer active. To code a prior disorder from which the client has recovered, the clinician can use the modifier "Prior History." For example, one client suffered a posttraumatic stress disorder with intrusive thoughts, increased arousal, disturbed sleep, and panic attacks after she witnessed a murder. Following a successful course of individual psychotherapy, her symptoms completely resolved. Because witnessing the murder was such a major event in this client's life, a clinician seeing her years later might wish to code her old diagnosis as Posttraumatic Stress Disorder (309.81), Prior History.

MODIFIERS FOR COURSE AND SEVERITY

(*DSM-IV*, p. 2–3)

As we saw with the diagnosis of major depression, the fifth digit can indicate the state of remission or the severity (mild, moderate, severe, psychotic) of the disorder. The modifier "In Partial Remission" implies that the client meets some of the criteria for the disorder, but no longer meets the full criteria that were present when the diagnosis was originally made. A diagnosis can also be labeled "In Partial Remission" when some signs and symptoms recur after a period of full remission. The modifier "In Full Remission" means that all of the signs and symptoms of the disorder have cleared, but that the diagnosis is still clinically significant. For example, a person on antidepressants for a major depressive episode may have a full remission of symptoms because of the antidepressant medication and may need ongoing evaluation and treatment to prevent a relapse of the disorder.

The severity modifiers — "mild," "moderate," and "severe" — imply that the client meets full criteria for a disorder. The factors that vary along the dimension of severity are the number and intensity of signs and symptoms of the disorder and the degree to which functioning is impaired. The clinician must use a measure of clinical judgment to assign the severity modifiers. Generally, a "mild" disorder indicates that a fairly minimal set of the full criteria to make the diagnosis are in evidence and that the level of impairment is modest. In contrast, a "severe" disorder meets many criteria beyond the minimal set required to make the diagnosis and that there is marked functional impairment. "Moderate" disorders fall in between "mild" and "severe."

The clinician is encouraged to apply the "mild, moderate, severe" modifiers to all of the official *DSM-IV* diagnostic categories. To aid the clinician in determining the severity and course modifiers of a particular diagnosis, *DSM-IV* often provides specific criteria.

THE "PRINCIPAL DIAGNOSIS/REASON FOR VISIT" MODIFIERS

(*DSM-IV*, p. 3)

DSM-IV diagnoses typically refer to the client's current clinical condition. With the shift in *DSM-III-R* and *DSM-IV* toward multiple diagnoses, clients are more likely to meet criteria for more than one disorder. In cases of multiple diagnosis, the clinician should identify which diagnosis brought the client to clinical attention and is likely to be the focus of treatment. *DSM-IV* provides the modifier "Principal Diagnosis" to identify which diagnosis is responsible for the psychiatric admission. Clinicians can use the qualifying phrase "Reason for Visit" to code which diagnosis prompts an outpatient service.

It can be difficult to select a principal diagnosis, especially when two disorders are active and causing symptoms. For example, many clients who suffer from schizophrenia also abuse psychoactive substances. Both disorders can present with psychotic symptoms and disorganized behavior, and both disorders may be simultaneous foci of treatment. In this same case, once the effects of the intoxicating substance wear off, the more chronic psychotic disorder becomes the primary focus of treatment.

When multiple current diagnoses exist, the convention is to list the principal diagnosis first with the modifier "Principal Diagnosis." The remaining diagnoses follow this principal diagnosis in order of their importance as foci of attention or treatment. Most often, the principal diagnosis is a major clinical syndrome coded on Axis I. In some cases, however, the principal diagnosis is a personality disorder coded on Axis II with the modifier "Principal Diagnosis/Reason for Visit." Whether the clinician chooses to report the diagnoses in multiaxial or in nonaxial format, he or she should follow the convention of placing the principal diagnosis first and listing any other diagnosis in order of their decreasing clinical significance.

The "Reason for Visit" modifier for outpatients is analogous to the "Principal Diagnosis" modifier for inpatient admissions. The qualifying phrase "Reason for Visit" is used to indicate which of several diagnoses is responsible for an outpatient or ambulatory service. The diagnosis that constitutes the "Reason for Visit" is usually the primary focus of attention or treatment for outpatient visits.

PROVISIONAL AND NOT OTHERWISE SPECIFIED (NOS) DIAGNOSES

(*DSM-IV*, pp. 3–5)

Sometimes diagnoses are uncertain. The clinician may have too little information. The client may be uncooperative, disorganized, mute, or otherwise unable to provide much personal history. When the client does not meet the full criteria for a disorder, but the clinician strongly suspects that, with more information or observation, full diagnostic criteria will be met, the presumed diagnosis can be given provisionally. To do so, the clinician simply writes the modifier "Provisional" after the name of the presumed but uncertain diagnosis.

Some disorders must be diagnosed provisionally because of the way they are defined, especially when a time course is required to make the diagnosis. Panic Disorder (300.01), for example, requires that at least one panic attack be followed by a month or more of persistent worry about having more panic attacks and about their consequences or significant behavioral changes due to the attacks. By definition, a client with panic attacks who worries or is behaviorally disordered for less than one month could only receive a provisional diagnosis.

Another example is Schizophreniform Disorder (295.40), which closely resembles schizophrenia. By definition, an episode of schizophreniform disorder lasts between one month and six months. Thus, a client who has had two months of ongoing prodromal and active symptoms at the time of evaluation could only receive a presumed diagnosis of "Schizophreniform Disorder, Provisional," if the clinician strongly suspected this diagnosis. A remission of symptoms must occur within six months to make a definitive schizophreniform disorder diagnosis.

In some cases the clinician may be in the right ballpark in making a diagnosis, but the clinical presentation may be so atypical that none of the standard diagnostic criteria sets for the class of disorder specifically applies. Because presenting clinical pictures can be so varied, the *DSM-IV* provides a Not Otherwise Specified (NOS) category for all of its major classes of mental disorders. There are four typical situations in which the clinician may choose the NOS diagnostic label, namely:

1. Cases that phenomenologically belong to a general class of disorder (e.g., mood disorder, psychotic disorder, anxiety disorder) but that are atypical, mixed, or do not meet the full criteria set for any of the specific types of the general class of disorder will receive an NOS diagnosis.

2. Cases of disorders that are not included in the *DSM-IV* may receive an NOS diagnosis. Some of these disorders may appear in the appendix to *DSM-IV*. Others may be syndromes peculiar to a particular culture or subculture. Believe it or not, *DSM-IV* does not include every mental disorder possible. In fact, critics of DSM-III have pointed out that researchers too often limit themselves solely to the criteria included in DSM instead of incorporating criteria from other systems.

3. When the cause of the disorder is uncertain, the NOS category can be used. In one clinical example, a woman with systemic lupus erythematosus (SLE, an inflammatory connective tissue disease) developed a disturbance of thought and mood while on corticosteroid therapy. It was not clear if the SLE was affecting her brain, if she was suffering from a steroid-induced mental disorder, of if she had a primary disorder of thought and mood that predated the onset of her SLE. In other words, the etiology of the mental disturbance could have been a primary mental disorder, a medical illness, or the result of a substance the patient was ingesting.

4. Finally, when the clinician does not have enough information to make a specific diagnosis, but is fairly certain that the disorder falls within a general class of disorders, the NOS category can be used. For example, in emergencies the clinician may be able to diagnose a psychotic disorder, but have insufficient time for a complete evaluation. In other cases, the client may be mute, uncooperative, or contradictory in supplying historical information.

In a lecture at the May 1994 APA convention in Philadelphia, Michael First, M.D., encouraged clinicians to make more use of the NOS category. He noted that in the past clinicians have felt somewhat ashamed to use the NOS category, as if the use of NOS somehow implied the clinician's ignorance or lack of diagnostic acumen. The reality is that patients in the real world often fall outside the strict bounds of *DSM-IV* criteria. Many clients present for evaluation with subthreshold conditions that do not meet full *DSM-IV* criteria sets. In such cases, the clinician can code the disorder as NOS;

or, if in the clinician's clinical judgement the disorder appears prototypic and meets most but not full *DSM-IV* criteria, the clinician can give the specific *DSM-IV* diagnosis.

Dr. First emphasized that the NOS category is especially useful in the following circumstances: (1) when subthreshold conditions exist that do not meet full *DSM-IV* criteria, (2) when it is not clear if the disorder is primary, substance induced, or secondary to a general medical condition, (3) when the available clinical data is incomplete, inconsistent, or contradictory, (4) when the clinician does not have access to relevant information, and (5) when the clinician confronts one of the new diagnoses or culture-bound syndromes described in the appendices of *DSM-IV*. Dr. First's take-home lesson was: don't be ashamed to code a disorder as "Not Otherwise Specified."

V CODES, UNSPECIFIED, DEFERRED, AND NO DIAGNOSIS CATEGORIES

(*DSM-IV*, pp. 4–5)

In addition to the use of provisional and NOS diagnoses, the clinician can indicate diagnostic uncertainty by using V codes, the "Unspecified" modifier, and the Deferred Diagnosis (799.9) category.

The V codes of *DSM-IV* are more extensive than those found in *DSM-III-R*. The V codes are placed in the section of *DSM-IV* entitled "Other Conditions" that may be a focus of clinical attention (*DSM-IV*, pp. 675–686). Medication-induced movement disorders have also been included in that section.

In the multiaxial diagnostic format, V codes are listed on Axis I. The V codes cover such problems for which people seek psychological therapy as Bereavement (V62.82), Partner Relational Problems (V61.1), and Acculturation Problems (V62.4). Initially, the clinician may only have enough information to make a V code diagnosis, but upon further evaluation may discover that the presenting difficulty is in fact related to a mental disorder.

When the evaluation reveals that no Axis I clinical syndrome diagnosis exists, the clinician should say so by listing "No Diagnosis or Condition" on Axis I (V71.09). However, when the clinician has inadequate information either to reasonably make or rule out an Axis

I diagnosis, then the proper coding is "Diagnosis or Condition Deferred" on Axis I (799.9).

Similarly, when the evaluation reveals that no Axis II personality disorder or mental retardation diagnosis exists, the clinician should say so by listing "No Diagnosis or Condition" on Axis II (V71.09). This is the same V code (V71.09) used for "No Diagnosis or Condition" on Axis I. However, when the clinician has inadequate information either to reasonably make or rule out an Axis II personality disorder diagnosis, then the proper coding is "Diagnosis Deferred" on Axis II (799.90). The same numerical code (799.9) is used for "Diagnosis or Condition Deferred" on Axis I.

A final option for expressing diagnostic uncertainty about a nonpsychotic disorder is to use the Unspecified Mental Disorder (nonpsychotic) category (300.9). For example, the clinician may be certain of the presence of a mental disorder, but have insufficient information to further categorize the disorder. With further evaluation, the diagnosis may be changed to a specific disorder. In other cases the disorder may not be part of the DSM-IV classification system or else the available NOS categories may not apply.

8

Multiaxial Assessment

"Let observation with extensive view,
Survey mankind, from China to Peru;
Remark each anxious toil, each eager strife,
And watch the busy scenes of crowded life."

Samuel Johnson, *The Vanity of Human Wishes* (1749)

The use of five axes to code clinical information about mental disorders began with *DSM-III*. Those who used the old *DSM-I* and *DSM-II* were aware that a single diagnostic label, like schizophrenia, was not comprehensive enough to capture a client's clinical status and allow the clinician to develop an adequate treatment plan or to predict a likely outcome.

There is often a heterogeneity among persons with the same psychiatric diagnosis, and clinical situations often vary enormously in their complexity. In addition, clinicians may overlook important clinical variables, such as personality traits or the presence of mental retardation in their assessment and treatment planning. In developing *DSM-III*, the consensus of expert opinion was that clinical status could be more accurately reported along several dimensions or axes.

The choice of five axes was arbitrary and had to do with making the diagnostic system clinically useful without being too intricate and cumbersome. The goal of the multiaxial approach was to provide a useful, comprehensive, and systematic overview of the clinical situation.

Each of the five axes depicts a different type of information. The first three "diagnostic" axes code traditional disorders, both psychiatric and medical, as well as personality disorders and V codes of other conditions that may be a focus of clinical attention.

Axis I comes first in the multiaxial system because it codes clinical syndromes, which are the most common reasons individuals come to clinical attention. Next, the personality disorders and mental retardation receive a separate axis (Axis II) to ensure that the clinician will consider these important personality variables as part of the clinical picture. Finally, Axis III allows the clinician to note general medical conditions that are relevant to the case.

The fourth and fifth "non-diagnostic" axes code areas of assessment other than clinical syndromes and medical illnesses. Included are psychosocial and environmental problems on Axis IV and a Global Assessment of Functioning (GAF) on Axis V. The former Axis IV of *DSM-III-R* was used to identify and rate the severity of psychosocial stressors. The authors of *DSM-IV* reconceptualized Axis IV as a way to list important psychosocial and environmental problems. The following outline should make these distinctions clear.

DSM-IV MULTIAXIAL ASSESSMENT

Diagnostic Axes I–III

(*DSM-IV*, pp. 25–28)

Axis I: Clinical syndromes, including all mental disorders in *DSM-IV*, except the personality disorders and mental retardation. This includes developmental disorders, which had been coded on Axis II in *DSM-III-R*.

Other conditions that may be a focus of clinical attention (V codes, psychological factors affecting medical condition, medication-induced movement disorders).
V71.09:   No diagnosis on Axis I.
799.9:   Diagnosis deferred on Axis I.

Axis II: Personality disorders.
Mental retardation.
Maladaptive personality traits.
Habitual defense mechanisms.
V71.09:   No diagnosis on Axis II.
799.9:   Diagnosis deferred on Axis II.

Axis III: General medical conditions relevant to understanding and managing the case.
ICD codes for medical condition are included.
Axis III: None (no medical conditions).
Axis III: Deferred.

Other Areas of Assessment:
Non-diagnostic Axes IV–V

(*DSM-IV*, pp. 29–31)
Axis IV: Psychosocial and environmental problems that may affect the diagnosis, treatment, or prognosis of the disorders on Axes I, II, and III.

Axis V: Global Assessment of Functioning (often reported as a single number between 1 and 100, using the GAF scale to rate current functioning).

The use of multiaxial *DSM* diagnosis for mental disorders has become the norm in the United States, but is by no means mandatory. *DSM-IV* allows the clinician to decide whether to code diagnoses in a multiaxial or in non-axial format (*DSM-IV* page 35). According to *DSM-IV*, clinicians who prefer a non-axial format should list the appropriate diagnoses, being certain to list the "Principal Diagnosis" or "Reason for Visit" first and to record all coexisting mental disorders, medical conditions, and other factors relevant to the care and treatment of the individual.

Page 34 of *DSM-IV* provides a sample "Multiaxial Evaluation Report Form" that clinicians may use or adapt for recording axial diagnoses. In the remainder of this chapter we will focus on multiaxial recording.

AXIS I

(*DSM-IV*, pp. 25–26)
Recall that *DSM-IV* provides sixteen broad classes of clinical syndromes and a seventeenth class, Other Conditions That May Be a Focus of Clinical Concern. Except for reporting mental retardation and personality disorders (which go on Axis II), Axis I is used for

recording all the remaining fifteen classes of clinical syndromes and the other conditions that may be a focus of clinical attention. We list below the sixteen general categories of clinical information that can appear on Axis I:

1. Disorders Usually First Diagnosed in Infancy, Childhood, or Adolescence. The exception is mental retardation, which is coded on Axis II.
2. Delirium, Dementia, Amnestic, and Other Cognitive Disorders.
3. Mental Disorders Due to a General Medical Condition Not Elsewhere Classified.
4. Substance-Related Disorders.
5. Schizophrenia and Other Psychotic Disorders.
6. Mood Disorders.
7. Anxiety Disorders.
8. Somatoform Disorders.
9. Factitious Disorders.
10. Dissociative Disorders.
11. Sexual and Gender Identity Disorders.
12. Eating Disorders.
13. Sleep Disorders.
14. Impulse Control Disorders Not Elsewhere Classified.
15. Adjustment Disorders.
16. Other Conditions That May Be a Focus of Clinical Attention.

When a person exhibits more than one Axis I disorder, the convention is to report the principal diagnosis first, appending the qualifying phrase "Principal Diagnosis/Reason for Visit" (see DSM-IV, p. 3) unless the principal diagnosis happens to be an Axis II mental retardation or personality disorder diagnosis. If a client displays both an Axis I and an Axis II diagnosis, the Axis I diagnosis is presumed to be the principal diagnosis/reason for visit unless the Axis II diagnosis is followed by the modifier "Principal Diagnosis/ Reason for Visit."

When the clinical evaluation reveals that there is no Axis I diagnosis, the clinician should note the absence of an Axis I disorder with the code V71.09.

When there is too little time or information to establish an Axis I diagnosis, the clinician can defer making the diagnosis by using the code 799.9 (Diagnosis Deferred), pending further evaluation.

Because many of the V codes represent psychosocial and environmental problems, they can appear on both Axis I as a focus of clinical attention and by name on Axis IV as an external stressor.

AXIS II

(*DSM-IV*, pp. 26–27)

Axis II is where the clinician records personality disorders and mental retardation. When an individual meets criteria for more than one personality disorder, they should all be listed. Axis II can also be used to report significant maladaptive personality traits and habitual defense mechanisms. There are no code numbers for personality traits or for defense mechanisms. Borderline Intellectual Functioning (V62.89) is also coded on Axis II.

DSM-IV identifies eleven categories of personality disorder that can be listed on Axis II. These are:

1. Paranoid
2. Schizoid
3. Schizotypal
4. Antisocial
5. Borderline
6. Histrionic
7. Narcissistic
8. Avoidant
9. Dependent
10. Obsessive-Compulsive
11. Personality Disorder Not Otherwise Specified

When clinical evaluation reveals no Axis II personality disorder or mental retardation, the clinician should note the absence of an Axis II disorder with the code V71.09.

When there is too little information to establish an Axis II diagnosis, the clinician can defer making the diagnosis by using the code 799.9 (Diagnosis Deferred), pending further evaluation.

In creating a separate axis to code personality disorders, the authors of *DSM-III* had the noble intention of encouraging clinicians not to overlook important clinical information in diagnosing psychiatric disorders. There was never any implication that Axis II disorders are fundamentally different from Axis I disorders. Nonetheless, managed care companies and health insurers are not fond of Axis II diagnoses because personality disorders often require intensive, long-term, and costly treatment.

At meetings of professional societies, one hears reports of clinicians being asked by managed care companies to invent Axis I diagnoses for patients whom they are treating solely for an Axis II disorder. The following dialogue took place early in 1994 between a psychiatrist and the representative of a national managed care company:

Managed care person: What is the patient's Axis I diagnosis?
Doctor: She doesn't have an Axis I diagnosis.
Managed care person: But we need an Axis I diagnosis.
Doctor: She really doesn't have an Axis I diagnosis. I'd have to make one up!
Managed care person: Okay. We don't like Axis II diagnoses. They take too long to treat.

AXIS III

(*DSM-IV*, pp. 27–28)

Persons with severe mental disorders have a higher incidence of medical illnesses than the general population. Axis III exists for reporting current general medical conditions relevant to understanding and managing the case. If the past medical history is important for current clinical understanding, it is also recorded on Axis III.

By providing a separate axis for medical conditions, the authors of *DSM-IV* did not intend to imply any fundamental distinction between mental and physical disorders. *DSM-IV* eschews a reductionistic mind/body dualism. According to *DSM-IV*, a separate Axis III exists for the sake of thorough assessment and enhanced communication among clinicians.

A significant medical condition is likely to have an impact on the psychological well-being of an individual. In addition, the medications used to treat medical disorders may interact with psychotropic medications and/or have adverse side effects with psychiatric consequences.

Sometimes the medical condition on Axis III will be the underlying cause of the mental disorder on Axis I. In such instances the medical disorder is recorded on both axes. For example, hypothyroidism can present with symptoms of a major depressive episode that clear once the thyroid condition is treated. In this case, hypothyroidism (*ICD-9-CM* code 244.9) is listed on Axis III as a general medical condition and is also mentioned on Axis I with the code 293.83, Mood Disorder Due to Hypothyroidism.

When evaluation reveals that no medical conditions exists, the clinician reports this as "Axis III: None."

When the clinician has insufficient information to adequately determine the presence or absence of a medical condition, the coding is "Axis III: Deferred."

The code numbers used on Axis III are taken from *ICD-9-CM*'s 999 categories of diseases. When *ICD-10-CM* becomes official in the United States toward the end of this century, its codes will supersede those of *ICD-9-CM*. For reference we list here the range of *ICD-9-CM* code numbers and the classes of medical conditions that they represent:

ICD-9-CM CODE Medical Condition

001–139	Infectious and Parasitic Diseases
140–239	Neoplasms
240–279	Endocrine, Nutritional, Metabolic, and Immunity Disorders
280–289	Blood and Blood-forming Organs Diseases
(290–319)	(Mental Disorders)
320–389	Nervous and Sense Organs Diseases
390–459	Circulatory System Diseases
460–519	Respiratory System Diseases
520–579	Digestive System Diseases
580–629	Genitourinary System Diseases
630–679	Complications of Pregnancy, Childbirth, and the Puerperium
680–709	Skin and Subcutaneous Tissue Diseases

710-739   Musculoskeletal System and Connective Tissue Diseases
740-759   Congenital Abnormalities
760-779   Certain Conditions Originating in the Perinatal Period
780-799   Symptoms, Signs, and Ill-defined Conditions
800-999   Injury and Poisoning

Although officially Axis III exists for recording *ICD-9-CM* names and code numbers of general medical conditions that are relevant to the client's mental disorder, some clinicians also use this axis to note significant physical signs and symptoms that need further evaluation. For example, a client might complain of "blurred vision" during the psychiatric evaluation. Visual blurring is often a side effect of psychotropic medication, but might also be due to some other medical problem. The clinician could then refer the client to an ophthalmologist as part of a comprehensive treatment plan.

AXIS IV

(*DSM-IV*, pp. 28-28)
Axis IV underwent a revision with the development of *DSM-IV*. In *DSM-III-R*, Axis IV was used to identify psychosocial stressors and to rate their severity. Many clinicians did not find such severity ratings particularly helpful. The authors of *DSM-IV* decided it would be more useful to use Axis IV to record those external psychosocial and environmental problems that might impact on the disorders listed on Axes I, II, and III.

By convention, Axis IV lists the psychosocial and environmental problems that have been clinically relevant during the year preceding the evaluation. A certain amount of clinical judgment is needed in cases where external stressors have occurred more than a year prior to the current evaluation. For example, some individuals develop a chronic pathological grief reaction leading to a prolonged major depressive episode years after the death of a significant person. In such cases, the death of the significant other, no matter how long ago, should be listed on Axis IV. In another example, a veteran who still suffers Posttraumatic Stress Disorder (309.81) because of witnessing atrocities in the Vietnam War should have the war experiences listed on Axis IV.

The literature on stress distinguishes between stresses due to positive events (eustress) and negative events (distress). Negative stressors, like the loss of a job or a death in the family, clearly belong on Axis IV. Positive stressors, like winning the lottery or the birth of a child, go on Axis IV only if they pose a clinically significant problem for the individual.

Many of the common stressors that people encounter have V codes attached to them in *DSM-IV*. Stressful events may represent both areas of clinical attention (Axis I) and psychosocial or environmental problems (Axis IV). The V codes for these stressors should appear on Axis I when the environmental factor or psychosocial stressor is a primary focus of clinical attention.

DSM-IV recommends that the clinician routinely consider the following nine categories of psychosocial and environmental problems when coding Axis IV (*DSM-IV*, pp. 29–30):

1. Problems with Primary Support Group:
   Childhood (V61.9)
   Adult (V61.9)
   Parent–Child (V61.20)
2. Problems Related to the Social Environment (V62.4)
3. Educational Problems (V62.3)
4. Occupational Problems (V62.2)
5. Housing Problems
6. Economic Problems
7. Problems with Access to Health Care Services
8. Problems Related to Interaction with the Legal System/Crime
9. Other Psychosocial and Environmental Problems

Most of these nine categories are self explanatory, but the first and second require some clarification. Most crisis situations involve a failure of the individual's support system. Problems with the primary support group include such events as a death in the family, the birth of a sibling, separation, divorce, remarriage, abuse, neglect, and illness in the family. Problems related to the social environment include items such as social isolation, the breakup of friendships, relocation, retirement, and problems due to cultural differences. The final "other" category can be used for stressors related to natural or man-made disasters, for problems related to professional caregivers, and for other stressors that do not fit within the other eight categories.

In addition to identifying which of the nine categories applies on Axis IV, the clinician should identify the specific stressors within each category. Complex clinical pictures usually involve multiple stressors, and the clinician should list all that apply on Axis IV. For example, a homeless Afro-American with schizophrenia, paranoid type (295.30), living on the streets of New York might have the following list of Axis IV diagnoses:

- Problems with Primary Support Group (estrangement from family).
- Problems Related to Social Environment (lack of friends, racial discrimination, physical abuse by a local gang of teenagers).
- Educational Problems (illiteracy).
- Occupational Problems (unemployment).
- Housing Problems (homelessness).
- Economic Problems (extreme poverty, not receiving entitlements).
- Problems with Access to Health Care (lack of any form of health insurance).
- Problems Related to Interactions with the Legal System/Crime (charged with shoplifting food from supermarket).
- Other Psychosocial Problems (Client's social worker was out due to personal illness.)

AXIS V: GAF SCALE

(*DSM-IV*, pp. 30–31)

The GAF scale has implications for clinical assessment, treatment planning, research, and reimbursement for services. At least one managed care company has decided to refuse to fund the treatment of patients who have a GAF score above 70.

Axis V underwent revision in *DSM-IV*. Research on the use of Axis V in *DSM-III* and *DSM-III-R* revealed that this axis had only modest reliability. According to the research, Axis V was a reasonably valid measure of adaptive functioning, but it was not being widely used in clinical settings.

Some critics of Axis V questioned the value in *DSM-III-R* of recording two separate measures of adaptive functioning on Axis V, one at the time of the evaluation and another for the highest level of adaptive functioning during the past year. The *DSM-IV* task force decided that, in most instances, limiting Axis V to a single rating at the time of the evaluation was the most clinically useful measure of adaptive functioning.

In *DSM-IV*, clinicians can use Axis V to record their assessment of the individual's current overall level of psychological, social, and occupational functioning at the time of the evaluation. Impairment due to physical and environmental limitations is excluded from Axis V.

DSM-IV provides a GAF scale that allows clinicians to express the level of functioning as a number from 1 to 100. *DSM-IV*'s GAF scale is a revision of the Global Assessment Scale published by Endicott, Spitzer, Fleiss, and colleagues in 1976. The GAF scale has been criticized because it confounds the severity of symptoms with the level of functioning. In addition, the GAF scale has the potential for being abused in forensic, disability, managed care, and insurance reimbursement situations.

A GAF score of 0 indicates that the clinician has inadequate information to assess functioning. GAF scores from 1 to 100 are divided into 10 point segments, each representing a different level of functioning. Scores from 1 to 10 indicate the lowest level of functioning at the low end of the scale, while scores from 90 to 100 code superior functioning at the top of the scale. Important points to remember about the GAF scale are that:

- GAF is a single measure of symptom severity and current functioning at the time of the evaluation, rated as a number from 1 to 100.
- GAF is a global measure of psychological, social, and occupational functioning and symptom severity.
- GAF does not measure impairment due to physical or environmental limitations.
- GAF measures level of functioning and symptom severity in 10 point segments whose interpretation we paraphrase as follows:
  0: Inadequate information.
  1–10: Lowest level of functioning.
  The MOST EXTREME level of impairment.

Failure of personal hygiene.
Persistent danger to self or others.
11–20: Some danger to self or others.
EXTREME impairment.
Grossly impaired communication.
Occasional failure of minimal hygiene.
21–30: Unable to function in most areas.
MODERATELY EXTREME impairment.
Seriously impaired communication or judgment.
Psychotic symptoms determine behavior.
31–40: MAJOR IMPAIRMENT in several areas.
Some impaired reality testing.
Some impaired communication.
41–50: SERIOUS symptoms or impairment.
(e.g., suicidal preoccupations, no friends)
51–60: MODERATE symptoms or impairment.
(e.g., blunted affect, few friends)
61–70: MILD symptoms or impairment.
Generally functions fairly well.
Some significant interpersonal relationships.
71–80: Transient symptoms.
Only SLIGHT impairment.
Symptoms are expectable reactions to stress.
81–90: Absent or MINIMAL symptoms.
Good functioning in all areas.
90–100: SUPERIOR functioning.
No symptoms.
A paragon of mental health.

Clearly the GAF scale requires the clinician to use clinical judgment. Once the clinician decides which 10-point spread applies to the person being evaluated, he or she can use the intermediate numbers in the spread to indicate where on the spectrum the client lies. Thus, a client with a GAF score of 52 would have moderate symptoms or impairment and would be functioning less well than a similar client with a GAF score of 59. In inpatient settings, the clients' GAF scores at the time of admission are likely to be 50 or less, as these scores represent serious to extreme symptomatology or impairment.

Perhaps the solar patriarchal authors of *DSM-IV* were thinking of themselves when they wrote the description for the range of 91 to 100 on the GAF Scale. The *DSM-IV* Draft Criteria (March 1, 1993, p. D:8) defines a GAF score of 91 to 100 as follows: "91–100: Superior functioning in a wide range of activities, life's problems never seem to get out of hand, is sought out by others because of his many positive qualities. No symptoms."

While the rest of the diagnostic manual scrupulously avoids the pronoun "his" when referring to individuals, the *DSM-IV* Draft Criteria's description of the highest level of functioning on the *GAF* scale talks of "his" and not of "her" many positive qualities. Is this a Freudian slip? Do the authors of *DSM-IV* secretly believe that only men can be paragons of mental health? (A historical note for clinicians trained after *DSM-III*: a Freudian slip refers to the antiquated notion that the objective descriptive words one uses sometimes reveal one's unconscious ideas about a subject.) The editors of the final (1994) draft of *DSM-IV* caught this error, and women are now allowed as many positive qualities as men in psychiatric nosology.

In addition to the GAF scale, *DSM-IV* provides three related scales in its *Appendix B*. Such scales may be useful in certain mental health care or rehabilitation settings. The three additional scales are:

1. The *SOFAS* (*DSM-IV*, pp. 760–761). The Social and Occupational Functioning Assessment Scale (SOFAS) allows clinicians to rate social and occupational functioning separate from the severity of psychological symptomatology. In other words, the SOFAS deals only with social and occupational functioning, whereas the GAF scale combines the overall severity of the symptoms and the level of impairment produced by the mental disorder. In assessing social and occupational functioning, the SOFAS includes impairments of both physical and mental functioning that are due to problems with mental and/or physical health. This scale may be useful in rehabilitation programs aimed at improving social and occupational functioning.

2. The *GARF* (*DSM-IV*, pp. 758–759). The Global Assessment of Relational Functioning (GARF) scale provides a measure of competence or dysfunction in the functioning of a relational unit rather than an individual. The GARF scale rates the functioning of a relational unit (family or similar social system) much as the GAF scale rates the functioning of an individual. Using the GARF scale, the clinician can

rate, on a scale from 1 to 100, how well a family or other ongoing relational unit meets the needs of its members along the dimensions of problem solving, organization, and emotional climate.

3. The *DFS* (DSM-IV, pp. 751–757). The Defensive Functioning Scale (DFS) provides a method to code the individual's defensive style. The DFS groups the various individual defense mechanisms (a.k.a. coping styles in *DSM-IV*) into seven "defensive levels," namely:

High Adaptive Level
Mental Inhibitions (compromise formation) Level
Minor Image-Distorting Level
Disavowal Level
Major Image-Distorting Level
Action Level
Level of Defensive Dysregulation

We refer the reader to *Appendix B* of *DSM-IV* for further details of the DFS ratings. The manual provides a glossary that defines the mechanisms of defense (*DSM-IV*, pp. 755–757).

GLOBAL ASSESSMENT OF FUNCTIONING SCALE (GAF) FROM *DSM-IV*

Finally, with permission we reproduce here the GAF scale from *DSM-IV* (see *DSM-IV*, p. 32).

Consider psychological, social, and occupational functioning on a hypothetical continuum of mental health-illness. Do not include impairment in functioning due to physical (or environmental) limitations.

Code (Note: Use intermediate codes when appropriate, e.g., 45, 68, 72.)

100   Superior functioning in a wide range of activities, life's problems never seem
 | to get out of hand, is sought out by others because of his or her many positive
91   qualities. No symptoms.

90   Absent or minimal symptoms (e.g., mild anxiety before an exam), good
 | functioning in all areas, interested and involved in a wide range of activities,
81   socially effective, generally satisfied with life, no more than everyday problems or concerns (e.g., an occasional argument with family members).

80 **If symptoms are present, they are transient and expectable reactions to**
| **psychosocial stressors** (e.g., difficulty concentrating after family argument); **no**
71 **more than slight impairment in social, occupational, or school functioning**
(e.g., temporarily falling behind in schoolwork).

70 **Some mild symptoms** (e.g., depressed mood and mild insomnia) **OR some**
| **difficulty in social, occupational, or school functioning** (e.g., occasional tru-
61 ancy, or theft within the household), **but generally functioning pretty well, has**
some meaningful interpersonal relationships.

60 **Moderate symptoms** (e.g., flat affect and circumstantial speech, occasional panic
| attacks) **OR moderate difficulty in social, occupational, or school functioning**
51 (e.g., few friends, conflicts with peers or co-workers).

50 **Serious symptoms** (e.g., suicidal ideation, severe obsessional rituals, frequent
| shoplifting) **OR any serious impairment in social, occupational, or school**
41 **functioning** (e.g., no friends, unable to keep a job)

40 **Some impairment in reality testing or communication** (e.g., speech is at times
| illogical, obscure, or irrelevant) **OR major impairment in several areas, such as**
31 **work or school, family relations, judgment, thinking, or mood** (e.g., depressed
man avoids friends, neglects family, and is unable to work; child frequently
beats up younger children, is defiant at home, and is failing at school).

30 **Behavior is considerably influenced by delusions or hallucinations OR serious**
| **impairment in communication or judgment** (e.g., sometimes incoherent, acts
21 grossly inappropriately, suicidal preoccupation) **OR inability to function in**
almost all areas (e.g., stays in bed all day; no job, home, or friends).

20 **Some danger of hurting self or others** (e.g., suicide attempts without clear
| expectation of death; frequently violent; manic excitement) **OR occasionally**
11 **fails to maintain minimal personal hygiene** (e.g., smears feces) **OR gross**
impairment in communication (e.g., largely incoherent or mute).

10 **Persistent danger of severely hurting self or others** (e.g., recurrent violence) **OR**
| **persistent inability to maintain minimal personal hygiene OR serious suicidal**
1 **act with clear expectation of death.**

0 **Inadequate information.**

9

The *DSM-IV* Diagnostic Interview

"No one can understand what ails a person without knowing that person."

"Who is this person and how does he come to be here?"

> Harry Stack Sullivan, *The Psychiatric Interview* (1954)

"Above all else, do no harm. *(Primum non nocere.)*"

> Hippocrates

The art of interviewing is best learned through apprenticeship with an experienced clinician. Diagnostic interviews come in many shapes and sizes. An interview conducted by a psychoanalyst or family therapist will differ from one conducted by a clinician seeking to make a *DSM-IV* diagnosis. The psychoanalyst will be interested in unconscious conflict and the patient's suitability for psychoanalysis. The family therapist will pursue family dynamics and the cross-generational transmission of family dysfunction and might even complete the Global Assessment of Relational Functioning (GARF) scale (DSM-IV, pp. 758–759). The goals of the interview determine its structure and process.

DSM-IV deals with mental disorders occurring in individuals rather than in families, groups, or society. *DSM-IV* is also theoretically atheoretical—that is, it tries to stick to empirical evidence and to avoid theoretical speculation about the causes of psychiatric disorders. To this end, it focuses on objective signs and symptoms while avoiding inferences about unconscious process or content. *DSM-IV* avoids dynamic formulations, not because unconscious factors are irrelevant to clinical work, but rather because psychodynamic diagnosis is based on a specific theory about mental life that is not part of the official *DSM* classification. *DSM-IV* seeks to make diagnoses based on a Kraepelinian approach of objective, empirically verifiable signs and symptoms of mental disorders.

Thus, the *DSM-IV* diagnostic interview will selectively address general areas, such as the following:

For Axis I (Clinical Syndromes and Other Conditions That May Be a Focus of Clinical Attention): Who is this person and how does he or she come to be here? What is the chief complaint or presenting problem? Why does the person present now for evaluation? What is the most pressing issue on the client's mind? Where does the client hurt? Does the client show signs and symptoms of any of the fifteen major classes of Axis I mental disorders, either during the narrative part of the interview or on formal mental status examination? Is there a prior history of a similar or related disorder? Were there any developmental difficulties in childhood? Is there a family history of major mental disorders? Could an Axis III general medical condition be causing the current disturbance? Could the presenting clinical picture be the result of substance use or abuse? Are there conditions other than clinical syndromes (e.g., V codes) that should be a focus of clinical attention? Which clinical syndromes or conditions will become the current focus of clinical attention? Which is the principal diagnosis or the reason for today's visit? Are there any provisional or uncertain diagnoses? What further information does the clinician need to establish a diagnosis? How will that information be obtained?

For Axis II (Personality Disorders and Mental Retardation): Does the client evidence any long-term pattern of maladaptive character traits that cause significant impairment or distress? Such a history may have to be obtained from friends and family, as the individual with a personality disorder may be unaware of his or her maladaptive traits. What are the client's habitual defense mechanisms? Does the client meet criteria for any of the ten specified *DSM-IV* personality disorders? Is there evidence of mental retardation?

For Axis III (General Medical Conditions): Are there any physical signs and symptoms present? Does the client have a documented history of any injuries or medical disorders? If so, what type of treatment is the client receiving? What, if any, prescribed medications is the client taking and do those medications have any psychological or psychiatric side effects? Does the client use illicit drugs that have medical consequences? Is there a history of a traumatic brain injury? Is there any significant family history of medical disorder? Could a general medical condition be causing the clinical problems noted on Axis I? Who is the client's doctor? When and why did the client visit a doctor last? When was the most recent complete physical examination and what did it reveal?

For Axis IV (Psychosocial and Environmental Problems): What psychosocial or environmental problems is the client facing? Why is the client presenting now for evaluation? What stressors are currently taxing the client's ability to cope? Because most crises involve a failure of the support network, what is the client's social support system and how well is it functioning? How is the client meeting such basic needs as survival, food, shelter, clothing, safety, education, employment, friendship, affection, social interaction, and self-esteem? Common stressors include losses and anniversaries of emotionally significant events.

For Axis V (Global Assessment of Functioning): How well is the client currently functioning in the psychological, social, and occupational aspects of his or her life? How severe are the current symptoms of the disorder? What score would the client receive on the GAF scale?

Does the client evidence impaired reality testing or major impairment in several areas, indicating a GAF score of 40 or below? Does the client's score fall in the serious symptom range of 41 to 50 or in the moderate symptom range of 51 to 60? Or is the client doing fairly well with some meaningful interpersonal relationships and only mild symptoms, indicating a score of 61 or above? The clinician will need to use the GAF scale (*DSM-IV*, p. 32) to arrive at the proper score.

The above paragraphs present an overview of the types of questions that clinicians should have in mind during a diagnostic interview. An interview concerned primarily with making a *DSM-IV* diagnosis, however, will invariably push some important clinical information into the background. The psychiatric literature after the inception of *DSM-III* in 1980 documents that clinicians steeped in the current *DSM*, to the exclusion of other systems of psychological thought, run the risk of conducting narrowly focused, mechanical, computer-like interviews.

The authors of *DSM-IV* recognized these risks and issued several important caveats to those wishing to use *DSM-IV*. The introduction to the diagnostic manual warns that *DSM-IV* is not to be applied mechanically by untrained individuals. *In fact, the DSM-IV diagnostic criteria are intended to serve as guidelines that always require clinical judgment and are not meant to be used in a cookbook fashion.*

Making a *DSM-IV* diagnosis is only a first step in the evaluation. A comprehensive treatment plan will require substantial information about the client beyond that needed to make the *DSM-IV* diagnosis. Clinicians and researchers need to bear in mind that the *DSM-IV* criteria represent only a consensus of current formulations of evolving knowledge about mental disorders. By no means does the *DSM-IV* encompass all conditions that may be a legitimate focus of clinical attention or research. A competent diagnostic interview will not only provide a *DSM-IV* diagnosis, but will also begin to gather a fair amount of additional information needed to provide adequate treatment to another human being.

Where does one begin? The best place to start is with the interviewer rather than with the patient. A good interviewer needs an attitude of openness, acceptance, and respect for the other person. Clinicians should have an interest in the varieties of human experience, a basic curiosity about humanity, and a fundamental desire to get to know other people as well as themselves. Such an attitude of genuine interest and respect for the patient has traditionally been called "bedside manner."

Clinicians should also know about psychopathology—about the characteristic presentations, signs and symptoms, and clinical course of the mental disorders. We can only see what our construct of reality allows us to see. If we do not know that something can exist, we are unlikely to notice it when it is before us. A solid grounding in *DSM-IV* descriptive diagnosis and in the major theoretical schools of psychopathology is essential for good clinical work.

Diagnostic interviewing requires a blend of art, interpersonal skill, talent at communication, and scientific knowledge. Alvan Feinstein, in his book *Clinical Judgment* (1967), gives an account of the requirements of a skillful interviewer. In the passage below, Feinstein follows the convention of referring to the generic clinician with the masculine pronoun "him." Feinstein was writing in the 1960s in a style that may sound sexist to contemporary ears. Even in the words of this compassionate and exemplary physician, we cannot escape the influence of solar patriarchal mythology on modern medicine as Feinstein (1967) describes the ideal clinical interview:

> The art of clinical examination comes from attitudes and qualities that are neither obtained nor easily detected by scientific procedures: the clinician's awareness of people and human needs; his ability to temper the rational aspects of his work with a tolerant acceptance of the irrationalities of mankind; his perception of faith, hope, charity, love and other elements of human spirit and human emotion. These properties of care and compassion, although sometimes dismissed as *merely* "bedside manner," are the fundamental and most important tools of any clinician. With them, he can often give healing or comfort where science fails or does not exist. Without them, his science is unsatisfactory, no matter how excellent. [p. 298]

Another excellent discussion of the art of clinical interviewing can be found in the classic text by Sullivan, *The Psychiatric Interview* (1954). Sullivan viewed the clinician as an expert in the field of interpersonal relations, and he saw the purpose of the psychiatric interview as "elucidating *characteristic patterns of living*" (p.4). Sullivan stressed the need to respect the client, to pay attention to issues of anxiety and self-esteem, and to conduct the interview strictly for the benefit of the client. He viewed the interviewer as a "participant observer" in the process and took the position that no one can understand a person without knowing that person.

Finally, Sullivan (1954) found the essential ingredient of a competent psychiatric interview to be "that the person being interviewed realizes, quite early, that he is going to learn something useful about the way he lives. . . . that the person will leave with some measure of increased clarity about himself and his living with other people" (pp. 18–19). What a strange idea to modern ears! That every interview is potentially therapeutic and will enhance the client's self understanding! Sullivan's suggestion is both an attitude and an ideal that we as clinicians can strive to achieve.

Spitzer (cited in Skodol 1989), one of the masterminds behind *DSM-III* and a seasoned teacher of clinical interviewing, humorously distinguishes three approaches to the diagnostic interview: the "checklist," the "smorgasbord," and the "canine" styles (pp. 4–5).

The caricatured "checklist" interviewers act like computers, devoid of warmth and the human touch, simply gathering data in a rote, closed-minded manner. Their major goal is to thoroughly note the presence or absence of *DSM* diagnostic criteria. No other aspect of the clinician/client interaction seems to matter. The problem is that checklist questions stop the spontaneous flow of conversation. Such questions give the impression that the interviewer is not interested in information that falls outside the categories provided. The checklist approach introduces interviewer bias into the inquiry, as it forces the clients to pigeonhole their responses categorically. Checklist interviewers tend to reify the *DSM* diagnoses and do not recognize, to quote Hamlet, that "there are more things in heaven and earth, Horatio, than are dreamt of in your philosophy."

A smorgasbord is a Swedish buffet of appetizers or sandwiches served at a long table. The "smorgasbord" interviewer takes a little taste of each type of clinical information without pulling the clinical picture together into a coherent whole or going into depth about particularly significant areas of clinical concern. The risk here is of not seeing the forest for the trees. The smorgasbord interviewer may be able to describe a little about early development, a little about job and marital history, a little about medical and psychiatric history, and a little about current functioning, but may be unable to formulate why the patient presents now with the current set of symptoms.

In contrast to the checklist and smorgasbord interviewers, Spitzer's "canine" interviewer does the best job in gathering diagnostic information. Such an interviewer seeks out relevant clinical data the way a dog sniffs out, discovers, and digs up the backyard in quest of its treasured and buried bone. Spitzer's dog metaphor resembles Sullivan's (1954) idea of considering impressions as hypotheses to be tested during the interview "by *clearly purposed exploratory activity* of some kind" (p. 122).

How does one arrive at hypotheses to be tested during the interview? In Spitzer's dog metaphor, what is the scent that the interviewer sniffs after? One important principle is to always follow the client's affect or emotional state during the interview. People tend to encode significant issues as a combination of three modes of representation of thought: ideationally as thoughts and images, affectively as feelings or emotions, and motorically as patterns of muscle or motor response (Horowitz 1970). For example, a woman who has been raped, when approached sexually, may experience an intrusive visual memory, feelings of panic, and a tightening of her muscles.

By following the client's affect and motor responses, the clinician can become aware of unexpressed ideas on the client's mind. Any incongruity between verbal and body language has a similar connotation. Some clients will say they feel fine, but look like they are about to cry. Others will complain of multiple woes, but appear to be in no distress. *La belle indifference* of grand hysteria is a classic example of incongruity between verbal and body language. Clients with conversion disorders often demonstrate such a "beautiful indifference" or lack of concern about their impairment.

There is a danger in taking Spitzer's dog metaphor too literally. A dog in pursuit of a bone will not attend to issues of respect, consideration, and the client's self-esteem. A dog has no sense that it is causing property damage by digging hole after hole in the backyard. One would expect clinicians to have more empathy for their clients than they do for their backyards.

The client, coming in pain to the mental health professional, expects relief from suffering through the empathic understanding of the interviewer. The clinician whose primary interest lies in sniffing out the diagnostic bone may end up with a juicy *DSM-IV* category, but no client to pin it on. Consider the nonclinical example of Erasmus Darwin (1731–1802), who was asked by someone whether he found his stammering inconvenient. Erasmus replied, "No, sir, because I have time to think before I speak, and don't ask impertinent questions."

According to Allen Enelow and Leta Adler (1979), a good diagnostic interview, aimed at the efficient gathering of detailed clinical information in a short time, requires

attention to rapport and to the development of the clinician-patient relationship and an attempt to facilitate the *emergence* of facts rather than their *extraction* from the patient, thereby creating the opportunity for less biased and more relevant information, both verbal and non-verbal. It relies on a differential use of the clinician's authority, never using more authority than is required to get the needed data, and on

the ability of the interviewer, through appropriate support and reassurance, to express his interest in helping the patient. [p. 60–61]

An interview typically begins with clinicians introducing themselves, indicating to the client where to sit, and explaining the
purpose of the interview if it is not obvious. The interview room
should be comfortable and private to assure confidentiality. The
interviewer seeks to create an atmosphere of trust and confidence and
to establish rapport and mutual collaboration. The most important
activity of the clinician during the interview is to listen empathically
and try to understand what ails the client.

It is useful early on to gather basic identifying data about the client:
name, age, gender, address, ethnicity, cultural background, country
of origin, marital status, children, living arrangements, employment,
level of education, military service, legal status, and so on. Such
demographic and identifying information provides a frame of reference for understanding the chief complaint developmentally and in
context of the unique life situation of the individual.

Most mental health clinicians use an open-ended approach to elicit
the chief complaint. The open-ended model begins by inviting the
client to discuss his or her reasons for seeking the consultation and
how he or she believes the interviewer might be of help. According to
Roger MacKinnon and Stuart Yudofsky (1986), "the most important
technique in obtaining the psychiatric history is to allow the patient to
tell his story in his own words and in the order he chooses" (p. 41).
Andrew Skodol (1989) recommends using opening comments, such
as "tell me how it is that you've come to be in the hospital," or "tell
me about what's been bothering you and how I can help." Enelow
and Adler (1979) suggest a broad opening question, such as, "What
kind of difficulties are you having?" Freud said to his patient
Katharina, "Well, what is it you suffer from?"

The client's response to the initial open-ended question can be
quite revealing. One young man, when asked what was bothering
him that he sought help at the mental health center, responded, "I
have running thoughts that debilitate my health physically to a point
of metaphysical being." This striking chief complaint led the clinician
to form several hypotheses about what might be troubling this young
man at this time. Some of the questions that ran through the
interviewer's mind included the following: Do the running thoughts

represent a hypomanic symptom? Does substance abuse play a role? Is the strange phrasing of the response evidence of a thought disorder? What concern does he have about his physical health?

As this client told his story, the interviewer learned that he was a 25-year-old male prostitute who had been HIV positive for four years and was being treated with AZT. He had a very low T-cell count and was concerned about dying of AIDS. Three years prior to the evaluation, he began to hear voices talking to each other about him and sometimes addressing him directly. He was a user of crack cocaine on almost a daily basis and supported his drug habit by prostitution. His mood was mildly depressed, and he suffered from poor sleep and diminished appetite. There was also a family history of his mother having auditory and visual hallucinations during one of her pregnancies.

While listening to the client's response to the initial open-ended inquiry, the interviewer should be wondering why the client presents at this particular time for an evaluation. Why now? The young man with HIV had been symptomatic with auditory hallucinations for three years. During the interview two acute stressors emerged that might account for his current presentation to the clinic. The first stressor was that his longstanding lover was about to be released from jail after serving a 15-month sentence for a drug-related offense. The second stressor was that, almost exactly a year before the current psychiatric evaluation, his internist had given him only five more years to live. The client presented for psychiatric evaluation on the first anniversary of his internist's prediction. A year had elapsed since the prediction, and the client was dealing with issues of dying from his disease. As mentioned previously, anniversary reactions are common reasons why people present to mental health professionals.

Open-ended questions tend to avoid introducing interviewer bias into the inquiry. Clinicians should not suggest an expected answer by their choice of words in phrasing questions and comments. For example, one clinician, who believed her client to have a multiple personality disorder (300.14) with a little girl alter, demanded of the client, "Come out and speak to me, little girl; I know you're in there." The emergence of a little girl alter at this point in the interview could simply be a sign of a suggestible client's wish to please a powerful authority, rather than evidence of a multiple personality disorder.

Emotionally charged words are best avoided. Clients often want to please the interviewer and tell clinicians what they want to hear. The ideal response, however, is the client's spontaneous formulation of a reply without regard to what the interviewer approves of or expects to hear. Clinicians should also be careful not to bias the communication by their tone of voice and body language, showing approval of one line of response while discouraging the client's telling of what they don't want to hear.

At an appropriate point in the interview, it is helpful to ask the clients about their hopes and expectations of the interview and of the interviewer. Clinicians might ask questions such as: "How do you hope I can be of help?" and "What were you expecting I (we) could do for you when you came in today?" The answers to such inquiries can be revealing. For example, one client, who came to a mental health center, responded to such questions with: "I really need someone to talk to, but I thought you probably just gave medications here."

Another useful inquiry is to ask clients whether they have any theory about what has happened to cause their current difficulty. A man presented to a hospital emergency room with severe diarrhea. During a medical interview, the doctor asked all the usual questions about the nature, duration, and severity of the symptoms. Only when the patient was asked if he had any idea how he got the diarrhea did the patient respond that he had just returned from Mexico and thought the intestinal ailment had something to do with the water he drank.

Each interviewer should speak naturally in his or her own style. It is best to talk simply and clearly in nontechnical language. In framing comments and questions, the interviewer needs to take into account the client's educational level, facility with English, native language, and social and cultural background.

An open-ended approach usually results in the spontaneous reporting of a broad range of clinically relevant history. The interviewer must listen to the client's story, forming hypotheses about diagnostic possibilities and deciding on ways to follow up clinical impressions with more focused inquiry later in the interview. The clinician is always striking a balance between facilitating communication, taking control of the interview to limit circumstantial chatter, and redirecting the client to discuss other clinically relevant topics.

For many clinicians, a useful technique is to visualize the patient's story as if one were watching a movie. This visualization technique not only aids in remembering the client's history, but also reveals clinically important gaps or inconsistencies that require further exploration. In applying one's visual imagination to the client's story, the clinician wonders silently, "What's missing or not right about this picture?"

The interviewer needs to attend to both the client's verbal and nonverbal communication. The verbal information includes the client's spontaneous telling of his or her story and the responses to the interviewer's comments and inquiries. Clients also convey much about themselves through their behavior, gait, posture, tone of voice, facial and eye expression, gestures, and body stance. As mentioned previously, any incongruence between body language and the verbal message is likely to be clinically significant.

Having elicited what the medical model terms the client's *chief complaint* in an open-ended manner, the clinician is next curious about how the current difficulties developed. In the medical model, this type of information is called the *history of the present illness*. In this part of the interview the clinician's knowledge of diagnosis and psychopathology is essential. When did the problem start? What signs and symptoms did the client experience? Does the symptom picture constitute an episode of any of the *DSM-IV* clinical syndromes? How severe is the disorder at the time of the evaluation? Could any medical condition or the use of substances account for the presenting complaints? Are any associated or related disorders present? Usually, a discussion of the client's chief complaint and history of present illness will identify external stressors (coded on Axis IV) associated with the development or exacerbation of the client's difficulties.

In forming hypotheses during the interview, it is useful to keep in mind the biopsychosocial model of mental disorders as a mnemonic for covering all the diagnostic bases. Virtually all mental disorders have biological, psychological, and social components. Could the client's difficulties be the result of a primarily biological disturbance, perhaps a general medical or neurological condition, a genetic disorder, or the ingestion of a substance? Confusion, disorientation, and poor cognitive functioning suggest brain dysfunction.

Although functional (versus medical or organic) disorders may have a firm biological substrate, the clinician needs to consider whether the client's chief complaint lies in the realm of the more psychological functional disorders. In common parlance, do the client's symptoms have more of an organic/physical/medical/ neurological basis or more of a "mental" basis? At the Greater Bridgeport Community Mental Health Center in Connecticut, families frequently bring in relatives for evaluation with the complaint, "You've got to see him, doc, he's mental."

Recall that the *DSM-IV* has only seventeen major categories. One of these is for the personality disorders of Axis II, and another is for conditions other than clinical syndromes that may be a focus of clinical attention. Of the remaining fifteen major categories, one is for disorders of childhood and adolescence and three have to do with predominantly organic disorders, namely, with cognitive disorders, with disorders due to general medical conditions, and with substance-related disorders. The remaining eleven disorders are predominantly functional in nature.

To aid in remembering the seventeen major *DSM-IV* categories, we outline them below.

The seventeen major categories of *DSM-IV* are:

I. Disorders Usually First Diagnosed in Infancy, Childhood, or Adolescence.
II. The Predominantly Organic Disorders (no longer called organic in *DSM-IV*). There are three major categories:
   A. Delirium, Dementia, Amnestic, and Other Cognitive Disorders
   B. Mental Disorders Due to a General Medical Condition
   C. Substance-Related Disorders
III. The Predominantly Functional Disorders (not referred to as functional in *DSM-IV*). There are eleven major categories:
   A. Schizophrenia and Other Psychotic Disorders
   B. Mood Disorders
   C. Anxiety Disorders
   D. Somatoform Disorders
   E. Factitious Disorders
   F. Dissociative Disorders
   G. Sexual and Gender Identity Disorders
   H. Eating Disorders
   I. Sleep Disorders
   J. Impulse Control Disorders Not Elsewhere Classified
   K. Adjustment Disorders
IV. Personality Disorders.
V. Other Conditions That May Be a Focus of Clinical Attention.

In considering the psychological aspect of the biopsychosocial model, the clinician runs through the personality disorders and through the eleven major functional disorders of *DSM-IV*. Does the clinical picture reveal psychotic disturbance, mood disorder, irrational anxiety, disturbance of physical functioning (somatoform), factitious symptoms, dissociation, sexual problems, eating disorder, sleep disturbances, lack of impulse control, adjustment to a stressor, or personality disorder?

Finally, consider the social aspects of the biopsychosocial model. Is the client's problem primarily rooted in social causes? What is the status of the person's provision for food, shelter, and clothing? Does the client live in an atmosphere of violence or abuse? Are there economic or occupational problems? Is the client trying to establish grounds to receive disability payments? Could the client be malingering? Is there a legal case pending? Is the support system adequate? Has the client suffered a recent loss or a death? People frequently seek help at mental health clinics because of grief reactions.

Having established a chief complaint and having detailed the history of the present illness, the next logical question is whether the client has had similar problems in the past. In the medical model, this type of information is called the past psychiatric history and includes prior diagnoses, previous types of treatment, and the history of past hospitalizations. Often the client's developmental and family history help to elucidate the present and past psychiatric history. While on the topic of past psychiatric history, some clinicians inquire about current and past medical history to round out the clinical presentation.

Throughout the interview, the clinician is also assessing the client's personality style and level of adaptive functioning. In the evaluation of personality functioning, the clinician should distinguish between enduring personality traits and the current clinical state of the client. Severely depressed individuals, for example, are often irritable, angry, moody, pessimistic, and difficult for family and friends to spend time with. Such irritability and moodiness usually disappear with successful treatment of the depression and do not constitute maladaptive personality traits. In addition, information about past relationships and job performance is helpful in making trait versus state distinctions.

One criticism of *DSM-IV* has been that it focuses primarily on what's wrong with the person rather than on the strengths and assets of the individual. The clinician should be alert to the client's areas of strength and coping skills that will assist in treatment planning. One clinician likened the clinical evaluation to the assessment of a flooded city. Some of the roads and structures will be damaged and in need of repair, but large sections of the city will remain intact and will be useful in restoring normal functioning. Typical assets include motivation for treatment, insight and judgment, psychological mindedness, relatedness, good impulse control, employment skills, education, avocational interests, cognitive abilities, intelligence, friendships, family and other social supports, religious affiliation, ability to live independently, and suitable housing.

Interviews rarely take place as neatly as described in the textbooks. Clinicians need to be adaptable and to go with the client's flow. At the same time, for the sake of thoroughness, the interviewer should have a mental map of the areas to be covered during the diagnostic interview and should come back to material that has not yet been discussed.

Time should be allowed for a proper ending of the diagnostic interview. During the closing phase the clinician usually summarizes the salient aspects of the patient's history, provides a formulation of the problem in nontechnical language, and explains any recommendations for further evaluation or treatment. The clinician tries to make sure that the client understands the formulation and recommendations and also asks if the client has any questions. Some clients find it helpful to be given the opportunity to read the section of *DSM-IV* that describes their diagnosis.

There are clients who regard the interview as a formality or rite of passage and save their real concerns until the very end. The following question often provides useful clinical information: "Is there anything we have not discussed that you think might be important for me to know?" It may happen that the clinician learns what is really on the client's mind only during the last few minutes of the interview.

Finally, the clinician tries to conclude the interview on a note of hope and optimism. Most likely the client has sought help out of worry or concern about a personal problem. The client wants assurance that help is available and that matters are not hopeless. Ideally, the client should leave with a sense of having been listened to respectfully and understood by the interviewer.

One issue that frequently comes up during the ending phase of the interview is that of secondary gain. The sick role confers certain advantages in our society, such as relief from responsibilities, disability benefits, monetary gain, attention from family and significant others, and professional services. In public clinics clients will often wait until the end of the interview to pull out papers to be completed by the clinician in order to qualify for city welfare or Social Security disability payments. Some of these clients may be malingering. Others have disabling mental disorders, but are seeking financial assistance rather than psychiatric treatment. In such cases, the answer to the question, "Why now?," is that the client needs papers signed to qualify for financial aid.

In today's climate of managed health care, time is often at a premium when doing a diagnostic interview. Many clinics, mental health centers, and hospital emergency rooms have limited resources and must restrict the time allotted for a psychiatric assessment. Clinicians need to become sufficiently expert at interviewing in order to conduct a psychiatric evaluation as efficiently as possible. We will conclude this chapter by reviewing some basic principles and techniques of interviewing.

Sullivan (1954) stressed that the psychiatric interviewer is an expert with an unusual grasp of the field of interpersonal relations. As an expert, the clinician knows how to facilitate communication and, when necessary, how to guide and limit the client's productions. This is done in an atmosphere of trust, respect, and mutual participation. The noted psychiatrist Otto Will (1970) summarized Sullivan's approach as follows:

> The interview is characterized by the coming together of two people, one recognized as an expert in interpersonal relations, the other known as the client, interviewee, or patient, who expects to derive some benefit from a serious discussion of his needs with this expert. The situation is designed to make clear certain characteristic patterns of the client's living with the prospect that such elucidation will prove useful to him. [p. ix]

In this book we are advocating an open-ended approach to the diagnostic interview that encourages the client to tell his or her story. Rather than focusing on the extraction of detailed facts, the interviewer seeks to facilitate spontaneous communication. To this end, the clinician exerts the least control early in the interview and more control in seeking information as the interview progresses. Any exercise of control or authority by the clinician runs the risk of biasing the client's responses.

The clinician has several methods available to facilitate communication. After asking an open-ended question to elicit a chief complaint, the interviewer should normally remain silent and attentive while allowing the patient to tell his or her story. The clinician's occasional facilitating gestures or comments may help the conversation to flow smoothly by inviting the client either overtly or tacitly to elaborate on a topic.

The interviewer usually asks for more detail to follow up on clinically significant material at the time it is presented. The clinician can then redirect the client back to the story line. This technique of following leads at the time of presentation and then returning to the flow of the interview conveys a sense of continuity and professionalism.

Sometimes clients have difficulty relating their stories. In such cases the interviewer may choose to use the technique of confrontation in which the clinician directs the client's attention to some aspect of his or her story or behavior in the interview. Confrontation is not a hostile or aggressive statement by the interviewer. It is a technical term that refers to the technique of confronting clients with some aspect of their behavior. The clinician is essentially saying to the client, "This is what you just said or did in the interview. Please take a look at it." The hope is that directing the client to examine a piece of current behavior will open the door to further relevant clinical material.

For example, a clinician might say to a client who looks tearful while describing how wonderful life is, "You look like you are about to cry even though you are saying how happy your life is" or, to a client who gets stuck while discussing a particular topic, "You seem to be uncomfortable discussing this matter." Clinicians should be especially sensitive to a client's sense of shame about issues such as sexual abuse. The interviewer might say to the abused client, "It is difficult to talk about some topics with a stranger," and allow the client the choice of whether to continue.

Some clients seem able to talk endlessly about a topic. In these cases the clinician will need to exert control of the interview to make a transition to a new topic. Such transitions should be respectful of the client while making use of the legitimate authority of the clinician to conduct the interview. A typical transitional comment might be, "I have a picture of what's been happening recently; have you had similar problems in the past?" At times the clinician will need to exert a high degree of authority by saying such things as, "Our time is limited and there are other areas we need to cover today; I would like to ask you now about your family history."

We have not yet mentioned the formal mental status examination as part of the diagnostic interview. Throughout the interactions with the client, the clinician is attending to the client's verbal and non-verbal communication. Much of the evaluation of mental status is done in this unobtrusive natural way. The interviewer is constantly assessing the client's appearance and behavior, speech, intelligence, orientation, memory, level of awareness, perceptions, judgment, thought process and content, mood, affect, impulse control, potential for harm to self and others, and so on. The clinician should make a transitional comment to introduce those aspects of the mental status exam that are not a smooth part of the interview. For example, the interviewer might say, "I would now like to ask you some questions to check if there are any difficulties with your memory or sense of orientation." In the next chapter we will review the formal mental status examination and its role in diagnostic interviewing.

10

The Mental Status Examination

"The more distinctly human the phenomenon, the more necessary is a human observer to discern the phenomenon adequately. Whatever can be distinguished only by human speech, sight , smell, touch, hearing, taste, movement, and cerebration cannot be discerned by inanimate devices, which lack the perception of human sensory organs and the ingenuity of a human brain."

Alvan Feinstein, *Clinical Judgment* (1967)

The mental status examination (MSE) is an essential part of a psychiatric evaluation. It consists of a systematic examination of the client's thinking process, feeling state, and behavior. In doing the mental status examination, the clinician performs an orderly assessment of the cognitive and emotional functioning that may be disturbed in patients with mental disorders.

The mental status examination derives from the medical model of assessment of psychiatric disorders. Just as a physician does a physical examination to check each organ system of the body, the mental health professional examines each major area of psychological and behavioral functioning. The typical psychiatric mental status examination notes the client's general appearance and behavior, cognitive functioning and intelligence, thought process and content, reality testing, affective functioning, suicidal or homicidal ideation, impulse control, judgment, and insight.

Textbooks artificially separate the formal mental status examination from history taking during the diagnostic interview. Such a distinction is useful in preparing a written report, but can be awkward during a clinical interview. The clinician gleans much of the information about mental status from the patient's presentation and spontaneous reporting. Some clinicians awkwardly split off the mental status assessment from the rest of the diagnostic session and even apologize for asking questions to evaluate mental status. Clients may wonder why they are being subjected to irrelevant inquiry.

Ideally, the mental status examination is an integral, seamless part of the interview. The clinician should introduce mental status examination inquiries in a way that makes sense to the client. For example, if the client complains of feeling confused, the clinician might say, "You say you are feeling confused; let me ask you some questions to check your memory and sense of orientation." The client then realizes the importance of the cognitive testing and is more likely to collaborate in a process to his or her own benefit.

Assessment of mental status goes on throughout the interview. The clinician constantly observes the client's behavior and communication, both verbal and nonverbal. The interviewer attends to content as well as process—that is, to both what and how the client communicates. While clients are telling their stories, the clinician is forming hypotheses about their current and past functioning. Much of the interviewer's activity during the interview will involve the testing of such hypotheses. Some of the clinician's questions will be answered by simply listening to the client's spontaneous reporting; others will require specific detailed inquiry by the interviewer. In cases of extremely guarded, mute, or uncooperative clients, the clinician may need to assess mental status through the observations of others who are able to describe the person's recent functioning. If no reliable informant is available, the clinician may not be able to achieve any degree of diagnostic certainty until such time as the client's mental status improves, a reliable source is found, or medical and/or psychiatric records are obtained.

We now present an outline of a typical written report of a mental status examination. This is but one possible outline for the mental status examination, and many other equally useful formats exist. The most informative way to document the mental status examination is to quote the client's comments verbatim, giving specific examples of the client's behavior during the interview.

To repeat, we present this mental status examination outline as one possible format for a written report and stress that it is not to be used as a series of steps to follow during the interview. The categorical divisions of this outline are arbitrary. One category may blend imperceptibly into another; for instance, it may be difficult to distinguish abnormalities of speech and language from disorders of thought process and content.

In conjunction with this chapter, we recommend that the reader review Appendix C of *DSM-IV*, the Glossary of Technical Terms (*DSM-IV*, pp. 763–771) , which defines many of the psychiatric terms used in the diagnostic manual.

THE MENTAL STATUS EXAMINATION IN PSYCHIATRY

I. General Description
   A. Appearance
      1. Dress and grooming
      2. Physical characteristics
      3. Posture and gait
   B. Attitude and interpersonal style
   C. Behavior and psychomotor activity
   D. Speech and language
      1. Rate
      2. Clarity, pitch, volume, tone, quality, and resonance
      3. Abnormalities
II. Emotions
   A. Mood
   B. Affect
   C. Neurovegetative signs of depression
III. Cognitive Functioning
   A. Orientation and level of consciousness
   B. Attention and concentration
   C. Memory
      1. Immediate registration, retention, and recall (a minute or less)
      2. Recent memory (a minute to days or weeks)
      3. Remote memory (weeks to years)
         a. Memory for recent past

           b. Memory for distant past
        4. Client's subjective report of memory difficulties
    D. Ability to abstract and generalize
    E. Information and intelligence
        1. Fund of knowledge
        2. Estimate of intelligence
IV. Thought and Perception
    A. Disordered perceptions
        1. Illusions
        2. Hallucinations
        3. Depersonalization and derealization
    B. Thought content
        1. Distortions
        2. Delusions
        3. Ideas of reference
        4. Magical thinking
    C. Thought process
        1. Flow of ideas
        2. Quality of associations
    D. Preoccupations
        1. Somatic
        2. Obsessions and compulsions
        3. Phobias
  V. Suicidality, Homicidality, and Impulse Control
  VI. Insight and Judgment
 VII. Reliability

The remainder of this chapter will flesh out the mental status examination outline, beginning with the general description of the client.

GENERAL DESCRIPTION

   I. General Description
    A. Appearance
        1. Dress and grooming
        2. Physical characteristics

3. Posture and gait
B. Attitude and interpersonal style
C. Behavior and psychomotor activity
D. Speech and language
    1. Rate
    2. Clarity, pitch, volume, tone, quality, and resonance
    3. Abnormalities

Appearance

The written report of the mental status examination starts with a general description of the client, including appearance and behavior, attitude toward the interviewer, and quality of speech. Consider the following clinical study by Sigmund Freud of the case of Katharina, who was the victim of incest by her father (Case 4, Volume II, p. 125, *The Standard Edition*):

> I was so lost in thought that at first I did not connect it with myself when these words reached my ears: "Are you a doctor, sir?" But the question was addressed to me, and by the rather sulky-looking girl of perhaps 18 who had served my meal and had been spoken to by the landlady as "Katharina." To judge by her dress and bearing, she could not be a servant, but must no doubt be a daughter or relative of the landlady's. . . . So there I was with the neuroses once again—for nothing else could very well be the matter with this strong, well-built girl with her unhappy look. . . . I report the conversation that followed between us just as it is impressed on my memory and I have not altered the patient's dialect.
> "Well, what is it you suffer from?"
> "I get so out of breath. Not always. But sometimes it catches me so that I think I shall suffocate."

Notice how Freud creates for his readers a vivid image of a sullen but healthy mountain girl who seeks his advice with an attitude of hopeful expectation. She speaks in a dialect, but her speech with its normal rate and volume appears to be polite, clear, and articulate. Note also how Freud uses an open-ended query to elicit the girl's chief complaint: "Well, what is it that you suffer from?" After listening to the young lady's spontaneous report and following up with some pointed inquiries, Freud concluded that she suffered from anxiety attacks that were part of a posttraumatic stress disorder, rooted, as Freud believed, in a sexual trauma.

An ideal description of a client should be full enough that it might allow another clinician to identify the client in the waiting room. The adjectives used should be objective and descriptive, free of value judgments and editorial comments. It is useful to describe the client's dress and grooming, hygiene, body build and salient physical characteristics, facial expression, eye contact, vocal qualities, posture, gait, agility, coordination, gestures, general behavior, sense of personal space, and level of psychomotor activity.

Certain physical signs will generate clinical hypotheses. For example, a patient with pinpoint pupils may be abusing narcotics. A client with scars on the face or head may have poor impulse control or a traumatic brain injury. Some people come to interviews reeking of alcohol.

Attitude and Interpersonal Style

The client's attitude toward the interviewer is of clinical importance. Chronic maladaptive attitudes are suggestive of a personality disorder. Some clients, like Freud's patient, may be polite, cooperative, and expectant of receiving help. Others may be friendly, frank, open, irritable, hostile, belligerent, demanding, sullen, evasive, passive, seductive, dramatic, manipulative, complaining, suspicious, accusatory, blaming, paranoid, guarded, withdrawn, defensive, playful, obsequious, ingratiating, and so on. The list of possible adjective runs the gamut of human behavior.

The clinician should note how the client relates to the interviewer as well as how the interviewer relates to the client. Is it possible to establish an empathic bond? Is the client able to make an emotional connection? Does the client have a sense of appropriate interpersonal boundaries? Is the client remote, detached, schizoid, or interpersonally disconnected?

The clinician's emotional reactions to the client may provide important clues. Experienced clinicians learn over time that certain types of disorders regularly trigger certain reactions in them. For example, clients with personality disorders may routinely evoke the same type of feelings in the people around them. In one significant study, J.M. Goodwin and colleagues (1979) demonstrated that medical patients whom doctors disliked were frequently either suicidal or suffering from organic brain damage. The doctors in this study were aware of their dislike of the patient, but remained unaware of the patient's suicidality or organicity.

Psychomotor Behavior

Psychomotor behavior, narrowly defined, refers to the quality and quantity of the client's motor activity. Severely depressed patients classically exhibit psychomotor retardation with a slowing of movement, speech, and thought. The psychomotor retardation of depressed clients can be so marked that they appear demented or cognitively impaired (the so-called pseudo-dementia of depression). The severely depressed person may also present with poor hygiene and grooming due to a lack of interest in self-care.

In contrast, manic patients show psychomotor excitement with physical and emotional hyperactivity and speeded responses. Anxious patients may exhibit psychomotor agitation or restlessness as they shift about and fidget during the interview. A patient with akathisia (an uncomfortable sense of motor restlessness) secondary to an antipsychotic medication may be unable to sit still. A severe akathisia may mimic a worsening of the patient's psychosis; in such cases, the unwary clinician may mistakenly increase the offending medication.

The interviewer should also note any stereotyped movements, twitches, tics, grimacing, dystonias, gestures, mannerisms, abnormal movements, fidgeting, pacing, restlessness, nail biting, tremulousness, agitation, or hyperactivity. A dystonia is an acute tonic spasm of a muscle, especially of the tongue, eyes, jaw, or neck, often secondary to antipsychotic medication. Acute dystonias usually occur early in the course of antipsychotic medication therapy; young males seem to be at highest risk for this side effect, but women are not immune.

Tardive Dyskinesia

Other movements seen among psychiatric patients on long-term neuroleptic (antipsychotic) medication are those of tardive dyskinesia

(TD), which literally means "late appearing abnormal movements." Tardive dyskinesia can involve the muscles of the face, mouth, tongue, limbs, and trunk. According to the *American Psychiatric Association's Psychiatric Glossary*, typical movements of tardive dyskinesia include "tongue-writhing and protrusion, chewing, lip-puckering, choreiform (brief, purposeless, involuntary) finger movements, toe and ankle movements, leg-jiggling, or movements of the neck, trunk, and pelvis" (p. 131). During the interview, patients with tardive dyskinesia may frown, blink, smile, or grimace; they may pout or smack their lips; or they may move their knees back and forth, tap their feet, bounce their heels up and down, or wiggle their feet. In severe cases the patient's neck, shoulders, hips and trunk may rock, twist, squirm, or gyrate.

The late appearing dyskinetic movements of tardive dyskinesia may be choreic or athetoid, or a combination of the two (choreoathetoid). Choreic movements are sudden, quick, jerky, involuntary, and without purpose. Some patients learn to merge their involuntary choreic movements into purposeful or semipurposeful actions to mask the underlying movement disorder. Athetosis refers to slow, irregular, complex, writhing, serpentine motions that blend continuously into a flowing stream of movement. Tremors, which are not part of the tardive dyskinesia spectrum, but which are common side effects of lithium carbonate and of tricyclic antidepressants, are repetitive, alternating, rhythmic movements produced by the regular contraction and relaxation of muscle groups.

Catatonic Behavior

Other uncommon abnormalities of motor behavior include catatonic rigidity and posturing, waxy flexibility, grimacing, catatonic excitement, mutism, negativism, echolalia, and echopraxia. Catatonic behavior may be seen in schizophrenia, catatonic type (295.2x), but in practice appears to be more common in the course of mood disorders than in schizophrenia. *DSM-IV* allows the clinician to specify whether the current manic or major depressive episode occurs with catatonic features.

Catatonic rigidity involves the maintenance of a rigid posture against efforts to be moved. Catatonic posturing refers to the patient's voluntarily assuming a bizarre or inappropriate posture. Waxy flexibility (*cerea flexibilitas*, in Latin) is the term used for the fact that the limb of a catatonic patient will remain in the position in which it is placed. Catatonic excitement stands in marked contrast to extreme catatonic immobility. The patient with catatonic excitement exhibits excessive purposeless motor activity that is uninfluenced by external stimuli. Echolalia is the parrot-like repetition of what the patient hears. Echopraxia is the imitative repetition or mimicking of the behavior of others.

Speech

Clinicians often describe the client's speech as a separate item of the mental status examination report. Speech is significant because it is the individual's primary means of communication and thus becomes the vehicle through which clinicians observe many of the signs of mental disorder. Speech is also the medium through which we usually observe the client's use of language and the nature of the client's thought.

Speech can be described in terms of its rate, clarity, pitch, articulation, volume, quality, quantity, impediments, use of words, and ability to get to the point. Manic patients typically exhibit pressure of speech as well as racing thoughts. Schizophrenic clients often speak in bizarre and stilted ways and may even coin entirely new words (neologisms) with uniquely personal and idiosyncratic meanings. Neologisms are also common in patients who are aphasic because of brain injury. Depressed patients may demonstrate poverty of speech. Clients who are being interviewed in a language other than their native tongue, especially if they are depressed, run the risk of being falsely assessed as suffering from poverty of speech.

Verbatim examples of the client's speech provide the most useful information for other clinicians reading the mental status examination report. For example, a man in his twenties suffering from chronic schizophrenia reported to his therapist in a flat and stilted manner how he learned of the recent death of his mother: "I received a letter from my sister in Ohio; one of the parents died." The patient stopped talking at that point, leaving the therapist wondering which parent had died. The stilted, overly abstract phrase "one of the parents died" conveys to other clinicians the schizoid style of communication of this troubled young man.

Language

Language is the basic tool by which people communicate. Disturbances of language occur routinely in cases of brain dysfunction. Some common causes of language deficits include strokes (cerebrovascular accidents), head trauma, and brain tumors. The presence of intact language ability is necessary for the clinician to be able to fully evaluate the client's cognitive functioning.

The mental health professional should be familiar with common neurological language disturbances and should be able to distinguish them from the loose associations of schizophrenia and from the flight of ideas of mania. For the reader's convenience, we list these neurological terms below with brief explanations.

Aphasia

Aphasia is the loss, due to brain damage, of the ability to understand or produce language. In the aphasic patient the damage is usually to the left cerebral hemisphere, which regulates such abilities as word choice, verbal comprehension, grammar, and syntax. In left-hand dominant persons and in some right-handed persons, the language cortex may be located in the right hemisphere.

The type and extent of aphasia depends on the location and extent of the brain injury. The most severe form of aphasia is global aphasia, in which the patient can neither understand nor speak; nor can the global aphasic patient read or write, repeat words, or name objects.

In Broca's aphasia ("expressive" aphasia), the patient can understand written and spoken language, but has difficulty expressing thoughts linguistically. The client's speech sounds like a telegram containing mostly nouns and verbs spoken in staccato. One woman who suffered brain damage due to toxic shock syndrome, when asked about an impending family visit, said, "Ah . . . son . . . come . . . son . . . yes . . . come."

Wernicke's aphasia ("receptive" aphasia) involves both the severe inability to understand language and the production of fluent but bizarre, nonsensical speech. Clients with Wernicke's aphasia often act strangely and may become agitated, paranoid, or euphoric. Inexperienced clinicians sometimes mistake the abnormal speech of

Wernicke's aphasia with a psychotic thought disorder. Unlike the aphasic patient, however, the typical client with schizophrenia will be able to understand written and spoken language and will be able to read, write, repeat spoken words, and name objects.

Dysarthria

Dysarthria refers to difficulty with the articulation of speech due to incoordination of the apparatus of speech production. It is caused by lesions in the inputs to the muscles of articulation. Patients with pure dysarthria will produce distorted and sometimes unintelligible speech sounds, but they will be able to read and write normally. Besides observing the articulation of the client's speech, the clinician can check for dysarthria by asking an English-speaking client to repeat a phrase like, "No ifs, ands, or buts."

Perseveration and Stereotypy

Perseveration is often a feature of brain dysfunction. In perseveration, the patient persists (perseveres) in repeating a verbal or motor response to a prior stimulus even when confronted with a new stimulus. For example, a perseverating client may continue to give the same answer to several different questions.

Stereotypy (stereotyped behavior) may occur with brain dysfunction (e.g., complex partial seizures), but is also seen in schizophrenia. Stereotypy refers to the constant repetition of speech or actions—for example, the repeated buttoning and unbuttoning of one's shirt or blouse. The constant repetition of a word or phrase is sometimes called *verbigeration*. Stereotypies and ritualistic behaviors are a feature of childhood autism.

EMOTIONS

II. Emotions
   A. Mood
   B. Affect
   C. Neurovegetative signs of depression

Mood and Affect

Mood has been likened to the enduring climate of a region, and affect to the daily weather fluctuations.

Mood refers to the dominant and enduring emotional tone of a person. The term mood emphasizes the pervading sustained quality of such feelings as depression, elation, expansiveness, anger, sullenness, dejection, irritability, and anxiety. Moods may vary in depth, intensity, and duration. In bipolar disorder, for example, mood can fluctuate from profound depression to ecstatic elation. Severely depressed patients frequently talk of feeling trapped when describing their overall mood.

Affect is the feeling-tone that accompanies a mental representation. Affects are the relatively brief outward expressions of a person's feelings and reflect the current but fleeting emotional state. People become aware of affect through body language, such as facial expressions, eye contact, gestures, posture, crying, laughing, tone of voice, and body movements. Clinicians use the phrase *full range of affect* to describe the affective responses of individuals whose affect varies appropriately during the interview in a way that matches the content of their speech and their interactions with the interviewer.

When affect shifts suddenly or rapidly during the interview, we speak of it as being labile. When the range and intensity of affective expression is diminished, we speak of restricted affect. When affective expression appears almost completely absent, we speak of blunted or flat affect. A person with flat affect may appear robotlike, speaking monotonously with no affective coloring as if the inner experience of emotion were totally absent. The affective flattening or blunting of schizophrenia is often accompanied by what *DSM-IV* calls avolition—that is, a kind of apathy, lack of persistence, or lack of energy and drive.

At times the expression of emotion will appear strange in the manner in which it does not match either the situation or the content of what the person is saying. There appears to be no connection between the verbal report and the emotional state of the patient. For example, a person may start laughing when nothing funny has occurred. This commonly occurs in schizophrenia, and in such cases we speak of the affect being inappropriate.

Neurovegetative and Other Signs of Depression

Patients with major depression commonly suffer disturbances in the normal regulation of body functioning. The clinician should inquire about sleep and appetite habits, energy level, interest in and ability to enjoy daily activities, sexual functioning, headaches and other pains, diurnal patterns in depressed mood, constipation, and weight changes. We will discuss these issues more fully in the chapter on mood disorders.

In asking about sleep, we usually ask if there has been initial, middle, or terminal insomnia. We commonly refer to these forms of insomnia as difficulty falling asleep (DFA), middle of the night awakening (MNA), and early morning awakening (EMA). Melancholic patients (see *DSM-IV*, pp. 383–384) frequently wake two or more hours before their customary hour of awakening and tend to feel most depressed in the morning. Some depressed patients, especially those with bipolar disorders, tend to sleep excessively (hypersomnia). Anhedonia, the inability to experience pleasure, is another common feature of depression.

In addition, depressed patients often lose or gain excessive amounts of weight (more than 5 percent of their body weight in a month). Appetite is commonly diminished in depressed individuals, but in some cases it may increase substantially. Loss of interest in sex is another common accompaniment of depression, and it is important for clinicians to take a sexual history as part of an evaluation.

COGNITIVE FUNCTIONING

III. Cognitive Functioning
   A. Orientation and level of consciousness
   B. Attention and concentration
   C. Memory
      1. Immediate registration, retention, and recall (a minute or less)
      2. Recent memory (a minute to days or weeks)
      3. Remote memory (weeks to years)

      a) Memory for recent past
      b) Memory for distant past
    4. Client's subjective report of memory difficulties
  D. Ability to abstract and generalize
  E. Information and intelligence
    1. Fund of knowledge
    2. Estimate of intelligence

Cognitive testing is an essential feature of the mental status examination. If a patient is significantly cognitively impaired, it may not be possible to perform a complete and accurate mental status examination. Medical and neurological conditions, which sometimes present as psychiatric disorders, often affect the functioning of the brain and of the special senses (vision, audition, smell, taste). Substance abuse can also cause brain dysfunction.

A careful assessment of cognitive functioning can lead the clinician to suspect and diagnose such disorders as delirium, dementia, general medical conditions, substance abuse, and medication toxicity. The clinician obtains much information about general attentiveness by simply observing the client's behavior and distractibility during the interview.

Because brain disease can initially present with emotional and behavioral changes, neurologists Richard Strub and F. William Black feel that a full mental status examination should be done on all psychiatric patients. The importance of careful cognitive testing is especially true when a mental disorder presents acutely in a client with a history of normal functioning. For example, the first appearance of a major depression in middle or late life may be the result of cortical atrophy, hydrocephalus, or a tumor in the frontal or temporal lobes.

In a critical review of the literature on the mental status examination, Martin Keller (1979) concluded that certain traditional tasks of the mental status examination are useful in detecting organic brain dysfunction, whereas others are not. According to Keller, the most helpful mental status examination items for differentiating organic from functional disorders among American clients are the following:

1. Orientation to time, place, and person.
2. Recall of remote personal events.

3. Recall of recent general events.
4. Recall of three objects after two minutes.
5. Fund of general knowledge, including past U.S. presidents, famous people, current events, and so on.

Keller also concluded that four traditional mental status examination tasks are not especially helpful in evaluating organicity or memory. These are:

1. Recall of recent personal events.
2. Subtraction of serial sevens. This task measures ability to sustain effort on a task.
3. Digits forward and backward. This task measures capacity to sustain effort and pay attention.
4. Proverbs and similarities. According to Keller, these are too influenced by education, intelligence, and culture to be reliable.

Not all clinicians agree with Keller's recommendations. Howard Benditsky, Ph.D. (personal communication [1994]), for example, argues that digit repetition, especially digits forward, is a useful way to gauge attention. He points out that it is useless to try to assess memory if attention is inadequate. Similarly, according to Benditsky, digits reversed, serial 7s, and proverb interpretation are useful measures of concentration and of immediate recall. In computer terminology, digit repetition, serial 7s, and proverbs test the clients available random access memory (RAM).

The Mini-Mental State Examination by Marshal F. Folstein and colleagues (1975) is a quick and useful standardized screening for cognitive difficulties that may be a result of brain dysfunction. For the reader's convenience, we have reproduced the Mini-Mental State examination at the end of this chapter. Scores on this exam range from 0 to 30. The test provides a convenient way to track cognitive functioning over time. The person being examined with the Mini-Mental State Examination should have at least nine years of education, or else false positives for cognitive impairment are likely to result. In addition, two items on the examination—specifically, naming a watch and a pencil and performing a simple reading task—do not adequately distinguish normal from organically impaired subjects.

Level of Consciousness

Evaluation of cognitive functioning begins with the clinician's assessment of the client's level of consciousness. The majority of psychiatric patients will be awake, alert, aware of internal and external stimuli, and able to cooperate with the examiner. Any drowsiness, inattentiveness, or clouding of consciousness is likely to be clinically significant and may suggest a medical, neurological, or substance-induced impairment. There are several technical terms to describe the varying degrees of diminished alertness, including, in order of worsening severity:

1. Lethargy (somnolence)
2. Obtundation
3. Stupor (semicoma)
4. Coma

In writing a mental status examination report, the clinician should not only include the descriptive term for the level of alertness, but also give a brief description of the client's actual behavior.

Lethargy

The lethargic or somnolent client has difficulty remaining alert and will drift off to sleep if allowed. When stimulated by the interviewer, the lethargic patient can be fairly readily aroused to alertness. Nonetheless, the somnolent client will have difficulty concentrating and attending to the interviewer's comments and will lose his or her own train of thought while speaking. In a written mental status examination report, it is insufficient to say simply, "The client was lethargic." Extremely lethargic patients are most often seen in medical settings, and the doctor could most clearly communicate the clinical picture with a description such as: "The patient would fall asleep unless I shook his shoulder. While awake, he would be able to answer only one or two brief questions before drifting back to sleep."

Obtundation

Unlike the lethargic patient, the obtunded client is difficult to arouse and must be repeatedly stimulated to maintain any level of alertness.

The obtunded patient is usually confused and unable to cooperate in formal cognitive testing.

Stupor

Stuporous (semicomatose) and comatose clients are typically evaluated by neurologists rather than mental health professionals. The stuporous patient is not self-arousing and can be roused by the examiner only with vigorous and persistent stimulation. Even when aroused, the semicomatose patient cannot interact normally with the examiner or participate in a mental status examination.

Coma

Coma is the most severe disturbance in the level of consciousness. Comatose patients are unarousable and, though alive, do not respond to stimulation. Obviously, clinicians will not be able to perform a mental status examination on comatose individuals.

Orientation

Clients with clouding of consciousness may exhibit disorientation, but impaired orientation can also occur with a clear sensorium. The mental status examination evaluates orientation in three areas: time, place, and person. Disturbances of consciousness typically affect sense of time first, sense of place second, and sense of person last. Recovery of orientation tends to occur in the reverse order.

In assessing orientation to time, the clinician might ask for the current date (day, month, year), the day of the week (Sunday through Saturday), the current time of day, the season of the year, and the client's sense of how long the interview has lasted or how long they have been in the hospital. Answers that are approximate but reasonably accurate are acceptable.

To evaluate orientation to place, the interviewer can ask where the client is now, the name and address of the place where the interview is taking place, the client's home address, the present city and state, if the client can give accurate directions from one familiar place to another, and other questions related to the client's sense of knowing his or her current whereabouts. The clinician should observe whether the client behaves as if he or she were in a different place. For example, a confused elderly man with Alzheimer's disease might act in the doctor's office as if he were at home in his own bedroom.

Finally, to examine orientation to person, the clinician inquires whether clients can identify themselves and the people around them. Does the client know personal identifying data, such as name, age, and date of birth? Can the client identify other people in the environment, and does the client understand his or her relationship to these other people? Disorientation to person is usually a sign of significant disturbance, such as delirium, dementia, a psychotic delusional state, or a severe dissociative disorder.

The ability to remain oriented to time and place requires an intact memory. Knowing where you are and what time it is depends on the continuous learning and retention of new information about the environment. Disorientation suggests that a significant memory deficit may be present, and the interviewer should test memory in detail in the disoriented client.

Attention and Concentration

Attention is the ability to stay focused on a stimulus without distraction. The client must be alert to be attentive, but an alert client is not necessarily able to pay attention. The interviewer should observe the client's behavior for any distractibility or inability to pay attention. To formally test the ability to sustain effort and pay attention, the clinician can use the digit repetition task described below.

Concentration (sometimes referred to as vigilance) is the ability to sustain attention for an extended period. The ability to concentrate is necessary for learning, for performance of intellectual tasks, and for academic success. The clinician should observe the client's ability to pay sustained attention during the interview. To formally test concentration, the interviewer can ask the client to perform mentally a complex intellectual task. Such tasks include the serial subtraction of 7s from 100 and the spelling of a five-letter word forward and backward. Like the repetition of digits forward and backward, the ability to subtract serial 7s mentally measures the ability to sustain effort on a task.

To test serial 7s, the interviewer gives an instruction such as: "Please start with 100 and subtract 7; then subtract 7 from your answer and keep subtracting 7 from each subsequent answer." The wording of the instruction should be commensurate with the client's intelligence and level of education. Subtracting serial 7s is a difficult task for most people and requires sustained attention and concentration. If the client has had academic difficulties, the serial 7s test may be invalid.

The clinician should be careful not to humiliate the illiterate or uneducated client by demanding intellectual performance beyond the capacity of the individual. If the serial 7s task is too difficult, the interviewer might ask the client to subtract serial 3s from 100. Other options include asking simple arithmetic calculations or asking the client to make change from $10 after a purchase, say, of $7.43. The idea is to test whether the client can sustain attention long enough to perform a complex intellectual task mentally for a period of at least 30 seconds.

Another useful bedside test for attention and concentration is the Mental Alternation Test (Jones et al. 1993). This quick test of cognition correlates well with the results of the Mini-Mental State Examination and with the Trailmaking Test. The clinician instructs the client to count from 1 to 20 and then to recite the alphabet. Finally, the client is asked to alternate the letters of the alphabet with their corresponding numbers for a period of 30 seconds, as follows: A-1, B-2, C-3, D-4, E-5, and so on. The clinician scores one point for each correct pair. Cognitively impaired clients will achieve a score of 14 or less. A score below 15 on the Mental Alternation Test, which correlates with an abnormal result on the Mini-Mental State Exam or on the Trailmaking Test, suggests the need for further evaluation.

Memory

Memory is a complex neuropsychological process involving both the neocortex and subcortical structures of the brain. Memory involves the ability to learn new material, to recognize and register sensory input, to retain and store that information, and to retrieve or recall the stored material. Memory difficulties may be the result of problems with either the registration and retention or the retrieval of stored information.

Psychologists divide memory into the two broad categories of short-term and long-term memory, which can occur in any of the sensory modalities. Clinicians tend to refer to short-term memory as immediate, to long-term memory as recent, and to very long-term memory as remote. Short-term memory has a limited capacity of about seven items and usually lasts for less than a minute. With the rehearsal of the incoming information, short-term memory can be converted to long-term memory. The transfer from short-term to long-term memory depends on the amount and intensity of the rehearsal.

The following table (Table 10–1) illustrates the terms commonly used by clinicians and research psychologists to describe types of memory.

Table 10–1

Duration between Input and Recall	Experimental Term	Clinical Term
Less than 1 second	Sensory memory	None
Less than 1 minute	Short-term memory	Immediate memory
Minute to a few weeks	Long-term memory	Recent memory
Weeks to years	Very long-term memory	Remote memory

Most likely the processes of short-term and long-term memory are carried out by different neurophysiological systems in the brain. Short-term memory (immediate recall) involves initial registration of information, short-term holding, recall, and repetition. Immediate verbal recall, which can be performed entirely by the language cortex around the sylvian fissure (Strub and Black 1977), does not require long-term storage or the formation of permanent memories. Problems with short-term memory are most often due to inattention; hence, it is important for clinicians to evaluate attention before trying to assess memory. Some neurological causes of immediate memory impairment include aphasia, dementia, and problems with sensory perceptual systems.

The storage of long-term memories occurs in the neocortex of the brain. However, subcortical structures like the limbic system (including the hippocampi, mammillary bodies, and dorsal medial nuclei of the thalamus) are essential for the storage and retrieval of information from the cerebral cortex. Without the limbic system's mechanism of storing and retrieving both verbal and nonverbal memories from the cortex, we would be unable to learn new material or recall memories of the recent past.

For example, a 45-year-old man was struck in the center of his forehead by an iron rod in an industrial accident in 1992. Following his injury, he was unable to learn new tasks and has no recall of events that have occurred since the accident. His long-term memory of events prior to the accident is intact. However, he cannot remember anything that has happened to him since 1992.

Understanding the neuroanatomy of memory can help the clinician understand the presentation of certain disorders. For example, in dementing illnesses such as Alzheimer's disease (with degeneration of the hippocampus) or Korsakoff's syndrome (due to the thiamine depletion of chronic alcoholism and destruction of the mammillary bodies and dorsal medial nuclei of the thalamus), there can be severe memory deficits because of destruction of cells in the limbic system.

The clinician should be alert to the possibility of confabulation, commonly seen in Korsakoff's amnestic syndrome secondary to alcoholism. Confabulation refers to the filling in of memory gaps with false information. The confabulating client is not deliberately lying, but believes the imagined happenings to be true. Such clients can be convincing in their reporting of fantasied experiences as true recollections. It is imperative to corroborate the client's reports with a reliable historian to determine whether the client is, in fact, confabulating.

On occasion neurosurgeons deliberately destroy brain tissue to control severe epilepsy. In one case of neurosurgery for intractable seizures that required the ablation of the hippocampi bilaterally, the patient became unable to acquire new memories. He had a normal digit span of seven items, but could not recall anything that happened more than a minute or two earlier. He could read the same newspaper over and over, unaware that he had read it earlier in the day. Despite his inability to consolidate new memories, this patient's very long term memory for people and events early in his life remained intact.

The mental status examination attempts to evaluate each of the processes (recognition, registration, retention, recall) that are essential to the proper functioning of memory. The inability to remember is called *amnesia*. A person who cannot learn new material suffers from *anterograde amnesia*, while a person who cannot recall recent past memories suffers from *retrograde amnesia*.

Many psychiatric patients have a history of head trauma (Bohnen and Jolles 1992). In fact, every minute in the United States approximately four people sustain a head injury (Swiercinsky 1987) . Intoxication with drugs or alcohol is a frequent contributing factor to traumatic brain injury.

Blows to the head can cause both temporary physiological disruption of neural systems and permanent damage to brain structures. Head injuries commonly concuss the temporal lobes and hippocampi against the bones of the middle fossa of the skull. The effect of such blunt trauma on brain tissue is diffuse axonal injury (axonal shearing), in which nerve cells are torn apart from one another, thus disrupting the normal transmission of nerve impulses in the brain. Such physiological disruption of the functioning of the hippocampi impairs the ability to store and retrieve information and creates a post-traumatic amnesia.

The most common memory deficits in brain-injured individuals are, in order of frequency, the inability to recall people's names, to recall recent events, to recall spoken messages, and to remember to do something. Fortunately for the interviewer, patients with head injuries, when asked, are usually able to describe the types of memory deficits they are experiencing. In addition, head-injured patients often report word-finding difficulties and loss of interest in sex. Repeated blows to the head can permanently damage memory circuits and cause an irreversible memory disturbance, as seen in "punch-drunk" boxers. Significant head injury can also lead to personality changes and to psychotic and affective disturbances.

A curious and dramatic memory disturbance is that of transient global amnesia. This disorder lasts from minutes to several hours and typically occurs in older individuals who experience sudden and extreme confusion, disorientation, and memory difficulties. Patients with transient global amnesia cannot lay down new memories during the episode and have retrograde amnesia for past events. They appear distraught and ask repeatedly where they are and what they are doing. When given the answers, they quickly forget and ask again. The cause appears to be a temporary insufficiency in the blood supply bilaterally to the posteromedial thalamus and hippocampi. Fortunately, most patients experience a total recovery.

Testing Memory on the Mental Status Examination

The first step in assessing memory impairment is to ask whether the client has been having any difficulties with memory. Family and friends may be able to confirm the memory impairments. Does the client have trouble remembering the names of people, have difficulty finding words when speaking (anomia, which may also reflect impairments other than memory disturbance), forget appointments and recent events, forget to do things, not know what day or time it is, get lost or disoriented when away from home, leave the stove on after cooking, or forget where he or she has put things? These are common experiences for people with memory impairment due to brain dysfunction.

The interviewer should also be attentive to any memory lapses the client displays during the interview. Does the client have difficulty recalling what the interviewer just said? Does the client forget topics that were discussed earlier in the session? Any such observations of memory difficulties should prompt a more thorough testing of memory on the mental status examination.

Testing Immediate Recall

Immediate recall (a minute or less) can be tested by the digit repetition task. The interviewer asks the client to listen to a list of random digits and then to repeat them. The interviewer speaks the digits in a normal tone of voice at a rate of one per second. The task begins with two digits and the interviewer keeps adding one digit to the list until the client fails to repeat them accurately. Clients are given two trials to complete the task accurately. Most people can repeat five to seven digits forward without difficulty. Inability to repeat at least five digits forward is abnormal and suggests deficits with sustained effort, attention, or immediate memory. A typical list might read as follows:

2-5

3-9-4

7-2-8-1

4-6-5-3

9-7-3-1-5-8

6-5-9-1-2-4-7

8-3-9-2-5-1-7-4

Digit repetition is a test of both ability to sustain attention and of immediate registration, short-term retention, and verbal repetition. The entire process can be carried out by the language cortex around the sylvian fissure and does not require the systems needed for long-term memory storage. Inattention, which may be due to anxiety or depression, is the most common reason for difficulty on this test.

Some clinicians ask the client to repeat the digits backwards as a further test of sustained attention, concentration, and immediate memory. The ability to repeat a list of digits backwards is a challenging intellectual task. It requires sustained concentration involving the registration of the digits, their retention in short-term memory, their mental manipulation, and their verbal recall and repetition in reverse order.

A similar task for assessing sustained concentration is to ask the client to spell a five letter word, like "world," both forward and backward. Illiterate clients are sometimes able to spell their first or last names. If so, the clinician can ask illiterate clients to spell their names forward and backward to test attention and concentration.

Testing Recent Memory

To test recent memory, the clinician can ask the client to recall events that have occurred from hours to days before the evaluation. The recall of personal events (like what the client ate for breakfast) must be validated by a reliable source. The clinician can also ask the client to recall something that was discussed earlier in the interview.

To test recent visual memory, clinicians can have clients watch them hide some objects and then ask the clients to locate them. Alternatively or additionally, clinicians can ask clients to recall a simple drawing as a gauge of recent visual recall.

In addition, the clinician can test recent verbal memory by asking the client to recall three or four unrelated words several minutes after hearing them for the first time. Typically, the clinician gives an instruction such as: "I am going to say three words that I want you to remember. Please repeat them for me now so I am sure you heard them, and in a few minutes I will check to see if you still remember them. The words are: apple, honesty, and dishwasher [or whatever unrelated words of different categories the clinician chooses]."

The clinician says the words clearly and in a normal tone of voice. The client should be able to repeat all three words, indicating the ability to register and immediately recall them. If the client has difficulty with immediate recall, the clinician should repeat the words and note the number of trials it takes for the client to learn them. The clinician then proceeds to a different part of the mental status examination, such as digit repetition or performing serial subtraction of 7 from 100, before asking the client to recall the three words. To check the adequacy of recent verbal memory, about three to five minutes should elapse between the initial registration and the subsequent recall of the three words. The average person should be able to recall three unrelated words after three to five minutes.

Testing Remote Memory

The literature does not offer a clear dividing line between recent and remote memory. The clinician can assess remote memory by asking the client about personal information and public events from both the recent (weeks to months) and remote (months to years) past. For reliable testing, any personal information must be verified by the interviewer. Typical personal questions include childhood events, changes of residence, schools attended, jobs held, military service, names of significant people in the past, important dates in the client's life, and so on. Inquiries about public historical information include the names of recent presidents of the United States, data about other public figures, major news stories, and other information (more than a few weeks old) that a reasonably informed member of the society or culture would know. The clinician needs to weigh the client's education, intelligence, and cultural background in making judgments based on the recall of historical facts.

Ability to Abstract and Generalize

The ability to think abstractly and make generalizations is one of the higher mental functions that separates humans from the rest of the animal kingdom. These abilities are traditionally tested through proverb interpretation and similarities testing. The client's responses to proverb interpretation and similarities testing are greatly influenced by intelligence and cultural background.

Proverbs

Proverb interpretation requires a reasonable fund of general knowledge and the ability to think abstractly when applying that knowledge to a novel situation. The instructions for proverb interpretation should go something as follows: "I am going to say a proverb or saying that you may or may not have heard before. I would like you to tell me in your own words what the saying means."

The interviewer then recites the proverb and judges how concrete or abstract the client's interpretation is. The clinician should quote the client's response verbatim in the mental status examination report. Consider the proverb, "People in glass houses shouldn't throw stones." A concrete response might be, "Stones will break the glass." An abstract response might be, "You shouldn't criticize others without considering your own faults."

In addition to indicating ability to think abstractly, the answers to proverb interpretation will sometimes uncover psychotic thinking or delusional ideas. A psychotic response to the "glass houses" proverb might be, "How did you know I broke the glass? Were you spying on me?"

Patients may be familiar or unfamiliar with the proverbs used on the mental status examination. Familiar proverbs may test learned responses rather than the capacity for abstract thinking. As yet, there is no good research to indicate whether it is preferable to test abstraction ability with familiar or unfamiliar proverbs. Rita Haynes and colleagues (1993) surveyed 333 English-speaking high school students in Cleveland to determine their familiarity with twenty-five proverbs. There were no differences in familiarity with proverbs between black and white students nor between male and female students. Thirty-seven clinicians who were surveyed had inaccurate beliefs about proverb familiarity in their patients. Until further research is available, Haynes and colleagues recommend using a mixture of familiar and unfamiliar proverbs to test abstraction on the mental status examination.

The following list of proverbs that is reasonably free of racial and gender bias is quoted with permission from the research of Haynes et al. (1993):

The Most Familiar Nondiscriminatory Proverbs:

1. The bigger they are, the harder they fall.
2. What goes around comes around.
3. Don't judge a book by its cover.
4. Two wrongs don't make a right.
5. Don't count your chickens before they hatch.

Unfamiliar Nondiscriminatory Proverbs:

1. There is no rose without its thorns.
2. The dogs may bark, but the caravan moves on.
3. A man who chases two rabbits catches neither one.
4. When the elephants fight, the grass gets trampled.

Similarities and Differences

The testing of similarities and differences involves asking the client to tell how two objects or situations are alike or different. To identify what two items do or do not have in common requires the ability to use abstract verbal categories, the analysis of relationships, and logical abstract thought.

A typical instruction to the client would be: "I am going to mention two objects that have something in common; I would like you to tell me how they are similar or alike." The interviewer then might ask, "What do an apple and a pear have in common?" A concrete answer might be, "You buy them in the grocery store." A more abstract answer would be, "They are both something to eat." A more verbally abstract answer would be, "They are both types of fruit."

To test differences, the clinician might ask, "How are a soldier and a policeman different?" or "What is the difference between a soldier and a policeman?"

The answers to similarities or differences testing often reveal other aspects of the client's thought process. One hypomanic woman, when asked how a fox and an elephant were alike, said, "They both have similar lifestyles," demonstrating her ability to make rapid humorous connections between ideas.

Information (Fund of Knowledge) and Intelligence

For both diagnosis and treatment planning, it is useful for the clinician to get a sense of the client's overall intelligence and store of general information. The client's use of language and vocabulary, ability to abstract, performance with calculations like serial sevens, and general fund of knowledge provide a basis for estimating intelligence.

Fund of knowledge can be tested by asking for information generally known by the population. Typical questions for American clients include the following:

Who were the last four or five U.S. presidents?
Who is the governor of this state?
How many weeks are in a year?
What is the distance from New York to California?
Why do we sweat more in the summer?
What is the capital of France?
Why do we pasteurize milk?
Who is Mark Twain?

In testing intelligence and fund of information, the clinician should be sensitive to the client's educational level, cultural background, and socioeconomic status. For example, a Peruvian client may never have heard of Mark Twain but might be thoroughly familiar with the poetry of César Vallejo. Without taking culture and education into account, the interviewer might form an invalid appraisal of the client's intelligence, general knowledge, and ability to abstract and generalize.

THOUGHT AND PERCEPTION

IV. Thought and Perception
  A. Disordered perceptions
    1. Illusions
    2. Hallucinations
    3. Depersonalization and derealization
  B. Thought content
    1. Distortions
    2. Delusions
    3. Ideas of reference
    4. Magical thinking
  C. Thought process
    1. Flow of ideas
    2. Quality of associations
  D. Preoccupations
    1. Somatic
    2. Obsessions and compulsions
    3. Phobias

The interviewer should assess how clients perceive themselves, others, the outer world, the roles they play vis-à-vis others, the content and process of their thoughts, and any preoccupations on their mind.

Perceptual Disturbances

Disorders of perception are often key factors in suggesting a possible diagnosis. Perception is the process of becoming aware of objects in the environment through sensory input. Common disturbances of perception include illusions, hallucinations, and dissociative perceptual phenomena.

An illusion is a misperception or misinterpretation of a sensory stimulus. For example, someone may mistake shadows for people or may interpret a household noise to be a human voice. Clients who are hard of hearing may fill in what they don't hear with personal material and sometimes give a paranoid slant to remarks they can't understand.

An hallucination is an apparent perception in the absence of an external stimulus. Many clients with schizophrenia will talk of hearing voices that no one else can hear. Hallucinations can occur in any sensory modality (sound, sight, touch, taste, smell, equilibrium, position sense, etc.). Sometimes they take the form of a voice commanding the client to do something. Such command hallucinations can be dangerous when they instruct patients to harm themselves or others.

Dissociative perceptions include depersonalization and derealization. In depersonalization, the client feels personally unreal, as if detached or estranged from the self. In derealization, the person feels detached from the environment, as if living in a dream world. Individuals who dissociate will often feel uncertain whether what they are experiencing is really happening.

Thought Content

The clinician should note the content of the client's thought. Careful listening to the client's story will reveal areas that might be important in ongoing treatment. For example, one man who had been given up for adoption at birth told the interviewer: "I have no feelings about my birth parents. I never met them and I have no desire to. In fact, if I ran them both over in the street and killed them with my car, I wouldn't even know it was them." Perhaps he did have feelings about his birth parents that he was unaware of.

Distortions

Some disorders are characterized by distortions of thought. For example, starving clients with anorexia may think of themselves as extremely obese, and hypochondriacal clients may regard every minor physical symptom as a sign of a life-threatening illness. Persons with antisocial personality disorder will distort reality to see themselves as blameless and attribute the cause of their antisocial behavior to the actions of other.

Delusions

Delusions are false beliefs about reality that are firmly held despite evidence to the contrary. Delusions are signs of a psychotic disorder. Common delusions include the fixed idea that one is being controlled by outside forces, the paranoid belief that one has been singled out for harassment or persecution, the grandiose delusion that one is very special and important, and the unshakable somatic complaint that one is dying of a fatal disease. Delusions may be either congruent or incongruent with the client's mood. Paranoid delusions are often extensive and organized in a systematic, interconnected manner (systematized).

Delusions that someone or something is controlling one's mind is common in schizophrenia. Some patients believe that thoughts are being put into or taken out of their minds—so-called thought insertion and thought withdrawal. Others are convinced that their thoughts are being broadcast to others (thought broadcasting) so that people know what they are thinking without having been told.

Ideas of Reference

Ideas of reference consist of false thoughts that one is being talked about or referred to by others. Such mildly paranoid ideation can become frankly delusional with the fixed belief that the actions of others are deliberately directed toward the client. Some patients with schizophrenia come to feel that messages or stories on the radio or TV are meant specifically for them.

Magical Thinking

Magical thinking is a mode of thought that attributes magical powers to a person's thoughts, words, and deeds. This type of thinking disregards the scientific mechanistic belief in cause and effect and is typical of children who have not yet fully developed reality testing. Magical thinking underlies superstitious practices such as knocking on wood, avoiding the thirteenth floor of a building, and consulting one's daily horoscope in the newspaper. Such thinking is consonant with the lunar mythological view of reality (discussed in Chapter 1 of this volume), but is denounced as dangerous by solar patriarchal types.

Magical thinking per se is part of normal human development and is not pathological. Such thinking underlies most religious systems and is culturally appropriate and acceptable in many situations. Magical thought becomes problematic when carried to extreme, as in obsessive-compulsive disorder, delusion formation, and schizotypal and borderline personality disorders.

Thought Process

Thought process includes the flow of ideas and the quality of the associations. The clinician should assess the client's stream of thought (flow of ideas) for the quantity and nature of the thoughts, the rate of thinking, and the coherence, connectedness, continuity, and goal-directedness of the thinking process.

Clients may have too many or too few ideas. For example, severely depressed patients often exhibit a poverty (paucity) of ideas. The number of ideas is associated with the rate of thinking. Depressed clients will display slowed thinking, whereas manic or hypomanic clients will exhibit rapid thinking, often described by the client as "racing thoughts."

Despite its commitment to simple, descriptive language, *DSM-IV* has introduced the pedantic term *alogia* (from the Greek *a* meaning "no" and *logos* meaning "word, reckoning, speech, calculation, or thought") to refer to the impoverished thinking that can accompany schizophrenia. The clinician makes an inference of alogia from the observation of poverty of speech (non-fluent empty talking) and poverty of content of speech (fluent empty talking).

Clients may communicate clearly and directly or may have trouble getting to the point. There are many ways to not get to the point, and politicians are expert at this art. Disturbances of the continuity of thought include evasiveness, irrelevance, incoherence, rambling, perseveration, blocking, circumstantiality, tangentiality, overintellectualizing, flight of ideas, clang associations, and stereotyped speech.

Eugen Bleuler (1950) regarded disturbances of associations as one of the core symptoms of schizophrenia. Loosening of associations is characteristic of schizophrenic thinking in which ideas shift from one subject to another in an apparently unrelated manner. Some textbooks refer to associative loosening as *derailment,* as if the schizophrenic ideas were like train cars that slipped off their tracks. In actuality, the associative loosening of schizophrenic thinking often makes sense to clinicians who become familiar with the private inner world of the patient. The problem is that in schizophrenia the associative links between ideas are idiosyncratic to the individual and do not follow ordinary, consensually accepted modes of continuity of thought.

Blocking refers to the sudden stopping of the flow of thought, which causes an interruption in the spontaneous flow of speech about a topic. When asked about the interruption, clients usually report being unable to recall what they wanted to say.

Circumstantiality involves the inclusion of a host of irrelevant details in getting to the point. The client has too many associated ideas in mind and speaks with too many digressions. They eventually say what they are trying to say, but only after regaling the listener with endless parenthetical comments. Circumstantiality is often a defense against recognizing troublesome feelings or impulses. For example, a psychiatrist wanted to tell the hospital staff that he had recently seen a patient who had eloped from the hospital. Instead of simply saying where and when he had seen the patient, the circumstantial doctor gave a detailed account of the route he took, why he took that route rather than another, why he was out of the hospital at midday and not in his office, and why he happened to be looking at pedestrians on the sidewalk while driving in traffic. After several minutes of such details, the psychiatrist finally got to the point that he had recently seen the missing patient on a downtown street. Like this psychiatrist, circumstantial clients take the scenic route rather than the direct highway to reach their goals.

Overintellectualization is similar to circumstantiality in that intellectualizing clients flood their minds with abstract ideas to avoid objectionable emotions. This type of thinking is allegedly characteristic of college sophomores ("wise morons"), who may spend endless hours pondering philosophical issues. Excessive intellectualization is also common in some personality disorders, obsessive-compulsive disorders, and schizophrenia.

Tangentiality refers to veering off on tangents while speaking. Such tangents take the speaker further and further away from the initial direction of thought so that the he or she never gets to the point. This type of difficulty with goal-directed thinking is common in mania and hypomania. The pun is a humorous form of tangential thinking.

Clang associations are an extreme form of tangentiality commonly seen in mania with flight of ideas. In clang associations, the sound of a word, rather than its meaning, triggers a new train of thought. Flight of ideas refers to the extremely rapid jumping from one idea to another based on clang associations, tangential connections, or chance rather than goal-directed associations.

Preoccupations

Preoccupations are thoughts and concerns that appear to take possession of the client's thinking. Common preoccupations include somatic concerns, obsessions and compulsions, and phobias. Preoccupations have an obsessive quality.

Somatic preoccupations are excessive hypochondriacal concerns about one's physical health and body functioning.

Obsessions are persistent, intrusive, unwanted thoughts that haunt or trouble the mind and do not yield to reason or logical analysis. The word *obsession* derives from the Latin *obsessio*, meaning the act of an evil spirit in possessing or besieging a person.

Compulsions are the action counterpart of obsessions. Compulsions are persistent, intrusive, unwanted urges to do something that runs counter to one's wishes or moral principles. Failure to perform the compulsion produces anxiety. Compulsions are often organized into repetitive ritualistic behaviors. Common compulsions include handwashing, checking locks, counting cracks, straightening picture frames, and so forth.

Phobias are irrational, intense, persistent fears of particular things or situations. Common phobias include fears of insects or animals, fear of heights, fear of flying, fear of closed spaces, and fear of leaving the safe familiar setting of one's home.

SUICIDALITY, HOMICIDALITY, AND IMPULSE CONTROL

For both clinical and legal reasons, the clinician needs to assess whether the client is suicidal, homicidal, or dangerously impulsive.

There are varying degrees of suicidality and homicidality. The clinician should look for the presence of suicidal or homicidal thoughts (ideation), plans, or intent. The mildest forms of ideation would be thoughts such as "the world would be better off without me," "sometimes I wish I would go to sleep and never wake up," or "I wish so-and-so would die and leave me alone." More serious is the situation in which the client is making plans, such as hoarding medications or buying a gun. The most serious situation is one in which the client has made a plan to harm self or others and expresses the clear intent to carry out the plan.

In assessing impulse control, the clinician should consider how the client deals with sexual and aggressive urges. How has the client managed stressful situations in the past? Is there a history of uncontrolled sexual expression or hostile behavior? Can the client delay gratification and tolerate frustration? Does the client get into fights, punch walls when frustrated, smash furniture when upset, cut his or her wrists when rejected, drink excessively or use illicit drugs, and so on? Is there a history of the triad of childhood fire setting, bed wetting, and cruelty to animals, which the psychiatric literature has associated with cruel behavior in adulthood?

INSIGHT AND JUDGMENT

The term *insight*, as used on the mental status examination, refers to the awareness and understanding that one is suffering from an illness or disorder. Some clients completely deny having any difficulties that require attention. Other clients have varying degrees of awareness that they are suffering from a disorder and recognition of the fact that they need evaluation and treatment.

Judgment refers to the client's ability to critically evaluate a situation and to decide on a reasonable course of action. Evidence of poor judgment includes a recent history of engaging in risky or potentially harmful behavior. Practicing unsafe sex or behaving in culturally unacceptable ways would be typical examples of poor judgment. The clinician tries to assess whether clients are able to understand the potential consequences of their behavior and plan accordingly.

In addition to assessing judgment based on the client's history, clinicians may wish to ask questions about hypothetical situations. Typical questions include: "What would you do if you spotted a fire in a movie theater?" and "What would you do if you found an uncancelled stamped, addressed envelope on the sidewalk?"

RELIABILITY (ACCURACY OF THE CLIENT'S REPORT)

The interviewer should state his or her impression of the reliability and accuracy of the client's report. A psychotic person, for example, may give a grossly distorted picture of the presenting situation. One woman presented in a state of terror to the emergency room of a general hospital with the following complaint: "You've got to help me doctor. It's those little furry things. They're coming from outer space and they've landed up the street. Soon they'll be at my house and they want to masturbate me."

The doctor felt that the woman who was being terrified by the little furry things from outer space was not a reliable historian.

It is, however, necessary to be careful about jumping to conclusions about reliability. For example, a middle-aged man with a long-standing diagnosis of paranoid schizophrenia presented to the crisis team of a mental health center with the complaint that his neighbor was trying to poison him. According to the patient, his neighbor had been connecting a hose to the exhaust of his car and was inserting it into the patient's bedroom window. Upon hearing this story, the clinician increased the patient's medication and gave him a follow-up appointment later in the week. A few days later the local newspaper reported that the patient's neighbor had been arrested when the police noticed a hose connected to the exhaust of his neighbor's car running into the window of the house next door.

Another common reason for historical unreliability is cognitive impairment. People suffering from dementia or delirium may simply be unable to remember what has been happening. Others may deliberately falsify their reports to qualify for disability payments or to achieve other secondary gains for their illnesses. Mental health professionals can, at times, be such trusting souls as to forget that some people deliberately lie to get what they want.

THE MINI-MENTAL STATE EXAMINATION

Adapted from M. F. Folstein and colleagues (1975), and used with permission.

Orientation:

A. (5 points) What is the (year) (season) (date) (day of the week) (month)?

B. (5 points) Where are we (country) (state) (city or town) (hospital) (floor of the building)?

Registration:

C. (3 points) The examiner names three unrelated objects, taking one second to say each. The patient is asked to repeat all three objects after the examiner has said them. Give one point for each correct answer. Repeat the objects until the patient learns all three. Record the number of trials.

Attention and Calculation:

D. (5 points) Serial 7s. One point for each correct answer. Stop after five answers. Alternatively, have the patient spell the word "WORLD" backwards, giving one point for each correct letter. For Spanish speaking clients, use the word "MUNDO."

Recall:

E.   (3 points)   Ask the client to recall the three objects learned in item C.

Language:

F.   (2 points)   The patient is shown a pencil and a watch and is asked to name each one.

G.   (1 point)   Ask the patient to repeat, "No ifs, ands, or buts." Listen for dysarthria.

H.   (3 points)   The patient is handed a sheet of paper and given a three-stage command: "Take this paper in your right hand, fold it in half, and put it on the floor."

G.   (1 point)   Show the patient a sign which reads "Close your eyes," and ask the patient to follow the command.

I.   (1 point)   Ask the patient to write a sentence.

Visual-motor integrity:

J.   (1 point)   The patient is asked to copy a Bender-Gestalt figure.

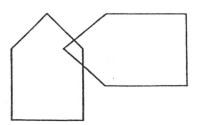

INTERPRETATION: According to Folstein, a score of less than or equal to 23 points in a person with at least nine years of education is evidence of cognitive impairment. False positive results often occur in persons with fewer than nine years of education.

11

Issues in the Assessment of Puerto Rican and Other Hispanic Clients, Including *Ataques de Nervios* (Attacks of Nerves)

by
José M. Méndez-Villarrubia, M.A.
in collaboration with
Anthony LaBruzza, M.D.

"Every culture has rules for translating signs into symptoms, for linking symptomatologies to etiologies and interventions, and for using the evidence provided by interventions to confirm translations and legitimize outcomes. The path a person follows from translation to socially significant outcome constitutes his sickness. *Sickness is, then, a process for socializing diseases and illness.*"

A. Young, The anthropologies of illness and sickness,
A Rev Anthrop 11, 257 (1982)

Hispanics, who comprise a sizable non-English-speaking minority population in the United States, are often in need of mental health and other social services. Unfortunately, the differences in language and culture, combined with a shortage of bilingual, bicultural Hispanic clinicians in the United States, often makes adequate assessment, treatment, and provision of services difficult.

The following case illustrates some of the issues that arise when a monolingual Hispanic client seeks social services in America. Héctor, a Puerto Rican man in his mid-40s, was applying for benefits at the welfare office in a New England city with a large Hispanic population. Héctor indicated to the welfare worker that he had previously received psychiatric treatment for depression and a suicide attempt. He was consequently referred for psychiatric evaluation as part of a special program at the welfare office to identify cases of psychiatric disability and refer them for treatment.

Because Héctor spoke only Spanish, the clinician and the psychiatrist who evaluated him needed to rely on the services of a translator. The findings of this initial assessment were that Héctor was hearing voices (command hallucinations) telling him to kill his family and himself. He was also described as having conversations with God and as being religiously preoccupied. As a result, Héctor was sent by ambulance for psychiatric admission to a hospital where he was evaluated by a bilingual, bicultural Spanish-speaking clinician who determined that Héctor was very religious, believed in the supernatural, and listened to the voice of God. He had experienced auditory hallucinations fifteen years earlier and had been hospitalized with both suicidal and homicidal ideation at that time. He currently had no psychiatric symptoms other than some mild insomnia. Remarkably, he was sent for hospitalization at this time because of an episode that had occurred much earlier in his life. His deeply held religious beliefs had been misinterpreted as psychosis, and the language barrier had prevented an accurate assessment.

This case dramatically underscores the need to attend to cultural and language differences in the assessment of psychiatric disorders. The consequences of Héctor's first psychiatric evaluation could have been devastating for this patient. He could have been involuntarily hospitalized and forced to take unnecessary psychotropic medications, running the risk of tardive dyskinesia. Although Héctor's case might seem to be a rare situation to some clinicians, it is unfortunately not at all uncommon for monolingual Hispanic patients.

Unlike its predecessors, *DSM-IV* has paid special attention to cultural issues in psychiatric diagnosis. *Appendix I* (*DSM-IV*, pp.

843–849) provides suggestions for developing a cultural formulation and gives a glossary of several culture-bound syndromes.

The psychiatric literature (Guarnaccia 1993) uses the terms *popular illness category* or *culture-bound syndrome* to refer to popular and indigenous categories used to explain coherent patterns of illness or distress that are specific to certain geographic localities or cultural groups. Culture-bound syndromes may resemble or overlap with particular *DSM-IV* categories, but rarely have a one-to-one relationship with *DSM-IV* diagnoses. Unlike the criteria sets of *DSM-IV* diagnostic categories,

. . . much cross-cultural research has found that symptoms are not necessarily the main criteria for diagnosis of popular illnesses and that social and moral characteristics of the ill individual and the kinds of social stresses that person faces may be equally important in identifying and treating illness. [Guarnaccia 1993, p. 159]

When assessing an individual from a different culture, the clinician must attend to any language barrier that might exist and assess how cultural differences affect the presentation of symptoms and the interpretation of the meaning of the illness. Some questions to consider in the assessment of an individual from a different culture include the following:

1. What is the client's ethnic and cultural background?
2. What is the country of origin, and when did the client migrate or immigrate to the United States? Is the client an illegal immigrant? Is the client a first or second generation immigrant? To what extent has the client become acculturated to the United States?
3. What is the client's native language? Has the client been able to learn English? If so, with what degree of proficiency? Is the client multilingual? What is the client's preferred language at the time of the evaluation? If an interpreter is needed, how familiar is the interpreter with mental health assessment?
4. What is the client's support system? Do other family members live in the area? Is the client involved with a church, religious group, or other social network? Does the client feel isolated and alone in a foreign land? What is the client's cultural and social reference group? What role does religion play in the client's life?

5. To what extent has the client remained involved with the native culture? What efforts, if any, has the client made to become involved with the mainstream culture of the United States?

6. How do language and cultural differences affect the clinician's ability to communicate with and understand what is troubling the client? In what ways does the clinician need to modify the interviewing technique to establish rapport and perform an adequate assessment?

7. Does the clinician share the majority culture's biases and stereotyped views of the client's culture? Does the minority client hold a culturally biased view of the clinician? Milton Bloombaum and colleagues (1968) found that negative attitudes based on cultural stereotypes held by psychotherapists are the same as those of the general population and cause therapists to remain socially distant from their minority clients. Lawrence Kline (1969) reported that Spanish-American clients in Colorado held culturally biased views of Anglo psychotherapists as cold, exploitative, and insincere.

8. What are the popular explanations for distress in the client's culture (e.g., *ataques* (attacks), *nervios* (nerves), *susto* (fright), and *embrujado (bewitchment)* among Hispanics)? How do the client's cultural reference groups (family, church, neighbors, etc.) interpret the meaning of the presenting symptoms and complaints? What are the familial and cultural explanations for the client's suffering? Although the client's symptoms or behaviors might be considered pathological in the dominant culture, would they be accepted as common or normal expressions of distress in the client's culture?

9. Where has the client sought help in the past for similar difficulties? A doctor? A priest? A spiritist? An astrologer? The family? What kind of treatment does the client's reference group recommend? What are the popular or indigenous types of treatment and sources of care?

10. What has the client's past experience been with visits to doctors and clinics? Was the client kept waiting for hours, given a "runaround," or made to feel discriminated against? Did the client expect immediate advice and direction (*consejo*) or a prescription for medication? Does the client view helping professionals as superior and authoritarian?

The above questions should be part of a cultural assessment of a Hispanic individual. The remainder of this chapter will focus on cultural, educational, and socioeconomic issues that affect the psychiatric assessment of Hispanic clients living in the United States. Consideration will be given to the different roles of men and women in the Hispanic culture and particularly to the syndrome of *ataque de nervios*, a prototypical popular illness category that is used to express distress among Hispanics from the Caribbean and from many South American and Latin Mediterranean countries.

The observations in this chapter are based on the author's own experience growing up in Puerto Rico and on his clinical work with indigent, predominantly Puerto Rican clients at the Greater Bridgeport Community Mental Health Center in Connecticut. The reader should bear in mind that, although Hispanics are united by a common language and culture, there exist many regional differences among Hispanics, including the peoples of the Caribbean, Mexico, and the countries of Central and South America. Amada Padilla and René Ruiz (1973) observed that most of the literature about Spanish-speaking, Spanish-surnamed communities deals with two major subgroups: Mexican Americans and Puerto Ricans. Generalizations based on experience with one group of Hispanic migrants or immigrants may not apply equally across all Hispanic groups in the United States (Scheck 1993). For example, native Mexicans and Mexican-Americans may express emotional distress more in terms of *susto* than of *ataques de nervios*. In addition, Mexican immigrants, unlike Puerto Ricans, who are already United States citizens, must frequently deal with the issue of being derogatorily viewed as "illegal aliens" whether or not they have legally immigrated to the United States.

Hispanic migrants and immigrants to the United States face many of the same problems that other non-English-speaking immigrant groups have faced before them. Some of the difficulties that Hispanics experience in this country are less reflective of the Hispanic culture than of lack of education, the language barrier, and lower socioeconomic status. In addition, the problems consequent to migration and uprooting from one's homeland and social support network are not unique to Hispanics who are newly settled in the U.S. mainland.

CULTURE

The word culture comes from the Latin *cultura*, which in turn derives from *colere*, a verb meaning to till, care for, or cultivate the soil; also, to produce, develop, improve, or promote growth. Culture is commonly understood to consist of all the concepts, habits, arts, skills, instruments, social conventions, and institutions of different character—religious, moral, aesthetic, scientific—that are proper to a given people in a particular era. Culture, which is in constant evolution, encompasses the totality of the lives of a group of people. It includes the attitudes and beliefs of a given civilization whose teleological content is influenced by and linked to the values and symbols of that group of people.

It was not until the seventeenth century that this higher understanding of culture was accepted throughout Europe and that culture came to be understood as the totality of all human creation throughout the years. The crucial point for psychiatric diagnosis is that culture is a way that a given group of people come to see, interpret, transform, and communicate their understanding of reality.

In a Grand Rounds given at the Greater Bridgeport Community Mental Health Center, psychoanalyst Michael Moskowitz, Ph.D., (June 1994) pointed out that the definition of culture is imprecise and ever-changing. He suggested that a helpful way to view cultural differences would be to use the categories of a culture of oppression and a culture of immigration. Members of the culture of oppression suffer discrimination and powerlessness in the society. Members of the culture of immigration have come to the United States seeking a better life for themselves and their families.

Individuals who belong to either oppressed or immigrant cultures frequently suffer adverse psychological consequences. Immigrants may have a profound sense of loss of family and homeland. Immigrant or migrant families are often split apart, with children being left in the care of relatives in the native land while their parents try to establish themselves in the United States. At times such stresses on the family lead to divorce.

Immigrants often also suffer from discrimination and oppression. The dominant culture's negative stereotypes of the immigrant group may constantly assault the immigrant's dignity and sense of identity in the new land. For example, a recent Peruvian immigrant who was trying to sell his wares on a street corner in New York City was ticketed by a New York City policeman, who happened to be black, for selling goods without a permit. When the Peruvian tried to explain in his limited English that he did not know about the requirement of a permit, the policeman demeaningly responded, "You people think you can come to this country and do whatever you want." In this example a member of an oppressed minority applies a pejorative stereotype to a member of the immigrant culture.

Critics have pointed out that the label "culture-bound syndrome" carries with it the risk of implying negative judgments about the character of individuals of a non–North American or non-European background. The concept of a syndrome being "culture-bound" focuses attention of the "otherness" of the non-dominant culture as if North American and European (*DSM-IV* or *ICD-10*) diagnostic categories were immune from cultural influences. That such may not be the case is argued by Joseph Westermeyer (1985), who proposed that bulimia is a culture-bound syndrome of North American women. Peter Guarnaccia (1993) argues convincingly that the term *popular illness category* (Good and Good 1982) is preferable to the label *culture-bound syndrome*. In dealing with clients of a different cultural background, clinicians would do well to keep in mind the observations of C. Hughes in the introduction to the book *Culture-Bound Syndromes* (Simons and Hughes 1985):

> It may well be that the dichotomy between "us" and "them" in regard to discussions of culture-bound syndromes has been too quickly drawn; between, that is, the non-Western peoples, the "underdeveloped" peoples, the "primitives" [who have the "exotic" and the "culture-bound" syndromes] and the western world, the "developed world," the "civilized world." [p. 11]

THE ROLE OF RELIGION
AND SPIRITUAL PRACTICES

Religion is integral to the Hispanic culture and forms an essential part of the support system of many Hispanic individuals. When Hispanics come for psychiatric help, they have often turned first to their priest, pastor, folk healer, or other spiritual advisor (e.g., *espiritista, santero, curandero*) for guidance and support. Clinicians should always inquire about which religion the individual practices.

The majority of Hispanics are Roman Catholic, and a large number of others are Protestant. In addition, complex spiritual belief systems (e.g., *santería, espiritismo*) are often deeply ingrained among members of the Caribbean and Brazilian communities. *Santería*, which represents a fusion of West African and Roman Catholic belief systems, was developed by slaves from Yorubaland (now Nigeria) as a way to continue to worship their own deities (orishas) in the New World. The Spanish brought *espiritismo* to the New World during their conquest of the Caribbean. *Espiritismo* derives from a medieval philosophical system that divides the spiritual world into levels ranging from the living to the spirits of the dead, pure spirits, and, finally, God. It is not uncommon to see church-front *centros* in Puerto Rican, Dominican, Cuban, or Brazilian communities where *espiritismo* is practiced.

Curanderismo, a complex spiritual system of folk healing commonly practiced by Mexican Americans, is a blend of Mayan and Aztec traditions, Roman Catholicism, Arabic medicine, and Spanish European witchcraft. According to Jerold Kreisman (1975), the *curandero* (practitioner of curanderismo) is "a very religious and highly respected member of the community who retains many of the customs of Mexico, maintaining cultural bonds for even the acculturated Mexican-American" (p. 81). During a consultation, the *curandero* takes a careful history from the client and is aided in making a diagnosis by seeing the client's aura and receiving messages from a spirit guide in dreams. In addition to perceiving natural, medical, and psychological causes of a client's malady, the *curandero* may also discover supernatural forces at work. For example, the client's problem may be attributed to *embrujado* (bewitching or possession by an evil spirit) or to *mal puesto* (an evil spell or hex).

Religion generally serves as a positive guiding principle and sustaining force throughout the life cycle of many Hispanic individuals. The clinician should assess the role that religion plays in the client's life and the attitude of the client's spiritual advisor and other church members toward mental health care. Such attitudes range from active encouragement of mental health services to condemnation of secular attempts to deal with one's difficulties. It goes without saying that, when the client's religious training devalues mental health care, the clinician must remain sensitive to and respectful of the client's alternative point of view. Psychoeducational efforts by the clinician are especially important for engaging such clients in treatment.

As mentioned, the degrees of sophistication about mental health treatment among Hispanic religious counselors is variable. Some priests and pastors accompany their parishioners to the mental health center and actively support the treatment. Other Hispanic religious counselors, however, may explain the client's problems exclusively in theological terms, viewing the root cause of the client's difficulties as the result of "sinfulness" and, at times, of "spirit possession." One client, for example, reported being advised to "pray, do sacrifice, and trust in God that everything will be all right." Some pastors or ministers will engage the client in a healing ritual involving the "laying (on) of hands." Hispanic clients at the Greater Bridgeport Community Mental Health Center have occasionally made comments such as, "I hope my pastor doesn't know I came here. He does not want me to come here."

Clinicians may feel especially challenged when clients report that their pastors have explained their psychiatric and depressive symptoms as works of the devil. Such clients may feel that their emotional suffering is due to lack of faith and poor intimacy with God. Depressed clients, especially, may focus on religious themes of sinfulness and lack of faith to explain their depressive sense of guilt and lowered self-esteem.

For example, the infant son of a Puerto Rican woman was hospitalized in Miami, Florida, for a severely debilitating illness. The doctors told her that her son was likely to die, but that if he survived he would most probably suffer permanent neurological damage. She turned to her pastor for support, and he advised her that her son's illness was due to her lack of faith in God. "If you truly believe in God, your son will be healed," he told her. When after a prayer service her son did not improve, the other parishioners blamed her son's continued illness on her lack of faith. The woman went on to develop a major depressive episode, frequently commenting, " . . . que si de verdad yo quisiera que mi nene se sanara tenía que confiar en Dios (. . . if I really wanted my son to be healed I would have to trust more in God)."

At times the clinician may have difficulty distinguishing psychiatric symptoms from religious beliefs or experiences and from the practices of espiritismo. Among Hispanics who engage in santería and espiritismo, for example, seeing visions or hearing the voices of saints or of deceased relatives are common and even welcome experiences.

In addition, these belief systems espouse divination, possession, and the reality of spiritual forces as causes of physical and psychosocial problems. From the client's point of view, orthodox psychiatry and psychology, which tend to debunk spirituality, are culturally deviant belief systems. Although the Roman Catholic church condemns such practices, both *santería* and *espiritismo* commonly coexist with Roman Catholicism. Individuals who belong to more fundamentalist sects (e.g., Seventh Day Adventists, Pentacostalists) are less likely to engage in *santería* and *espiritismo* because they fervently regard such practices as evil or the work of the devil.

The case of Héctor at the beginning of this chapter illustrates how religious beliefs can be misinterpreted as psychosis. When Hispanic clients say they believe in spirits, visions, possessions, and supernatural forces, the clinician must consider that these may be culturally normative experiences. Because families are often involved together (Goldman 1993) in *santería* and *espiritismo*, an interview with family members can help the clinician determine how normative or bizarre the individual client's beliefs are in the context of his or her culture.

Latinos who regularly consult *santeros*, *curanderos*, or *espiritistas* will come with certain expectations to a clinical interview. *Espiritistas* typically make a "diagnosis" by asking a series of yes or no questions that progressively narrow down the diagnostic possibilities. Having made her diagnosis, the *espiritista* then gives specific advice and detailed instructions about how to remedy the problem. Mental health professionals, in contrast, tend to ask open-ended questions and do not generally give detailed advice about personal problems. Hispanic clients often complain about mental health interviewers: "All they do is ask me questions, and they don't tell me anything." Nonetheless, by remaining nonjudgmental, culturally sensitive, empathic, and accepting, the clinician might be able to engage the Hispanic client in orthodox treatment.

Actually, the spiritually based folk healing practices engaged in by Hispanic clients often "closely parallel contemporary behavior therapy, chemotherapy, dream interpretation, family therapy, hypnotherapy, milieu therapy, and psychodrama" (Krippner and Welsh 1992). James Dow's study of the Otomi shamans of Mexico (1986) revealed striking similarities between shamanic healing practices and Western psychotherapy. Stanley Krippner and Patrick Welsh (1992) point out that for shamans the spiritual dimension of healing is extremely important while the contemporary physician and psychotherapist typically ignore it. Shamans often retrieve lost souls, communicate with spirits, emphasize the interconnectedness of their patients with the community and the earth, facilitate spiritual purification for those who have violated social taboos, explain dreams and visions, and stress the importance of spiritual growth, life purpose, and being of service to humanity and to nature.

SOCIOECONOMIC FACTORS

The Hispanic population in the United States has grown significantly within the last decade. The Institute for Puerto Rican Policy, Inc., (March 1992) estimates that 62 percent of this country's Hispanic population is of Mexican origin, followed by Central and South Americans, who comprise 14 percent, Puerto Ricans, who account for 11 percent, other Hispanics, who account for 8 percent, and, finally, Cubans, who comprise 5 percent. The poverty rates, sorted by racial and ethnic groups, reveal that Puerto Ricans are the poorest, followed by Mexicans, Central and South Americans, other Hispanics, and, finally, Cubans, who are the most well-to-do Hispanics in the United States.

The socioeconomic, political, and educational conditions of Hispanic immigrants have improved more slowly than those of the average American. Because the coping skills of this immigrant group are often inadequate, these individuals frequently suffer from homelessness, drug and alcohol abuse, broken marriages, sexual abuse, AIDS, lack of health care services, unemployment, violence, and crime. In addition, immigrant Hispanics often have to deal with anti-Hispanic prejudice or racism in the United States.

Unfortunately, some Hispanics are frightened to enter hospitals, mental health centers, clinics, and other health care institutions. Some lack health insurance or financial resources. Others fear being stigmatized because of mental illness. In addition, Hispanics seeking mental health services must face the reality that very few services are available in the Spanish language.

In addition, Padilla and Ruiz (1973) suggested that many Hispanics feel that their presence is unwelcome at traditional mental health service centers. Mental health professionals and institutions discourage Hispanics from seeking services through direct and indirect means, including geographical inaccessibility, not providing services in Spanish, and "inaccurate diagnostic and treatment decisions based on middle-class values" and on "cultural differences." They also pointed out that therapists are subject to prejudice, cultural stereotyping, excessive social distance, and "reliance upon a physical symptom model of inquiry which omits consideration of potentially significant ethnographic data" (p. 21).

Like other impoverished urban minorities, many inner-city Hispanics live in an environment of poverty, homelessness, unemployment, hunger, and physical and sexual abuse. These individuals do not receive the medical and psychiatric care they need. A significant number of Hispanics believe that going to a mental health center means they "are crazy" (estar loco). Hispanics are especially likely to share the stereotype of mental illness as degrading, self-lowering, and shameful.

Hispanics tend to live in close-knit communities and often do not want their neighbors or public agencies to know their business, especially if they have a mental illness. They continuously endeavor to conceal this aspect of their lives and do not want to make it public. Like most people, Hispanics hold in high regard such characteristics as honesty, integrity, morality, good reputation, esteem, and respect. They fear being viewed by others as insignificant, negligible, inferior, or second-rate because their community might regard them as "crazy" (loco) or genetically defective. For example, Kreisman (1975) points out that

> the Mexican-American family is typically tightly knit; distrust of agencies outside this unit prevails. Since illness may be perceived as a hereditary defect, the family strives to determine that a member's illness is due to external, extrafamilial factors, often seeking the services of a curandero (healer), who will support such an etiology. [p. 81]

HISPANICS—A BRIEF HISTORICAL OVERVIEW

Hispanics are commonly a blend of Spanish, indigenous Indian, and African ancestry. In addition, in certain countries of Latin America,

Hispanics are descended from German, Italian, French, Portuguese, and other nationalities. Argentina, for example, is like the United States in being a melting pot of many immigrant groups. Usually, however, Hispanics (whether predominantly white, black, Indian, or mixed) will not identify themselves with a Spanish, Indian, African, or other ancestry. Their ethnic identification will be that of their country of origin, with no other qualification given.

In the Caribbean, the indigenous Indians' life-style faded shortly after the invasion by Spain in the late fifteenth century. According to historians, the native Puerto Rican Indians were enslaved during the Spanish invasion, and their wives became consorts for the Spanish settlers. According to Padilla and Ruiz (1973), "with colonization, the native inhabitants of the island were virtually eliminated and replaced by Negro slaves" (p. 6). The influence of this native Puerto Rican Indian culture can be seen today in the emphasis on parentage, the expectation of obedient and peaceable conduct among children (Bluestone and Vela 1982), and dependence on each other as a group in contemporary Puerto Rican society. The indigenous Puerto Rican Indians emphasized group rather than individual identity. In contemporary Puerto Rico, for example, when an individual builds a cement house, the entire extended family and social network often volunteer to help with the heavy labor of laying the floor and ceiling.

Marriage in traditional Hispanic culture tends to be as much a union of two families as of two individuals. The societal expectation is that both families of origin will provide help in strengthening the relationship between the married couple. Siblings and extended family are also expected to help in child rearing, a task that other cultures typically leave more exclusively to the wife and mother.

When the marriage takes place without the consent of both families, the most visibly affected person is the wife. Without help from her extended family, the wife turns to her husband for help. Hispanic husbands tend to resent such requests because they force the husband into a role that is outside the culturally defined norms of the society. The husband's resentment about adopting an unaccustomed role may lead to arguments and distance or to such behaviors as drinking, extramarital affairs, and domestic violence.

Hispanic families, especially those of the lower and lower-middle classes, are likely to be dominated by the man of the house. In Hispanic culture, as in many other cultures, the husband is expected to be in control of his wife and children and to make all important financial decisions. Regardless of social class, the Hispanic husband is identified as the provider. He is expected to supply whatever the family needs. Padilla and Ruiz (1973) observed that the literature identifies a "typical" pattern of family structure among Hispanics studied that includes "an authoritarian father and a submissive mother, mutual acceptance of the doctrine of male superiority, and child-rearing practices which include indulgent affection and harsh punishment" (p.35).

Feminism, imported from the United States, is at odds with this traditional role of the Hispanic male. As in the United States, feminism has increasingly influenced the role of middle- and upper-class Caribbean, Central, and South American women who now wish to work and to have a profession. As Hispanic women become Americanized and more autonomous, Hispanic men feel threatened by their perceived loss of authority. Hispanic women are becoming less and less "convinced of the intellectual, biological, and social superiority of the male" (Padilla and Ruiz 1973, p. 43).

As parents, Hispanic men are often authoritarian and do not treat children as individuals with minds of their own. Spankings, which demonstrate the parents' power and superiority, are widely accepted as a way to teach respect, discipline, and responsibility. Good behavior often goes unacknowledged because parents fear losing their children's respect (faltar el respeto). In the Hispanic culture, respect (respeto) of one's elders is highly valued.

Culturally, Hispanic men fear losing control at home and in the eyes of their community. If they feel they are losing control, they may display sudden aggressive outbursts. Generally, such aggression is controlled by persuasion from the group, the extended family, and in most cases by the compadrazco connection with the men whom they have chosen as godfathers for their children. The social rule that children must respect their parents is held in high regard. When children act disrespectfully, the parents lose face in their community.

As happens in other cultures that place a high premium on social acceptance, the outward dignity that Hispanics try to maintain is usually accompanied by suppression and repression of feelings and psychological needs (Rothenberg 1964) . The expression of anger is a particularly problematic area. Hispanic men usually release anger within their group through heated arguments about politics and religion. Hispanic women, on the other hand, tend to channel their anger and aggression into gossip and psychosomatic illness.

MACHISMO AND MARIANISM

Machismo is a major factor in the sense of identity of most Hispanic individuals. According to the *American Heritage Dictionary* (1980), machismo refers to "an exaggerated sense of masculinity stressing such attributes as physical courage, virility, domination of women, and aggressiveness or violence." Padilla and Ruiz (1973) state that machismo denotes "a latent capacity for violence, sensitivity to insult or affront, and a tendency to manifest male superiority and dominance through multiple sexual conquests" (p. 45). The machismo of the Hispanic culture is reinforced by the teachings of the Bible, which imply that men are superior to women. For example, Paul wrote to the Ephesians:

> Let wives be subject to their husbands as to the Lord; because a husband is head of the wife, just as Christ is head of the Church, being Himself savior of the body. But just as the Church is subject to Christ, so also let wives be to their husbands in all things. (Ephesians 5:22–24)

Marianism goes hand in hand with machismo as a factor in Hispanic identity formation. The cult of the Virgin Mary among Roman Catholics has done much to define feminine identity in Hispanic culture. For many Hispanic Roman Catholics, the Virgin Mary is the central religious figure. She intervenes as a heavenly mother directly with God the Father on behalf of the supplicant. The assumption is that God will not deny a request made by the Blessed Virgin. For example, in the New Testament story of the wedding at Cana, Mary convinces her son Jesus to change water into wine, despite Jesus' comment that "my time has not yet come."

Mary is so central to Hispanic Catholicism that in Puerto Rico, for example, the entire months of May and October are devoted to honoring the Blessed Mother with rosaries, novenas, and special religious ceremonies. During the season of Lent and especially during Holy Week, the preaching often includes the maternal suffering and voluntary solitude of Mary upon the loss of her son Jesus. Mary is so culturally significant that many Hispanics feel the ideal woman should resemble the Virgin Mary—sexually pure, holy, caring, maternal, peaceable, faithful, handmaiden of the Lord, subservient to the will of a masculine God. The *machista* husband rules his universe with his wife's compliant obedience and support.

Hispanic men, especially from the lower and middle classes, usually make all the major decisions. They tend to disregard their wives' ideas and often do not even confer with them. The husband sees his major responsibility as providing for the family and feels a strong need to be regarded by the community as a distinguished, hardworking *macho*. Hispanic men struggle to maintain their image of manliness, working hard to gain respect and a socially acceptable position in the community.

Machismo in the Hispanic culture is a blend of ideals and virtues, such as endurance, masculine pride, tenacity, virility, control, sexual prowess, bravery, and vengefulness when dishonored. The macho husband is not expected to help with child rearing. Women take control of the family environment only when their husbands are not around and report back to the husband when he returns. Although many Hispanic women need to work outside the home to "help my husband provide" for the family, the Hispanic culture regards the primary role of women as raising the children, preparing meals on time, cleaning, and meeting the needs of their husbands. So long as wives do not challenge or confront their husbands, the household and the marriage remain peaceful. As one Hispanic male client said to his wife, "Respect between husband and wife means that as a wife you must be loving, considerate, and never have negative thoughts about me" (quoted by Garcia-Preto 1982, p.171).

Clinical Vignette

Naomi and Jorge, a Puerto Rican couple in their late twenties, had recently moved from New York to Bridgeport, where they presented at the clinic seeking a renewal of Naomi's medication. They had come to New York from Puerto Rico two years previously. Naomi had been started on Haldol (an antipsychotic medication) in Puerto Rico in her late teens when she had begun to hear voices and to fear that she was being followed. The doctor inquired whether the current dose of

Haldol was effective. Naomi responded that she was doing well and did not think that people were following her. Her husband interrupted, complaining that the medication was not helping Naomi and requesting that the doctor prescribe a new medication. When the doctor asked Jorge why he felt that the Haldol was ineffective, Jorge explained, "Because she doesn't do what I tell her anymore." The doctor explored Jorge's complaint further and learned that Naomi had begun to act more independently after the couple had moved to New York. Jorge had become frustrated by his wife's lack of traditional obedience and began to hit her when she disobeyed. Following this discussion of Jorge's aggression, Naomi and Jorge accepted a referral for marital therapy with a Spanish-speaking clinician.

As a husband, the Hispanic man feels he must give the impression of always being ready for sex. Women, in contrast, tend to regard sex as an obligation. The Hispanic man typically maintains a double standard about sex. Women are expected to be virgins on their wedding day, but there is no similar requirement for men. The husband expects his wife to be totally faithful, despite the cultural view of women as defenseless and vulnerable to seduction by the sexually attractive man. An unfaithful wife runs the risk of being severely injured or even killed if she is discovered. Men, on the contrary, are expected but not required to be faithful, and the consequences of male infidelity are not nearly as severe. Ironically, some women learn to accept the infidelity of their husbands and at times adapt to their husband's infidelity without much resistance. Hispanic women often accept the husband's double standard with a profound sense of suppressed or repressed anger. The acceptance of the husband's double standard could be a result of financial hardship, social conflict/status, as well as cultural and religious values deeply ingrained in the society (e.g., the prohibition against divorce).

Clinical Vignette

Marcelo, a 60-year-old Hispanic man, was brought by his medical social worker to the mental health center for psychiatric evaluation. During his medical examination, he had revealed to his doctor that he had a plan to kill himself because he had just found out that his current girlfriend had been unfaithful. During the psychiatric evaluation, he took pride in boasting about his sexual prowess and potency. He said that he had been involved with numerous women throughout his marriage and had fathered more than thirty children, twenty-three of whom bore his name. He also reported having left his homeland ten years earlier when he learned that his *esposa principal* (principal wife) had cheated on him and he was afraid that he might kill her. Marcelo explained, *"A mi no me gusta que mi esposa me ponga cuernos"* ("I don't like my wife to cheat on me").

THE CONSEQUENCES OF MACHISMO AND MARIANISM

Historically, Hispanics have been dominated by external forces (e.g., Spaniards, Americans, the Roman Catholic Church). Consonant with years of colonization and oppression, many Latinos have adopted a submissive, passive, and dependent life-style. Such passivity is even reflected linguistically in Spanish grammar in such constructions as *"Se me rompió la taza"* (I broke the cup; literally translated, the cup broke itself for me). Submissiveness to authority has become culturally rewarded and is considered respectable behavior. Obedience is taught as an important moral value in the cultural, religious, and personal development of most Hispanic individuals. Marvin Karno (1966) noted traits such as passivity, silence, deference, and politeness among Mexicans living in Los Angeles, and Rogelio Díaz-Guerrero (1975) reported greater passivity among Mexicans when compared with Americans. Anthropologists have pointed out that in Puerto Rico "the good child was the one who was quiet and obedient and did not get involved in fights" (Bluestone and Vela 1982, p. 277). Resentment about such socioculturally enforced docility may be repressed and emerge in symptomatic behavior during the course of the life cycle.

Traditional Hispanic submissiveness and passivity can cause problems when the Hispanic individual enters a different culture. Writing about Puerto Ricans, Nydia García-Preto (1982) states that "conflict and anxiety are experienced when they confront a society that frowns on passivity and expects independent individualistic behavior" (p. 175).

The submissiveness of Hispanics in American culture contributes to stress in the Hispanic family, group, and individual. When the Hispanic man, for example, becomes part of a larger society that values autonomy and independence, he may not fit in and may consequently become dysfunctional. The Hispanic man may not understand the individualistic behavior of the dominant culture as opposed to his own more submissive, group-oriented culture. There is also a tendency to be a passive participant in an effort to be accepted in the dominant culture, or a tendency to "play the game" that the dominant culture plays. In an individualistic society, the judgment of the Hispanic man might be in jeopardy because Hispanic men usually make decisions within the extended group or family.

Hispanic men, like most immigrants, experience culture shock upon arrival in the United States. They undergo a mental conflict because they are living between two cultures, both of which are partially accepted, each providing contradictory standards and opposing loyalties. This culture shock may lead to psychological and social maladjustment. If the Hispanic man joins a group composed of individuals from different cultures, he tends to attribute to the new group the same qualities and expectations that he attributed to his native Hispanic group-oriented network. He may be unaware that the values and morals of the non-Hispanic cultures may be radically different from his own.

Traditional Hispanic submissiveness may be interpreted by the host culture as acceptance. Such acceptance may lead Hispanics to adopt behaviors that are new or that have not been explained to them, but that, in their need to belong to the group, they may carry out, perhaps suppressing their unwillingness. The Hispanic individual is especially in danger when the new social group uses or abuses substances, especially substances requiring intravenous administration.

For a man, assuming the role of "macho" usually leads to success within his native Hispanic culture; however, the role of "macho" might become merely a way of survival in the United States because of an ever increasing desire to be accepted, acknowledged, and highly regarded by the group. This wish for acceptance by the group is a cultural value that affects Hispanics in this country. Recall that Hispanic men turned to the group in their native land to alleviate tension, frustration, and aggression.

"KNOWING" AND PERSONALISMO

The concept of "knowing" is important for the Hispanic male. To the Hispanic individual, "knowing" means trusting someone, caring, sharing, guiding, being a companion, being a friend, being well-connected, and being part of the family *(personalismo)*. "Knowing" means giving up what you have to help the other and "knowing" who to contact *(tener palancas)* when you need to find a job or get something done. "Knowing" is the pride of the Hispanic man. Consequently, the more people you "know," the more groups you will belong to and the more likely it is that you will be highly respected, accepted, and regarded. "Knowledge" of many social groups and many people will make the Hispanic male's social status worthy of envy by many. Ultimately, "knowing" means connection with the group.

In his cultural milieu the Hispanic man prides himself in "knowing" what he does and personally "knowing" the members of his group. It is the group's responsibility to provide support, strength, and new ways to regulate tension, aggression, and frustration in a functional way. The traditional cultural values of the Hispanic population in the United States pose a threat to their lives by virtue of the desire to be highly regarded by society and the need to gain and save face in the community where they live. Hispanic men, in their need to be part of a group and gain respect in the community, are adopting behaviors that put them, their wives, and children at risk of drug abuse or other illegal behaviors.

However, for the Hispanic man, connection with a group outside his own culture can have negative consequences. Hispanics often have difficulty seeing themselves separately from the roles they play in society. To put it in term of a simple equation:

$$\text{Friends (the group)} + \text{Family} = \text{Self}$$

This equation can be understood as a positive interaction between parties contributing to the development of the individual. Hispanics believe that their "knowing" of their friends implies a strong, almost familial, connection *(personalismo)* between the individuals.

MORAL AND RELIGIOUS DILEMMAS

Hispanics love to celebrate life, and spirituality plays a prominent role in Hispanic families. Hispanics are willing to sacrifice material satisfaction for spiritual goals. "For them being is more important than doing or having" (García-Preto 1982, p. 168). Hispanics, though not resigned to fate, are accepting of it. Catholic rituals, such as masses, rosaries, and novenas (prayers to the saints), are common practices of popular spirituality in the Hispanic culture.

The widely accepted and respected teachings of the Catholic church sometimes run counter to the efforts of mental health professionals. Contraception, for example, is forbidden by the Catholic church. A problem arises when case managers try to instruct Hispanic clients about safe sexual practices. To teach a traditional or even a non-practicing Hispanic Catholic to use a condom is a complex task. Before introducing such topics, one must first address and respect the religious, moral, and marital values of Hispanic clients.

SEX AND CULTURAL DILEMMAS

Machismo also plays a significant role when a man is asked to use a condom during sexual activity. One typical response among Hispanic men is, "she is my wife and I want to have natural sex." Like many men, Hispanics often complain, "it doesn't feel the same." Use of a condom might provoke the Hispanic man to experience guilt, shame, a sense of decreased manliness, loss of control, intense feelings of sinfulness, fear of God's punishment, and disconnection from God. Decisions are constantly filtered through religious belief systems in the Hispanic culture.

As in many other cultural groups, there exists a taboo against an open discussion of sexual matters in Hispanic families. Both cultural and religious factors underlie this taboo. It generally takes great courage for Hispanics to go to a store to buy condoms. Obtaining condoms from public service agencies (e.g., clinics, mental health centers) is often considered embarrassing because of all the questions that clients may be asked about their sexuality and sexual practices.

THE SUPPORT NETWORK

When Hispanics experience distress, they commonly turn for support to one (or more) of four sources:

1. Their families—Families may provide advice and emotional support. In addition, they usually encourage the individual to see a physician.
2. The physician—Hispanics with emotional difficulties often go to physicians with physical complaints. They usually expect to receive the doctor's direct advice and possibly some medication. If the physician cannot clearly determine the nature of the problem, the individual is likely to question the competence of the doctor and seek assistance elsewhere.
3. The clergy—Hispanics visit the clergy when there are issues of guilt, shame, sin, and disrespect for their elders.
4. Other advisors, including folk healers, *curanderos*, *santeros*, *espiritistas* (spiritists or mediums who can contact spirits), and, on occasion, astrologers (Kloppenburg 1983)—When there is no clear physical cause for a problem or illness, the difficulty is considered supernatural or spiritual.

SPIRITISM

Spiritists and spiritualists provide mental health services to many segments of the Hispanic community. The importance of spiritism has been well-documented among Puerto Ricans and other people from the Caribbean (Rogler and Hollingshead 1961, Sandoval 1979). It is estimated that more than 60 percent of Puerto Ricans visit a spiritist at some time in their lives (Krippner and Welsh 1992). Spiritists are believed to have special powers to control spirits, and Hispanics frequently visit spiritists for help with psychosomatic ailments that the medical doctor has been unable to alleviate. Among Chicanos (Mexican-American), "curanderos often attribute an illness to an agent whose existence must be taken on faith because it cannot be detected with medical instruments" (Krippner and Welsh 1992, p. 15).

Unlike some narrowly focused treatment models, a fundamental tenet of spiritism is to take into account the entire family situation, cultural milieu, and social environment. Spiritists seek to decrease anxiety and provide cognitive guidance aimed at putting the individual back in control. Physical ailments are reframed as an attempt to alleviate the dysfunctional behavior. A positive restructuring of the whole environment of the individual is sought.

Lloyd Rogler and August Hollingshead (1961) drew a parallel between the gathering of people around a spiritist and a group therapy session. During the spiritist session, the medium (spiritist) attempts to contact the spirit world to discover which spirits are influencing the behavior of the individual and inflicting psychosomatic ailments. The medium then attempts to make peace with the spirits and to find positive ways to satisfy the patient's needs. The spiritist's job is to redirect the spirits to assist rather than harm the individual. The medium tries to restructure the client's milieu so that the client can resume normal functioning.

A major difference between the spiritist session and group psychotherapy lies in how they view personality-disordered behavior, hallucinations, visions, and overt psychotic symptoms. Unlike the psychotherapist, the spiritist will understand and reframe such "psychopathological" behaviors as spiritual gifts that can enable the individual to communicate better with the spirits. The spiritist will define symptoms and strange behaviors as meaningful personality variables rather than "sick" patterns of adaptation. Another difference between group therapy and the spiritist session lies in the composition of the group. The spiritist group is usually composed of friends and family members. Within this cultural climate of toleration of unusual behavior, the client's problems are examined, understood, and accepted, and solutions are sought.

SPANISH-SPEAKING PEOPLE AND THE SEARCH FOR MENTAL HEALTH TREATMENT

As mentioned previously, when Hispanics seek treatment in the United States, there is often a language barrier. Like other non-English-speaking immigrant groups, Hispanics are frequently accompanied by a neighbor or a child who speaks English and becomes the

Hispanic adult's link to the new culture. The dynamic of an adult needing a child to translate creates a sense of powerlessness in the Hispanic adult.

Given the role that children play in the Hispanic culture, for a child to translate for an adult during a psychiatric or psychological evaluation runs counter to cultural beliefs and violates parent/child boundaries in the family. In addition, the content of the evaluation may be beyond the child's comprehension, and the child may inadequately translate the information or be unable to translate at all. Clinicians may be unable to obtain the information they need to provide the proper mental health services. Furthermore, psychotherapy under such circumstances is impossible.

When the clinician needs to request non-fluent Hispanic individuals to speak in English, clients often feel humiliated by being asked to repeat themselves over and over again to make the clinician understand what they are saying. Such constant repetition creates a frustrating sense of distance. Communication rather than clinical information becomes the major task of the interview. Among some Hispanic clients, the communication impairment creates a sense of second-class status. The clinician runs the risk of having the client not return for treatment. Clients may complain: "They make me speak English. They speak English to me and I do not understand. I don't think they understand me either."

Luis R. Marcos and colleagues (1973) studied the effects of interviewing psychiatric patients in English versus their native Spanish language. In this study Hispanic patients who were interviewed in English were judged to have more psychopathology, misunderstood the interviewer more often than in Spanish interviews, gave briefer responses than in Spanish, exhibited speech disturbances due to anxiety, and spoke more slowly with more silences than in Spanish. According to Marcos and colleagues:

> . . . patients were less communicative, more concise and formal, and more emotionally withdrawn in English than in Spanish. . . . When a patient must be interviewed in a language in which he is less competent the clinician must make every effort to assure that the patient understands what is expected: he must introduce redundancy to facilitate communication and he ought not to accept laconic responses as evidence of withdrawal or uncooperativeness. [p.659]

The conceptualization of time is another factor that influences the Hispanic client's receiving of mental health services. Hispanics often do not fully understand the value placed on "being on time" by North American mental health professionals. Bluestone and Vela (1982), for example, reported that Puerto Ricans in New York City, regardless of their social class, are lax in their sense of time. The idea of an appointment beginning precisely at a given time is culturally foreign, and the thought of paying for a missed appointment is often inconceivable. This lax sense of time is most likely related to difficulties and delays in communication and transportation in underdeveloped countries. In addition, as Bluestone and Vela (1982) point out:

> The Puerto Rican poor come to therapy with a set of expectations derived from their experience with other doctors, clinics, or agencies. They . . . may never have been seen at their appointment time. They may have been made to wait for hours in an emergency room or walk-in clinic or may have spent whole days in a welfare office. [p. 274]

PERSONALISMO AND COMMUNICATION WITH HISPANIC CLIENTS

The Hispanic culture places a premium on the group with social involvement characterized by warm, friendly interactions. The term *personalismo* refers to this cultural ideal of forming affectionate, familiar, personal relationships. To establish a therapeutic alliance, clinicians will need to take the time to "join" the Hispanic client's group by engaging in a warm, family-like conversation at the beginning of an evaluation. Doing so will make a tremendous difference to the Hispanic client. Only after connecting in this way with the individual and the family in crisis can a fruitful discussion of the problem take place.

Writing about Puerto Rican clients in New York City, Bluestone and Vela (1982) caution that

> Because of the Puerto Rican patient's marked need to form a rather affectionate and familiar relationship with the therapist, special caution must be taken to preserve a therapeutic stance. The patient may

> perceive the attitude adopted by many therapists with American and European patients as being cold, removed, and sometimes even rude when compared to the patient's previous social interactions, which are usually warmer in the Puerto Rican culture. . . . the patient may leave therapy in the early stages if his therapist appears too cold or remote. Thus, being spontaneous and empathically warm, but maintaining a therapeutic stance at all times, becomes imperative. [p. 276]

It appears that Hispanic clients need to make the interview environment like that of their reference group—warm, friendly, and trusting—and to make the mental health professional a member of the group. Such personalized relationships *(personalismo)* are idealized in Hispanic culture, and older Hispanic clients will often refer to their clinicians as *hijo* (son) or *hija* (daughter). Once Hispanic patients feel that the clinician has joined their group, they can begin to tell their stories and confide personal information.

As is generally true, once the assessment is completed, the clinician should provide the client with a clear and precise explanation of the evaluation. Explaining the findings of the evaluation is especially important because Hispanic clients need to "know" what is going on and wish to receive something specific and concrete for their efforts. When a Hispanic client presents for psychiatric evaluation, the most salient question on the client's mind is likely to be, "Am I crazy or not?" A clear and empathic explanation of the clinician's evaluation will alleviate much anxiety and help the client to resume an adaptive level of functioning.

COMMON REASONS WHY HISPANICS COME FOR PSYCHIATRIC EVALUATION

Hispanics seek treatment primarily for medical complaints and for symptoms such as insomnia, suicidal urges, recurrent nightmares, unexplained crying, silent brooding, fugue states, and difficulty with interpersonal relationships. Brain ache *(dolor en el cerebro)*, chest pressure *(el pecho apretado)*, backache, and tiredness are other symptoms frequently reported by Hispanics. Life transition and social readjustment, as well as fears of being diagnosed with a fatal illness, are other reasons that lead Hispanics to treatment.

Somatization is a common idiom for expressing emotional and psychological distress among many Hispanic clients. Patients from a lower socioeconomic background or with minimal education are especially likely to express depression through somatization, perhaps because of poorly developed expressive language skills. In contrast, wealthier, better educated individuals tend to express affect more directly rather than somatically. Guarnaccia and colleagues (1989) point out that some patients somatize their depressive feelings or psychosocial distress in clinical settings for "strategic" reasons based on prior experiences with physicians and the stigma of mental illness.

Somatic complaints appear to be especially common among Puerto Rican clients. Guarnaccia and colleagues (1989) noted a higher incidence of somatization disorder and a greater number of symptoms reported in the somatization section of the Diagnostic Interview Schedule in a study conducted in Puerto Rico in 1984 when compared with the Epidemiological Catchment Area studies (Robins et al. 1981). When Maritza Rubio-Stipec and colleagues (1989) compared the results from Puerto Rico with those of Anglo-Americans and Mexican-Americans in the Los Angeles Epidemiological Catchment Area study, they found a unique somatization factor in the Puerto Rico study. It may be that the increased prevalence of somatic symptoms among Puerto Ricans is related to the wider acceptance of *ataques de nervios* as an idiom of distress in the Puerto Rican community. Vicente Abad and Elizabeth Boyce (1979) reported that, among Puerto Ricans who had migrated to New Haven, Connecticut, the most common complaints were

. . . depression, anxiety, somatic concerns, hallucinations, and actual or feared loss of control. Patients rarely report depression as such, but rather complain of symptoms of insomnia, eating problems, fatigue, headaches, body aches, and feelings of weakness and exhaustion. Similarly, anxiety, in and of itself, may not be recognized by patients although manifested in reports of heart palpitations, dizziness, and fainting. Anger *(coraje)* may be expressed as nervousness or malaise. . . . The most widely pervasive single theme reported by the Puerto Rican patients we have seen has been that of actual or feared loss of impulse control. [p. 30]

Other issues that bring Hispanics to seek clinical intervention include the problems of acculturation of the Hispanic individual in the urban setting, employment issues, and the dynamics of the family system in the life of the individual. Frequently, social equilibrium may be restored by addressing such issues with family members in a session.

DIFFERING CONTENT AND STYLE
OF DREAMS

Night dreams often reveal much about an individual's emotional makeup. In one study, researchers investigated the manifest content in the dreams of the Hispanic-American and other Americans of both sexes (Brenneis and Roll 1975). The Hispanics spoke Spanish at home and identified themselves as Chicanos, Hispanic-Americans, or Mexican Americans. The Hispanic women's dreams made limited use of space, a response consistent with the traditional idea of Hispanic women being confined to their homes. Hispanic women also reported frequent scenes of friendly activities and interactions within the boundaries of their homes. The Hispanic men's dreams showed a higher incidence of activities outside their homes. Hispanic men reported sexual and aggressive behavior more frequently than the Hispanic women did.

Another study (Brenneis and Roll 1976) comparing Hispanic-American students with other American students found that

1. Hispanic-American students dreamed more often about familiar things than did American students.
2. A relatively greater number of characters were reported in the dreams of Hispanic individuals (the group).
3. While relating the dreams, Hispanic-Americans discussed affect and sensory impressions more often than their American counterparts.

Samuel Roll and colleagues (1976) looked at disclaimed activity in the dreams of Chicanos and Anglos. By disclaimed activity, they meant the deflecting of responsibility for one's behavior onto someone or something else (including one's body, mind, fate, or objects). They found that the manifest content of the dreams of their Hispanic subjects reflected a greater emphasis on disclaimed activity, passivity, and deflection of responsibility. They concluded that Hispanics tend to react more passively than do Anglo-Americans when confronted by stress and problem situations.

Abad and Boyce (1979) point out that Hispanic patients' reports of their dreams may be mistaken as signs of psychosis. Puerto Ricans, for example, typically regard dreams as premonitions or omens of future events. Non-Spanish-speaking clinicians may at times misinterpret dream reports by Hispanics as evidence of hallucinations, delusions, or psychotic thinking.

CRISIS INTERVENTION

Psychiatric assessment often merges with crisis intervention therapy because Hispanic clients most often come for assessment in the context of a crisis. Typically the crisis has taken place just days or weeks prior to coming for an initial evaluation. On occasion the symptoms will have been ongoing for months or years. Often a cultural dilemma or stigma attached to mental health services has kept the Hispanic individual from coming sooner for treatment.

In assessing the Hispanic client, especially in a crisis situation, the clinician should keep in mind such questions as:

Why did you come today instead of last week or two months ago?

What has changed in your life that made you decide to look for help?

What have you done to try to alleviate the situation?

Has anyone been helping you? Who is that person? How is that person helping? What do you do together to help ease the symptoms? Have you visited a spiritist?

How do you deal with your anger?

Is there meaningful verbal communication with family members?

What is your usual response when you are in a crisis?

Is there any family support available?

Does your pastor (if person goes to church) know that you came here?

While conducting the crisis interview, the therapist should also consider the following questions: What is the socioeconomic situation of the individual? Is there a history of suicidality, homicidality, or suicidal/homicidal ideation? Is there a medical condition from which the patient is suffering? Who is more in crisis—the family or the identified patient?

It is also important to review the financial situation of the family. Hispanic men, as husbands, parents, providers, and heads of the household, sometimes magnify problems in the hope of being relieved of the pressure of not being able to meet their roles within the family and sociocultural environment. While avoiding stereotyping patients, clinicians should nonetheless consider whether the individual is seeking mental health services as a requirement for state welfare or Social Security benefits. A fact of life in the inner city is that impoverished Hispanics and non-Hispanics alike will at times seek mental health services not because they need treatment, but rather because they are experiencing financial difficulties. For example, after a long interview in which the author had established a good empathic connection, a male Hispanic client confided:

> This is between you and me. I don't want this to be in the record. You know, I can work, but if I go looking for a job I will not make enough money and I have children and there are a lot of bills to pay. Now my daughter wants to go to college and I need some money. What I am doing is applying for Social Security Disability and as soon as I get it I will also look for a job under the table . . .

In addition, many Hispanic clients worry about the potential adverse effects of treatment. One client expressed this concern as follows:

> . . . people tell me that if I continue coming to the mental health center I will turn crazy (loco). They say that the medication that they give here make people crazy (loco). I know someone who was coming here and the medication he was given by you (ustedes, the formal plural of you) made him worse than when he first came here. He had to stop the medication. Are you sure that the medication will not make me crazy (loco)?"

CONCLUSIONS

Before proceeding to a survey of the syndrome of *ataques de nervios*, it may be useful to summarize the major points made thus far about the clinical assessment of Hispanic clients:

The docility and submissiveness of the indigenous Indians is still a part of the makeup of many Hispanic individuals and may be connected to cultural difficulties with the expression of anger.

Cultural and religious values of the Hispanic population are highly influential in the life structure of the Hispanic household.

The husband continues to dominate the family environment of the lower- and middle-class Hispanic household. In these same households, the Hispanic women adopt a subservient role vis-à-vis their husbands. The popular image of the Virgin Mary as the handmaiden of God serves as the feminine ideal for many Hispanic individuals.

Machismo continues to influence the behavior of Hispanic men as enforced by the group and family system. As a consequence, machismo has negative consequences when the Hispanic man tries to adapt to the American culture.

The cultural need of Hispanics to belong to a group and gain face in the community may have negative personal, family, and social consequences.

Language, class, and cultural barriers prevent the Hispanic population in the United States from obtaining adequate mental health treatment.

Treatment models that take into account cultural and socioeconomic aspects of the Hispanic community can be highly beneficial. Psychotherapeutic treatments that appear to be most congruent with the cognitive styles of poor inner-city Hispanic clients tend to be short term, directive, and action oriented. Once acculturation occurs and socioeconomic status improves, as Bluestone and Vela (1982) observe, "therapy with second generation Puerto Rican professionals in New York City approximates therapy with professionals of other ethnic groups" (p. 270).

Because of poverty and a language barrier, the Hispanic community in the United States is in a mental health crisis.

During the assessment, the clinician should stress familialism, take the necessary time to engage in conversation with the client, and refrain from criticizing or challenging existing cultural and religious beliefs.

ATAQUES DE NERVIOS—A PROTOTYPICAL FOLK ILLNESS CATEGORY

"Doña Concepción was having an 'ataque.' The four-poster rocked with it. The whole house vibrated to it. A purple and gilt image of Mary hanging against the blue wall of the head of the bed was particularly agitated. It seemed likely to fall and smash at any moment."

Edith Robert, *Candle in the Sun* (1939)

Clinical Vignette

"*Aguántenme, aguántenme que me da el ataque* (Hold me up, hold me up, I'm having an *ataque*)," said Carmen when her misbehaving son came home with bad news. "*Vas a matarme de un disgusto* (You're going to kill me with all the trouble you cause)," she used to say before experiencing an *ataque de nervios*.

Her husband Fermín came home completely drunk. He took his machete and held his children and wife hostage, threatening to kill them. He went out onto the balcony and screamed: "I am going to kill them all." The police were called and Fermín was arrested. Shortly after her husband's arrest, Carmen screamed out while biting her arm, "*Aguántenme que me da el ataque*." She soon fell to the floor and appeared to be convulsing. Her family ran to her assistance, and her *ataque* became the day's topic of conversation.

Definition of *Ataque de Nervios*

Ataques de nervios (attacks of nerves) is a popular or folk illness category used primarily by Spanish-speaking people from the Caribbean. Descriptions of *ataques* have appeared in the anthropological and psychiatric literature for over thirty years. Fiction writer Edith Robert described an *ataque* in her 1937 novel *Candle in the Sun*. Early professional articles (Fernández-Marina 1961, Mehlman 1961) referred to *ataques de nervios* as the *Puerto Rican Syndrome*, a term now considered pejorative of Puerto Ricans (Guarnaccia 1993). Although the early reports about *ataques* focused on Puerto Rican soldiers, the individuals who are most likely to suffer *ataques de nervios* on the island of Puerto Rico tend to be "female, older, less educated, and formerly married" and "to suffer from a combination of social disadvantage, psychiatric disorder, and poor perceived health" (Guarnaccia 1993, p. 164–165). Interestingly, in reviewing the epidemiology of *ataques* in Puerto Rico, Guarnaccia argued that "nervios and ataques cannot be usefully categorized as a culture-bound syndrome as they are not unique to a clearly defined cultural group" (p. 166).

María Oquendo, Ewald Horwath, and Abigail Martínez (1992) have proposed diagnostic criteria for *ataques de nervios*. According to the authors, the essential feature of an *ataque de nervios* is:

> . . . a sudden, though transient, change in behavior that occurs after a major stress. The stress may range from a break-up with a boyfriend or girlfriend to the death of a child. Though it is usually in the interpersonal arena, it is not invariably so. Following the stress, psychotic symptoms may ensue, most frequently incoherence or auditory hallucinations of the voice of a loved one. Dissociative experiences are common and include changes in the level of consciousness and amnesia. Sudden or impulsive behavior such as suicide attempts, falling to the floor, assaultiveness and seizure-like activity may bring the person to medical attention. [p. 368]

Oquendo and colleagues (1992) also state that there is no clear age of onset for an *ataque de nervios*. In his research, Guarnaccia and colleagues (1989) found that an *ataque* can occur at any age, ranging from adolescence to adulthood, more frequently in people over 45. *Ataques de nervios* may last from several hours to a week, followed by a return to premorbid levels of functioning. The transitory impairment that individuals experience during an *ataque* ranges from moderate to severe and sometimes includes self-harm. The actual prevalence of *ataques de nervios* is unknown because many cases do not come to medical attention.

Among certain Hispanic groups, an *ataque de nervios* is considered a culturally acceptable way to respond to distress. An *ataque de nervios* is often the physical expression of emotional pain related to grief, loss, family controversy, or a perceived threat. In most cases, individuals suffering an *ataque de nervios* have been experiencing difficulties with personal, family, or social situations that have gone largely unspoken or have been repressed or suppressed. At times an *ataque de nervios* results from an inability to carry out a social role.

Ataques may present with a variety of symptoms, such as tremors, jerks, increased heart beat, a sensation of warmth that migrates from the chest to the head, lethargy, lightheadedness, weakness, impediments in moving limbs, body parts that feel numb or *dormidas* (fallen asleep), the mind going blank, disrobing, and shaking of the head. Individuals suffering *ataques* may also exhibit uncontrollable shouting, self-mutilation, violent attitudes (verbal and physical), and catatonic posturing. Regardless of what form the *ataque* takes, the social contexts of these experiences are similar across the Americas (Guarnaccia et al. 1989).

In the Caribbean, *ataques* commonly present with seizure-like episodes and loss of consciousness. During the pseudoseizures of *ataques*, there is no urinary incontinence and the thumbs of the "seizing" individual are usually held inside the clenched fists. According to Guarnaccia (1993), the *ataques de nervios* of Central and South Americans, which may or may not involve convulsions or seizure-like activity, can be better conceptualized as "acute onset" *nervios*, a popular illness category referring to disease of the nerves.

Ataques typically occur suddenly and without warning. Those suffering *ataques de nervios* may become temporarily confused, have difficulty with speech or word finding, and briefly lose consciousness. When they regain self-awareness, most individuals claim amnesia, stating that they have no recollection for what happened.

Common circumstances under which individuals experience *ataques de nervios* include wakes, interment or burial, accidents, family altercations, marital arguments, and unexpected upsetting news. Guarnaccia (1993) reported that experiences frequently associated with *ataques* were deaths of loved ones, conflicts with spouse and partners, and loss of family support, often related to migration. According to Oquendo and colleagues (1992):

> The sociocultural context of ataque de nervios is crucial to the diagnosis. The syndrome usually begins in the presence of family members, often at home. Through this culturally condoned coping mechanism, the afflicted member relinquishes his or her social roles. The family then mobilizes to provide support and, if possible, to remove the stressor. [p. 369]

In a summary of the data of a psychiatric epidemiological survey conducted in 1987, Guarnaccia (1993) outlined the presentation of *ataques de nervios* on the island of Puerto Rico. Of the 145 people who reported suffering *ataques*, 72 percent were women and 28 percent were men. The women tended to be over 45 years of age, formerly married, and unemployed with less than a high school education. Interestingly, 63 percent of those who suffered *ataques* also met criteria for one or more psychiatric disorder, including generalized anxiety, alcoholism, dysthymia, depression, posttraumatic stress, and panic disorders.

The most common symptoms of the *ataques* were shouting, crying, nervousness, trembling, breaking things, getting "hysterical," loss of consciousness, intense anger *(coraje)*, and "fright" *(susto)*. The *ataques* tended to occur in situations of marital or family arguments, drunkenness of a family member, death or a life-threatening accident of a close relative, or a natural disaster, such as the Puerto Rican mud slides of 1985. The individuals who reported *ataques* often felt easily overwhelmed and were generally dissatisfied with their social and emotional lives, especially with their relationship with a spouse. These individuals also sought help for their problems from several sources.

AN OVERVIEW OF THE LITERATURE ON
ATAQUES DE NERVIOS

As mentioned previously, the early reports on *ataques de nervios* focused on Puerto Rican recruits in the American armed forces in the

1950s who were diagnosed with the Puerto Rican Syndrome (Rubio et al. 1955, Fernández-Marina 1961). Because they were American citizens, Puerto Ricans were the first Latino group to be inducted into the armed forces in large numbers. These Puerto Rican recruits underwent basic training, became familiar with weapons, and were relocated overseas in emotionally distressing ways. Under stress, some of these soldiers suffered *ataques de nervios* and were treated in VA hospitals and other psychiatric institutions, where they were diagnosed with anxiety, psychopathologic reactions, hysterical and other personality disorders, schizophrenic turmoil, conversion disorders, and malingering. Under such circumstances *ataques* were introduced into mainstream American psychiatry and were pejoratively labeled the Puerto Rican Syndrome. Had Dominicans been recruited in large numbers instead, *ataques* might well have been called the Dominican Syndrome.

Mauricio Rubio, Mario Urdaneta, and John Doyle (1955) reported "psychopathologic reaction patterns" among Puerto Rican personnel in the Antilles Command for the period from January through December 1954. Such reactions followed minor stressors, lasted from a few hours to several days, and were often accompanied by secondary gains, including special privileges and removal from the source of stress. The authors (1955) described five reaction patterns among Puerto Rican recruits, the most common consisting of

> a transient state of partial loss of consciousness, most frequently accompanied by convulsive movements, hyperventilation, moaning and groaning, profuse salivation, and aggressiveness to self or others in the form of biting, scratching, or striking; and of sudden onset and termination. [p. 1767]

Such patients experienced mild dissociation from the environment, and serious injury to self was avoided. Another reaction pattern consisted of sudden outbursts of hostility *(mal de pelea)*. A third pattern involved regression to infantile behaviors. A fourth pattern centered around dramatic pseudosuicidal gestures, and a final fifth pattern involved a day or two of cognitive impairment characterized by mild dissociation, poor concentration, forgetfulness, preoccupation, and decreased interest in self-care.

Rubio and colleagues (1955) reported that most of the Puerto Rican recruits in his sample were diagnosed with "character disorders," with the *ataques* being labeled "hysterical personality reactions." The personal history of these recruits revealed "remarkable similarities," including an extremely strong attachment to and dependence on the mother, a lack of identification with the father and an inadequate male role model, and a lack of experience with the "highly competitive culture" of the United States mainland. Some of the stressors that precipitated the *ataques* included induction into the armed forces, basic training exercises, prolonged hikes, not being allowed to go home on pass, the possibility of being sent overseas, reprimands from officers, and the prospect of discharge with "consequent return to a smaller income and lower living standards."

Ramón Fernández-Marina (1961), taking a psychoanalytic view, believed that the "hysterical attacks" of the Puerto Rican Syndrome were ego defenses against threatened psychotic decompensation. He felt that *ataques de nervios* served to limit "extreme regression" and ego disorganization. Fernández-Marina viewed the hyperkinetic episodes of *ataques* as the expression of intense emotions that had been cut off and rendered unconscious, only to reappear in the form of hysterical (conversion, dissociative, and somatic) reactions. He speculated that the repressed material was sexual in nature.

Fernández-Marina (1961) outlined a series of axioms, based on Freudian ego psychology, to explain the development of the Puerto Rican Syndrome. He postulated that the principles of ego psychology and the nature of Puerto Rican child-rearing practices could explain both the symptom patterns of the Puerto Rican Syndrome and the alleged infrequency of extreme regression in Puerto Rican schizophrenics.

Puerto Rican children, according to the authors, live in large, crowed quarters in a climate that is mild throughout the year. The children are fondled, caressed, and handled by older siblings, grandparents, aunts, and neighbors, as well as by their mothers. Children often sleep in the same bed with adults or other children, increasing the likelihood of being involuntarily fondled and caressed. Fathers, in their effort to show off their son as *macho completo* (complete he-man) may play with the child's genitals. The reader should bear in mind that this description applied to Puerto Rican child rearing in the 1950s and may be less typical today.

Fernández-Marina believed that the constant handling, fondling, and over-stimulation of Puerto Rican children by multiple caregivers affects the development of the child's arousal system. Because the zones of the arousal system are not differentiated prior to psychosexual development, Freud called the infant "polymorphously perverse." In many other cultures, the infant develops an anaclitic relationship with the mother, who is the sole identified, predictable, and consistent caregiver of early childhood. In contrast, Puerto Rican infants develop a "heteroclitic" dependency in which multiple caregivers fondle, caress, and handle the infant. This heteroclitic relationship becomes the basis for the hyperkinetic episodes of the Puerto Rican Syndrome.

Fernández-Marina reported that, because the polymorphously perverse infant shares sleeping quarters with others, he or she is often exposed to situations that prompt sexual tension for which he or she utilizes hyperkinetic discharge to achieve a vicarious orgasm. He suggested that adult Puerto Ricans experiencing *ataques de nervios* regress to this polymorphous perverse way of discharging repressed emotions. Presumably the repeated handling of the infant by multiple persons "fixes tension discharge mechanisms polymorphously at this primitive level" and "as an adult, the same person regresses to this polymorphous primitive discharge if either the threshold of other anxiety-discharging mechanisms is surpassed quantitatively or these mechanisms are not adequate qualitatively" (Fernández-Marina 1961, p. 82).

E.C. Trautman (1961), in the article "The Suicidal Fit," offers another perspective on *ataques de nervios*. Trautman divides the fit of *ataque* into two phases: 1) flight from a stressful scene, followed by 2) an impulsive suicide attempt. Each phase is characterized by sudden onset, inability to communicate, and action-oriented results. The family reacts to the suicidal fit with guilt and a show of affection, support, and attention. If a family or marital conflict triggered the suicidal reaction, the *ataque* may actually lead to a resolution of the problem.

Captain Robert D. Mehlman, M.D., Chief of the Psychiatric Section at the Rodriguez U.S. Army Hospital in Fort Brooke, Puerto Rico, described (1961) *ataques* as "bizarreness combined with extreme fright, agitation and personal violence" (p. 328). He felt that patients with *ataques de nervios* were suffering from "acute dissociative reactions of a hysterical sort." Mehlman also noticed that physicians commonly diagnosed Puerto Rican Syndrome in areas where a significant number of Puerto Rican citizens resided—that is, on the island of Puerto Rico, in New York, and in the armed forces.

In his article, Mehlman was concerned that Puerto Rican men in the armed forces were being too readily diagnosed with Puerto Rican Syndrome when they were, in fact, suffering from psychotic processes (e.g., schizophrenia), acute conversion symptoms, or other psychiatric disorders. Mehlman urged a more careful investigation of the precipitants of the episode to distinguish *ataques de nervios* from psychiatric disorders. According to Mehlman (1961),

> to invent or use a term which tends to class all these individuals in one category poses the ever present danger, first of failing to be aware of what the real disease process is; secondly, the failure to understand the difference amongst these various syndromes makes it impossible to apply the appropriate means of treatment. [p. 330]

He also cautioned his medical colleagues against "over-generalization, over-simplification, over-modernization that takes us away from the patient" (p. 331). In Mehlman's view, the term Puerto Rican Syndrome was a misnomer because it did not describe a single or unique disease entity. Rather, according to Mehlman, the Puerto Rican Syndrome is "a collection of various disease processes that tend to be superficially deceivingly similar in a particular culture" (p. 332).

Mehlman believed that *ataques de nervios* were linked to powerful unresolved feelings of anger with the individual's parents or other authority figures. He noted that those who suffered *ataques* returned quickly to their premorbid level of functioning without dealing with their repressed anger. As part of the treatment, Mehlman recommended helping these recruits to accept responsibility for their actions and to deal more adaptively with their anger.

Garcia-Preto (1982) shared Mehlman's formulation that *ataques* are often expressions of unresolved anger. She stated that, by means of the *ataque*,

> anger, which is usually precipitated by discord in social relationships, is discharged, and secondary gains, such as being able to exercise control over one's family or to receive protective care and attention from others, may result. Whatever guilt may be associated with the aggressive behavior is alleviated by claiming amnesia.

In Garcia-Preto's view, an *ataque de nervios* might allow highly stressed Puerto Rican women to make peace with their husbands or other family members.

In the Hispanic culture, and especially among Puerto Ricans, somatization becomes a means of expressing psychological and emotional concerns. Psychosomatic symptoms are used to express both distress and genuine concern about family, social, and personal problems. For example, one commonly hears Hispanic clients make comments such as, "Ay . . . that daughter of mine gives me a lot of headaches." Experiencing headaches may be the culturally sanctioned way for a rural woman of low socioeconomic status to express either genuine concern or anger about an estranged child.

Albert Rothenberg (1964) attributed *ataques de nervios* among Puerto Ricans to a defect in the expression of anger. He postulates that Puerto Rican mothers bottle feed their children for prolonged periods of time to avoid dealing with the child's anger at the weaning process. In Rothenberg's view, such a mother-child interaction produces a personality "defect" in the healthy expression of anger that, in turn, results in a pattern of hysterical reactions when Puerto Ricans face severe stress in adult life. Rothenberg thus subscribes to a deficit model in which the hysterical *ataque* is viewed as pathological.

Rothenberg further links the problem of expression of anger among Puerto Ricans with the island's history of violence and oppression during the period of Spanish colonialism. He draws a parallel between the violence of the armed forces and the long period of oppression that the inhabitants of the island experienced after the arrival of the Spanish at the end of the fifteenth century. In Rothenberg's view, violence is a symbol of colonial oppression, and the *ataque de nervios* serves as a symbolic expression of resistance against and anger at an oppressive system, whether it be the family or a social institution.

The early studies of *ataques* focused on their description and theories of causation. Albert Rubel (1964) advocated the development of an epidemiology of folk illnesses. He wanted to introduce a syndromal definition of folk illness as a collection of symptoms that tend to appear and cohere together in individuals of a given community in a patterned way. Although the anthropological literature explained how cultural groups understood, diagnosed, and treated various folk illnesses, Rubel pointed out that there were as yet, in

1964, insufficient epidemiological studies to identify who was at risk and under what circumstances the folk illnesses tended to occur.

Rubel (1964) described the folk illness category of *susto* (fright), which may manifest with a cluster of depressive symptoms such as listlessness, restlessness, disturbed sleep, loss of appetite, loss of interest in hygiene, depressed mood, and social withdrawal. The indigenous Indians of Mexico attribute *susto* to "soul loss," which results from an offense against an animistic spirit guardian of the earth. Non-Indian Mexicans explain *susto* in terms of a severe fright associated with a sudden traumatic event.

NERVIOS

The Spanish conquistadors brought to the New World an archaic conceptualization of mental illness called *nervios*, or disease of the nerves of the body (Tissot 1795) . This antiquated European-Spanish notion of emotional problems as strictly biological or organic in origin contributes to the tendency toward somatization of psychological conflict, especially among undereducated Hispanics in the Americas.

In a paper delivered at the Annual Meeting of the American Psychiatric Association in San Francisco (May 1993), Roberto Lewis-Fernández discussed *ataques de nervios* as being "nested in the broader idiom of distress *nervios* (nerves)." *Nervios* is popularly conceptualized as a subacute or chronic vulnerability of the anatomical nervous system that puts the subject at risk for physical, psychological, and emotional ailments. Typical symptoms of *nervios* include chronic somatic complaints, persistent anxiety or sadness, and even psychotic features.

Peggy Barlett and Setha Low (1980) described the syndrome of *nervios* in rural Costa Rican society. Regardless of social class, age, or gender, *nervios* is a signal of intense psychosocial distress. Family disruption or the breakdown in family relations may precipitate *nervios*. According to Barlett and Low, *nervios* illustrates how a symptom connects an individual's personal experience with the family and health care system in a culturally meaningful way.

The Costa Rican culture connects well-being with a calm living environment in which the individual is whole, as evidenced by a well-balanced social, physical, and psychological makeup. *Nervios,* which stands in opposition to well-being, implies a disruption of personal well-being and an inability to experience life in a meaningful and tranquil way. Francisco Escobar, a Costa Rican sociologist, believes that *nervios* is linked to an inability to "fulfill normal duties because of a personal crisis such as loss of a loved one, economic disaster, or insult to one's pride" (Low 1980, p. 27).

Low (1981) gave seven illustrations of circumstances that are explained in terms of *nervios:*

1. A crisis of *nervios* was said to be the result of the marriage of a son to a socially undesirable woman.
2. A woman was reported to get sick with *nervios* when her illegitimate child was born.
3. A child was thought to have *nervios* because her unmarried mother was very upset during the pregnancy, did not go out of the house, and did not want to see people.
4. A man blamed his *nervios* on a traumatic impoverished childhood and an alcoholic father.
5. *Nervios* and bronchial asthma allegedly resulted in a woman when her husband did not come home on time.
6. A mother had a *derrame* (stroke) when one of her grandchildren was killed by a car and when ten days later another child was born yellow (jaundiced). The child born yellow now suffers from *nervios.*
7. A young woman developed *nervios* because of an alcoholic father who fought with her and did not provide financially.

These examples illustrate that *nervios* within Costa Rican society occurs during crises related to marriage, undesirable social situations, feelings of being out of control, family disagreements, unresolved grief, alcoholic parents, problematic pregnancies, sexual issues, and tragic events. Costa Rican doctors usually diagnosed their patients with *nervios* as suffering from anxiety, anxious depression, or conversion disorders. They understood their patient's *nervios* as reflecting

family or economic factors, female reaction to husband inattention or abandonment, an attempt to obtain affection from individuals outside the family network, a reaction to hostility or guilt created by over-dependency, "boredom" in the countryside, or sexual problems. [Low 1981, p. 36]

Nervios is also an idiom of distress among Mexicans. In her report "The Meaning of Nervios," Low (1981) notes that Mexicans receiving psychiatric outpatient treatment did not spontaneously mention *nervios* as the primary source of their illness. However, when they were questioned about the cause of their disorder, 70 percent reported that *nervios* was part of their affliction as noted by Fabrega (1967).

Nervios also plays a role in the Nicaraguan community. The folk medical terms of Nicaragua identify two types of *nervios: nervios regados* and *nervios resentidos*. *Nervios regados* (from the Spanish verb *regar*, meaning to scatter, sprinkle, or strew in all directions) is a generalized nervousness, accompanied by periodic excitability, muscle pain, and insomnia. *Nervios resentidos* (from the Spanish verb *resentirse*, meaning to suffer, to be weakened, to remain weak, to feel hard done by, to have a chip on one's shoulder) is a chronic or fixed state in which it is difficult for the individual to alleviate or moderate pain, anger, passion, and feelings of melancholia.

Víctor De La Cancela and colleagues (1986), in an article entitled "Psychosocial Distress Among Latinos: A Critical Analysis of Ataques de Nervios," hypothesize that *ataques de nervios* are precipitated and understood through "socioeconomic circumstances of colonialism experienced by the *ataque* sufferers" (p. 432). They identify three major components of the *ataque de nervios*: (1) release of anger, (2) secondary gain, and (3) rebellion against repressive conditions. They suggest that *ataques* must be understood holistically in the framework of economic issues, ideology, and social struggle.

De La Cancela and colleagues (1986) distinguished among *nervios*, *ataques*, and *ataques de nervios*. They described *nervios* as the internal experience of distress, *ataque de nervios* as an individual "response to an outside stressor," and an *ataque* as "a particular kind of ataque de nervios in which the person experiences a seizure-like episode often involving loss of consciousness" (p. 434). The authors (1986) also cautioned against overlooking the social, historical, and economic contributions to *ataques de nervios*, stating:

> As such, ataques de nervios are considered pathological, related to paranoid or schizophrenic processes, sexual over stimulation, maternal

over protectiveness, and alienation from fathers. This model subscribes to a deficit model of behavior which masks the social-historical origins and socioeconomic order nurturing the psychological and behavioral manifestations of ataques. [p. 436]

Mario Rendón (1984) and Abad and Boyce (1979), writing about Puerto Rican clients, focused on the family dynamics of *ataques*, pointing out that *ataques de nervios* are socioculturally recognized expressions of emotion that often communicate about family relationships. Vivian Garrison (1977) also linked *ataques de nervios* to family struggles, conflicts and arguments, and to spiritual factors, including *espiritismo*.

In an attempt to clarify the concept of *nervios*, Peter Guarnaccia and Pablo Farias (1988) distinguished between *nervios* as "illness" and *nervios* as "sickness." *Nervios* as illness combines both physical and emotional factors. The patient with the "illness" of *nervios* is prevented from achieving life's goals and harmony. On the other hand, the issues involved in *nervios* as "sickness" center around the effects of family conflict, violence, politics, powerlessness, hopelessness, financial stress, and migration on the life of the individual.

Guarnaccia and Farias (1988) looked at gender differences in the experience of *nervios* among Salvadorans residing in the United States. For Salvadoran men, the major issues that precipitated *ataques de nervios* were estrangement from the family, marital friction, loneliness, isolation, and homesickness. The *ataques* of Salvadoran men were typified by dizziness, fainting spells, fear of falling, and a feeling that the floor was moving. Other symptoms included nightmares, violent fantasies, flashbacks, and feelings of being out of control. These men felt insecure and expressed a great sense of responsibility for supporting their families in their native land. Isolation and anger, according to Guarnaccia and Farias, were the two most common emotions displayed. The Salvadoran men explained all of their symptoms within the cultural construct of nervios.

In the same study, the authors found that Salvadoran women identified abuse and abandonment as the two most common precipitants of *nervios*, followed closely by a concern about loss of respect by their children. These women reported intense feelings of loss of family bonds and difficulty adapting to the new social environment in the United States. Their physical symptoms included headaches, chest tightness, difficulty breathing, a sense of choking, dizziness, fainting spells, and fear of falling (less frequently than reported by the men). Fear and crying spells were also common in this population. Like the Salvadoran men, these women understood their symptoms as aspects of *nervios*.

Guarnaccia and colleagues (1989), in "The Multiple Meanings of Ataques de Nervios in the Latino Community," described *ataques de nervios* as comprising a network of experiences charged with meaning and giving voice to internalized anger and intense feelings of sadness. In this view, *ataques de nervios* are ways to express powerful feelings and depict the personal impact of stressful life events. The events or crises that trigger an *ataque de nervios* usually lead to change in the unfolding of the individual's life.

As the literature suggests, clinicians should pay special attention to the events that trigger an *ataque de nervios*. The context of an *ataque* gives a picture of the psychosocial environment of the individual, the personal meanings of the symptoms, the individual's intimate relationships, and often the individual's religious dynamics. The clinician should try to understand the *ataque* sufferer's background, including sociocultural, psychosocial, familial, religious, and environmental factors, as well as the role that the individual plays in all of these.

ATAQUES DE NERVIOS AMONG PUERTO RICAN WOMEN IN BRIDGEPORT, CONNECTICUT

José Villa, M.D., (unpublished paper presented at the Greater Bridgeport Community Mental Health Center 1993) described a group of Hispanic women who presented with *ataques de nervios* at the Center. The patients were primarily Puerto Rican women over the age of 40 who were separated, widowed, or divorced. They often had adult children who resided a considerable distance from them. Throughout their lives these women had, for the most part, been emotionally stable. Some of them, however, had experienced chronic depression or had long histories of emotional suffering. As a group, they tended to have poor social and coping skills and were easily overwhelmed by relatively minor stressors. These individuals had a history of interpersonal difficulties, including unsatisfying intimate relationships with male partners who were often abusive or alcoholic. The women in Villa's sample did not meet full criteria for histrionic or borderline personality disorders.

Among these Puerto Rican women living in Bridgeport, a typical episode of *ataque* usually began after a stressful or unexpected situation that flooded the person with anxiety. Lacking the necessary coping skills to deal with a stressful situation, the individual developed "premature closure." By premature closure, Villa meant that these clients lacked adequate cognitive abilities to assess and cope with the stressor so that they experienced a sense of loss of control. Feeling out of control, the clients in this sample displayed a variety of psychomotor, anxiety, dissociative, and pseudopsychotic symptoms, including:

I. Psychomotor/Anxiety symptoms:
   1. Psychomotor agitation or catatonic-like posturing.
   2. Uncontrollable sobbing and crying.
   3. Hyperventilation, which may lead to dizziness and to tingling in the extremities.
   4. Discharge of pent-up anger.
II. Dissociative symptoms:
   1. Perplexity, confusion, disorientation.
   2. Inability to respond appropriately to questions.
   3. Asking or saying: Where am I? I want to die. I will kill myself.
   4. Flashbacks of betrayal.
III. Pseudopsychotic manifestations:
   1. Scanning the environment in a paranoid manner.
   2. An autistic preoccupation with the inner world.
   3. Reporting hallucinations, such as hearing voices or seeing things.
   4. Apparent delusional ideation.

Interestingly, the seizure-like phenomena that often characterize *ataques de nervios* in the Caribbean were not part of the clinical picture of these Puerto Rican women in Connecticut. Villa speculated that acculturation may have altered the form the *ataque* takes in this New England city. In addition, through acculturation, many Puerto Ricans in the United States seem to experience panic attacks rather than the full-blown *ataque* (e.g., with hyperkinesis and destructive behavior) that might have occurred on the island.

There was a variety of precipitants for the *ataques* in this sample. Common triggers of the attacks were family illnesses or deaths, funerals, legal problems, assaults, muggings, separations, abandonment, children leaving home, loss of social support, the vacation of a case manager, family discord, a conflict of loyalties, and engaging in a relationship disapproved of by the family. The secondary gains of *ataques* were often the reuniting of a family, a reconciliation, public atonement for guilty feelings, public demonstration of devotion to a deceased person, forgiveness from a family member, recognition from family members of the emotional pain of the patient, and the disclosure of a new but potentially unacceptable person in this patient's life. A major function of the *ataque de nervios* appeared to be the activation of the social support system of the individual.

In Villa's experience the following recommendations were helpful for clinicians dealing with a person undergoing an *ataque:*

1. As in any other crisis situation, do not overreact or make hasty decisions.
2. If possible, spend a significant amount of time with the patient and the family members. A thorough, well-conducted outpatient crisis intervention session can often avoid the need for hospitalization.
3. Acknowledge the feelings the individual is expressing. Sympathy is a key factor.
4. Do not say "I know how you feel," since the person knows things that you don't know.
5. Do not ask too many questions. Just be with the person. It sometimes helps to put your hand on the patient's shoulder or to touch his or her hand.
6. If there is more than one staff member in the room and the patient begins to respond, observe who the patient makes eye contact with, as this is the person who will best be able to do further assessment later on.
7. Have another staff member meet with the family to assess any family discord or any other family problems that may have precipitated the *ataque.*
8. As the patient begins to emerge from the confusional state, ask if he or she wants to talk to any particular family member. It is sometimes necessary to ask the rest of the family members to leave.

9. Offer something to drink, or possibly a minor tranquilizer, if the person appears controllably upset.
10. As the psychomotor agitation decreases or the patient begins to come out of the perplexed state, evaluate for suicidality, homicidality, and psychosis.
11. Do not rely solely on the information given by the patient. The family and significant others can usually offer valuable current and past historical information.

DIFFERENTIAL DIAGNOSIS

According to Guarnaccia and colleagues (1993), *ataques de nervios* cannot be subsumed within one specific *DSM* diagnostic category and should not be treated as a culturally based version of a particular psychiatric disorder. *Ataques de nervios* may resemble many of the *DSM-IV* psychiatric disorders, but *ataques* are transitory, related to specific psychosocial stressors, and are not viewed culturally as requiring long-term psychiatric treatment. Following the resolution of an *ataque de nervios,* usually within hours to a few days, the individual typically returns to premorbid levels of functioning.

At a discussion of *ataques* at the 1993 American Psychiatric Association meetings in San Francisco, Anthony LaBruzza pointed out that the severe *ataques de nervios* that he had treated in Bridgeport, Connecticut, often met *DSM-III-R* criteria for Brief Reactive Psychosis (298.80). Oquendo and colleagues (1992) had also reported that patients with *ataques de nervios* who present with psychotic symptoms may meet criteria for Brief Reactive Psychosis. "The sudden onset of perceptual and communication disturbances, abrupt change in behavior, or dissociative experiences should suggest the diagnosis of ataque de nervios when seen in a Hispanic person from the Caribbean islands" (p. 369).

In addition, Oquendo and colleagues (1992) point out that cases of *ataques de nervios* whose symptoms include disturbed consciousness, mutism, incoherence, or amnesia may mimic organic or substance use disorders *(DSM-III-R).* In such cases a toxicology screen and medical evaluation will help to establish the diagnosis. Oquendo also notes that episodes whose predominant symptoms are dissociative suggest a diagnosis of Dissociative Disorder. Furthermore, according to the authors (1992), *ataque de nervios* may occur recurrently in clients with Borderline Personality Disorder.

Factitious disorders (300.16, 300.19) pose a more difficult differential diagnostic problem. Unlike factitious disorders, *ataques* are not intentional or under the individual's conscious control. *Ataques* can also be expressions of an adjustment disorder. According to Oquendo and colleagues (1992): "the diagnosis of Adjustment Disorder may apply in the absence of dissociative experiences, communication disturbance, and psychotic symptoms."

Appendix I of *DSM-IV* (p. 845) notes that *ataques* may resemble panic attacks. In addition, *DSM-IV* suggests that clients with *ataques* may meet criteria for or be associated with various anxiety, mood, dissociative, and somatoform disorders. Marvin Karno and Robert Edgerton noted (1969) that 90 percent of Anglo psychiatric residents associated "hearing voices" with "being crazy," in contrast with only 16 percent of Mexican-American high school students who made a similar association.

Abad and Boyce (1979) emphasized the clinical importance of distinguishing between psychotic and nonpsychotic hallucinations in Puerto Rican clients in New Haven, Connecticut, stating that "While hallucinatory experiences are a common part of the symptomatology of the Puerto Rican psychotic, borderline, or neurotic patient, they also appear among normal individuals who have suffered some stress, such as the loss of a relative or friend" (p. 32).

According to Abad and Boyce, nonpsychotic hallucinations generally occur transitorily in response to an acute stress and may be either vague and ill-defined or centered around a religious theme or the appearance of a deceased relative. Ill-defined hallucinations include hearing one's name called, hearing footsteps or noises around the house, and seeing *celajes* or cloud-like, shadowy figures passing by. Such hallucinations are often "hysterical" phenomena that reflect the cultural beliefs in spiritism and supernatural forces. In contrast, Abad and Boyce point out that the psychotic hallucination "tends to be accusatory, threatening, and ego dystonic. Frequently, the patient has disruptive auditory experiences of voices calling him derogatory names or commanding him to hurt himself or other people. A patient often appears to struggle with such commands" (p. 33).

In summary, the psychiatric and anthropological literature suggests that *ataques de nervios* may be associated with:

Affective disorders, especially major depressive episodes and dysthymic disorder.

Anxiety disorders, including panic disorder, generalized anxiety disorder, agoraphobia, acute stress disorder, posttraumatic stress disorder, and specific and social phobias.

Dissociative disorders.

Somatoform disorders, especially somatization and conversion disorders.

Personality disorders.

Psychotic disorders, especially brief psychotic disorder .

CLINICAL ILLUSTRATIONS

This chapter concludes with two case examples that illustrate rather typical *ataques de nervios* in middle-aged Puerto Rican women.

María's *Ataque de Nervios*

María is a 46-year-old married Puerto Rican woman who lives on the island. She is a devout Roman Catholic and the mother of seven children. María has a second grade education, but her lack of formal education has not been an obstacle for her. She is hard-working and has always prided herself on being self-sufficient and, contrary to cultural norms, in control of the family finances. She has worked in a factory for several years and has been able to achieve most of her material goals in life, including a nice house and a family car.

It was a Monday and she woke up, as usual, at 5:30 in the morning. She went to check on her 20-year-old son, Raúl, to make sure that he had come home the previous night. Raúl had been getting in late during the previous few months because he was spending time with his new girlfriend. Soon after she noticed that her son had not come home, she began to tremble, sob hysterically, and experience hot and cold flashes. As a result, she took to her bed. When Raúl arrived fifteen minutes later, the rest of the family was gathered around her, lending support and trying to get her to calm down. The next door neighbor, who was her *comadre*, was also present. When Raúl entered his mother's room, his mother began to punch him, shouting and yelling uncontrollably. Soon afterward María fell on the bed and was trembling with her eyes closed. She appeared to have fainted. During this plateau period, the family telephoned relatives living abroad to make them aware of what had happened. An hour later María got up and began her daily routine. Later that day she telephoned her children in the United States and asked each of them to counsel her son Raúl not to make her suffer so much.

María has a long history of medical and psychiatric treatment and has been prescribed Valium, Ativan, and Prozac at various times. She has sought help from many different sources, including spiritists, for what medical doctors have diagnosed as psychosomatic complaints. Her major symptoms have been headaches, backaches, brain ache, *dejadez* (apathy), sadness, lightheadedness, fainting spells, difficulty falling asleep, and intermittent nighttime awakening. Thorough medical examinations have not shown evidence of major medical illnesses. During the last few years she has been seeing a psychiatrist who prescribed Xanax.

Just prior to this *ataque de nervios*, two of María's children had moved away from home. One had just departed for the United States and another had recently gotten married. She had also recently quit her job because she "needed a rest." María reported having had three other *ataques de nervios* similar to the one just described. One had occurred when her father died, another when her friend's son was killed in a car accident, and the third when she learned that the son to whom she felt closest was moving to France. When this son went to France, María experienced numbness and neck and back pains and had to be taken to a hospital emergency room because the family thought she was having a stroke or a heart attack. Now when María goes to wakes or when there are family conflicts, she takes a Xanax to avoid having another *ataque de nervios*. María's psychiatric records reveal that she has been diagnosed at various times with generalized anxiety disorder, somatoform disorder, dysthymia, and chronic depressive disorder.

Elsa's *Ataque de Nervios*

Elsa is a 45-year-old divorced Hispanic female with a second grade education. She comes from a poor socioeconomic background. Her mother died when she was 10 years old. She married Jaime when still quite young and had two children with him. Jaime began to abuse her from the very first day of the marriage. He literally held her hostage for a year and a half, frequently tying her to the bed, raping and sexually abusing her. While she was tied to the bed, he often beat the children in front of her. She divorced him eight years before her psychiatric evaluation. One year prior to her psychiatric evaluation, her ex-husband died of AIDS.

During her ex-husband's wake and funeral, she experienced two *ataques de nervios*. She described her *ataque* at the wake as follows:

> Everyone was gone home and I went closer to the casket. I started thinking on all the things Jaime did to me and on how he damaged my entire life. I wanted to tell him how much I hated him and that I'll never forgive him for what he did to me and my children. "Now you are dead," I told him, "but I am left behind with all this suffering. . . . " I remember telling him all of that, then I felt that he was coming out of the casket to get me. . . . I do not remember anything else but my family tells me that I started to scream and shout out loud uncontrollably, punching him, and beating him. They say I was breathing very fast and shaking a lot. I broke everything that was around me, they said, and wanted to take him out of the casket. I don't remember anything. When they tried to calm me down they said I became like crazy and I was very strong. They say that when I was having the ataque I was telling him a lot of bad things I wanted to tell him for a long time but I was afraid to tell him. I cursed him really bad.

Elsa also reported that, on the day of the Jaime's burial, she was told by fellow mourners that she had experienced a similar *ataque* for which she has no recollection. The last event she remembers is seeing "the casket being put in the ground."

GLOSSARY OF SPANISH TERMS RELATED TO THIS CHAPTER

Ahijado: Godchild.
Ataque: An attack; a tantrum.
Ataque de nervios: A sudden temporary change in behavior following a stressful event, especially among Latinos from the Caribbean.

Brujería: Witchcraft, hexing, casting spells.

Celajes: Shadowy, cloud-like figures; illusions seen passing by out of the corner of the eye.

Centro: A "center" where *espiritismo* is practiced.

Comadre: Godmother; female neighbor or friend; someone related through one's godparents; female co-parent.

Compadre: Godfather; buddy, friend; someone related through one's godparents; male co-parent.

Compadrazgo: Close friendship; kinship; relationship through one's godparents. This is an important supportive relationship.

Consejo: Advice, counsel.

Controlar los nervios: To control one's nerves.

Coraje: Rage, intense and poorly suppressed anger (sometimes expressed as nervousness or malaise; Abad and Boyce 1979, p.30).

Curanderismo: A spiritualistic system of folk healing.

Curandero: A practitioner of *curanderismo.*

Debilidad en el estómago: Queasiness, nausea, "weak stomach."

Dejadez: Apathy, neglect, slovenliness, laziness.

Derrame: Stroke; brain hemorrhage.

Desgaste cerebral: Brain exhaustion caused by too much of an activity, such as sex, reading, study, etc. (Similar to *brain fag, DSM-IV* p. 846).

Despojamientos: Expelling of bad or evil spirits.

Despojo: Removing an evil spirit who possesses an individual; dispossession.

Disgusto: Annoyance, trouble, vexation, chagrin, blow.

Dolor: Pain.

Dolor de (en el) cerebro: Brain ache; however, patients often point to the back of the neck when complaining of *dolor de cerebro.*

Dolor en el pecho: Chest pain.

Dormido: Asleep.

Embrujado: Bewitched; possessed by an evil spirit.

Embrujamiento: The casting of spells.

Espiritismo: A spiritual belief system about the levels of spiritual beings derived from medieval Spanish and European traditions.

Espiritista: A spiritist leader of *espiritismo.*

Estar en carne viva: Literally, "to be in living flesh," a phrase often used to describe a particularly raw emotional experience that feels like an open wound.

Estar saludable: To be well; to enjoy a state of well-being. Similar phrases include *ser feliz, sentirse como un cañón, estar como coco, estar sano,* and *estar o sentirse fuerte.*

Faltar el respeto: To lack respect, to disrespect (one of the worst "sins" Hispanic children can commit against their parents).

Fiesta santera: A religious gathering in *santería* that may involve possession of practitioners by the *orisha* saints. The ceremony may include the drinking of rum, the smoking of cigars, and the offering of fruits and the sacrifice of animals to the saints.

Gritar sin control: To shout uncontrollably.

Hombre de la casa: The man of the house.

Llorar: To cry.

Locura: Madness, craziness, insanity.

Machismo: Masculine pride; overvaluation of masculinity.

Machista: Full of machismo or male pride; very masculine; male chauvinistic.

Macho completo: Complete he-man.

Mal de pelea: The "disease of fighting," characterized by sudden outbursts of verbal and physical aggression, destructiveness *(romper cosas),* assaultiveness, and persecutory ideation.

Mal (de) ojo: The "evil eye."

Mal puesto: A hex or evil spell.

Mareos: Dizziness with occasional vertigo.

Nacer nervioso: To be born nervous.

Nervios: "Nerves." A state of vulnerability to nervous ailments that may be inborn or a response to stressful conditions.

Orisha (Oricha): A West African saint worshiped in *Santería.* Olodumare-Olofi is believed to be the creator of the universe. The identity of the *orisha* saints is based on a combination of beliefs in African gods and Roman Catholic saints and deities. For example, Jesus Christ is regarded as a manifestation of the orisha Obtalá and the Virgin Mary is considered to be a manifestation of the orisha Yemayá. Each *orisha* saint has special attributes connecting it to particular body parts, maladies, or natural phenomena (Alonso and Jeffrey 1988).

Padecer de los nervios: To suffer from "nerves."

Padrino: Godfather.

Pecho apretado: Tightness and pressure in the chest.

Perder el alma: To lose one's soul following a frightening event (see *susto*).

Perder el conocimiento: To lose consciousness.

Perder el juicio: To go crazy; literally, to lose one's capacity for judgment.

Perder la cabeza: To lose one's head or mind; to go crazy.

Persona nerviosa: Nervous person.

Personalismo: The ideal of forming warm, affectionate personal relationships.

Ponerse histérica: To get hysterical.

Ponerse nervioso: To get nervous.

Regado: Strewn about, scattered.

Resentido: Having a chip on one's shoulder, resentful.

Respeto: Respect, consideration, high regard.

Romper cosas: To break things.

Salud mental: Mental health—an Anglo notion that "does not exist as a concept" for Hispanics who make "no separation between the psychological and total well being of the individual" (Padilla and Ruiz 1973, p. 14).

Santería: A spiritual belief system that combines worship of West African deities (*orishas*) with Roman Catholicism and the cult of the Catholic saints.

Santerismo: An amalgamation of *santería* with local customs.

Santero: A leader of the *santería* spiritual practices.

Susto: Fright; soul loss due to a frightening event. Also known as *espanto, pasmo, pérdida del alma, tripa ida.*

Tener palancas: To have connections with people who can assist one in finding a job or getting things done; literally "to have crowbars."

Tranquilo: Calm, at peace.

Trincadismo: A spiritualist system based on the teachings of the Spanish engineer and philosopher Joaquín Trincado.

Tristeza: Sadness, sorrow, melancholy.

Volverse loco: To go crazy.

12

Disorders Usually First Diagnosed in Infancy, Childhood, or Adolescence

"My mother loved children—she would have given anything if I had been one."

Groucho Marx

"The Child is father of the Man."

William Wordsworth, "My Heart Leaps Up" (1807)

MENTAL RETARDATION (coded on Axis II):
317   Mild Mental Retardation
           (IQ from 50–55 to about 70)
318.0   Moderate Mental Retardation
           (IQ from 35–40 to 50–55)
318.1   Severe Mental Retardation
           (IQ from 20–25 to 35–40)
318.2   Profound Mental Retardation
           (IQ below 20–25)
319   Mental Retardation, Severity Unspecified

LEARNING DISORDERS (ACADEMIC SKILLS DISORDER):
315.00   Reading Disorder (Developmental Reading Disorder)
315.1   Mathematics Disorder (Developmental Arithmetic Disorder)
315.2   Disorder of Written Expression (Developmental Expressive Writing Disorder)

(For 315.0, 315.1, and 315.2, code any general medical condition or sensory deficit on Axis III.)

315.9   Learning Disorder Not Otherwise Specified

MOTOR SKILLS DISORDER:
315.4   Developmental Coordination Disorder

COMMUNICATION DISORDERS:
(Code any speech-motor or sensory deficit or neurological problem on Axis III.)

315.31   Expressive Language Disorder
          (Developmental Expressive Language Disorder)
315.31   Mixed Receptive-Expressive Language Disorder
          (Developmental Receptive Language Disorder)
315.39   Phonological Disorder
          (Developmental Articulation Disorder)
307.0   Stuttering
307.9   Communication Disorder Not Otherwise Specified

PERVASIVE DEVELOPMENTAL DISORDERS:
299.00   Autistic Disorder
299.80   Rett's Disorder
299.10   Childhood Disintegrative Disorder
299.80   Asperger's Disorder
299.80   Pervasive Developmental Disorder Not Otherwise
          Specified (including Atypical Autism)

DISRUPTIVE BEHAVIOR AND ATTENTION-DEFICIT DISORDERS:
Attention-Deficit/Hyperactivity Disorder (ADHD):
314.00   predominantly inattentive type
314.01   predominantly hyperactive-impulsive type
314.01   combined type
314.9   Attention-deficit/Hyperactivity Disorder Not Otherwise
          Specified (NOS)
312.8   Conduct Disorder
          Specify type of onset:
              Childhood onset type (before age 10)
              Adolescent onset type (age 10 or older)

Specify severity:
Mild
Moderate
Severe
313.81 Oppositional Defiant Disorder
312.9 Disruptive Behavior Disorder Not Otherwise Specified (NOS)

FEEDING AND EATING DISORDERS OF INFANCY AND EARLY CHILDHOOD:
307.52 Pica
307.53 Rumination Disorder
307.59 Feeding Disorder of Infancy or Early Childhood

TIC DISORDERS:
307.23 Tourette's Disorder
307.22 Chronic Motor or Vocal Tic Disorder
307.21 Transient Tic Disorder
Specify if: Single Episode or Recurrent
307.20 Tic Disorder Not Otherwise Specified (NOS)

ELIMINATION DISORDERS:
307.7 Encopresis without Constipation and Overflow Incontinence
787.6 Encopresis with Constipation and Overflow Incontinence
307.6 Enuresis (Not Due to a General Medical Condition)
Specify type:
Nocturnal Only
Diurnal Only
Nocturnal and Diurnal

OTHER DISORDERS OF INFANCY, CHILDHOOD, OR ADOLESCENCE:
309.21 Separation Anxiety Disorder
Specify if: early onset (before age 6)
313.23 Selective Mutism (Elective Mutism)
313.89 Reactive Attachment Disorder of Infancy or Early Childhood

Specify type:
   Inhibited type
   Disinhibited type
307.3   Stereotypic Movement Disorder
         (Stereotypy/Habit Disorder)
         Specify if: With Self-Injurious Behavior
313.9   Disorder of Infancy, Childhood, or Adolescence Not
         Otherwise Specified (NOS)

Children may suffer from most of the same mental disorders that affect the adult population. Affective, anxiety, and psychotic disorders are not uncommon in childhood and adolescence. Nowadays, unfortunately, the substance-related disorders are becoming commonplace among large segments of the teenage and preteen population, especially in the inner cities.

In this chapter of the manual, *DSM-IV* has grouped together a set of disorders that typically arise during infancy, childhood, and adolescence in contrast with adulthood. Many of these disorders reflect an aberration in the normal development of cognitive, language, social, or motor skills. *DSM-IV* has grouped the disorders usually first diagnosed in childhood in a single section as a matter of convenience. There is no implication that "childhood" disorders are clearly distinct from "adult" disorders, as the two frequently overlap.

Clinicians need special training to learn how to diagnose and treat many of the childhood disorders. Assessment of children requires specialized techniques like play therapy and direct observation. Consultation with families, teachers, and significant others is the norm. Psychological and educational testing as well as a comprehensive physical examination are usually part of a complete evaluation.

DSM-IV has made a change in the axial coding of the childhood disorders. According to the March 1994 *DSM-IV Update*: "Pervasive developmental disorders, learning disorders, motor skills disorders and communications disorders, which were coded on Axis II in *DSM-III-R*, are coded on Axis I in *DSM-IV*. For *DSM-IV*, only personality disorders and mental retardation are still coded on Axis II" (p. 2).

MENTAL RETARDATION (CODED ON AXIS II)

(*DSM-IV*, pp. 39–46)

Mental retardation (MR) has onset before age 18. The essential features of mental retardation are: (1) significantly below average intelligence (an IQ below about 70), and (2) significantly impaired adaptive functioning. *DSM-IV* requires that the mentally retarded individual demonstrate impairment in at least two skill areas, such as communication, living skills, interpersonal skills, academics, health/safety. General intellectual functioning is measured in terms of IQ. An IQ of 70 is two standard deviations below the population mean. The severity of intellectual impairment in mental retardation is coded as follows:

317   *Mild Mental Retardation*
        (IQ from 50–55 to about 70)
        The majority of cases of mental retardation (about 85 percent) fall in the Mild Mental Retardation category. Such individuals are "educable" in that they are able to develop social and communication skills, attend special classes, and function in the community. With support they can often live independently or in a supervised setting.

318.0   *Moderate Mental Retardation*
        (IQ from 35–40 to 50–55)
        About 10 percent of cases fall in the Moderate Mental Retardation category. In the past such individuals were called "trainable" because they could learn to communicate, perform self-care, and handle minor financial transactions. The term "trainable" has fallen out of favor because it falsely implies that individuals with moderate MR cannot benefit from educational programs. They generally adapt well to life in supervised settings in the community.

318.1   *Severe Mental Retardation*
        (IQ from 20–25 to 35–40)
        About 4 percent of cases fall in the Severe Mental Retardation category. They may be able to perform

simple tasks under supervision and are often able to live in group homes or with their families.

318.2　*Profound Mental Retardation*
(IQ below 20–25)
About 2 percent of cases fall in the Profound Mental Retardation category and may require institutional care. There is usually a concurrent neurological disorder that accounts for the profound mental retardation.

319　*Mental Retardation, Severity Unspecified*
Such individuals are presumed to be mentally retarded, but are not testable by standard intelligence tests.

The possible causes of mental retardation are legion. The most common etiology is Down's syndrome (trisomy 21). Several inborn errors of metabolism and genetic defects can also lead to mental retardation; examples include Tay-Sachs disease and phenylketonuria. The intellectual development of the child is also affected by prenatal maternal illness (e.g., rubella), substance abuse, and exposure to toxins. In addition, the developing brain of the fetus or newborn can be damaged by trauma, infection, exposure to toxins, malnutrition, and abuse or neglect.

Other childhood disorders frequently coexist with mental retardation. Thus, the retarded child may exhibit psychosis, mood disorder, attention deficit symptoms, autism, or learning disabilities. Seizure disorders are also common among the mentally retarded.

LEARNING DISORDERS (ACADEMIC SKILLS DISORDER)

(*DSM-IV*, pp. 46–53)

The learning or academic skills disorders, sometimes called learning disabilities, refer to specific areas of difficulty in learning one or more of the specific skills required for academic subjects, such as reading, writing, and arithmetic, at a level consonant with the individual's age, IQ, and educational level. The learning difficulty is evident on an individually administered standardized test and interferes with the child's academic achievement and/or with daily activities that require the use of that skill.

If a visual or hearing deficit exists, the learning difficulty is more severe than would normally be expected because of the sensory deficit. The clinician should code any coexisting medical/neurological condition or sensory deficit on Axis III. The typical individual with a learning disorder has average or above average intelligence, but is unable to master aspects of academic subjects at an age- and intelligence-appropriate level.

Learning disabilities tend to run in families and may represent an inherited neurodevelopmental defect affecting the area of the brain associated with a specific skill, such as perceptual organization, auditory sequencing, or memory storage or retrieval. When the learning disability goes unrecognized, the affected child may suffer lowered self-esteem, feel "stupid" and frustrated, and begin to act out or refuse to attend classes. Early educational intervention may prevent long-term problems with personality development.

Some difficulties with learning are due to emotional conflicts or specific phobias. A depressed child may present clinically with inadequate school performance. Some children develop phobias, like math phobia, for specific subject areas. Such learning problems are not rooted in neurodevelopmental deficits nor in specific difficulties with particular learning skills. Neuropsychological testing is usually necessary to isolate and define the nature of the specific learning difficulty.

DSM-IV specifies three learning disorders and also provides a Not Otherwise Specified category:

315.00   *Reading Disorder*
           (*DSM-IV*, pp. 48–50)
           (Developmental Reading Disorder)
           There is evidence of performance significantly below
           what would be expected for the person's age,
           educational level, or IQ on an individually administered
           standardized test of reading achievement. This lack of
           reading achievement interferes with the individual's
           academic performance or activities of daily living. In
           addition, the learning difficulty exceeds what would be
           expected from any associated sensory deficits that might
           coexist.

315.1   *Mathematics Disorder*
(*DSM-IV*, pp. 50–51)
(Developmental Arithmetic Disorder)
There is evidence of performance significantly below
what would be expected for the person's age,
educational level, or IQ, on an individually administered
standardized test of mathematical ability. This lack of
mathematical achievement interferes with the
individual's academic performance or activities of daily
living. In addition, the difficulty with learning
mathematics exceeds what would be expected from any
associated sensory deficits that might coexist.

315.2   *Disorder of Written Expression*
(*DSM-IV*, pp. 51–53)
(Developmental Expressive Writing Disorder)
There is evidence of performance significantly below
what would be expected for the person's age,
educational level, or IQ, on an individually administered
standardized test of written language achievement. This
lack of writing achievement interferes with the
individual's academic performance or activities of daily
living. In addition, the difficulty with writing skills
exceeds what would be expected from any associated
sensory deficits that might coexist.

315.9   *Learning Disorder Not Otherwise Specified*
(*DSM-IV*, p. 53)
This residual category allows the clinician to code
learning disorders that do not meet criteria for any of the
specific learning disorders above. For example, a child
may have a learning disability for spelling.

MOTOR SKILLS DISORDER

(*DSM-IV*, pp. 53–55):

315.4   *Developmental Coordination Disorder*
(*DSM-IV*, pp. 53–55)

Some children are especially clumsy and uncoordinated. They may be so clumsy that it interferes with their school performance or activities of daily life. They do not have cerebral palsy, muscular dystrophy, hemiplegia, or any general medical or neurological condition that would account for their clumsiness. Such clumsy children, whose motor coordination is significantly below what one would expect for their age and intelligence, suffer from developmental coordination disorder. They may be slow to reach developmental milestones for motor development. They may be poor at athletics, at gross and fine motor activities, and at handwriting or printing. As with the learning disabilities, these difficulties with motor coordination can lead to lowered self-esteem and have a negative effect on personality development.

COMMUNICATION DISORDERS

(*DSM-IV*, pp. 55–65):
Some children exhibit difficulties with the development of expressive or receptive language, with nonverbal intellectual abilities, and/or with the articulation of speech. *DSM-IV* classifies such problems under the rubric of Communication Disorders and provides four specific categories: Expressive Language Disorder, Mixed Receptive/ Expressive Language Disorder, Articulation Disorder, and Stuttering.

When diagnosing communication disorders, the clinician should also code any speech-motor or sensory deficit or neurological condition that exists on Axis III.

315.31   *Expressive Language Disorder*
(*DSM-IV* pages 55–58)
(Developmental Expressive Language Disorder)
Some children have adequate nonverbal intellectual abilities and adequate receptive language development, but have difficulty expressing themselves in language. They may be unable to retrieve words for objects or to organize words into coherent age-appropriate sentences.

For example, the child who wants ice cream might say, "Cold ice eat." Their expressive language problems show up on standardized tests of language functioning. When this problem with expressive language development causes significant impairment, an expressive language disorder is diagnosed. The child must not meet criteria for mixed receptive/expressive language disorder (below). In addition, the problems with language expression must be in excess of those connected with any coexisting associated disorder, such as mental retardation, motor or sensory deficits, inadequate schooling, environmental deprivation, or neurological disorder.

315.31   *Mixed Receptive-Expressive Language Disorder*
(*DSM-IV*, pp. 58–61)
(Developmental Receptive Language Disorder)
Some children have difficulty with both receptive and expressive language development. They have problems both with verbal expression and with understanding verbal communication at an age-appropriate level. For example, a child might become confused because of trouble understanding the sequential aspects of even simple directions or understanding spacial relationships expressed in language. These language difficulties are evident on standardized tests of language functioning and are not part of a pervasive developmental disorder. When these problems with language development cause significant impairment, a mixed receptive/expressive language disorder is diagnosed. In addition, the problems with language expression must be in excess of those connected with any coexisting associated disorder, such as mental retardation, motor or sensory deficits, inadequate schooling, environmental deprivation, or neurological disorder.

315.39   *Phonological Disorder*
(*DSM-IV*, pp. 61–63)
(Developmental Articulation Disorder)
Some children may have difficulty with the development of normal age-appropriate articulation of speech. For example, they may not be able to accurately produce the

sounds of their language or dialect, they may use one sound in place of another, or they may omit some sounds altogether. To meet criteria for the diagnosis, the problems with sound production must cause significant impairment in functioning. In addition, the articulation difficulties must be in excess of those expected from any coexisting associated disorder, such as mental retardation, other developmental disorders, motor or sensory deficits, or environmental deprivation.

307.0   *Stuttering*
(*DSM-IV*, pp. 63–65)
We are all familiar with people who stutter. If the stuttering significantly impairs functioning, a stuttering disorder is diagnosed. *DSM-IV* provides specific criteria for diagnosing the disruption of the normal fluency of speech. The degree of stuttering must be in excess of any associated motor or sensory deficit that might exist and contribute to the disturbed normal fluency of speech. When this problem with expressive language development causes significant impairment, an expressive language disorder is diagnosed. The child must not meet criteria for mixed receptive/expressive language disorder (below). In addition, the problems with language expression must be in excess of those connected with any coexisting associated disorder, such as mental retardation, motor or sensory deficits, inadequate schooling, environmental deprivation, or neurological disorder.

307.9   *Communication Disorder Not Otherwise Specified (NOS)*
(*DSM-IV*, p. 65)
This residual category allows the clinician to code disorders of communication that do not meet criteria for any of the above specific communication disorders.

PERVASIVE DEVELOPMENTAL DISORDERS

(*DSM-IV*, pp. 65–78)
The pervasive developmental disorders are childhood disorders characterized by significantly impaired development in several areas.

Typically these children display severe restrictions or difficulties with social interactions, communication, imagination, interests, activities, and symbolic play. They also may engage in rigid patterns of behavior that tend to be repetitive and stereotyped. In the past such atypical development was sometimes labeled childhood schizophrenia, childhood psychosis, or symbiotic psychosis. *DSM-IV* divides the pervasive developmental disorders into Autistic Disorder, Rett's Disorder, Childhood Disintegrative Disorder, and Asperger's Disorder. These last three disorders (Rett's, Childhood Disintegrative, and Asperger's Disorders) were added to maintain compatibility with *ICD-10*.

299.00   *Autistic Disorder*
          (*DSM-IV*, pp. 66–71)
          In the film *Rain Man*, actor Dustin Hoffman portrayed an
          autistic man named Raymond Babbitt who suffered from
          a restricted ability to interact socially, impaired
          communications skills, an abnormal use of language,
          stereotyped or ritualistic patterns of behavior, and
          restricted interests and activities. The developmental
          delays and abnormal behaviors of autism typically begin
          before age 3. Autistic children appear aloof, detached,
          mechanical, and withdrawn and seem unable to bond to
          their caregivers. Frequently they develop strong
          attachments to unusual inanimate objects like sticks or
          pieces of paper rather than teddy bears or dolls. They
          often engage in self-stimulation through body rocking or
          head banging. Their activities may be repetitive and
          highly routinized. *DSM-IV* gives a convenient checklist
          of signs and symptoms for making the diagnosis.
          Autism is most likely due to a brain abnormality. It runs
          in families and may have an autosomal recessive
          inheritance. The majority of autistic children (about 70
          percent) also meet criteria for mental retardation. About
          25 percent of autistic children also have a seizure
          disorder. In the differential diagnosis, autistic disorder
          must be differentiated from Rett's disorder, childhood
          disintegrative disorder, schizophrenia in childhood,
          severe sensory deficits, mental retardation,
          communication disorders, stereotypic movement

disorders, and schizoid or schizotypal personality disorders.

299.80   Rett's Disorder
(DSM-IV, pp. 71–73)
Rett's disorder is a pervasive developmental disorder in which children develop normally for the first 5 months of life. Then, sometime between 5 and 48 months of age, these children show signs of hampered development. Their heads stop developing normally, and measurements of head circumference show a deceleration of head growth. There are losses in previously acquired abilities to use their hands purposefully and to engage socially. Their movements become uncoordinated and they display psychomotor retardation. Their language skills (both receptive and expressive) are delayed or impaired.

299.10   Childhood Disintegrative Disorder
(DSM-IV, pp. 73–75)
Childhood disintegrative disorder is a pervasive developmental disorder in which children develop normally for the first two years of life. Then, sometime after age 2, they show a loss of previously acquired skills as well as impaired functioning in communication skills, social interactions, and/or the development of rigid stereotyped behaviors or interests. DSM-IV provides a specific checklist for making the diagnosis. Childhood disintegrative disorder must be differentiated from childhood schizophrenia (in which there are psychotic symptoms), from a profound language disorder, and from other specific pervasive developmental disorders.

299.80   Asperger's Disorder
(DSM-IV, pp. 75–77)
Asperger's disorder is a pervasive developmental disorder in which cognitive and language development are preserved while impairments occur in social interactions and in behavioral patterns and interests. Such children may be unable to make friends or engage in reciprocal social interactions. They have problems with nonverbal aspects of communication. Their

behavior and interests become rigid, repetitive, and stereotyped. By definition, Asperger's disorder does not meet criteria for any other specific pervasive developmental disorder.

299.80   *Pervasive Developmental Disorder Not Otherwise Specified (Including Atypical Autism) (DSM-IV, pp. 77–78)*

This is a residual category for severe pervasive developmental disorders of childhood that affect social interactions, communication skills, interests, activities, and behavior and that do not meet criteria for a specific pervasive developmental disorder. *DSM-IV* lists Atypical Autism (late onset, atypical symptoms, etc.) as an example of this category.

DISRUPTIVE BEHAVIOR AND ATTENTION-DEFICIT DISORDERS

(*DSM-IV*, pp. 78–85)

The disruptive behavior and attention-deficit disorders are the bread and butter of child psychiatry. Children with these disorders come to clinical attention because of their behavior, which is often difficult to manage and frustrating for parents and teachers. *DSM-IV* distinguishes three broad groups of such acting-out behavior disorders: Attention-Deficit/Hyperactivity Disorder, Conduct Disorder, and Oppositional Defiant Disorder.

ATTENTION-DEFICIT/HYPERACTIVITY DISORDER (ADHD)

(*DSM-IV*, pp. 78–85)

Attention-Deficit/Hyperactivity Disorder (ADHD) begins before age 7 and is characterized by (1) inattention, or (2) hyperactivity and impulsivity, or both. Inattentive children have trouble attending to tasks, organizing themselves, and following through. They are frequently unable to focus on specific tasks because of difficulty screening out extraneous stimuli. As a result, they are distractible and often forgetful. Hyperactive children have trouble sitting still, being motorically very active. Even though they are often able to pay attention, they may find it necessary to keep moving. Impulsive children can't wait. They may blurt out answers out of turn in class and find themselves unable to wait in lines or wait their turns.

To meet criteria for the diagnosis, the maladaptive symptoms must be present for at least six months in two or more situations. In addition, the symptoms must not be part of a pervasive developmental disorder, a psychotic disorder, an affective disorder, an anxiety disorder, a dissociative disorder, or a personality disorder or a result of the ingestion of substances. Many adults with substance abuse or antisocial personality disorder met criteria for ADHD as children.

DSM-IV specifies three types of ADHD (*DSM-IV*, p. 80):
314.00   Predominantly Inattentive Type
314.01   Predominantly Hyperactive-Impulsive Type
314.01   Combined Type
          Specify if: In Partial Remission (i.e., having some symptoms, but not meeting full criteria).
314.9   *Attention-deficit/Hyperactivity Disorder Not Otherwise Specified (NOS)*
          (*DSM-IV*, p. 85)
          This residual category allows the clinician to code disorders with symptoms of ADHD that do not meet full criteria for ADHD.
312.8   *CONDUCT DISORDER*
          (*DSM-IV*, pp. 85–91)
          Specify type of onset:
            Childhood Onset Type (before age 10)
            Adolescent Onset Type (age 10 or older)
          Specify severity:
            Mild
            Moderate
            Severe
          The essential feature of conduct disorder is a disturbance of conduct in which a child under age 18 regularly violates the rights of others or acts against the major

age-appropriate norms and rules of society for a period of at least six months. Such children repeatedly engage in antisocial behavior, such as lying, stealing, fighting, cruelty, fire setting, truancy, running away from home, and destruction of property. In the popular press, children with this disorder are referred to as "juvenile delinquents." After age 18 these individuals can often be re-diagnosed as having antisocial personality disorder (301.7).

DSM-IV provides a checklist of fifteen specific types of antisocial behavior to assist in making the diagnosis. Individuals must display at least three out of the fifteen behaviors to meet criteria for the disorder. The clinician can specify the type as mild, moderate, or severe, depending on the number and seriousness of the antisocial behaviors involved.

The typical individual with conduct disorder exhibits shallow interpersonal relationships, lack of empathy, and an impaired ability to feel guilt. Such children are often angry, resentful, and suffer from feelings of worthlessness. There is often a history of parental rejection, abuse, or abandonment as well as a family history of substance abuse, antisocial personality disorder, affective disorder, and academic skills disorders. Children with conduct disorder commonly meet criteria for other *DSM-IV* disorders, including learning disorders, mood disorders, and attention-deficit/hyperactivity disorder (ADHD). Generally, the earlier the age of onset of conduct disorder, the worse the prognosis and the more likely the association with aggression, male gender, and adult antisocial personality disorder.

313.81   *Oppositional Defiant Disorder*
(*DSM-IV*, pp. 91–94)
Oppositional defiant disorder is a new diagnosis that made its debut in *DSM-III-R* to allow clinicians to diagnose children who exhibited hostile, negativistic, or defiant behavior, but whose conduct did not regularly violate the rights of others or the norms and rules of

society. Such children are typically touchy, irritable, argumentative, annoying, oppositional, defiant, resentful, angry, vindictive, and prone to temper outbursts. *DSM-IV* provides a specific list of eight annoying behaviors to assist with diagnosis. To meet criteria, the child must exhibit four out of the eight difficult behaviors and not meet criteria for conduct disorder or, if over age 18, for antisocial personality disorder. The behavior must cause significant impairment in functioning. In addition, the disruptive behavior cannot be part of a mood or psychotic disorder. Oppositional defiant disorder may coexist with attention-deficit/hyperactivity disorder.

312.9 *Disruptive Behavior Disorder Not Otherwise Specified* (*DSM-IV*, p. 94)
This residual category allows the clinician to diagnose conduct or oppositional-defiant behaviors that do not meet criteria for a specific conduct disorder or oppositional defiant disorder.

FEEDING AND EATING DISORDERS OF INFANCY AND EARLY CHILDHOOD

(DSM-IV, pp. 94–100)
Some children engage in abnormal eating or feeding behaviors. *DSM-IV* provides three specific categories for feeding and eating disorders of infancy and early childhood.

307.52 *Pica*
(*DSM-IV*, pp. 95–96)
Children with pica persistently eat nonnutritive substances for at least a month. Commonly they eat paint chips, plaster, dirt, bits of cloth, hair, sand, leaves, pebbles, and even animal feces. Such unusual eating behavior is neither culturally sanctioned nor age appropriate. Parental neglect and mental retardation predispose to this disorder. Complications include lead

poisoning from paint, intestinal obstruction from hair or cloth balls, and toxoplasmosis from dirt or animal feces.

307.53   *Rumination Disorder*
(*DSM-IV*, pp. 96–98)
Children with rumination disorder repeatedly regurgitate their food, chew it again, and either spit it out or re-swallow it. This behavior persists for at least a month and is not due to a gastrointestinal disorder nor to a general medical condition, such as pyloric stenosis, esophageal reflux, or gastrointestinal illness. The affected children often strain and arch their backs while holding their heads back. The onset of this rare disorder is typically between 3 and 12 months of age. Weight loss or failure to gain weight and malnutrition are associated features.

307.59   *Feeding Disorder of Infancy or Early Childhood*
(*DSM-IV*, pp. 98–100)
Feeding disorder of infancy or early childhood begins before age 6 and consists of a persistent failure to eat adequately for at least a month with significant weight loss or failure to gain weight. The feeding disturbance is not due to another mental disorder nor to a general medical condition.

TIC DISORDERS

(*DSM-IV*, pp. 100–105):
Tics are brief, rapid, involuntary, stereotyped movements or vocalizations. They are repetitive but not rhythmic and may be simple (e.g., eye blinking) or complex (e.g., resembling normal behavior). Simple tics, like eye blinking, may be nervous habits or the result of emotional conflicts. Other tics may be part of a major disorder like Gilles de la Tourette syndrome. *DSM-IV* distinguishes three specific tic disorders: Tourette's Disorder, Chronic Motor or Vocal Tic Disorder, and Transient Tic Disorder.

307.23   *Tourette's Disorder*
(*DSM-IV*, pp. 101–103)

Tourette's disorder is a variably penetrant hereditary autosomal dominant motor and vocal tic disorder that begins in childhood (before age 18). It is more common in males with about a 3:1 male/female ratio. During the course of the illness, there are multiple motor tics and one or more vocal tics that occur intermittently or several times daily for more than a year. The disorder often begins with simple tics and progresses to more complex tics, including those of respiration and vocalization. Both motor and vocal tics occur at some time in the course of the disorder. The vocal tics may sound like grunting or barking, and in 50 percent of cases they progress to *coprolalia,* the involuntary speaking of scatological or obscene utterances. The tics are not due to substance use or to a general medical condition like Huntington's chorea or encephalitis. Tourette's disorder tends to co-transmit genetically with obsessive compulsive disorder (OCD), and OCD symptoms are a common associated feature of Tourette's. Many Tourette's patients also meet criteria for attention-deficit/hyperactivity disorder.

307.22   *Chronic Motor or Vocal Tic Disorder*
          (DSM-IV, pp. 103–104)
          Chronic motor or vocal tic disorder begins before age 18 and shares with Tourette's syndrome the presence of either motor or vocal tics. A major difference, however, is that either motor or vocal tics, but not both types, have occurred at some time during the disorder. The tics occur several times a day or intermittently for at least a year. The tics are not part of Tourette's disorder and are not the result of substance use or of a general medical condition.

307.21   *Transient Tic Disorder*
          (DSM-IV, pp. 104–105)
          Specify if: Single Episode or Recurrent
          In transient tic disorder there are single or multiple tics of the motor or vocal variety beginning before age 18. These tics occur several times daily or almost daily for at least four weeks, but for less than twelve consecutive months (hence, transient). The person does not meet criteria for Tourette's disorder or for chronic motor or

vocal tic disorder. In addition, the tics are not due to substance use or to a general medical condition. Transient tic disorder may present with a single episode or may be recurrent.

307.20   *Tic Disorder Not Otherwise Specified (NOS)*
(*DSM-IV*, pp. 105–106)
This residual category allows the clinician to code tic disorders that do not meet criteria for any of the specific tic disorders.

ELIMINATION DISORDERS

(DSM-IV, pp. 106–110)
Some children have difficulty controlling their bladders and their bowels. *DSM-IV* distinguishes two types of elimination disorders, according to whether the child exhibits an inappropriate passage of urine or of feces.

307.7   *Encopresis without Constipation and Overflow*
Incontinence
787.6   *Encopresis with Constipation and Overflow Incontinence*
In encopresis, the child has bowel movements in inappropriate places. Parents may complain, "My son soils himself" or "shits in his pants." Some children may pass feces onto the floor. Such behavior may or may not be voluntary. To meet criteria for the diagnosis, the child must be at least 4 years old, have one inappropriate fecal passage a month for at least three months, and not have a general medical condition that would account for the abnormal bowel behavior. The presence of constipation and overflow incontinence is indicated by different four-digit codes (307.7 and 787.6).
307.6   *Enuresis (Not Due to a General Medical Condition)*
Specify type:
Nocturnal Only
Diurnal Only
Nocturnal and Diurnal

Children with enuresis urinate in their beds or clothing at least twice weekly for at least three consecutive months or in such a way that they suffer significant distress or impairment. Parents may complain that the child "wets the bed" or "pisses in his pants." To meet criteria for the diagnosis, the child must be at least 5 years old and must not have a general medical condition that would account for the urinary problem.

OTHER DISORDERS OF INFANCY, CHILDHOOD, OR ADOLESCENCE

(*DSM-IV*, pp. 110–121)

309.21   *Separation Anxiety Disorder*
(*DSM-IV*, pp. 110–113)
Specify if: Early Onset (before age 6)
Separation anxiety disorder is the most common anxiety disorder seen in children. Part of normal development includes an experience of the fear of being separated from one's parents. In separation anxiety disorder this fear becomes excessive and causes significant distress or impairment. By definition, the disorder begins before age 18 and the anxiety symptoms have a duration of at least four weeks. The anxiety does not occur exclusively as part of a psychotic disorder or a pervasive developmental disorder. Typical features of separation anxiety include fear of being separated from one's parents, worry that harm will come to the parents, fear of being alone, refusal to attend school, fear of sleeping without a parent nearby, nightmares, and somatic complaints. *DSM-IV* provides a convenient checklist to assist in making the diagnosis.

313.23   *Selective Mutism (Elective Mutism)*
(*DSM-IV*, pp. 114–115)
Some children know how to speak, but refuse to do so in certain specific situations in which they are expected

to speak. This mutism may happen at school and interfere with their academic performance. To meet criteria for the disorder, the failure to speak must last for at least a month (other than the first month of school). The child typically speaks in some circumstances, but refuses to do so in others.

313.89   *Reactive Attachment Disorder of Infancy or Early Childhood* (*DSM-IV* pages 116–118)
Specify type:
    Inhibited Type
    Disinhibited Type
This disorder begins before age 5 and is the result of disturbances in caregiving early in the life of the child. Many of these children were neglected so that their basic physical and/or emotional needs were never adequately met. Often these children have suffered through frequent changes in foster care, in which they could not form stable attachments because of their all too rapidly changing caregivers. As a result, they do not learn how to relate normally to other people. Some become excessively inhibited and almost frozen in social interactions. Others become overly gregarious and socially disinhibited, exhibiting indiscriminate sociability. To qualify for the diagnosis, the disturbed social relatedness must not be due to mental retardation, a developmental delay, or a pervasive developmental disorder.

307.3   *Stereotypic Movement Disorder* (*DSM-IV*, pp. 118–121)
(Stereotypy/Habit Disorder)
Specify if: with Self-injurious Behavior
Stereotypies are repetitive movements or motor habits that seem driven and serve no useful function. Examples include head banging, rocking, picking at oneself, biting oneself, hitting oneself, and so on. Stereotypic movements must be distinguished from the compulsive ritualistic behaviors of obsessive compulsive disorder, from the tics of tic disorder, and from the hair pulling of trichotillomania. This disorder is diagnosed when the

motor behavior lasts for at least four weeks and causes clinically significant impairment or bodily self-injury. If the disorder causes or would cause self-harm requiring medical attention, the specifier "With Self-Injurious Behavior" is added to the diagnosis. This diagnosis can be made in the presence of mental retardation or a pervasive developmental disorder if the stereotypic motor behavior is severe enough to warrant its own treatment.

313.9   *Disorder of Infancy, Childhood, or Adolescence Not Otherwise Specified (NOS)*
(*DSM-IV*, pp. 121)
This is a residual category for disorders of infancy, childhood, or adolescence that do not meet criteria for any of the specific disorders covered in this section of *DSM-IV*.

13

Delirium, Dementia, Amnestic, and Other Cognitive Disorders

"You are old, Father William," the young man said,
"And your hair has become very white;
And yet you incessantly stand on your head—
Do you think at your age, it is right?"
"In my youth," Father William replied to his son,
"I feared I might injure the brain;
But now that I'm perfectly sure I have none,
Why I do it again and again."

Lewis Carroll (1884–1898), *Alice's Adventures in Wonderland*

"The term 'organic mental disorders' has been eliminated from *DSM-IV*, however, as it implies that other disorders in the manual do not have an 'organic' component."

DSM-IV Update, p. 6, APA, March 1994

DELIRIA

293.0   Delirium Due to a General Medical Condition
(If delirium is superimposed on a preexisting dementia, code as the type of dementia, "with Delirium.")

---.--   Substance-Intoxication Delirium
          (Refer to specific substance for code.)
---.--   Substance-Intoxication Delirium
          (Refer to specific substance for code.)
---.--   Delirium Due to Multiple Etiologies
          (Use multiple codes based on specific etiologies.)
780.09   Delirium Not Otherwise Specified (NOS)

DEMENTIAS

Dementia of the Alzheimer's Type (290.xx):
(Also code for Alzheimer's Disease 331.0 on Axis III.)
Dementia of the Alzheimer's Type, with Early Onset:
(onset at age 65 or below)
290.10   Uncomplicated
290.11   With Delirium
290.12   With Delusions
290.13   With Depressed Mood
          Specify if:
          With Behavioral Disturbance

Dementia of the Alzheimer's Type, with Late Onset:
(onset after age 65)
290.0   Uncomplicated
290.3   With Delirium
290.20   With Delusions
290.21   With Depressed Mood
          Specify if:
          With Behavioral Disturbance

Vascular Dementia (290.4x):
(formerly Multi-infarct Dementia)
(Code cerebrovascular condition on Axis III.)
290.40   Uncomplicated
290.41   With Delirium
290.42   With Delusions
290.43   With Depressed Mood
          Specify if:
          With Behavioral Disturbance

Dementia Due to Other General Medical Conditions:

294.9   Dementia Due to HIV Disease
           (Code HIV as 043.1 on Axis III.)
294.1   Dementia Due to Head Trauma
           (Code head injury as 854.00 on Axis III.)
294.1   Dementia Due to Parkinson's Disease
           (Code Parkinson's as 332.0 on Axis III.)
294.1   Dementia Due to Huntington's Disease
           (Code Huntington's as 333.4 on Axis III.)
290.10   Dementia Due to Pick's Disease
           (Code Pick's as 331.1 on Axis III.)
290.10   Dementia Due to Creutzfeldt-Jakob Disease
           (Code Creutzfeldt-Jakob as 046.1 on Axis III.)
294.1   Dementia Due to Other General Medical Condition
           (Name the medical condition on Axis I and also code it
           on Axis III.)
---.--   Substance-Induced Persisting Dementia
           (Refer to specific substance for codes.)
---.--   Dementia Due to Multiple Etiologies
           (Use multiple codes based on specific etiologies.)
294.8   Dementia Not Otherwise Specified (NOS)

Amnestic Disorders:

294.0   Amnestic Disorder Due to a General Medical Condition
           Specify if:
           Transient (a month or less)
           Chronic (longer than a month)
---.--   Substance-Induced Persisting Amnestic Disorder
           (Refer to specific substance for code.)
294.8   Amnestic Disorder Not Otherwise Specified (NOS)

294.9   Cognitive Disorder Not Otherwise Specified (NOS)

In *DSM-III-R* this chapter was entitled "Organic Mental Syndromes and Disorders." The authors of *DSM-IV* decided to drop the term *organic* from psychiatric diagnosis because it might imply that the other mental disorders are not organic. The former "organic mental syndromes" are now called Cognitive Disorders and include Delirium, Dementia, and Amnestic Syndrome. What *DSM-III-R* called the "Organic Mood, Anxiety, Delusional, and Personality Syndromes" have been returned to their phenomenological homes in the Mood, Anxiety, Delusional, and Personality Disorders sections of *DSM-IV*, respectively. In addition, in *DSM-IV* the new label "Vascular Dementia" has replaced the older term "Multi-infarct Dementia."

DELIRIUM

(*DSM-IV*, pp. 124–133)

The core problem in delirium is an impairment in consciousness that develops over a brief time period and tends to fluctuate during the course of the day. The typical delirious patient has a reduced level of awareness, cannot readily focus or sustain attention, has memory difficulties, is disoriented, and suffers disturbances in language and perception. These cognitive deficits and difficulties develop over a matter of hours or days and vary in severity at different times of the day. There is also historical, laboratory, or physical examination evidence of the existence of a general medical condition that underlies the delirium. The general medical condition should be coded on Axis III. The Mini-Mental State Examination by Folstein and colleagues is a useful method to document and follow the fluctuating levels of consciousness seen in delirium.

When the medical evidence confirms that substance intoxication or withdrawal underlies the delirium, the diagnosis of substance-intoxication or substance-withdrawal delirium is made.

When the medical evidence points to the existence of more than one medical condition or a medical condition plus a substance-related etiology, the diagnosis of delirium due to multiple etiologies is made. This is a new category in *DSM-IV*.

When a delirium is superimposed upon a preexisting dementia, the clinician should code the presence of the delirium as a subtype of the dementia.

The Delirium Not Otherwise Specified (780.09) category allows the clinician to code deliria whose medical or substance-induced etiology is suspected but not yet verified or to code deliria due to other causes, such as sleep or sensory deprivation.

DEMENTIAS

(*DSM-IV*, pp. 133–155)

Unlike delirium, dementia has a gradual, insidious onset and follows a course of progressive cognitive decline. The essential features of dementia are 1) memory impairment and 2) at least one of four specific disturbances of higher cortical function, including aphasia, apraxia, agnosia, and impaired executive functioning.

Memory impairment refers to the inability to learn new material and to retrieve previously learned information. Aphasia refers to the loss of a previously possessed ability to comprehend or produce language that is not due to sensory or motor defects. Apraxia is the loss of a previously possessed ability to perform skilled motor behaviors that is not due to muscle weakness or abnormal muscle tone or that occurs despite intact motor functioning. Agnosia is the inability to recognize or identity objects presented to the senses that is not due to defective sensory functioning. Executive functioning refers to the higher mental functions of judgment, planning, organizing, thinking ahead, sequencing, abstracting, and taking account of consequences.

The cognitive deficits in dementia represent a significant decline from a prior level of cognitive functioning. They do not occur exclusively as part of a delirium, and they cause a marked impairment in social and occupational functioning. The core cognitive disturbances of dementia may be accompanied by delirium, delusions, hallucinations, depressed mood, perceptual disturbances, behavioral disturbances, and/or communication disturbances. Because of its lack of specificity, personality change, which had been a diagnostic feature of dementia in *DSM-III-R*, has been moved to the "Associated Features" of the dementia section of *DSM-IV*.

DSM-IV sought to make its criteria more consistent with those of the National Institute of Neurologic and Communicative Disorders (NINCD) and with the Alzheimer's Disease Group. The old *DSM-III-R* term "Primary Degenerative Dementia" was replaced in *DSM-IV* by "Dementia of the Alzheimer's type," with early or late onset rather than presenile or senile. *DSM-IV* distinguishes five specific types of dementias, including:

1. *The Alzheimer's type* (290.−)
   (*DSM-IV*, pp. 139–143)
   In Alzheimer's dementia the memory impairment and cognitive deficits are not due to other central nervous system conditions that cause dementia (e.g., Huntington's disease), to systemic conditions that cause dementia (e.g., HIV brain infection), or to sub-

stance-induced conditions. The clinician should also code Alzheimer's Disease (331.0) on Axis III.

2. *Vascular Dementia* (290.4x)
   (*DSM-IV*, pp. 143–146)
   In vascular dementia there are etiologically related focal neurological signs and symptoms and/or medical laboratory evidence of cerebrovascular disease. The clinician should code the cerebrovascular condition on Axis III. Vascular dementia used to be called "Multi-Infarct Dementia" in *DSM-III-R*.

3. *Dementias Due to Other General Medical Conditions*
   (*DSM-IV*, pp. 146–152)
   In this type of dementia there is evidence of the existence of a medical illness that is judged to be etiologically related. For example, there may be historical, laboratory, or physical examination evidence that the dementia is related to HIV disease (294.9), Head Trauma (294.1), Parkinson's Disease (294.1), Huntington's Disease (294.1), Pick's Disease (290.10), Creutzfeldt-Jakob Disease (290.10), or to another General Medical Condition (294.1). The clinician should also code the general medical condition on Axis III.

4. *Substance-Induced Persisting Dementia*
   (*DSM-IV*, pp. 152–154)
   There is medical evidence that substance use or abuse, medications, or exposure to toxins are etiologically related to the dementia. The specific substance should be coded, for example, Alcohol (291.2), Inhalants (292.82), Sedative/Hypnotic/Anxiolytics (292.82), or Other/Unknown (292.82).

5. *Dementia Due to Multiple Etiologies*
   (*DSM-IV*, pp. 154–155)
   There is evidence that the dementia has more than one etiology. For example, it is not uncommon for individuals with chronic alcoholism to suffer multiple head traumas, both of which contribute to dementia.
   In addition, *DSM-IV* provides a Dementia Not Otherwise Specified category (*DSM-IV*, p. 155) for dementias in which there is not enough evidence to establish a definite etiology.

A Note on *AIDS Dementia Complex*

Of the above types of dementia, mental health professionals are becoming increasingly aware of dementia due to HIV disease. This form of dementia has also been called AIDS dementia complex (ADC) and results directly from infection of the central nervous system by HIV. Unfortunately, ADC often goes undiagnosed because it is not considered in differential diagnosis.

The diagnosis of ADC is based on the appearance of core symptoms and the exclusion of other neurological disorders that commonly affect AIDS patients. The principal symptoms of ADC involve cognition (especially attention and concentration), motor speed and accuracy (timed performance), and behavior. ADC usually occurs with diffuse rather than focal symptoms.

Early cognitive changes in ADC include forgetfulness and problems with the processing of complex information. Individuals may forget appointments, have trouble with arithmetic, make mistakes balancing their checkbooks, have difficulty concentrating, and not be able to recall material they have read. They may need to repeat cognitive tasks several times. In severe cases clients may become mute and have difficulty with speech and thought. Cognitive changes are often accompanied by apathy and a lack of zest. The Mental Alternation Test by Jones, Teng, and Folstein (see Chapter 10 of this text) is a useful screening device.

Early motor impairments include slowing and imprecision as seen, for example, in difficulty with rapid, purposeful movements. If ADC affects the spinal cord, there can be spastic-ataxic gait. The motor slowing and imprecision commonly affects the limbs and the eyes bilaterally. There may also be abnormal deep tendon reflexes, including the knee jerks and ankle jerks. Frontal release signs, like the snout reflex, are commonly present. The motor and reflex abnormalities of ADC (unlike those of many other neurological disorders) are bilaterally symmetrical and diffuse (affecting head and extremities). Focal and one-sided or unilateral neurological abnormalities (e.g., aphasia, hemiplegia, hemianopsia) argue against a diagnosis of ADC. Brain imaging in ADC reveals cerebral atrophy and a pattern of diffuse or patchy increased water signal in the white matter on the magnetic resonance imaging (MRI). The cerebrospinal fluid is usually tested to rule out other diagnoses, such as neurosyphilis and meningitis of cryptococcal or other origin.

The differential diagnosis of ADC includes, in the milder stages, toxic/metabolic encephalopathy as well as psychiatric disorders, such as the anxiety and depressive disorders. In the later stages, ADC resembles primary central nervous system lymphoma, toxoplasmosis, cryptococcal meningitis, and other viral infections, such as cytomegalovirus (CMV) and herpes simplex virus (HSV).

AMNESTIC DISORDERS

(*DSM-IV* pages 155–163):
It is possible to suffer from memory impairments without being demented. When the primary feature of a disorder is the inability to learn new information or to retrieve previously learned information, the diagnosis of amnestic disorder can be made. The memory difficulty must be severe enough to impair social or occupational functioning, and the individual must demonstrate a marked decline from a prior level of cognitive functioning. To meet criteria for amnestic disorder, the memory problems must not solely be part of a delirium or a dementia.

When there is medical evidence that the inability to learn or recall previously learned information is due to a general medical condition, the clinician can diagnose Amnestic Disorder due to a General Medical Condition (294.0). This disorder can be further classified as *transient* if the memory difficulty lasts for a month or less or as *chronic* if the memory problems persist for more than a month.

When there is medical evidence that the inability to learn or recall information is due to substance use or abuse, medications, or exposure to toxins, the diagnosis of substance-induced persisting amnestic disorder can be made. The clinician should code the specific substance involved—e.g., Alcohol (291.1), Sedative/Hypnotic/Anxiolytic (292.83), or Other/Unknown (292.83).

If there is not enough evidence to establish a specific etiology of the memory impairment, the clinician can use the diagnosis of Amnestic Disorder Not Otherwise Specified (294.8).

COGNITIVE DISORDER NOT OTHERWISE SPECIFIED (294.9)

(*DSM-IV*, p. 163)
This is a residual category for cognitive disorders that are apparently due to substance use or to a general medical condition, but that

are not Delirium NOS, Dementia NOS, or Amnestic Disorder NOS and do not meet criteria for any of the specific cognitive disorders above.

Appendix B of *DSM-IV* includes criteria for a *Mild Neurocognitive Disorder* (DSM-IV, pp. 706–708), whose essential feature is the development of mild neurocognitive dysfunction as a result of a general medical condition. The proposed neurocognitive changes can include impairments of memory, attention, executive functioning, perceptual-motor skills, and language.

Appendix B also includes criteria for a *Postconcussional Disorder* (*DSM-IV*, pp. 704–706), whose essential features are cognitive dysfunction (memory and concentration impairment) and neurobehavioral changes due to a cerebral concussion suffered during a closed head injury.

14

Mental Disorders Due to a General Medical Condition Not Elsewhere Classified

"Speak in French when you can't think of the English for a thing."
Lewis Carroll (1832–1898), *Through the Looking-Glass*

The authors of *DSM-IV* decided to include most of the eleven Mental Disorders Due to a General Medical Condition in those sections of the manual that describe the predominant clinical feature of the disorder. Only three of the eleven mental disorders due to general medical conditions are not classified elsewhere, namely:

293.89   Catatonic Disorder Due to a General Medical Condition
         (Indicate the medical condition.)
310.1   Personality Change Due to a General Medical Condition
         (Indicate the medical condition.)
         Specify type:
            Labile (affective lability)
            Disinhibited (poor impulse control)
            Aggressive
            Apathetic (apathy and indifference)
            Paranoid (suspiciousness and paranoia)
            Other type
            Combined type
            Unspecified type
293.9   Mental Disorder Not Otherwise Specified (NOS) Due to
         a General Medical Condition
         (Indicate the medical condition.)

The remaining eight of the eleven Mental Disorders due to a General Medical Condition are included phenomenologically in those sections of the manual with which they share symptomatology. These eight disorders, which are classified elsewhere in *DSM-IV*, are as follows. In the Delirium, Dementia, Amnestic, and Other Cognitive Disorders section:

293.0   Delirium Due to a General Medical Condition (*DSM-IV*, p. 127)

---.--   Dementia Due to a General Medical Condition (*DSM-IV* page 139)

294.0   Amnestic Disorder Due to a General Medical Condition (*DSM-IV*, p. 158)

In the Schizophrenia and Other Psychotic Disorders section:

293.8x   Psychotic Disorder Due to a General Medical Condition (*DSM-IV*, p. 306)

In the Mood Disorders section:

293.83   Mood Disorder Due to a General Medical Condition (*DSM-IV*, p. 366)

In the Anxiety Disorders section:

293.89   Anxiety Disorder Due to a General Medical Condition (*DSM-IV*, p. 436)

In the Sexual Disorder section:

---.--   Sexual Dysfunction Due to a General Medical Condition (*DSM-IV*, p. 515)

In the Sleep Disorders section:

780.5x   Sleep Disorder Due to a General Medical Condition (*DSM-IV*, p. 597)

THE THREE MENTAL DISORDERS DUE TO A GENERAL MEDICAL CONDITION NOT ELSEWHERE CLASSIFIED

(*DSM-IV*, pp. 165–174)

Catatonic Disorder Due to a General Medical Condition (293.89)

(*DSM-IV*, pp. 169–171)

The authors of *DSM-IV* added this category to the manual because it is a frequent explanation of catatonia and is thus important in differential diagnosis.

The syndrome of catatonia refers to a severe disturbance of psychomotor functioning that may include muscle rigidity, motor inflexibility, posturing, stupor, negativism, mutism, purposeless excitability, and other peculiarities of voluntary speech and movement (e.g., echolalia and echopraxia). Catatonic patients may appear immobile, rigid, mute, and unreactive and may resist any attempts to move them. They may hold their limbs in any position in which the examiner places them (waxy flexibility, cerea flexibilitas). At other times they may be wildly and purposelessly active and excited. They may repeatedly imitate the words (echolalia) or the movements (echopraxia) of others.

To meet criteria for catatonic disorder due to a general medical condition, the patient must display a catatonic syndrome that is judged to be causally related to an established medical/neurological condition. The catatonia must not be part of another mental disorder (e.g., affective or psychotic disorder) and must not occur solely as part of a delirium.

Catatonia is commonly seen in affective disorders and may also be seen in somatoform disorders and schizophrenia. Medical conditions that produce catatonia include carbon monoxide poisoning, encephalitis, and brain tumors. Catatonia may also be a feature of factitious disorders and malingering.

Personality Change Due to a General Medical Condition (310.1)

(*DSM-IV*, pp. 171–174)

More than two millennia ago, Hippocrates (cited in Andreasen and Black 1991) observed that from the brain "come joys, delights, laughter, and sports; and sorrows, griefs, despondency, and lamentations. . . . and by the same organ we become mad and delirious, and fears and terrors assail us, some by night and some by day. . . . all these things we endure from the brain when it is not healthy" (p. 101). Today we know that many medical and neurological conditions that affect the brain can lead to persistent personality disturbances, behavioral changes, or deviations from normal development. Some common causes include traumatic brain injury (head trauma), brain tumors, temporal lobe epilepsy, multiple sclerosis, and cerebrovascular disease.

In *DSM-IV* a Personality Change Due to a General Medical Condition (formerly Organic Personality Syndrome) refers to a clinically significant and persistent change in personality that is causally related to an established medical or neurological condition. Such a personality disturbance is not due to another mental disorder and does not occur solely as part of a delirium or a dementia. Children with this disorder may display abnormal development or disturbed behavior and must be symptomatic for at least a year to meet criteria for the diagnosis.

When a personality change occurs as a result of a general medical condition, the clinician should further specify its type. Specifically, *DSM-IV* adds the following list of types:

- Labile (affective lability)
- Disinhibited (poor impulse control)
- Aggressive (hostile, belligerent)
- Apathetic (apathy and indifference)
- Paranoid (suspicion and paranoia)
- Other type (e.g., associated with epilepsy)
- Combined type (more than one of the above)
- Unspecified type

Mental Disorder Not Otherwise Specified Due to a General Medical Condition (293.9)

(*DSM-IV*, p. 174)

This NOS category allows the clinician to code mental disorders that are due to an established medical/neurological condition, but do not meet criteria for any of the specific mental disorders due to a general medical condition. *DSM-IV* gives as examples postconcussion syndrome and dissociative symptoms that occur during complex partial seizures. The criteria for a *Postconcussional Disorder* (*DSM-IV* Appendix B, pp. 704–706) include cognitive dysfunction (memory and concentration impairment) and neurobehavioral changes (e.g., headache, fatigue, dizziness, affective symptoms, insomnia, personality changes) due to a cerebral concussion suffered during a closed head injury.

15

Substance-Related Disorders

"We were to do more business after dinner; but after dinner is after dinner—an old saying and a true, 'much drinking, little thinking.' "
Jonathan Swift (1667–1745), *Journal to Stella* (February 26, 1712)

"Fact: Philip Morris does not believe cigarette smoking is addictive. People can and do quit smoking all the time. According to the 1988 Surgeon General's Report, there are more than 40 million former smokers in the United States and 90% quit on their own, without any outside help."
Advertisement of the Philip Morris Company, in *USA Today* (April 15, 1994, p. 6A)

This section of *DSM-IV* considers problems related to the use of substances in the following categories:

Alcohol
Amphetamines or Related Substances
Caffeine
Cannabis
Cocaine
Hallucinogens
Inhalants
Nicotine
Opioids
Phencyclidine or Related Substances
Sedative, Hypnotic, or Anxiolytic Substances
Polysubstance Use
Other or Unknown Substance Use

Under each substance is a list of the various clinical syndromes that have been clinically associated with the use or abuse of that substance. Such disorders may include:

Dependence
  Specify if:
    With physiological dependence
    With psychological dependence
  Specify course:
    Remission:
      Early remission (the first year)
        Early full remission
        Early partial remission
      Sustained remission (after one year of early remission)
        Sustained full remission
        Sustained partial remission
Abuse
Intoxication
Withdrawal
Persisting Perceptions
Delirium
Dementia
Amnestic Disorder
Psychotic Disorder with Delusions
Psychotic Disorder with Hallucinations
Mood Disorder
Anxiety Disorder
Sexual Dysfunction
Sleep Disorder
Disorders Not Otherwise Specified

Note that in addition to the modifiers for the course of substance dependence in remission (early or sustained), *DSM-IV* suggests two other modifiers to describe the course of those clients who are in treatment programs. The clinician can specify if the patient with a substance-related disorder is "On Agonist Therapy" or is "In a Controlled Environment," like a restricted treatment setting where the availability of substances is strictly prohibited.

Below is an outline of the substance-related disorders described in *DSM-IV*.

ALCOHOL USE DISORDERS:
303.90   Alcohol Dependence
          (*DSM-IV*, p. 195)
305.00   Alcohol Abuse
          (*DSM-IV*, p. 196)

ALCOHOL-INDUCED DISORDERS:
303.00   Alcohol Intoxication
          (*DSM-IV*, p. 196)
291.8   Alcohol Withdrawal
          (*DSM-IV*, p. 197)
          Specify if: With perceptual disturbances
291.0   Alcohol Intoxication Delirium
          (*DSM-IV*, p. 129)
291.0   Alcohol Withdrawal Delirium
          (*DSM-IV*, p. 129)
291.2   Alcohol-Induced Persisting Dementia
          (*DSM-IV*, p. 152)
291.1   Alcohol-Induced Persisting Amnestic Disorder
          (*DSM-IV*, p. 161)
291.5   Alcohol-Induced Psychotic Disorder with Delusions
          (*DSM-IV*, p. 310)
          Specify if:
              With onset during intoxication
              With onset during withdrawal
291.3   Alcohol-Induced Psychotic Disorder with Hallucinations
          (*DSM-IV*, p. 310)
          Specify if:
              With onset during intoxication
              With onset during withdrawal
291.8   Alcohol-Induced Mood Disorder
          (*DSM-IV*, p. 370)
          Specify if:
              With onset during intoxication
              With onset during withdrawal
291.8   Alcohol-Induced Anxiety Disorder
          (*DSM-IV*, p. 439)

Specify if:
With onset during intoxication
With onset during withdrawal

291.8   Alcohol-Induced Sexual Dysfunction
          (*DSM-IV*, p. 519)
          Specify if: With onset during intoxication

291.8   Alcohol-Induced Sleep Disorder (*DSM-IV*, p. 601)
          Specify if:
          With onset during intoxication
          With onset during withdrawal

291.9   Alcohol Use Disorder Not Otherwise Specified (NOS)
          (*DSM-IV*, p. 204)

AMPHETAMINE USE DISORDERS:

304.40   Amphetamine Dependence
          (*DSM-IV*, p. 206)

305.70   Amphetamine Abuse
          (*DSM-IV*, p. 206)

AMPHETAMINE-INDUCED DISORDERS:

292.89   Amphetamine Intoxication
          (*DSM-IV*, p. 207)
          Specify if: With perceptual disturbances

292.0   Amphetamine Withdrawal
          (*DSM-IV*, p. 208)

292.81   Amphetamine Intoxication Delirium
          (*DSM-IV*, p. 129)

292.11   Amphetamine-Induced Psychotic Disorder with Delusions
          (*DSM-IV*, p. 310)
          Specify if: With onset during intoxication

292.12   Amphetamine-Induced Psychotic Disorder with
          Hallucinations
          (*DSM-IV*, p. 310)
          Specify if: With onset during intoxication

292.84   Amphetamine-Induced Mood Disorder
          (*DSM-IV*, p. 370)
          Specify if:
          With onset during intoxication
          With onset during withdrawal

292.89   Amphetamine-Induced Anxiety Disorder
          (*DSM-IV*, p. 439)
          Specify if: With onset during intoxication
292.89   Amphetamine-Induced Sexual Dysfunction
          (*DSM-IV*, p. 519)
          Specify if: With onset during intoxication
292.89   Amphetamine-Induced Sleep Disorder
          (*DSM-IV*, p. 601)
          Specify if:
              With onset during intoxication
              With onset during withdrawal
292.9   Amphetamine-Related Disorder Not Otherwise Specified
          (NOS) (*DSM-IV*, p. 211)

CAFFEINE-INDUCED DISORDERS:
305.90   Caffeine Intoxication
          (*DSM-IV*, p. 212)
292.89   Caffeine-Induced Anxiety Disorder
          (*DSM-IV*, p. 439)
          Specify if: With onset during intoxication
292.89   Caffeine-Induced Sleep Disorder
          (*DSM-IV*, p. 601)
          Specify if: With onset during intoxication
292.9   Caffeine-Related Disorder Not Otherwise Specified
          (NOS) (*DSM-IV*, p. 215)
          Appendix B Caffeine Withdrawal
          (*DSM-IV*, pp. 708–709)

CANNABIS USE DISORDERS:
304.30   Cannabis Dependence
          (*DSM-IV*, p. 216)
305.20   Cannabis Abuse
          (*DSM-IV*, p. 217)

CANNABIS-INDUCED DISORDERS:
292.89   Cannabis Intoxication
          (*DSM-IV*, p. 217)
          Specify if: With perceptual disturbances

292.81   Cannabis Intoxication Delirium
          (*DSM-IV*, p. 129)
292.11   Cannabis-Induced Psychotic Disorder with Delusions
          (*DSM-IV*, p. 310)
          Specify if: With onset during intoxication
292.12   Cannabis-Induced Psychotic Disorder with Hallucinations
          (*DSM-IV*, p. 310)
          Specify if: With onset during intoxication
292.89   Cannabis-Induced Anxiety Disorder
          (*DSM-IV*, p. 439)
          Specify if: With onset during intoxication
292.9   Cannabis-Related Disorder Not Otherwise Specified
          (NOS) (*DSM-IV*, p. 221)

COCAINE USE DISORDERS:
304.20   Cocaine Dependence
          (*DSM-IV*, p. 222)
305.60   Cocaine Abuse
          (*DSM-IV*, p. 222)

COCAINE-INDUCED DISORDERS:
289.89   Cocaine Intoxication
          (*DSM-IV*, p. 223)
          Specify if: With perceptual disturbances
292.0   Cocaine Withdrawal
          (*DSM-IV*, p. 225)
292.81   Cocaine Intoxication Delirium
          (*DSM-IV*, p. 129)
292.11   Cocaine-Induced Psychotic Disorder with Delusions
          (*DSM-IV*, p. 310)
          Specify if: With onset during intoxication
292.12   Cocaine-Induced Psychotic Disorder with Hallucinations
          (*DSM-IV*, p. 310)
          Specify if: With onset during intoxication
292.84   Cocaine-Induced Mood Disorder
          (*DSM-IV*, p. 370)
          Specify if:
             With onset during intoxication
             With onset during withdrawal

292.89   Cocaine-Induced Anxiety Disorder
          (*DSM-IV*, p. 439)
          Specify if:
          With onset during intoxication
          With onset during withdrawal
292.89   Cocaine-Induced Sexual Dysfunction
          (*DSM-IV*, p. 519)
          Specify if:
          With onset during intoxication
292.89   Cocaine-Induced Sleep Disorder
          (*DSM-IV*, p. 601)
          Specify if:
          With onset during intoxication
          With onset during withdrawal
292.9   Cocaine-Related Disorder Not Otherwise Specified
          (NOS) (*DSM-IV*, p. 229)

HALLUCINOGEN USE DISORDERS:
304.50   Hallucinogen Dependence
          (*DSM-IV*, p. 230)
305.30   Hallucinogen Abuse
          (*DSM-IV*, p. 231)

HALLUCINOGEN-INDUCED DISORDERS:
292.89   Hallucinogen Intoxication
          (*DSM-IV*, p. 232)
292.89   Hallucinogen Persisting Perception Disorder (Flashbacks)
          (*DSM-IV*, p. 233)
292.81   Hallucinogen Intoxication Delirium
          (*DSM-IV*, p. 129)
292.11   Hallucinogen-Induced Psychotic Disorder with Delusions
          (*DSM-IV*, p. 310)
          Specify if: With onset during intoxication
292.12   Hallucinogen-Induced Psychotic Disorder with
          Hallucinations
          (*DSM-IV*, p. 310)
          Specify if: With onset during intoxication
292.84   Hallucinogen-Induced Mood Disorder

(*DSM-IV*, p. 370)
Specify if: With onset during intoxication
292.89   Hallucinogen-Induced Anxiety Disorder
(*DSM-IV*, p. 439)
Specify if: With onset during intoxication
292.9   Hallucinogen-Related Disorder Not Otherwise Specified
(NOS) (*DSM-IV*, p. 236)

INHALANT USE DISORDERS:
304.60   Inhalant Dependence
(*DSM-IV*, p. 238)
305.90   Inhalant Abuse
(*DSM-IV*, p. 238)

INHALANT-INDUCED DISORDERS:
292.89   Inhalant Intoxication
(*DSM-IV*, p. 239)
292.81   Inhalant Intoxication Delirium
(*DSM-IV*, p. 129)
292.82   Inhalant-Induced Persisting Dementia
(*DSM-IV*, p. 152)
292.11   Inhalant-Induced Psychotic Disorder with Delusions
(*DSM-IV*, p. 310)
Specify if: With onset during intoxication
292.12   Inhalant-Induced Psychotic Disorder with Hallucinations
(*DSM-IV*, p. 310)
Specify if: With onset during intoxication
292.84   Inhalant-Induced Mood Disorder
(*DSM-IV*, p. 370)
Specify if: With onset during intoxication
292.89   Inhalant-Induced Anxiety Disorder
(*DSM-IV*, p. 439)
Specify if: With onset during intoxication
292.9   Inhalant Use Disorder Not Otherwise Specified (NOS)
(*DSM-IV*, p. 242)

NICOTINE USE DISORDERS:
305.10   Nicotine Dependence
(*DSM-IV*, p. 243)

NICOTINE-INDUCED DISORDERS:
292.0   Nicotine Withdrawal
          (*DSM-IV*, p. 244)
292.9   Nicotine-Related Disorder Not Otherwise Specified
          (NOS) (*DSM-IV*, p. 247)

OPIOID USE DISORDERS:
304.00   Opioid Dependence
          (*DSM-IV*, p. 248)
305.50   Opioid Abuse
          (*DSM-IV*, p. 249)

OPIOID-RELATED DISORDERS:
292.89   Opioid Intoxication
          (*DSM-IV*, p. 249)
          Specify if: With perceptual disturbances
292.0   Opioid Withdrawal
          (*DSM-IV*, p. 250)
292.81   Opioid Intoxication Delirium
          (*DSM-IV*, p. 129)
292.11   Opioid-Induced Psychotic Disorder with Delusions
          (*DSM-IV*, p. 310)
          Specify if: With onset during intoxication
292.12   Opioid Psychotic Disorder with Hallucinations
          (*DSM-IV*, p. 310)
          Specify if: With onset during intoxication
292.84   Opioid-Induced Mood Disorder
          (*DSM-IV*, p. 370)
          Specify if: With onset during intoxication
292.89   Opioid-Induced Sexual Dysfunction
          (*DSM-IV*, p. 519)
          Specify if: With onset during intoxication
292.89   Opioid-Induced Sleep Disorder
          (*DSM-IV*, p. 601)
          Specify if:
            With onset during intoxication
            With onset during withdrawal
292.9   Opioid-Related Disorder Not Otherwise Specified (NOS)
          (*DSM-IV*, p. 255)

PHENCYCLIDINE USE DISORDERS:
304.90   Phencyclidine Dependence
           (*DSM-IV*, p. 256)
305.90   Phencyclidine Abuse
           (*DSM-IV*, p. 257)

PHENCYCLIDINE-INDUCED DISORDERS:
292.89   Phencyclidine Intoxication
           (*DSM-IV*, p. 257)
           Specify if: With perceptual disturbances
292.81   Phencyclidine Intoxication Delirium
           (*DSM-IV*, p. 129)
292.11   Phencyclidine-Induced Psychotic Disorder with
           Delusions
           (*DSM-IV*, p. 310)
           Specify if: With onset during intoxication
292.12   Phencyclidine-Induced Psychotic Disorder with
           Hallucinations
           (*DSM-IV*, p. 310)
           Specify if: With onset during intoxication
292.84   Phencyclidine-Induced Mood Disorder
           (*DSM-IV*, p. 370)
           Specify if: With onset during intoxication
292.89   Phencyclidine-Induced Anxiety Disorder
           (*DSM-IV*, p. 439)
           Specify if: With onset during intoxication
292.9   Phencyclidine-Related Disorder Not Otherwise Specified
           (NOS) (*DSM-IV*, p. 261)

SEDATIVE, HYPNOTIC, OR ANXIOLYTIC USE DISORDERS:
304.10   Sedative, Hypnotic, or Anxiolytic Dependence
           (*DSM-IV*, p. 262)
305.40   Sedative, Hypnotic, or Anxiolytic Abuse
           (*DSM-IV*, p. 263)

SEDATIVE-, HYPNOTIC-, OR ANXIOLYTIC-INDUCED DISORDERS:
292.89   Sedative, Hypnotic, or Anxiolytic Intoxication
           (*DSM-IV*, p. 263)

292.0   Sedative, Hypnotic, or Anxiolytic Withdrawal
          (*DSM-IV*, p. 264)
          Specify if: With perceptual disturbances

292.81   Sedative, Hypnotic, or Anxiolytic Intoxication Delirium
          (*DSM-IV*, p. 129)

292.81   Sedative, Hypnotic, or Anxiolytic Withdrawal Delirium
          (*DSM-IV*, p. 129)

292.82   Sedative-, Hypnotic-, or Anxiolytic-Induced Persisting
          Dementia
          (*DSM-IV*, p. 152)

292.83   Sedative-, Hypnotic-, or Anxiolytic-Induced Persisting
          Amnestic Disorder
          (*DSM-IV*, p. 161)

292.11   Sedative-, Hypnotic-, or Anxiolytic-Induced Psychotic
          Disorder with Delusions
          (*DSM-IV*, p. 310)
          Specify if:
            With onset during intoxication
            With onset during withdrawal

292.12   Sedative-, Hypnotic-, or Anxiolytic-Induced Psychotic
          Disorder with Hallucinations
          (*DSM-IV*, p. 310)
          Specify if:
            With onset during intoxication
            With onset during withdrawal

292.84   Sedative-, Hypnotic-, or Anxiolytic-Induced Mood
          Disorder
          (*DSM-IV*, p. 370)
          Specify if:
            With onset during intoxication
            With onset during withdrawal

292.89   Sedative-, Hypnotic-, or Anxiolytic-Induced Anxiety
          Disorder
          (*DSM-IV*, p. 439)
          Specify if: With onset during withdrawal

292.89   Sedative-, Hypnotic-, or Anxiolytic-Induced Sexual
          Dysfunction
          (*DSM-IV*, p. 519)
          Specify if: With onset during intoxication

292.89   Sedative-, Hypnotic-, or Anxiolytic-Induced Sleep
           Disorder
           (*DSM-IV*, p. 601)
           Specify if:
             With onset during intoxication
             With onset during withdrawal
292.9   Sedative-, Hypnotic-, or Anxiolytic-Related Disorder Not
           Otherwise Specified (NOS)
           (*DSM-IV*, p. 269)

POLYSUBSTANCE-RELATED DISORDER:
304.80   Polysubstance Dependence
           (*DSM-IV*, p. 270)

OTHER (OR UNKNOWN) SUBSTANCE USE DISORDERS:
304.90   Other (or Unknown) Substance Dependence
           (*DSM-IV*, p. 176)
305.90   Other (or Unknown) Substance Abuse
           (*DSM-IV*, p. 182)

**OTHER (OR UNKNOWN) SUBSTANCE-INDUCED
DISORDERS:**
292.89   Other (or Unknown) Substance Intoxication
           (*DSM-IV*, p. 183)
           Specify if: With perceptual disturbances
292.0   Other (or Unknown) Substance Withdrawal
           (*DSM-IV*, p. 184)
           Specify if: With perceptual disturbances
292.81   Other (or Unknown) Substance Delirium
           (*DSM-IV*, p. 129)
292.82   Other (or Unknown) Substance-Induced Persisting
           Dementia
           (*DSM-IV*, p. 152)
292.83   Other (or Unknown) Substance-Induced Persisting
           Amnestic Disorder
           (*DSM-IV*, p. 161)
292.11   Other (or Unknown) Substance-Induced Psychotic
           Disorder with Delusions
           (*DSM-IV*, p. 310)

Specify if:
With onset during intoxication
With onset during withdrawal

292.12 Other (or Unknown) Substance-Induced Psychotic
Disorder with Hallucinations
(*DSM-IV*, p. 310)
Specify if:
With onset during intoxication
With onset during withdrawal

292.84 Other (or Unknown) Substance-Induced Mood Disorder
(*DSM-IV*, p. 370)
Specify if:
With onset during intoxication
With onset during withdrawal

292.89 Other (or Unknown) Substance-Induced Anxiety
Disorder
(*DSM-IV*, p. 439)
Specify if:
With onset during intoxication
With onset during withdrawal

292.89 Other (or Unknown) Substance-Induced Sexual
Dysfunction
(*DSM-IV*, p. 519)
Specify if: With onset during intoxication

292.89 Other (or Unknown) Substance-Induced Sleep Disorder
(*DSM-IV*, p. 601)
Specify if:
With onset during intoxication
With onset during withdrawal

292.9 Other (or Unknown) Substance-Related Disorder Not
Otherwise Specified (NOS)
(*DSM-IV*, p. 272)
This "Other or Unknown" category includes substances
not listed above as well as unlabeled medications.
Examples include over-the-counter medications,
prescription medications, anabolic steroids, nitrous oxide
or "laughing gas," nitrite inhalants or "poppers,"
anti-Parkinson agents (like Cogentin), antihistamines,
and natural intoxicants (like catnip, betel nut, and kava).

The use of mind-altering drugs is part of the human condition. Psychoactive substances are compounds that alter one's mental state, and the most common reason people use drugs is to make themselves feel better than they did before they took the drug. In recent times, substance abuse has become a major social problem that is affecting the quality of life in the United States as well as the economic status of the nation.

The substance use disorders are among the most common psychiatric disorders in the general population. Ronald C. Kessler and his colleagues (1994) reported that in the United States the prevalence of any substance abuse/dependence in a national sample was about 27 percent over the course of a lifetime and approximately 11 percent in any one year period.

Alcohol dependence accounts for the bulk of the substance-related disorders. In any given year, about 11 percent of men and 4 percent of women in the United States suffer from alcohol dependence. In the course of a lifetime, approximately 20 percent of men and 8 percent of women meet criteria for alcohol dependence.

Substance-related disorders can mimic most of the major mental disorders and have become one of the primary reasons why people with disordered behavior, emotions, or cognition present to hospital emergency rooms. To ensure that clinicians will consider substance-related disorders as part of every differential diagnosis, *DSM-IV* has included them in each section dealing with a specific class of clinical psychiatric disorders. For similar reasons, *DSM-IV* has included Mental Disorders Due to a General Medical Condition in each clinical chapter of the diagnostic manual. Clinicians should rule out possible substance-related and medical etiologies as a routine part of every psychiatric evaluation.

Certain key concepts run across all the substance-related disorders. Such concepts include substance dependence, substance abuse, physiological dependence (tolerance and withdrawal), intoxication, persistence, and remission.

Physiological tolerance (*DSM-IV*, pp. 176–177) refers to the need for ever greater amounts of a substance in order to either become intoxicated or achieve a desired effect. Physiological tolerance also encompasses the diminishing effect of a substance with the continued consumption of the same dose of the substance.

Physiological withdrawal (*DSM-IV*, p. 177) refers to a clinical syndrome, peculiar to a particular class of substances, of physical and mental symptoms that occur in response to withdrawing (removing or reducing the dosage of) an addictive substance from an individual who has become habituated to the substance. Some typical (though not universal) withdrawal symptoms include craving for the substance, vomiting, insomnia, nervousness, tremulousness, agitation, sweating, alterations in pulse and blood pressure, and so on.

Physiological dependence (*DSM-IV*, p. 179) on a substance refers to the presence of both physiological tolerance and withdrawal.

Intoxication is a reversible clinical syndrome, peculiar to a particular class of substances, of maladaptive physical and/or mental symptoms that occur in response to consumption of a substance. Some typical (though not universal) symptoms of intoxication include an altered level of consciousness, impaired judgment, impaired motor performance, and changes in pulse and respiration.

Persistence refers to the lasting nature of a substance-induced disturbance after the acute effects of substance intoxication or withdrawal have worn off.

Substance dependence (*DSM-IV*, pp. 176–181) is a maladaptive pattern of substance use that causes clinically significant distress or impairment and that may or may not involve physiological dependence. To diagnose substance dependence, *DSM-IV* requires the presence of at least three out of seven items characteristic of substance dependence at some time during the same twelve-month period. The seven *DSM-IV* substance dependence criteria (there were nine in *DSM-III-R*) include items such as physiological tolerance, withdrawal, increasing consumption, persistent desire or else inability to reduce substance use, drug-seeking behavior, giving up normal activities because of substance use, and refusal to stop using the substance despite obvious adverse physical or psychological consequences. The *DSM-III-R* duration requirement for substance dependence was dropped from *DSM-IV* because, as stated above, at least three *DSM-IV* dependence criteria must be met in the same twelve-month period. With the exception of caffeine, substance dependence can occur with all the substances covered in the *DSM-IV* chapter on substance-related disorders.

DSM-IV has added the subtype "With Physiological Dependence" to indicate the diagnosis of Substance Dependence with evidence of either tolerance or withdrawal. If there is no evidence of tolerance or withdrawal, the specifier "Without Physiological Dependence" is used.

In addition, *DSM-IV* has expanded the course modifiers for Substance Dependence to allow clinicians to differentiate between early and sustained remission and between partial and full remission. Clinicians can also identify by subtype whether the client has been receiving agonist therapy or has been staying in a controlled environment like a substance treatment program. These course modifiers apply only to dependence.

DSM-IV defines clients as *in remission* (*DSM-IV*, pp. 179–180) if they have not met any of the criteria that define substance dependence or abuse for a period of at least one month. According to *DSM-IV*, the remission categories require a transitional month during which the client does not meet criteria for substance abuse or dependence.

Early remission (*DSM-IV*, pp. 179–180) refers to the first twelve months of remission. During the first year of remission, individuals with substance abuse or dependence are at high risk for relapse. An individual who meets none of the criteria for substance dependence or abuse for the previous one to twelve months is said to be in *early full remission*. Some clients will be able to achieve only a partial remission during the first year. Specifically, during early remission, an individual who has not met full criteria for substance dependence for the previous one to twelve months and who has met at least one criterion for substance dependence or abuse is said to be in *early partial remission*.

An individual who remains in remission after the twelve months of early remission is said to be in *sustained remission* (*DSM-IV*, pp. 179–180). As with early remission, there can be *sustained full remission* (continues to meet no criteria for dependence or abuse) and *sustained partial remission* (meets at least one criterion, but not full criteria for dependence or abuse).

For clients who are in substance treatment programs, *DSM-IV* also allows the clinician to specify whether the person with a substance-related disorder is "On Agonist Therapy" or is "In a Controlled Environment," such as a restricted treatment setting where the availability of substances is strictly prohibited.

DSM-III-R had modified the narrower *DSM-III* concept of "substance dependence" to emphasize the individual's inability to control substance use while de-emphasizing physiological dependence (tolerance and withdrawal). Critics argued that the broader *DSM-III-R* definition of substance dependence was overly inclusive and muddied the concept of substance abuse. The *DSM-IV* field trials confirmed that substance dependence does, in fact, take place in the absence of physiological dependence (tolerance and withdrawal). The field trials also revealed that subtyping substance dependence according to the presence of tolerance and withdrawal is clinically useful. Furthermore, empirical evidence suggested that substance abuse can be distinguished from substance dependence by its adverse social consequences.

Substance abuse (*DSM-IV*, pp. 182–183) is a maladaptive pattern of substance use, occurring in the absence of substance dependence, which leads to adverse consequences causing significant distress or impairment. To diagnose substance abuse, *DSM-IV* requires the presence of one out of four characteristic features of substance abuse. The *DSM-IV* criteria for abuse include recurrent behaviors involving not performing one's role obligations, exposing self or others to physical risk because of substance use, substance-related legal difficulties, and substance-related problems with relationships. By definition, the diagnosis of substance abuse requires that the individual has never met criteria for substance dependence for the particular class of substance.

The *DSM-IV* definitions of Substance Abuse and Substance Dependence establish a hierarchical relationship between the two disorders. The definition of Substance Abuse stresses only the adverse consequence of repeated substance use. The definition of Substance Dependence implies the preexistence of abuse of a specific substance accompanied by tolerance, withdrawal, and/or compulsive use of the substance.

In other words, individuals who have ever met criteria for dependence on a specific substance should not also be diagnosed with abuse of that substance. The diagnosis of substance dependence implies preexisting abuse and therefore preempts the diagnosis of substance abuse. To paraphrase a line from the movie *Love Story*, abuse means never having to say you were dependent. Because dependence contains abuse as part of its definition, the clinician must consider the criteria of both substance abuse and dependence to determine the type of remission from dependence.

DSM-IV defines *substance intoxication* (*DSM-IV*, pp. 183–184) as "the development of a reversible substance-specific syndrome due to recent ingestion of (or exposure to) a substance." Each substance or class of substances produces a particular intoxication syndrome. *DSM-IV* provides extensive lists of the various signs and symptoms of the specific substance intoxication syndromes. Intoxication, by definition, involves substance-induced alterations of the central nervous system, leading to adverse behavioral or psychological consequences. The diagnosis requires that the signs and symptoms attributed to substance-related intoxication not be due to a general medical condition or to another mental disorder.

Substance withdrawal (*DSM-IV*, pp. 184–185) is "the development of a substance-specific syndrome due to the cessation of, or reduction in, the intake of a substance that the person previously used regularly." The definition also requires that the withdrawal syndrome cause significant distress or impairment and not be due to a general medical condition or to another mental disorder. For each substance or class of substances, *DSM-IV* provides lists of the various signs and symptoms of the specific substance withdrawal syndromes.

DSM-IV provides the specifier "With Perceptual Disturbances" for many of the intoxication and withdrawal syndromes. Perceptual disturbances include sensory illusions (e.g., auditory, visual, or tactile illusions), altered perceptions, and hallucinations in which reality testing is preserved.

Polysubstance dependence (304.80) (*DSM-IV*, p. 270) refers to the use of at least three categories of substances for a period of at least six months, so that the individual meets criteria for substance dependence for the group of substances, but not for any one substance individually.

We refer the reader to the appropriate sections of *DSM-IV* for further details of each of the specific substance-related disorders. *Appendix B* of *DSM-IV* contains proposed criteria for "Caffeine Withdrawal" whose essential feature is a headache that may be accompanied by fatigue, anxiety or depressive feelings, nausea, or vomiting, following a marked reduction in chronic caffeine intake (*DSM-IV*, pp. 708–709).

This chapter concludes with a vivid autobiographical account of substance abuse and dependence contributed by writer C. Adam Richmond, who chronicled his own experience with drug addiction in the book *Twisted* (1992). We highly recommend Richmond's book to anyone who wishes to understand the inner world of the addicted individual.

PERSONAL ACCOUNT OF SUBSTANCE DEPENDENCE BY C. ADAM RICHMOND

I was nineteen when I began using heroin. I was in college then, living on my own, in my own apartment. I was holding down a 3.73 grade point average at the university and looking at options for graduate school. I had a part-time job at a nearby psychiatric institute as a mental health worker. All the while I was whacking cocaine and heroin on a daily basis, drinking, and taking a variety of pills. You see, I had always been fascinated by drugs, by the idea that I could change what I felt, alter it, *control* it somehow.

When I was in nursery school, I used to spin around until I was dizzy, and then hold my breath while another child wrapped his arms around me and squeezed my chest. I used to love the way that made me feel. As a boy I remember the family doctor making house calls when I was sick. I thought he was God. He had syrups that could make me feel better, shots that could make me well. He would come into my bedroom and lay his huge black bag on the bed and I would look at it, dreaming of the mysteries contained, knowing that it was full of wonder and power and magic. My mother, too, had a magic box. She was a diabetic, and here contained little plastic vials of blood pressure and heart medications, anticonvulsants, sedatives, tranquilizers, and narcotics. Sometimes, I took things from my mother's magic box. Just to see what they would do to me.

At a very young age I was introduced to antibiotics, antidiarrheals, antiemetics, mild sedatives, narcotics, and alcohol, mostly from mother and the family doctor, and sometimes, too, I received medication from my grandfather (who just so happened to be a pharmacist). I learned that if I didn't like the way I felt—I could change it—and that if I didn't want to feel it—I didn't have to. This theory even worked for events in my life like being molested by three older boys when I was nine. I didn't have to think about it, you see. I could make it disappear. There was magic in the world. And it came in doctors' bags, little plastic vials, syringes, and the glassine envelopes I could buy from the older kids who hung out on the corner.

Winding up a junkie, for me at least, was inevitable. The reason junkies do junk in the first place is to manipulate their feelings.

By my early teens, I was smoking marijuana and drinking daily. By twenty, I was hooked on heroin and cocaine.

No one plans on getting strung-out, you see. It's not like that. You go for years, messing around with the stuff, dabbling here and there, and nothing. Life is fine and you're having a good time. You convince yourself that you're invincible. *What? Me? A drug addict?* It's the kind of thing you think will never happen to you.

But addiction is insidious and clever. It's deceptive. Suddenly, you wake up one day and discover that you've stepped over the line. You've got a problem. A big one. Only now it's too late to go back. When it hits, it comes down on you like a freight train. It hurts. And it scares the shit out of you. So you try any number of things to try and disguise it. Hide it. To make it go away and just leave you alone. Forever, maybe. You try anything to tell yourself you're not *that* bad.

When the consequences of my illicit activities became too much and it looked like I really might be a *real* drug addict, I had an array of physical ailments which I could conjure up and use to manipulate the medical profession into legitimizing my drug use: I had a bad back, a cervical condition, a blown knee, impacted wisdom teeth, migraine headaches, a deviated septum, painful sinuses, and I suffered with chronic stress. Or so I told them. The medical community provided me with painkillers and sedatives—Percodan, mostly, sometimes codeine, Talwin, Demerol, Xanax, and Valium—for my discomforts. I had only to dress in a suit and perform a lot of moaning and grimacing, and I could get my drugs legally now. It's a lot like being an actor, I suppose: I could con an emergency room physician in a New York minute and get a controlled substance. It wasn't the doctor's fault; I was just good at it, that's all. And when they didn't offer the drugs to me, I simply called in or wrote the orders for the narcotics, myself. It was easy. I only had to steal their prescription pads or abscond with a viable DEA number.

But I was already on the merry-go-round. There was no getting off now. It had begun. And it was spinning wildly. Sick one day, not sick the next. I wanted badly to get off. And couldn't. It hurt too much. And then it didn't hurt enough. I hated riding the fucking merry-go-round.

All the time you're on it, you lie to the ones you love. You steal from them. You look into their eyes—you know that *they know* the truth about you—but you tell them how wrong they are for even thinking it about you. You cry. You fight. You wake up every morning with demons in your head, sobbing with remorse over what you had to do yesterday and then screaming in horror over what you know you're going to have to do today. The demons try to drive you mad. And they will. Unless you can quiet them. Unless you can shut them up with another shot and get a few moments peace from the madness.

I tried to quit. I saw shrinks, I went to programs. Ask me how many times I detoxed on Methadone, how many clinics I was in, how many times I swore off it for good . . . only to go back to it the next day. Or the next week. Or the next month. I lost family, friends, a wife, cars, money. I got in trouble with the law. I tried to control it by switching from heroin to cocaine and tranquilizers, to booze, back to oral narcotics, then to booze and pills again, then to just narcotics alone, then back to booze, coke, dope—but all that did about as much good as changing seats on the Titanic.

Inevitably, what began at age nine and continued through my twenties as a way to transcend the pain I felt life had to offer became by the time I was thirty a living, breathing horror movie. Life went from a little cocaine and a little heroin while riding home from the college library on my motorcycle—to robbing Seven-11s so that I could support a three-hundred-dollar-a-day drug habit in the South Bronx. It happens. I suppose it's the progressive nature of the beast. I lost all control. Suicide became a daily option. Perhaps if I had been stronger, I might have accomplished it.

I wish I could say that it was a magic pill I took somewhere along the line, or some magic words someone said that finally sobered me up, but I can't. About all I remember about the whole thing was being locked in jail cell one minute and facing nine years in a federal penitentiary, and the next minute I was in a hospital being taken care of by some pretty fine doctors and nurses. I think I remember seeing angels while I was in the jail cell too. It was pretty weird.

In the final analysis, I tell myself that it was an act of grace that sobered me up. That, and going to meetings finally. I guess I had just been beaten up so bad, for so long, that I was ready to let go. I was really sick and tired of being sick and tired.

Oh, there was treatment. A *lot* of treatment. It got to the point where it became almost a semiannual event: *Oh, you mean him? Oh. He's in treatment again. You know. For his drug addiction.* Maybe, too, it was a combination. Of compassionate people and a little willingness on my part, some time, and a good measure of God's grace. Then, too, there were those funny angels.

Because I'll tell you one thing: When I look back on it all, on the sheer amounts, and overdoses, and close calls, and potentially lethal combinations of the drugs I took, and the dangerous places my addiction took me to and the horrible things it made me do . . . it's a wonder I'm even alive right now to write about it. For the longest time I was traveling on a one-way track, hell-bent straight for the morgue. And it's just a miracle that I ever managed to get off.

C. Adam Richmond
May 18, 1994

16

Schizophrenia and Other Psychotic Disorders

"Your noble son is mad.
Mad I call it; for to define true madness,
What is't but to be nothing else but mad?"

Shakespeare, *Hamlet*, Act II, Scene ii

SCHIZOPHRENIA AND THE OTHER PSYCHOTIC DISORDERS:

295.30   Schizophrenia, Paranoid Type
295.10   Schizophrenia, Disorganized Type
295.20   Schizophrenia, Catatonic Type
295.90   Schizophrenia, Undifferentiated Type
295.60   Schizophrenia, Residual Type
295.40   Schizophreniform Disorder
          Specify if:
            Without good prognostic features
            With good prognostic features (brief prodromal period, confusion, good premorbid adaptation, absence of flat affect)
295.70   Schizoaffective Disorder
          Specify type:
            Bipolar type
            Depressive type
297.1   Delusional Disorder
          Specify type:
            Erotomanic (de Clerambault's syndrome)
            Grandiose

	Jealous
	Persecutory
	Somatic
	Mixed
	Unspecified
298.8	Brief Psychotic Disorder
	Specify if:
	With marked stressor(s) (brief reactive)
	Without marked stressor(s)
	With postpartum onset
297.3	Shared Psychotic Disorder (*Folie à Deux*)
293.81	Psychotic Disorder Due to a General Medical Condition with Delusions
293.82	Psychotic Disorder Due to a General Medical Condition with Hallucinations
---.--	Substance-Induced Psychotic Disorder (refer to specific substances for codes)
	Specify if:
	With onset during intoxication
	With onset during withdrawal
298.9	Psychotic Disorder Not Otherwise Specified (NOS)

SCHIZOPHRENIA (295. –)

(*DSM-IV*, pp. 274–290)

Subtypes:

295.30	Schizophrenia, Paranoid Type (*DSM-IV*, p. 287)
295.10	Schizophrenia, Disorganized Type (*DSM-IV*, pp. 287–288)
295.20	Schizophrenia, Catatonic Type (*DSM-IV*, pp. 288–289)
295.90	Schizophrenia, Undifferentiated Type (*DSM-IV*, p. 289)
295.60	Schizophrenia, Residual Type (*DSM-IV*, pp. 289–290)

The term *schizophrenia* derives from the Greek *schizein*, to cut or cleave, and *phren*, meaning mind. The schizophrenic individual suffers from a shattered or fragmented mind. The schizophrenic process causes a fragmentation of many facets of the personality and affects most aspects of human functioning.

Schizophrenia is one of the major health concerns in the world today. This psychotic disorder or group of disorders affects approximately 1 percent of the population. Its current economic burden in the United States totals more than $70 billion dollars annually in direct and indirect costs, not including the human suffering of the affected individuals, their friends, and their families.

Throughout history there are descriptions of severely deranged or psychotic individuals whom we would diagnose today as schizophrenic. In 1852 Benedict Morel reported cases of *demence precoce*— that is, progressive intellectual deterioration beginning in adolescence. In 1896 Emil Kraepelin used a similar term, *dementia praecox*, to label individuals who developed chronic progressive functional impairment in early adulthood, often accompanied by intellectual deterioration, hallucinations, and delusions. Kraepelin distinguished dementia praecox (schizophrenia) from "manic-depressive psychosis" and from "paranoia" (delusional disorder). Manic-depressive psychosis could have had onset throughout the life cycle, could have had periods of relatively normal functioning during remissions, and have had a more episodic course than dementia praecox. Paranoia was characterized by persistent persecutory delusions without the functional impairment or florid psychotic symptoms of dementia praecox. In Kraepelin's view, dementia praecox had an early onset and a chronic deteriorating course.

In 1911 Eugen Bleuler coined the term *schizophrenia* to emphasize the splitting of psychic processes that he believed to be at the core of this group of disorders. Bleuler de-emphasized the florid psychotic symptoms of dementia praecox and instead focused on four primary features that came to be called Bleuler's four A's: loose associations, autistic thinking, ambivalence, and affective blunting. Bleuler felt that his four A's were present throughout the disorder, whereas the florid hallucinations and delusions were secondary and occurred only during periods of relapse. Bleuler's definition broadened the concept of schizophrenia and allowed clinicians to diagnose many individuals as schizophrenic who did not follow the chronic deteriorating course of dementia praecox.

In 1933 J. Kasanin used the term *schizoaffective* to describe patients with both significant psychotic and affective symptoms. Kasanin's concept of schizoaffective illness became a source of controversy. (See the section on Schizoaffective Disorder below.)

In 1959 Kurt Schneider, reacting against the overly broad Bleuler-ian concept of schizophrenia, suggested a narrower definition based on a set of specific hallucinations and delusions, the so-called Schneiderian "first-rank" symptoms. He sought to define a set of symptoms that reflected the core schizophrenic experience of a loss of a sense of autonomy over the self and a blurring of the boundaries between the self and the not-self. According to Schneider's concep-tion, schizophrenic individuals suffer a fundamental loss of a sense of who and what they are and of where they end and outside reality begins. Anyone who has become engrossed in the movie *Invasion of the Body Snatchers* will have a sense of what Schneider regarded as the core schizophrenic experience.

Schneider believed that the following experiences were pathogno-monic for schizophrenia: thought broadcasting, thought insertion or withdrawal, bizarre delusions, hearing one's thoughts spoken aloud, hearing a voice or voices conversing about one's behavior or thoughts in the third person, hearing two or more voices having a running commentary with each other, having somatic hallucinations in which the individual believes that bodily sensations are produced by outside forces, and the delusion of being controlled by outside agents. Schneider also described a set of "second-rank" symptoms which could indicate the diagnosis of schizophrenia in the absence of first-rank symptoms. Second-rank symptoms include such items as perplexity, emotional blunting, other types of hallucinations, and affective symptoms.

While the earlier research focused on the more flagrant "positive" psychotic symptoms of schizophrenia, more recent investigators have pointed out the "negative" symptoms of the disorder. Timothy J. Crow (1985) distinguished between a positive (Type I) syndrome of hallucinations, delusions, and conceptual disorganization, and a negative (Type II) syndrome of flat affect, withdrawal, and dimin-ished volition.

The notion of positive and negative symptoms derives from the work of British neurologist Hughlings Jackson. Positive symptoms represent distortions or exaggerations of normal functioning. Negative symptoms reflect a diminution of normal functions. The negative symptoms of schizophrenia account for much of the social and occupational impairment seen in this group of disorders.

In 1987 Stanley R. Kay and colleagues suggested viewing schizophrenia along four dimensions: a positive syndrome, a negative syndrome, a depressive syndrome (feelings of guilt and depression), and an excitement/impulsivity syndrome (excitement, tension, poor impulse control). Kay's Positive and Negative Symptom Scales (PANSS) have become useful research measures.

The Positive Symptom Subscale of the PANSS consists of:

- Delusions
- Conceptual disorganization
- Hallucinations
- Excitement
- Grandiosity
- Suspiciousness/persecution
- Hostility

The Negative Symptom Subscale of the PANSS includes:

- Blunted or flat affect
- Emotional withdrawal
- Poor rapport
- Passive/apathetic social withdrawal
- Difficulty with abstract thinking
- Lack of spontaneity and flow of conversation
- Stereotyped thinking

According to a report by Nancy Andreasen (1987) in the *Schizophrenia Bulletin*, the most common positive symptoms of schizophrenia include auditory hallucinations, hearing voices commenting or conversing, visual hallucinations, persecutory delusions, delusions of reference, delusions of being controlled, delusions of mind reading, tangential thinking, and loose associations (derailment).

In the same study of 111 patients with schizophrenia, Andreasen found the most frequent negative symptoms to be an unchanging facial expression, a paucity of peer relationships, few recreational interests or activities, lack of persistence at school or at a job, poor grooming and hygiene, lack of expressiveness, low energy (anergia), and difficulty forming close or intimate relationships.

This brief historical overview suggests that schizophrenia is a heterogeneous, phenomenologically diverse, and difficult-to-define disorder. Many clinicians and researchers believe that schizophrenia represents a group of disorders with various etiologies and a variety of clinical presentations. In its definition of schizophrenia, the *DSM-IV* has sought to acknowledge Kraepelin's emphasis on chronicity and deterioration, Schneider's notion of characteristic hallucinations and delusions, Bleuler's idea of fundamental symptoms, and the more recent recognition of the importance of negative symptoms as part of the active disease process. *DSM-IV* has added two negative symptoms ("alogia" and "avolition") to its criteria set and has included new course modifiers that the authors of *DSM-IV* have adapted from *ICD-10*.

In defining schizophrenia, *DSM-IV* requires the presence of at least two out of five "active phase symptoms" that *DSM-IV* identifies as characteristic of schizophrenia. The five *DSM-IV* pathognomonic symptoms are:

1. delusions,
2. hallucinations,
3. disorganized speech,
4. grossly disorganized or catatonic behavior, and
5. negative symptoms. (*DSM-IV*, p. 285)

As examples of negative symptoms, *DSM-IV* gives flat affect, alogia (poverty of speech or poverty of content of speech), and avolition (lack of drive or energy, apathy). These symptoms must be present for a significant part of the time for at least a month. (*DSM-IV* has increased the duration requirement for active phase symptoms from *DSM-III-R's* one week to one month to reduce false positive diagnoses and to enhance compatibility with *ICD-10*.)

The *DSM-IV* definition of schizophrenia emphasizes the importance of negative symptoms as part of the active phase of the disorder. In doing so, *DSM-IV* implies that negative symptoms, which account for much of the social morbidity of schizophrenia, are a core feature of the disorder and are worthy of active treatment. By defining certain schizophrenic behaviors (withdrawal, apathy, lack of drive) as active phase negative symptoms, *DSM-IV* helps clinicians and families to avoid labeling such dysfunctional behaviors as "laziness" or other character flaws. *Appendix B* of *DSM-IV* includes a proposal for the diagnosis of *Simple Schizophrenia* whose essential feature is functional decline accompanied by the predominance of the negative symptoms of schizophrenia (*DSM-IV* pp. 713–715).

In deference to Schneider, *DSM-IV* allows the presence of only one of its five characteristic active phase symptoms of schizophrenia if that one symptom is a Schneiderian first-rank symptom. Specifically, a single active phase psychotic symptom can indicate the diagnosis of schizophrenia if that symptom is (a) a bizarre delusion, (b) an auditory hallucination of a voice making a running commentary on one's thoughts or behavior, or (c) an auditory hallucination of multiple voices conversing with one another.

In deference to Kraepelin, *DSM-IV* also requires the presence of impaired social and/or occupational functioning "for a significant portion of the time since the onset of the disturbance" (*DSM-IV*, p. 285) and a duration of at least six months during which "continuous signs of the disturbance persist" (*DSM-IV*, p. 285). During the six months of continuous signs of disturbance, there must be at least one month of the active phase symptoms as described above. There may also be prodromal and/or residual symptomatology, including negative symptoms and milder active psychotic symptoms (strange beliefs, oddities of perception, etc).

The *prodromal phase* of schizophrenia refers to a period of deteriorating functioning preceding the development of active phase symptomatology. The *residual phase* of schizophrenia follows the period of active symptoms and is characterized by the persistence of some symptomatology that may include negative symptoms and/or attenuated forms of active psychotic experiences. Typical symptoms of the prodromal and residual phases include social withdrawal, impaired functioning, blunted affect, apathy, and oddities of speech, thought, and/or behavior.

To qualify for the diagnosis of Schizophrenia, *DSM-IV* also requires the exclusion of certain disorders. Thus, the psychotic symptomatology must not be due to a Schizoaffective Disorder, a Mood Disorder, a General Medical Condition, or the Use of a Substance.

DSM-IV allows the clinician to specify the course of schizophrenia. These course modifiers, which were adapted from *ICD-10*, are as follows:

- Continuous (no remission during the period being described)
- Episodic, with progressive development of negative symptoms between psychotic episodes
- Episodic, with persistent, nonprogressive negative symptoms between psychotic episodes
- Episodic (remittent): full or almost complete remission between psychotic episodes
- In partial remission following a single episode
- In full remission following a single episode
- Other pattern
- Period of observation less than one year

DSM-IV also distinguishes five subtypes of Schizophrenia: Paranoid, Disorganized, Catatonic, Undifferentiated, and Residual. The Paranoid type is characterized by preoccupation with systematized delusions or with frequent auditory hallucinations dealing with a single theme. The essential features of the Disorganized type are flat affect and disorganized speech and behavior. As the name implies, the Catatonic type is characterized by the presence of a catatonic syndrome (catatonic immobility or hyperactivity, negativism, posturing, stereotyped movements, echolalia, and/or echopraxia). In the Undifferentiated type, there are significant psychotic symptoms that do not fit neatly into one of the previous three categories or that have combined features of paranoia, disorganization, and/or catatonia. Finally, the Residual type refers to a clinical picture in which the individual no longer meets criteria for active phase psychotic symptoms, but continues to suffer from symptomatology in the form of negative symptoms (withdrawal, apathy, blunting, etc.) or attenuated positive symptoms (odd speech or behavior, unusual perceptions, strange or illogical thinking, etc.).

Appendix B of *DSM-IV* proposes alternative dimensional descriptors for schizophrenia (*DSM-IV*, p. 710). The authors of this section feel that the classical subtyping described above is too limited. Instead, or in addition, they suggest a model consisting of three dimensions: (1) psychotic (hallucinations and delusions), (2) disorganized (disorganized speech and behavior, inappropriate affect), and (3) negative or deficit symptoms (blunted affect, alogia, avolition, anhedonia, lack of spontaneity, etc.)

SCHIZOPHRENIFORM DISORDER (295.40)

(*DSM-IV*, pp. 290–292)
    Specify if:

—Without good prognostic features
—With good prognostic features (brief prodromal period, confusion, good premorbid adaptation, absence of flat affect)

Except for the duration requirement of an episode of schizophreniform disorder lasting at least one month but less than six months, the diagnostic criteria for Schizophreniform Disorder are the same as those for Schizophrenia. As with schizophrenia, the episode of illness may include prodromal, active phase, and residual symptoms. By definition, patients with schizophreniform disorder recover completely within six months. If the clinician must diagnose this disorder without waiting the six months for recovery, only a "Provisional" diagnosis of Schizophreniform Disorder can be given. If the psychotic episode lasts less than one month and there is complete recovery, the diagnosis of Brief Psychotic Disorder should be used.

The clinician should further specify whether the disorder occurs with or without good prognostic features. Indications of a good prognosis include a brief prodromal period (less than four weeks), confusion during the phase of active psychotic symptoms, good premorbid adaptation, and the absence of flat affect.

SCHIZOAFFECTIVE DISORDER (295.70)

(*DSM-IV*, pp. 292–296)
    Specify type:

—Bipolar type
—Depressive type

In 1933 J. Kasanin introduced the term *schizoaffective* to describe a group of individuals who suffered from significant affective as well as schizophrenic symptoms. Kasanin's patients tended to have a good prognosis, a history of precipitating stressors, an acute onset of the disorder, and a family history of an affective disorder. Because of the prominent psychotic symptoms that accompanied the mood disturbance, Kasanin believed his patients to be suffering from a subtype of schizophrenia.

Other researchers have grouped schizoaffective disorders under the rubric of mood or affective disorders. The literature contains so much unclarity and controversy surrounding this diagnosis that some researchers believe schizoaffective disorder is not a valid diagnosis. It may be that some individuals diagnosed with schizoaffective disorder suffer from a mood disorder with psychotic features and that others with the same diagnosis suffer from a schizophrenic disorder with an associated disturbance of mood.

The authors of *DSM-IV* have chosen to define Schizoaffective Disorder in terms of an uninterrupted episode of illness (rather than a lifetime pattern of symptoms) during which the individual meets criteria for Schizophrenia and, at the same time, meets criteria for either a Major Depressive Episode with depressed mood or for a Manic Episode.

DELUSIONAL DISORDER (297.1)

(*DSM-IV*, pp. 296–301)
  Specify type:

  −Erotomanic (de Clerambault's syndrome)
  −Grandiose
  −Jealous
  −Persecutory
  −Somatic
  −Mixed
  −Unspecified

Some individuals develop persistent non-bizarre delusional beliefs or systematized delusions in the absence of any signs of an affective disorder, a schizophrenic or other psychotic disorder, or a psychosis induced by a medical condition or substance use. Despite their otherwise logical, organized, and coherent thinking, these delusional persons hold adamantly to their false beliefs, which have a ring of truth and reasonableness, but are based on incorrect assessments of reality. Their false ideas are not consistent with their cultural or religious background nor their level of intelligence. These individuals refuse to alter their false beliefs even when presented with reasonable or incontrovertible evidence of their inaccuracy. Instead, they will often invent further delusional explanations to account for the apparent discrepancies between their beliefs and consensual reality.

The comedy *Arsenic and Old Lace* features a man who believes he is Teddy Roosevelt and a couple of little old ladies (sisters) who share the belief that it is merciful to poison their male visitors and bury them in the basement. The characters in this play seem to function normally outside of the sphere of their delusional preoccupations.

In the past, delusional disorders were often called "paranoid disorders" from the Greek *para nous* for "mind beside itself." The concept of paranoia was introduced into Western psychiatry by the German physician Johann Christian Heinroth in 1818 when he used the term *Verrücktheit* ("craziness") to describe a disorder of intellect involving severely impaired reality testing. The influential French psychiatrist Jean Etienne Esquirol, in 1838, used the term *monomania* to describe a disorder characterized by delusions with preservation of logical reasoning and normal behavior. In 1921 Kraepelin described a similar delusional disorder that he called *paraphrenia* to distinguish it from schizophrenia because paraphrenia lacked the hallucinations, disorganized thinking, and personality deterioration seen in schizophrenia.

To diagnose Delusional Disorder, *DSM-IV* requires the presence of "nonbizarre delusions of at least one month's duration" (*DSM-IV*, p. 301). Except for the areas of functioning related to the delusional thinking, other aspects of functioning and behavior must be relatively normal. Any episodes of mood disturbance that have occurred with the delusions must be relatively brief so that the delusions are not considered part of a Mood Disorder. In addition, the individual must never have met criteria for the characteristic symptoms of Schizophrenia, and the delusions must not be substance induced or due to a general medical condition.

DSM-IV describes seven subtypes (five specific subtypes, a mixed subtype, and an unspecified subtype) of Delusional Disorder, based on the predominant theme of the delusions, as follows:

Erotomanic: the delusion that someone, often a celebrity, is in love with the delusional person.

Grandiose: the delusion of markedly exaggerated self-importance, power, knowledge, or influence, or of a special relationship to God or to a very important person.

Jealous: the delusion of one's partner's infidelity.

Persecutory: the delusion of being persecuted or deliberately maltreated.

Somatic: the delusion of having a medical illness or physical malady or defect.

Mixed: more than one of the above delusions coexist.

Unspecified: the delusion is not specified.

BRIEF PSYCHOTIC DISORDER (298.8)

(*DSM-IV*, pp. 302–304)
    Specify if:

–With marked stressor(s) (brief reactive)
–Without marked stressor(s)
–With postpartum onset (within four weeks postpartum)

The husband of a middle-aged woman brought her to a psychiatrist for evaluation. She was a language teacher who was highly functioning and well respected by her students. A few days earlier she had begun to say bizarre things, to appear restless and agitated, and to diminish her self-care. The husband could identify no precipitant for this behavior. By the time of the psychiatric evaluation, the woman was mute, catatonic, and appeared to be visually hallucinating. There was no history of schizophrenia or of a mood disorder, but the husband did report that his wife had suffered a similar condition years before that had responded quickly to a low dose of an antipsychotic medication.

The psychiatrist placed the woman on the same medication that had helped her in the past and scheduled an appointment for two days later. The woman came by herself to the next visit. There was a dramatic change in her appearance and demeanor. She was bright, intelligent, thoughtful, articulate, and insightful. Her mood was euthymic and there was no trace of the state of disorganized behavior or thinking of the previous session. She had no idea of what had caused her disorganization, but wanted to meet for brief crisis-oriented psychotherapy to try to understand her five days of psychotic regression. She appeared to have suffered a Brief Psychotic Disorder (298.8). Other names in the literature for similar conditions are "brief reactive psychosis," "hysterical psychosis," and the French term *bouffée délirante*.

In the course of the next few sessions, the woman reviewed what had been happening prior to her brief psychotic disorder. Her father, who had recently changed doctors because his company had changed insurance carriers, had become ill. The woman needed to bring her father to his medical appointment. Her father's new doctor bore a striking resemblance to a man she had met years previously as a college student traveling through an Asian country. This man had befriended her and then raped her in a frightening and traumatic way. She had developed symptoms of PTSD after the rape and had sought psychotherapy to deal with the trauma. The chance meeting of a man who strongly resembled the rapist had re-evoked the painful repressed memories and had flooded her with temporarily unmanageable affect, leading to a state of brief psychotic disorganization.

According to *DSM-IV*, Brief Psychotic Disorder requires the presence of at least one of four prominent psychotic symptoms (hallucinations, delusions, psychotically disorganized speech, or extremely disorganized or catatonic behavior) that last at least one day but no more than a month. Eventually the patient must have a full recovery to a previous level of functioning. The diagnosis cannot be made if the psychotic symptoms represent a culturally sanctioned response. In addition, the psychotic reaction must not be part of a Mood Disorder, a Schizophrenic Disorder, a Psychotic Disorder due to a General Medical Condition, or a Substance-Induced Psychotic Disorder.

The *DSM-IV* definition of Brief Psychotic Disorder is a broadening of the *DSM-III-R* definition, which focused on brief reactive psychosis and required the etiological factor of a severe stressor. In *DSM-IV*, the clinician can code the presence of a triggering stressor with the subtype "With Marked Stressor(s)" or "Brief Reactive." *DSM-IV* has also extended the *DSM-III-R* duration requirement from a few hours to a full day of psychotic symptoms.

Some clinicians view brief psychotic disorder, especially the reactive type, to be a type of dissociative disorder or possibly a type of conversion disorder with mental symptoms rather than the typical conversion symptoms or deficits of the voluntary motor or sensory organ systems.

SHARED PSYCHOTIC DISORDER
(FOLIE A DEUX) (297.3)

(*DSM-IV*, pp. 305–306)

Shared psychotic disorder is a rare condition that also goes by the names of *Folie à Deux*, "double insanity," or "psychosis of association." It was first described in 1877 by the French psychiatrists Ernest Lasègue and Jules Falret and most commonly affects two members of the same family who share very similar delusional beliefs. Typically, a more submissive or dependent person comes to share the established delusion of a more dominant individual. In some instances three or more closely knit individuals may share the same delusion.

According to *DSM-IV*, the diagnosis of Shared Psychotic Disorder requires two individuals—one who has an established delusion and another who develops a similar delusion in the context of a close relationship with the already delusional individual. The newly developed delusion must not be better accounted for by another psychotic disorder, by a general medical condition, or by the use of a substance. Two acquaintances who share the same delusional ideas simply as a matter of coincidence do not meet criteria for this disorder.

PSYCHOTIC DISORDER DUE TO A GENERAL
MEDICAL CONDITION (293.8–)

(*DSM-IV*, pp. 306–310)

293.81   with Delusions
293.82   with Hallucinations

Certain medical disorders may have prominent psychotic symptoms as part of their clinical presentation. Delusions, for example, have been reported in certain individuals with temporal lobe epilepsy. Patients with diabetes mellitus may appear bizarre and thought-disordered during episodes of hypoglycemia.

According to *DSM-IV*, the characteristic symptoms of a Psychotic Disorder due to a General Medical Condition are prominent hallucinations or delusions for which there exists evidence of a medical etiology through the medical history, physical examination, or laboratory tests. In addition, the hallucinations or delusions must not occur solely during a delirium or dementia and must not be better explained by another mental disorder. The medically induced psychotic disorder is coded by whether delusions or hallucinations predominate the clinical picture.

SUBSTANCE-INDUCED PSYCHOTIC DISORDER

(*DSM-IV*, pp. 310–315)
  Specify if:

  −With onset during intoxication
  −With onset during withdrawal

Many substances can induce psychotic symptoms. Paranoia, for example, may occur as part of cocaine intoxication. Visual hallucinations are classic symptoms of the delirium tremens of alcohol withdrawal. In the 1960s many individuals ingested LSD for its hallucinogenic properties. To facilitate differential diagnosis, *DSM-IV* has included the category of Substance-Induced Psychotic Disorder along with Psychotic Disorder due to a General Medical Condition in the Schizophrenia and other Psychotic Disorders section.

According to *DSM-IV* criteria, a Substance-Induced Psychotic Disorder is characterized by prominent hallucinations or delusions that develop within a month of significant substance intoxication or withdrawal. There must be evidence from the medical history, physical examination, or laboratory tests that substantiate the diagnosis of substance intoxication or withdrawal. An independent general medical or mental disorder must not better account for the hallucinations or delusions, and the psychotic symptoms must not occur solely as part of a delirium or a dementia.

If a substance-specific intoxication or withdrawal coexists with the substance-induced psychotic disorder, the clinician should code the substance intoxication or substance dependence separately. The clinician should also specify if the substance-induced psychotic disorder occurs "With Onset During Intoxication," or "With Onset During Withdrawal."

The specific codes for Substance-Induced Psychotic Disorder are as follows:

291.5	Alcohol with delusions
291.3	Alcohol with hallucinations
292.11	Amphetamine or related substance with delusions
292.12	Amphetamine or related substance with hallucinations
292.11	Cannabis with delusions
292.12	Cannabis with hallucinations
292.11	Cocaine with delusions
292.12	Cocaine with hallucinations
292.11	Hallucinogen with delusions
292.12	Hallucinogen with hallucinations
292.11	Inhalant with delusions
292.12	Inhalant with hallucinations
292.11	Opioid with delusions
292.12	Opioid with hallucinations
292.11	Phencyclidine or related substance with delusions
292.12	Phencyclidine or related substance with hallucinations
292.11	Sedative, Hypnotic, or Anxiolytic with delusions
292.12	Sedative, Hypnotic, or Anxiolytic with hallucinations
292.11	Other or unknown substance with delusions
292.12	Other or unknown substance with hallucinations

PSYCHOTIC DISORDER NOT OTHERWISE SPECIFIED (298.9)

(*DSM-IV*, p. 315)

This residual NOS category allows the clinician to code psychotic disorders that do not meet criteria for any of the specific psychotic disorders in *DSM-IV*. In addition, this NOS category may be used to code a psychotic presentation for which there is insufficient or contradictory information on which to base a more definitive diagnosis.

An example would be the presence of hallucinations, delusions, or extremely bizarre behavior in an individual with a general medical illness or a history of substance abuse. On initial evaluation, it may not be clear whether the psychotic symptoms represent a primary psychotic disorder, a psychosis secondary to medical illness, or a substance-induced psychotic disorder.

SIMPLE DETERIORATIVE DISORDER
(SIMPLE SCHIZOPHRENIA)

(*DSM-IV*, pp. 713–715)

Appendix B of *DSM-IV* proposes criteria for *Simple Schizophrenia* or *Simple Deteriorative Disorder*. The essential feature of this condition is marked impairment and the progressive development of prominent negative symptoms of schizophrenia over the course of at least a year without prominent positive schizophrenic symptoms. Individuals who meet the research criteria for Simple Schizophrenia would be diagnosed as Unspecified Mental Disorder (300.9) in *DSM-IV* (see *DSM-IV*, p. 687).

17

Mood Disorders

"Those who have become eminent in philosophy, politics, poetry, and the arts have all had tendencies toward melancholia."

Aristotle (4th century B.C.)

DEPRESSIVE DISORDERS:

296.2x   Major Depressive Disorder, Single Episode
296.3x   Major Depressive Disorder, Recurrent
300.4   Dysthymic Disorder
         Specify if:
           Early onset (before age 21)
           Late onset (age 21 or older)
           With atypical features
311   Depressive Disorder Not Otherwise Specified (NOS)

BIPOLAR DISORDERS:

Bipolar I Disorder:
296.0x   Single Manic Episode
296.40   Most Recent Episode Hypomanic
296.4x   Most Recent Episode Manic
296.6x   Most Recent Episode Mixed
296.5x   Most Recent Episode Depressed
296.7   Most Recent Episode Unspecified
Bipolar II Disorder:
296.89   Bipolar II Disorder (Recurrent Major Depressive Episodes with Hypomania)

Specify current or most recent episode was:
Hypomanic
Depressed
Cyclothymic Disorder:
301.13   Cyclothymic Disorder
Bipolar Disorder Not Otherwise Specified:
296.80   Bipolar Disorder NOS
293.83   Mood Disorder Due to a General Medical Condition
Specify type:
With depressive features
With major depressive-like episode
With manic features
With mixed features
‒‒‒.‒‒   Substance-Induced Mood Disorder (refer to specific
substances for codes)
Specify type:
With manic features
With depressive features
With mixed features
Also, specify if:
Onset during intoxication
Onset during withdrawal
296.90   Mood Disorder Not Otherwise Specified

SEVERITY, PSYCHOTIC, and REMISSION SPECIFIERS:
(*DSM-IV*, pp. 380–381)
Fifth Digit Codes for Current State of Major Depressive Disorders
and Bipolar Disorders:
296.x0:   Unspecified
296.x1:   Mild
296.x2:   Moderate
296.x3:   Severe, without Psychotic Features
296.x4:   Severe, with Psychotic Features
Mood-congruent Psychotic Features
Mood-incongruent Psychotic Features
296.x5:   In Partial Remission
296.x6:   In Full Remission

CROSS SECTIONAL SYMPTOM FEATURES:
For the most recent Manic Episode or Major Depressive Episode:
Specify if: With catatonic features
 (*DSM-IV*, p. 382–383)
For Major Depressive Episodes:
Specify if: With melancholic features
 (*DSM-IV*, pp. 383–384)
For the most recent Major Depressive or Dysthymic Episode:
Specify if: With atypical features
 (*DSM-IV*, pp. 384–386)

COURSE SPECIFIERS:
POSTPARTUM ONSET (*DSM-IV* pp. 386–387):
For: Bipolar I Disorder
 Bipolar II Disorder
 Major Depression
 Brief Psychotic Disorder
 Specify if: With postpartum onset (within four weeks)

LONGITUDINAL COURSE (*DSM-IV*, pp. 387–389):
For: Major Depressive Disorder
 Specify longitudinal course:
 With full interepisode recovery
 Without full interepisode recovery
For: Bipolar I or Bipolar II Disorders
 Specify longitudinal course:
 With full interepisode recovery
 Without full interepisode recovery

SEASONAL PATTERN (*DSM-IV*, p. 389):
For Major Depressive Episodes occurring in:
 Bipolar I Disorder
 Bipolar II Disorder
 Major Depressive Disorder, Recurrent
 Specify if: With seasonal pattern

RAPID CYCLING (*DSM-IV*, pp. 390–391):
For: Bipolar I Disorder

Bipolar II Disorder
Specify if: With rapid cycling (four episodes in the past year)

The Mood Disorders are divided into two major groupings: the Depressive Disorders and the Bipolar Disorders. *DSM-III* used the term Affective Disorders for this class of syndromes. The essential feature of these disorders is a disturbance of mood with accompanying symptoms of a depressive or manic syndrome. Mood disorders may be either primary or secondary to a general medical condition or to the use of substances. Mood refers to the pervasive and sustained emotional state of an individual. One's mood is the persisting affective lens through which one views the world.

Affective disorders are among the most common and disabling psychiatric disorders in the general population. Ronald Kessler and his colleagues (1994) reported that in the United States the prevalence of mood disorders in a national sample was about 19 percent for a lifetime and 11 percent for a one-year period. Major depressive episodes accounted for the bulk of the affective disorders. In any given year, about 8 percent of men and 13 percent of women in the United States suffer a major depressive episode. In the course of a lifetime, approximately 13 percent of men and 21 percent of women will have one or more major depressive episodes. Social role theorists have argued that women are at almost twice the risk of suffering a major depressive episode as men because their sense of identity develops in a society that devalues the female gender role.

DSM-IV begins its chapter on mood disorders by defining several types of "mood episodes," including Major Depressive Episode, Manic Episode, Mixed Episode, and Hypomanic Episode. The various mood disorders are defined in terms of the type of presenting episode. The various specifiers further define the nature of the current mood episode or the course of recurring episodes.

A *Major Depressive Episode* (*DSM-IV*, pp. 320–327) consists of at least two weeks of either depressed mood or anhedonia (loss of interest or pleasure), accompanied by clinically significant distress or impairment. Oddly, *DSM-IV* allows for irritable rather than depressed mood only in the case of children and adolescents despite the fact that in office-based practice many adults (especially elderly males) suffer major depressive episodes with predominantly irritable mood. *DSM-IV* also requires the presence of at least four out of nine characteristic symptoms of a depressive syndrome, including neurovegetative changes in weight and/or sleep, psychomotor agitation or retardation, feelings of guilt or worthlessness, preoccupation with death or suicide, decreased energy, and poor concentration. The depressive symptoms must not be due to Bereavement (V62.82, *DSM-IV* pp. 684–685), to substance use, or to a general medical condition. In addition, the patient must not satisfy criteria for a Mixed Mood Episode.

A *Manic Episode* (*DSM-IV*, pp. 328–332) is characterized by a period, lasting at least one week (or less if the patient is hospitalized), of "persistently elevated, expansive, or irritable mood," accompanied by clinically significant distress or impairment. In addition, the patient must demonstrate at least three (four if the mood is only irritable) of *DSM-IV*'s list of seven characteristic symptoms of mania. Typical manic symptoms include grandiosity, lessened need for sleep, pressured speech, flight of ideas, distractibility, psychomotor agitation, and engaging in risky behaviors. The manic symptoms must not be due to substance use or to a general medical condition. Finally, the patient must not meet criteria for a Mixed Mood Episode.

The reader should note that *DSM-IV* has taken the somewhat controversial stance of not allowing the occurrence of a manic episode caused by antidepressant treatment to be counted in making the diagnosis of Bipolar I Disorder. Antidepressant treatment includes antidepressant medication, ECT, and phototherapy. A manic syndrome precipitated by antidepressant medication is diagnosed in *DSM-IV* as a Substance-Induced Mood Disorder.

DSM-IV has reinstated the old *DSM-III* criteria of one week's duration for a Manic Episode. The one week criteria had been dropped from *DSM-III-R*. In addition, *DSM-IV* requires at least two months without significant symptoms of hypomania or mania to delineate the manic episodes.

A *Mixed Episode* (*DSM-IV*, pp. 333–335) is an episode of affective disturbance consisting of rapid mood swings that, except for duration, meets criteria for both a Major Depressive Episode and a Manic Episode almost daily for the period of at least one week. As with manic episodes, a Mixed Mood Episode caused by antidepressant treatment does not count toward the diagnosis of Bipolar I Disorder.

A *Hypomanic Episode* (*DSM-IV*, pp. 335–338) is essentially an attenuated nonpsychotic manic episode that is not due to substance use or to a general medical condition. *DSM-III-R* did not provide a separate criteria set for hypomanic episodes and regarded hypomania as a less severe form of mania. To diagnose hypomania, *DSM-IV* requires a duration of at least four days of a distinct change in both mood and functioning that is observable or apparent to others. Unlike mania, hypomania is not psychotic and does not cause significant impairment nor necessitate hospitalization.

According to *DSM-IV*, a Hypomanic Episode refers to a distinct period of at least four days of elevated, expansive, or irritable mood that is observable by others. There is a definite and atypical change in the person's functioning. In addition, the individual must display three (or four if the mood is only irritable) of *DSM-IV*'s list of seven characteristic symptoms of mania. Unlike mania, the Hypomanic Episode does not cause marked functional impairment.

DEPRESSIVE DISORDERS

Major Depressive Disorder

DSM-IV, pp. 339–345)
    MAJOR DEPRESSIVE DISORDER, SINGLE EPISODE (296.2x)
    MAJOR DEPRESSIVE DISORDER, RECURRENT (296.3x)
    The essential feature of major depressive disorder is the occurrence of one or more major depressive episodes in the absence of a history of manic, hypomanic, or mixed mood episodes. Major depressive disorder, however, can be diagnosed if there have been manic, hypomanic, or mixed mood symptoms that were clearly due to a substance, medication, or a general medical condition.

Significant depressive syndromes that are substance-induced or due to a general medical condition are diagnosed separately from Major Depressive Disorder in *DSM-IV* as Substance-induced Mood Disorder and as Mood Disorder due to a General Medical Condition, respectively.

If a clinically significant or a full depressive syndrome (meeting criteria for a major depressive episode) occurs during the course of delusional disorder, schizophrenia, or psychotic disorder NOS, then the diagnosis of Depressive Disorder NOS should be given. Depressive syndromes that occur as part of a schizoaffective disorder do not warrant a separate diagnosis of Major Depressive Disorder.

Major depressive disorder can consist of a single episode or be recurrent. By definition, recurrence means the occurrence of two or more major depressive episodes separated by a period of at least two months in which the patient satisfies none of the criteria of a major depressive episode.

For the current or most recent major depressive episode, the clinician should further specify all the following that apply:

- Severity/Psychosis/Remission
- Chronic
- With catatonic features
- With melancholic features
- With atypical features
- With postpartum onset

For recurrent major depressive episodes, the clinician should also specify:

- Longitudinal course (with/without interepisode recovery)
- With seasonal pattern

Dysthymic Disorder (300.4)

(*DSM-IV*, pp. 345–349)
Specify if:

- Early onset (before age 21)
- Late onset (age 21 or older)
- With atypical features

Some individuals appear to have a chronic, low-grade depression that does not meet criteria for a major depressive episode. These mild depressive symptoms often date back to early childhood. In the older literature, such clients were diagnosed with depressive neurosis or dysthymia.

DSM-IV defines Dysthymic Disorder as a syndrome consisting of at least two years of depressed mood occurring a good part of the day and most of the time. For children and adolescents, *DSM-IV* allows the mood to be irritable rather than depressed and shortens the duration to one year. In addition, the affected individual must display two or more of six characteristic symptoms of dysthymic disorder. These symptoms include neurovegetative changes, such as sleep and appetite disturbances and lack of energy, poor self-esteem, difficulty concentrating and/or making decisions, and hopelessness. In addition, the depressed or irritable mood and other symptoms must cause significant distress or impairment.

Patients with dysthymic disorder may go on to suffer a major depressive episode. The *DSM-IV* criteria, however, do not allow the diagnosis of Dysthymic Disorder if a major depressive episode has occurred during the first two years (one year for children and adolescents) of chronically depressed mood. The patient with dysthymic disorder may have suffered a major depressive episode earlier in life, and *DSM-IV* requires at least a two-month symptom-free period between the major depressive episode and the onset of the dysthymic disorder.

DSM-IV has a number of exclusion criteria for Dysthymic Disorder. The symptoms must not be due to substance use or to a general medical condition. The individual must never have met criteria for a cyclothymic disorder and must have no history of a manic, hypomanic, or mixed episode. Finally, the dysthymic disturbance must not occur solely during the course of a chronic psychotic disorder, such as schizophrenia or delusional disorder.

DSM-IV has dropped the older *DSM-III-R* distinction between primary and secondary dysthymic disorders because of lack of supporting evidence.

There is controversy in the literature about which symptoms best define dysthymic disorder. *Appendix B* of *DSM-IV* provides "Alternate Research Criterion B for Dysthymic Disorder" (*DSM-IV*, p. 718). Ongoing research will help determine which symptoms of dysthymia are most characteristic.

Depressive Disorder Not Otherwise Specified (NOS) (311)

(*DSM-IV*, p. 350)

DSM-IV provides this NOS category for disorders with prominent depressive features that do not meet criteria for major depressive disorder, dysthymic disorder, or adjustment disorders with depressed mood or with mixed anxiety and depressed mood. The clinician can also use this category to code disorders where there is as yet diagnostic uncertainty about the type or etiology of the depressive disorder.

Appendix B of *DSM-IV* contains proposals for four new depressive diagnoses that can be coded as Depressive Disorder NOS. They are:

1. *Postpsychotic Depressive Disorder of Schizophrenia (DSM-IV,* pp. 711–712): a major depressive episode occurring during the residual phase of schizophrenia.

2. *Premenstrual Dysphoric Disorder (PMDD) (DSM-IV,* pp. 715–718): significant sad or anxious mood, tenseness, emotional lability, hopelessness, distressing irritability, loss of interest, suicidal ideation, and so on, occurring regularly in the last week of the luteal phase and beginning to remit within a few days of the onset of the follicular phase with no symptoms during the week after menses. The distressing irritability is the most common reason women with this disorder seek treatment. Because women with PMDD often appear hypomanic during the follicular phase, some researchers feel that premenstrual dysphoric disorder is a variant of bipolar disorder. A history of postpartum depression is not uncommon. Some women's groups are concerned about the potential for abuse of this diagnosis.

3. *Minor Depressive Disorder (DSM-IV,* pp. 719–721): essentially an attenuated form of Major Depressive Disorder. The depressive episodes last as long as major depressive episodes, but with fewer symptoms and less impairment.

4. *Recurrent Brief Depressive Disorder (RBDD) (DSM-IV* pp. 721–723): essentially the same as Major Depressive Disorder except for the two-week duration requirement. The episodes of RBDD occur at least once a month for at least twelve months and have a duration of two days to two weeks with a typical length of two to four days. In addition, the episodes of RBDD are not related to the menstrual cycle.

5. *Mixed Anxiety-Depressive Disorder (DSM-IV,* pp. 723–725): at least one month of dysphoric mood accompanied by four out of ten symptoms of a mixed anxiety/depression spectrum.

THE BIPOLAR DISORDERS

(DSM-IV, pp. 350–366)

All four types of bipolar disorders (Bipolar I, Bipolar II, Cyclothymia, and Bipolar Disorder NOS) involve the presence of hypomanic or manic symptoms that constitute one "pole" of a disturbance of mood. Opposite the hypomanic/manic pole lies the depressive/anhedonic pole of mood dysfunction. Some of the bipolar disorders require the presence of depressive pole symptoms (e.g., Cyclothymic Disorder), while others do not (e.g., Bipolar I Disorder, single manic episode). Students sometimes get confused by the fact that one can diagnose a bipolar disorder when symptoms of only one pole (hypomanic/manic symptoms) have ever been present.

DSM-IV has changed the organization and terminology of the bipolar disorders from *DSM-III-R*. There are now Bipolar I and Bipolar II Disorders. Bipolar I Disorders are subdivided into a single manic episode subtype and other subtypes in which the most recent episode was hypomanic, manic, mixed, depressed, or unspecified. Bipolar II Disorder refers to a clinical history of at least one major depressive episode and at least one hypomanic episode in the absence of any history of a manic episode.

BIPOLAR I DISORDER:
(*DSM-IV*, pp. 350–358)
296.0x   Single Manic Episode
296.40   Most Recent Episode Hypomanic
296.4x   Most Recent Episode Manic
296.6x   Most Recent Episode Mixed
296.5x   Most Recent Episode Depressed
296.7   Most Recent Episode Unspecified

Bipolar I Disorder consists of one or more manic or mixed episodes that may or may not occur with a history of major depressive episodes. *DSM-IV* excludes from the definition of Bipolar I Disorder the occurrence of mood disorders that are due to substances or to a general medical condition. In addition, the mood episodes of Bipolar I Disorder may not be part of a schizoaffective disorder and may not be superimposed on a psychotic disorder such as schizophrenia, delusional disorder, schizophreniform disorder, or psychotic disorder NOS.

If there has been only one manic episode in the absence of a history of any major depressive episodes, the diagnosis is Bipolar I Disorder, Single Manic Episode. If the symptoms of this disorder meet the criteria for a Mixed Mood Episode, then the specifier "Mixed" should be added to the diagnosis. The "Single Episode" subtype was added to *DSM-IV* to increase specificity and to be compatible with *ICD-10*.

If the current or most recent mood episode is hypomanic and there is a history of at least one prior manic episode, then the diagnosis is Bipolar I Disorder, Most Recent Episode Hypomanic. This is also a new subtype added to *DSM-IV* to increase specificity.

If the current or most recent mood episode is a manic episode and there is a history of at least one major depressive, manic, or mixed episode, then the diagnosis is Bipolar I Disorder, Most Recent Episode Manic.

If the current or most recent mood episode is a mixed episode and there is a history of at least one Major depressive, manic, or mixed episode, then the diagnosis is Bipolar I Disorder, Most Recent Episode Mixed.

If the current or most recent mood episode is a major depressive episode and there is a history of at least one manic or mixed episode, then the diagnosis is Bipolar I Disorder, Most Recent Episode Depressed.

Bipolar I Disorder, Most Recent Episode Unspecified, refers to the fact that the most recent or current mood episode meets all but the duration criteria for a manic, hypomanic, mixed, or major depressive episode. In addition, there is a history of at least one manic or mixed mood episode. This subtype allows the clinician to record the onset of a new episode of mood disturbance before the full duration criteria are met.

For each subtype of Bipolar I Disorder, the clinician should use the *DSM-IV* mood specifiers appropriate to the type of the most recent mood episode.

Bipolar II Disorder (296.89)

(Recurrent Major Depressive Episodes with Hypomania)
(*DSM-IV*, pp. 359–363)
Specify: Current or most recent episode was:

−Hypomanic
−Depressed

Bipolar II Disorders, new in *DSM-IV*, are characterized by hypomanic episodes that alternate with major depressive episodes. Full-blown manic episodes are not part of Bipolar II disorders. In *DSM-III-R*, Bipolar II Disorder was diagnosed as Bipolar Disorder NOS. Like most *DSM-IV* disorders, the symptoms of Bipolar II Disorder must cause clinically significant distress or functional impairment.

According to *DSM-IV*, the diagnosis of Bipolar II Disorder requires the occurrence of at least one major depressive episode and at least one hypomanic episode during the course of the disorder. In addition, there must never have been either a manic or a mixed episode. As with Bipolar I Disorder, the mood episodes of Bipolar II Disorder may not be part of a schizoaffective disorder and may not be superimposed on a psychotic disorder, such as schizophrenia, delusional disorder, schizophreniform disorder, or psychotic disorder NOS.

The clinician should code whether the current or most recent episode of Bipolar II Disorder is "Hypomanic" or "Depressed." In addition, the clinician should use the depressive episode specifiers to further categorize the most recent or current major depressive episode in Bipolar II Disorder, Depressed. Finally, the clinician should include the appropriate course specifiers as part of the diagnosis.

Cyclothymic Disorder (301.13)

(*DSM-IV*, pp. 363–366)

Cyclothymic Disorder refers to chronic alterations of mood between depressive and hypomanic poles. The hypomanic symptoms do not meet criteria for a manic episode and the depressive symptoms do not meet criteria for a major depressive episode.

For the diagnosis of Cyclothymic Disorder, *DSM-IV* requires that, for at least two years (one year for children and adolescents), the periods of mood disturbance do not satisfy criteria for a major depressive episode and that the individual is not free of depressive or hypomanic mood symptoms for more than two months at a time. In addition, during the first two years of the disorder, there hasn't been a major depressive, manic, or mixed mood episode. After the first two years of cyclothymic disorder, individuals may go on to develop manic, mixed, or major depressive episodes and, if so, will receive an additional diagnosis or Bipolar I or Bipolar II Disorder according to the nature of the major mood episode.

In addition, as with Bipolar I and Bipolar II disorders, the mood episodes of Cyclothymic Disorder may not be part of a schizoaffective disorder and may not be superimposed on a psychotic disorder, such as schizophrenia, delusional disorder, schizophreniform disorder, or psychotic disorder NOS. Nor can the cyclothymic disorder symptoms be the result of substance use or of a general medical condition.

Bipolar Disorder Not Otherwise Specified

(*DSM-IV*, p. 366)
296.80   BIPOLAR DISORDER NOS

DSM-IV provides this NOS category for disorders with bipolar features that do not meet criteria for any of the specific *DSM-IV* Bipolar Disorders. An example might be a patient who suffers recurrent discrete episodes of hypomanic symptoms without any history of a depressive disorder. In addition, the clinician can use this category to express diagnostic uncertainty when the exact nature or etiology of the bipolar disorder is as yet undiscovered.

Mood Disorder Due to a General Medical Condition (293.83)

(*DSM-IV*, pp. 366–370)
    Specify type:

—With depressive features (not meeting full criteria for a major depressive episode)

—With major depressive-like episode (meets full criteria for a major depressive episode, except the exclusion criterion for being due to a general medical condition)

—With manic features

—With mixed features

Certain general medical conditions can induce a disturbance of mood (including depressed, expansive, irritable, hypomanic, or manic mood, or marked anhedonia without predominant depressed mood) through changes in body physiology that are part of the medical disorder. For example, the first sign of carcinoma of the head of the pancreas may be the occurrence of a profound melancholic depressive syndrome.

DSM-IV diagnoses a Mood Disorder Due to a General Medical Condition when there is evidence from medical history, examination, or laboratory tests that the mood disturbance is caused by the physiological changes that are part of the medical disorder. As with other mental disorders, there must be significant distress or functional impairment. In addition, *DSM-IV* excludes from the definition those mood disturbances that occur solely during a delirium or that are better explained by the presence of another mood disorder.

In multiaxial coding, the medical condition is coded on Axis III, and the name of the medical condition is also used to further specify the type of mood disorder on Axis I (e.g., Mood Disorder Due to Carcinoma of the Head of the Pancreas, with Major Depressive-Like Episode). For depressive symptoms that are part of a dementia, the clinician should code the appropriate subtype of dementia.

Substance-Induced Mood Disorder

(*DSM-IV*, pp. 370–375)
    (Refer to specific substances for codes.)
    Specify type:

    −With manic features
    −With depressive features
    −With mixed features

Also, specify if:

    −Onset during intoxication
    −Onset during withdrawal

Certain substances of abuse as well as prescribed medications can provoke disturbances of mood (including depressed, expansive, irritable, hypomanic, or manic mood, or marked anhedonia without predominant depressed mood). *DSM-IV* diagnoses a Substance-Induced Mood Disorder when there is evidence from medical history, examination, or laboratory tests that the mood disturbance began within a month of substance intoxication or withdrawal or when a medication has caused the mood difficulty. As with other mental disorders, there must be significant distress or functional impairment. In addition, *DSM-IV* excludes from the criteria mood disturbances that occur solely during a delirium or that are better explained by the presence of another mood disorder.

Note that episodes of manic or hypomanic symptoms that are clearly caused by antidepressant medication (or by light therapy or ECT) do not count toward the definition of Bipolar I or Bipolar II disorders.

Mood Disorder Not Otherwise Specified (296.90)

(*DSM-IV*, pp. 318 and 375)

As usual, *DSM-IV* provides a residual category for disorders whose predominant symptom is a disturbance of mood that does not meet criteria for any of the specific mood disorders in this section of *DSM-IV*, including Depressive Disorder NOS and Bipolar Disorder NOS. For example, a client may present in an agitated, possibly hypomanic, and simultaneously depressive state. If the syndrome does not meet criteria for any of the specific mood disorders and the clinician is unable to decide between Depressive Disorder NOS and Bipolar Disorder NOS, then a diagnosis of Mood Disorder NOS is given.

Severity, Psychotic, and Remission Specifiers

DSM-IV, pp. 376–382):
Fifth Digit Codes for Current State of Major Depressive Disorders and Bipolar Disorders:
296.x0: Unspecified
296.x1: Mild
296.x2: Moderate

296.x3:   Severe, Without Psychotic Features
296.x4:   Severe, with Psychotic Features
           Mood-congruent Psychotic Features
           Mood-incongruent Psychotic Features
296.x5:   In Partial Remission
296.x6:   In Full Remission

DSM-IV allows the clinician to specify the severity of the mood episode according to the number of criteria met, the degree of distress and functional impairment, the severity of the symptoms, and the need for supervision by another person.

The clinician should also code for the presence or absence of psychotic symptoms (hallucinations, delusions, etc.) during the mood episode. The psychotic symptoms themselves can be further categorized as *Mood-Congruent* or *Mood-Incongruent*. For example, congruent depressive features might include delusions or hallucinations related to worthlessness (e.g., a voice saying "You're no good"), decay, illness, or punishment. Congruent manic psychotic features might be delusions of grandeur or special powers, being an agent of God, hearing a voice telling the individual to lead the nation to victory, and so on. In contrast, a schizophrenic young man, who became depressed, developed the noncongruent delusion that his father had become a bus seat.

Remission refers to recovery from an episode of the disorder. By definition, full remission in *DSM-IV* requires at least two months of no significant signs of the mood episode. Partial remission refers to full remission of less than two months duration or to partial recovery in which the individual suffers some mood symptoms, but does not meet full criteria for a mood episode.

CROSS SECTIONAL SYMPTOM FEATURES

Catatonic Features

(*DSM-IV*, pp. 382–383):
    For the most recent manic episode or major depressive episode:
    Specify if: With catatonic features

The new subtype *With Catatonic Features* emphasizes the clinical finding that the syndrome of catatonia is often associated with the mood disorders. In the past, catatonia was thought of mainly as a subtype of schizophrenia. The catatonic syndrome consists of motor symptoms (rigidity, posturing, stereotypies, immobility, excitement), negativism, stupor, echolalia, and echopraxia.

Melancholic Features

(*DSM-IV*, pp. 383–384):
For major depressive episodes:
Specify if: With melancholic features

Classically, individuals with melancholia were full of black bile and thus constitutionally (biologically) unable to enjoy life. Nothing would give them any pleasure. The specifier *With Melancholic Features* has a similar meaning. This specifier applies only to the current or most recent major depressive episode of a mood disorder.

After carefully reviewing the literature on melancholia, the authors of *DSM-IV* decided that the *DSM-III* definition of melancholia was superior to the one proposed in *DSM-III-R*. The new *DSM-IV* criteria for melancholia are almost the same as those from the 1980 *DSM-III* version, except that *DSM-IV* requires either a loss of pleasure or a lack of reactivity to pleasurable stimuli rather than the presence of both factors.

According to *DSM-IV*, the essential feature of melancholia is either a loss of interest or pleasure in most activities or an inability to react pleasurably to enjoyable happenings. In addition to the loss of pleasure or lack of reactivity, *DSM-IV* requires the presence of three out of six additional symptoms of the melancholic syndrome. These symptoms include a distinct quality of the depressed mood (i.e., the depressed mood feels qualitatively different from ordinary sadness or grief), excessive guilt, and certain neurovegetative features. For example, the melancholic individual may present with significant psychomotor retardation or agitation, may regularly awaken two or more hours earlier than usual (early morning awakening or EMA), may experience a marked loss of weight or appetite (anorexia), and may report feeling worst or most depressed in the morning rather than later in the day (diurnal variation).

Atypical Features

(*DSM-IV*, pp. 384–386):
For the most recent major depressive or dysthymic episode:
Specify if: With atypical features

This new subtype of *With Atypical Features* reflects the clinical literature on the existence of depressive syndromes that have an atypical symptom pattern of mood reactivity, reverse neurovegetative symptoms, and rejection sensitivity. Reverse vegetative symptoms include increased appetite, weight gain rather than loss, excessive sleep rather than insomnia, and "leaden paralysis," a heavy "leaden" feeling in the extremities. Diagnosing atypical mood disturbances may affect the choice of antidepressant medication used to treat the disorder.

COURSE SPECIFIERS

Postpartum Onset

(*DSM-IV*, pp. 386–387)
For: Bipolar I Disorder
Bipolar II Disorder
Major Depression
Brief Psychotic Disorder
Specify if: With postpartum onset (within four weeks)

The subtype *With Postpartum Onset* is new in *DSM-IV* and was included because it has implications for treatment and prognosis. By definition, this specifier means that the most recent or current major depressive, manic, or mixed mood episode began within four weeks of having a baby.

An episode of a mood disorder with postpartum onset differs from the common "baby blues," which is a brief period of dysphoric mood following delivery and lasting up to a week. Postpartum mood episodes may include troubling psychotic symptoms, command hallucinations to kill the baby, suicidal ideation, obsessions about harming the child, anxiety, panic attacks, initial or other types of insomnia, agitation, and failure to bond with the newborn. The condition occurs in about 1 in every 500 to 1000 births and carries with it the risk of the mother killing the newborn and/or herself.

Longitudinal Course

(*DSM-IV*, pp. 387–389)
For: Major Depressive Disorder, and for Bipolar I or Bipolar II Disorders
Specify: Longitudinal course:

−With full interepisode recovery
−Without full interepisode recovery

The longitudinal course specifiers allow the clinician to code the type of remission (full or partial) between the two most recent episodes of major depressive disorder, Bipolar I disorder, or Bipolar II disorder. Clinicians should also note whether the episode of major depressive or Bipolar I or II disorder is superimposed on a preexisting dysthymic disorder by separately coding the Dysthymic Disorder (300.4). Individuals with both dysthymic disorder and major depressive disorder are often said to suffer from *double depression*. *DSM-IV* (on p. 388) provides helpful diagrams to illustrate the lifetime patterns of recurrent mood episodes with and without antecedent dysthymic disorder.

Seasonal Pattern

(*DSM-IV*, pp. 389–390):
For major depressive episodes occurring in:

Bipolar I Disorder
Bipolar II Disorder
Major Depressive Disorder, Recurrent
Specify if: With seasonal pattern

DSM-IV has made several changes in the seasonal pattern specifier from *DSM-III-R*. The clinician can now apply the specifier "With

Seasonal Pattern" only to major depressive episodes that occur in the course of Bipolar I, Bipolar II, or recurrent major depressive disorders. It is no longer used to describe manic episodes. In addition, *DSM-IV* has eliminated *DSM-III-R*'s sixty-day window for the appearance of symptoms.

The idea of a seasonal pattern is that some individuals regularly experience major depressive episodes during certain seasons of the year. The fact that this pattern is more common in younger individuals living at higher latitudes suggests the likelihood of an interaction between the individual's biology and the environment. One hypothesis has been that the total duration of daylight affects the amount of melatonin in the brain, which, in turn, affects the regulation of mood. In addition, seasonal mood episodes are frequently associated with lack of energy, an excessive need for sleep, weight gain, and a craving for carbohydrates.

The clinician must consider the lifetime pattern of the affected individual's major depressive episodes. The majority of such episodes will have occurred in relation to a particular season (e.g., every autumn). The clinician cannot count episodes as seasonal if they occur in relation to an annual psychosocial stressor, such as unemployment every spring.

To qualify for the "Seasonal Pattern" specifier, *DSM-IV* requires the occurrence of a seasonal pattern of major depressive episodes with either full remission or a switch to a manic-spectrum episode that occurs at another characteristic season of the year. There must also be a history over the previous two years of at least two seasonal major depressive episodes and the absence of any nonseasonal major depressive episodes during the same two-year period.

Although not mentioned in *DSM-IV*, the senior author has noticed in his practice a pattern of bipolar mood episodes occurring regularly in relation to the two annual equinoxes. One bipolar patient, for example, suffered severe major depressive episodes every fall. When the patient reviewed the history of his multiple psychiatric hospitalizations, he discovered that they had all occurred in late September or early October, within two weeks of the Fall Equinox. In working with this patient for more than a decade, the author has observed a yearly pattern of dysphoric and psychotic symptoms beginning in late August, peaking in late September, and remitting around Christmastime. The author has treated other patients who regularly become acutely confused and manic within two weeks of the Spring Equinox. Documenting such patterns has been extremely helpful in treatment planning and preventing further hospitalizations. Clinicians may wish to mark the Fall and Spring Equinoxes on their calendars and pay attention to these *equinoctial mood episodes* (not a *DSM-IV* category).

Rapid Cycling

(*DSM-IV*, pp. 390–391):
   For: Bipolar I Disorder
   Bipolar II Disorder
   Specify if: With Rapid Cycling (four episodes in the past year)

The essential feature of this new subtype "With Rapid Cycling" is the occurrence of four or more major depressive, manic, hypomanic, or mixed mood episodes during the past year. To qualify for the "With Rapid Cycling" specifier, the individual must also have two months of partial or full remission between episodes or else must switch poles from a major depressive episode to a manic, hypomanic, or mixed episode, or vice versa.

Clinical experience suggests that the rapid cycling subtype has treatment implications. For individuals with bipolar disorder, rapid cycling is associated with a poorer long-term prognosis. It occurs in up to one-sixth of bipolar disorders and appears to be more common among women. Conditions associated with rapid cycling include a history of head trauma, mental retardation, hypothyroidism, neurological disorders, and treatment with antidepressant medications. One hypothesis is that our current antidepressant drugs may induce rapid cycling in predisposed bipolar individuals.

18

Anxiety Disorders

"Let me assert my firm belief that the only thing we have to fear is fear itself."

Franklin D. Roosevelt (1882–1945)
First Inaugural Address (March 4, 1933)

THE ANXIETY DISORDERS:

300.01	Panic Disorder without Agoraphobia
300.21	Panic Disorder with Agoraphobia
300.22	Agoraphobia without History of Panic Disorder
300.29	Specific Phobia (Simple Phobia)

Specify type:
Animal type
Natural environment type
Blood, injection, injury type
Situational type
Other type

300.23	Social Phobia (Social Anxiety Disorder)

Specify if: Generalized type (fear of most social situations; consider Avoidant Personality Disorder)

300.3	Obsessive-Compulsive Disorder

Specify if: Poor insight type (client has minimal recognition of the unreasonableness or excessive nature of the symptoms)

309.81	Posttraumatic Stress Disorder

Specify duration:
Acute (less than three months)
Chronic (three months or longer)
Specify if: With delayed onset (6 or more months after the stressor)

308.3   Acute Stress Disorder
300.02   Generalized Anxiety Disorder (including Overanxious
          Disorder of Childhood)
293.89   Anxiety Disorder due to a General Medical Condition
          Specify if:
            With generalized anxiety
            With panic attacks
            With obsessive-compulsive symptoms
---.--   Substance-Induced Anxiety Disorder (refer to specific
          substances for codes)
          Specify if:
            With generalized anxiety
            With panic attacks
            With obsessive-compulsive symptoms
            With phobic symptoms
          Specify if:
            With onset during intoxication
            With onset during withdrawal
300.00   Anxiety Disorder Not Otherwise Specified (NOS)

The anxiety disorders (along with the mood disorders and substance-related disorders) are among the most common psychiatric disorders in the general population. Kessler and his colleagues (1994) reported that in the United States the prevalence of any anxiety disorder in a national sample was 24.9 percent for a lifetime and 17.2 percent for a one-year period.

Social phobia accounted for the majority of the anxiety disorders in Kessler's study. In any given year, about 7 percent of men and 9 percent of women in the United States suffer from social phobia. In the course of a lifetime, about 11 percent of men and about 16 percent of women meet criteria for social phobia. Simple (called "Specific" in *DSM-IV*) phobias were a close second in prevalence to the social phobias. The lifetime prevalence of simple (specific) phobia is about 7 percent for men and 16 percent for women. The twelve-month prevalence of simple (specific) phobia in the United States is 4 percent for men and 13 percent for women.

The anxiety disorders are defined in terms of cognitive, somatic, and behavioral symptoms. Cognitive features include fears, worries, intrusive thoughts, obsessions, preoccupations, dissociation, and numbing. Somatic symptoms include motor tension, the startle response, autonomic hyperarousal, and other physical sensations or complaints. The behavioral aspects of the anxiety disorders include avoidance of evocative stimuli, compulsions, rituals, and compensatory behaviors.

PANIC DISORDER
WITHOUT AGORAPHOBIA (300.01)

(*DSM-IV*, pp. 394–403)

A panic attack does not a disorder make. Panic attacks may occur during several of the anxiety disorders, including panic disorder, obsessive-compulsive disorder, separation anxiety disorder, simple phobia, social phobia, acute stress disorder, and posttraumatic stress disorder. Panic attacks may also accompany other major Axis I disorders.

Panic attacks (*DSM-IV*, pp. 393–395) are discrete episodes of intense anxiety, terror, fear, or discomfort that begin suddenly and reach peak intensity within ten minutes. Panic attacks are accompanied by numerous physical and/or psychological symptoms that may include sweating, shortness of breath, rapid heart rate, palpitations, chest pain, chest discomfort, feelings of choking or smothering, tremulousness, nausea, upset stomach, urinary frequency, dizziness, giddiness, lightheadedness, numbness and tingling of the skin, chills, and hot flashes. Individuals suffering a panic attack often feel they are having a heart attack and rush to the nearest hospital emergency room. There may be feelings of loss of control or of impending doom. Some patients believe they are dying or losing their minds. *DSM-IV* lists thirteen typical panic symptoms in order of frequency and requires the presence of four out of the thirteen for the diagnosis of a panic attack.

Panic attacks may be either begin spontaneously or be triggered by environmental cues. *DSM-IV* refers to spontaneous attacks as "unexpected" or "uncued" and to triggered attacks as "situationally bound" or "cued." Unexpected panic attacks come "out of the blue" and are typical of those seen in panic disorder. Cued attacks occur in response to or in anticipation of a situational trigger. By definition, individuals with panic disorder have uncued or unexpected panic attacks, but they may suffer from situationally bound panic as well.

DSM-IV also describes a third type of panic attack according to onset, the so-called "situationally predisposed" panic attack. Such attacks are more likely to occur in response to an environmental stimulus, but do not invariably follow exposure to a situational cue, hence the idea of a "situational predisposition" to having the panic episode. Situationally predisposed panic attacks occur frequently in panic disorder, but may also be seen in simple and social phobic disorders, in PTSD, and in acute stress disorder.

To summarize, *DSM-IV* distinguishes three types of panic attacks according to onset and situational cues:

1. Unexpected or Uncued Panic Attacks (characteristic of panic disorder).
2. Situationally Bound or Cued Panic Attacks (common in phobic and stress disorders).
3. Situationally Predisposed Panic Attacks (may occur in many of the anxiety disorders).

To meet criteria for Panic Disorder Without Agoraphobia, *DSM-IV* requires the presence of recurring, unexpected panic attacks in the absence of agoraphobia. *DSM-IV* has changed the old *DSM-III-R* requirement of four attacks in four weeks or one attack followed by a month of fear of having another attack. Instead, according to the March 1994 *DSM-IV* Update, the definition now requires that the recurrent unexpected panic attacks be accompanied "by a month or more of persistent concern about having additional attacks or about the implications of the attacks, or a significant change in behavior related to the attacks" (p. 10). In addition, the panic attacks should not be more appropriately accounted for by substance use, by a general medical condition, or by another mental disorder.

PANIC DISORDER
WITH AGORAPHOBIA (300.21)

DSM-IV, pp. 393–403)

The term *agoraphobia* derives from the Greek, meaning "fear of the marketplace," and in psychiatric parlance has come to mean a fear of separation from one's source of security. *DSM-IV* has modified the

DSM-III-R definition of agoraphobia to emphasize that the agoraphobic fears typically involve a characteristic cluster of situations, such as being outside the home alone or standing in a line. *DSM-IV* defines agoraphobia as anxiety about being in a situation from which escape might prove embarrassing or difficult or where help might not be available should one have a panic attack. Many agoraphobic patients with a history of one or more panic attacks live in dread of having another panic episode. Other common agoraphobic concerns include being alone and away from home, increasing one's distance from home, standing in line at a store, experiencing medical symptoms such as diarrhea or fainting in public, feeling trapped in a small space such as a vehicle or elevator, being on a bridge, and being in a crowd. Some agoraphobic individuals report suffering anxiety in response to cloudy, depressing weather.

To meet criteria for Panic Disorder with Agoraphobia, the individual must suffer from both panic disorder (as described above) and agoraphobia. In addition, the affected individual must avoid the agoraphobic situations (e.g., become housebound, restrict travel) or endure the feared situations with distress or anxious anticipation of having a panic attack or require the accompaniment of a companion.

AGORAPHOBIA WITHOUT HISTORY OF PANIC DISORDER (300.22)

(*DSM-IV*, pp. 403–405)

To meet criteria for Agoraphobia without History of Panic Disorder, the individual must suffer from agoraphobia (as described above) in the absence of any history of a panic disorder. The affected individual must avoid the agoraphobic situations (e.g., become housebound, restrict travel) or endure the feared situations with distress or anxiety about suffering a panic attack or require the accompaniment of a companion. The anxiety and phobic avoidance must not be due to another mental disorder, and the anxiety must not be caused by substance use or a general medical condition. If there is a concomitant medical condition, the fear of suffering medical symptoms in public must be in excess of that usually associated with the condition. (*DSM-III-R* had provided no guidance on the issue of phobic avoidance associated with a general medical condition.)

SPECIFIC PHOBIA (FORMERLY SIMPLE PHOBIA) *(300.29)*

(DSM-IV, pp. 405–411)
Specify type:

- —Animal type
- —Natural environment type
- —Blood-injection-injury type
- —Situational type
- —Other type (e.g., phobic avoidance of diagnostic manuals)

A phobia is an irrational fear of an object, place, activity, or situation. The anxiety in phobic disorders is situationally bound, that is, cued by exposure to a dreaded stimulus.

To maintain compatibility with *ICD-10, DSM-IV* changed the name of Simple Phobia *(DSM-III-R)* to Specific Phobia in *DSM-IV.* Some common specific phobias include an irrational fear of spiders, snakes, insects, blood, heights, loud noises, and lightning or thunder. Nosologists (no doubt suffering from neologophilia) love to coin obscure Greek terms for each specific phobia (e.g., kakorrhaphio-phobia for fear of failure). Rather than list dozens of such Greek neologisms, *DSM-IV* provides a sensible list of general subtypes (animal type, natural environmental type, etc.) to specify the focus of the phobia.

To meet criteria for Specific (Simple) Phobia, an individual must have a marked, persistent, excessive or unreasonable fear of a specific object or situation. Except in the case of children, the phobic individual must recognize that the fear is unreasonable or excessive. When exposed to the phobic stimulus, the individual suffers symptoms of anxiety or panic. As a result, individuals avoid the phobic stimuli or endure them with severe anxiety or distress. As with other mental disorders, the symptoms produce significant distress or impaired functioning. Finally, another mental disorder must not better account for the symptoms of anxiety, panic, and phobic avoidance seen in this disorder.

The differential diagnosis of Specific Phobia includes other mental disorders characterized by anxiety, panic, and phobic avoidance. In OCD there may be specific fears and avoidance of dirt or contamination. In PTSD there is avoidance of stimuli associated with the traumatic event. Children with separation anxiety disorder fear leaving their mothers and avoid attending school. Individuals with social phobia stay away from social situations out of a fear of embarrassment. Agoraphobic individuals avoid being alone or going far away from home. Those with panic disorder suffer severe anxiety and panic attacks.

SOCIAL PHOBIA (SOCIAL ANXIETY DISORDER) (300.23)

(DSM-IV, pp. 411–417)

Specify if: Generalized type (fear of most social situations; also consider avoidant personality disorder)

To meet criteria for Social Phobia, an individual must have a marked, persistent, excessive or unreasonable fear of being humiliated or embarrassed in social or performance situation(s) involving strangers or scrutiny by others. Except in the case of children, the phobic individual must recognize that the fear is unreasonable or excessive. When exposed to the phobic stimulus, the socially phobic individual experiences anxiety or panic. As a result, individuals avoid social or performance situations or else endure them with severe anxiety or distress. As with other mental disorders, the symptoms produce significant distress or impaired functioning. The social anxiety and/or avoidance are not due to substance use, a general medical condition, or another mental disorder.

The DSM-IV category of Social Phobia now subsumes the DSM-III-R category of Avoidant Disorder of Childhood. The presentation of social phobia may differ from the clinical picture seen in adulthood. Children often express anxiety through crying, temper tantrums, frozen behavior, or social withdrawal. To meet criteria for the disorder, the child must have demonstrated a capacity for social relations with familiar individuals and must exhibit anxiety in situations involving peers.

OBSESSIVE-COMPULSIVE DISORDER (OCD) (300.3)

(*DSM-IV*, pp. 417–423)
Specify if: With Poor insight (client has minimal recognition of the unreasonableness or excessive nature of the symptoms)

"Out, damned spot! out I say!"

Lady Macbeth, *Macbeth*, Act V, Scene i

"The Tempter came upon me again, and that with a more grievous and dreadful Temptation than before. And it was, *To sell and part with this most blessed Christ, to exchange Him for the things of this life, for anything.* The Temptation lay upon me for the space of a year, and did follow me so continually that I was not rid of it one day in a month, no, not sometimes one hour in many days together, unless when I was asleep. . . .

Sometimes it would run in my thoughts, not so little as a hundred times together, *Sell Him, Sell Him*; against which I may say, for whole hours together, I have been forced to stand as continually leaning and forcing my spirit against it, lest haply, before I were aware, some wicked thought might arise in my heart that might consent thereto. . . ."

John Bunyan, *Grace Abounding to the Chief of Sinners*

The above two quotations refer to literary figures who suffered from obsessive-compulsive symptoms. Obsessions refer to certain recurrent mental processes that cause anxiety or distress, and compulsions refer to thoughts or behaviors intended to reduce the distress of the obsession or to undo the harm to oneself or to others suggested by the obsessive thought. In other words, *DSM-IV* views obsessions as causing marked anxiety or distress and compulsions (including compulsive mental acts) as preventing or diminishing the anxiety or distress.

Obsessions consist of distressing, recurrent, unwanted thoughts, impulses, or images that intrude into the mental life of an individual who recognizes them as products of his or her own mind. Obsessions are persistent and inappropriate mental products that the individual tries to ignore, suppress, counteract, control, or neutralize with alternate thoughts or activities. Obsessive mentations are often, but not invariably, viewed as unreasonable, excessive, or senseless by affected individuals. Obsessions are not simply excessive worries about real concerns, nor are they intrusive thoughts, such as thought insertion, that are part of a psychotic process. In the *DSM-IV* field trials, the majority of people who were diagnosed with OCD were not certain whether their obsessions and compulsions were unreasonable or excessive. Because insight into the unreasonableness of obsessive-compulsive symptoms occurs on a continuum, *DSM-IV* allows the clinician to code a "poor insight" type.

The most common obsessions deal with themes of aggression, contamination, and arrangement or symmetry. Doubt and worry usually accompany the obsessive thinking. Individuals may have intrusive thoughts about suicide, homicide, accidents, injury, or the death of someone. Sometimes there is a persistent urge to be violent toward a loved one or an unrealistic fear of having hurt someone. There may be intrusive ideas about illness due to germs, HIV infection, or other contaminants, and often there are worries about becoming infected by touching another person. The asymmetry of paintings on a wall or of books on a shelf may cause intense discomfort until they are put into an orderly arrangement.

Other themes found in obsessional thinking include concerns about sexuality, sexual identity, dirt, germs, toxins, excrement, hoarding and collecting items, inability to discard useless possessions, feeling overly responsible for the safety of others, concern with bodily secretions, religious preoccupations, blasphemous thoughts, sinfulness, and somatic concerns about appearance or health. Some individuals experience the unwanted intrusion into consciousness of nonsensical sounds, words, numbers, images, or of profane and irreligious thoughts during prayer. Many superstitious beliefs (e.g., lucky and unlucky numbers, avoiding black cats) are obsessional in nature and are characterized by magical thinking.

Compulsions are thoughts or behaviors that a person uses to reduce the distress caused by obsessive symptoms or to avert a dreaded event that the individual fears may occur if the compulsive act or thought is not carried out. Such compulsive thoughts and behaviors are typically repetitive and ritualistic and bear only the most remote realistic relationship to the distressing obsession or dreaded situation. The individual feels driven to complete compulsive acts according to an exacting set of rules. People with OCD often know that their symptoms are irrational, but feel unable to control them.

In the *DSM-IV* field trials, the majority of persons with OCD reported suffering both mental and behavioral compulsions. Common compulsive behaviors include handwashing, bathing, touching, cleaning, checking, hoarding, counting, avoiding stepping on cracks, and arranging things in an orderly manner. Typical compulsive mentations include praying, repeating words or phrases silently, repeatedly performing the same activity, and counting. The rituals provide short-term relief at the cost of long-term and time-consuming repetitions of the ritualistic behaviors. Usually the rituals follow an exact set of rules, and if the patient makes a mistake, he or she must start the whole process over. For example, one patient felt a bump in the road while driving. He became obsessed with the idea that he had run over a pedestrian and had to repeatedly retrace his automobile route to reassure himself that he had not struck anyone.

To meet criteria for the diagnosis of OCD, *DSM-IV* requires the presence of obsessions or compulsions that at some point the adult sufferer regards as either excessive or unreasonable (this excessive/unreasonable criterion does not apply to children). By definition the symptoms must cause significant distress or impairment, and *DSM-IV* also requires that the symptoms consume more than an hour a day of the individual's time. The content of the obsessions or compulsions must not be restricted solely to another Axis I disorder, and the symptoms must not be due to substance use or to a general medical condition.

Because individuals with OCD may not regard their obsessions or compulsions as excessive or unreasonable, *DSM-IV* provides the specifier "Poor Insight Type" to further categorize OCD.

Genetic, behavior, psychoanalytic, and neurobiological theories have been advanced to explain the origins of OCD. There is much support for a biological substrate of OCD. Family studies reveal a high prevalence of OCD among first-degree relatives of OCD sufferers. In addition, Tourette's disorder and major depression appear to be linked to OCD. Psychotropic medications that affect serotonin systems in the brain by blocking serotonin reuptake (e.g., clomipramine/Anafranil, fluoxetine/Prozac) can dramatically reduce obsessive-compulsive symptomatology.

Impairment from OCD ranges from mild to severe. In some cases the symptoms can be immobilizing. People with OCD often feel demoralized and frequently suffer recurrent major depressive episodes. According to the OC Foundation, Inc., (P.O. Box 70, Milford, CT 06460-0070), about 5 million Americans suffer from OCD at some time in their lives.

The differential diagnosis of OCD includes the many other psychiatric disorders that overlap with OCD. Severe obsessions sometimes resemble the delusional thinking seen in schizophrenia and other psychotic disorders. As mentioned above, major depression is a common accompaniment of OCD. Other anxiety disorders may coexist with OCD. Childhood disorders like Tourette's (tic) syndrome, autism, and trichotillomania (compulsive hair pulling) often have obsessive-compulsive features. The intrusive traumatic memories of posttraumatic stress disorder resemble obsessions. Individuals with body dysmorphic disorder become obsessively preoccupied with minor or imagined bodily defects, and people with hypochondriasis occupy their minds with unfounded fears of having a serious illness. In addition, the ritualistic behaviors seen in anorexia nervosa are similar to the compulsions of OCD. Unlike the compulsive behaviors seen in pathological gambling, overeating, or substance abuse, the compulsions of OCD are not inherently pleasurable.

Obsessive-compulsive personality disorder and obsessive-compulsive disorder appear to be distinct entities. Although many OCD patients report premorbid obsessive-compulsive traits, a significant number of OCD patients do not meet criteria for premorbid obsessive-compulsive personality disorder. There is not a one-to-one relationship between the two disorders.

POSTTRAUMATIC STRESS DISORDER (PTSD) (309.81)

(DSM-IV, pp. 424–429)
The authors of *DSM-IV* deleted the *DSM-III-R* criterion that a stressor must be "outside the range of normal human experience" because it was shown in the field trials and in data reanalysis and literature review to be both unreliable and inaccurate. It is a sad comment on contemporary American society that the types of stres-

sors capable of provoking a posttraumatic stress disorder are well within the range of normal human experience for much of the population. For example, the senior author gave a talk on stress disorders to a group of sophomores at a high school in Bridgeport, Connecticut. Eight out of the twenty-one high school students attending the lecture had suffered gunshot wounds simply growing up and playing on the streets of Bridgeport!

In PTSD the individual has experienced a traumatic event that involves a threat of "death or serious injury, or a threat to the physical integrity of oneself or others" (*DSM-IV*, p. 427) (e.g., rape) and has reacted with feelings of horror, extreme fright, or helplessness. The individual repeatedly reexperiences the traumatic event, avoids anything that evokes remembrance of the event, experiences a sense of emotional numbing or unresponsiveness, and has symptoms of hyperarousal. Commonly, individuals with PTSD have intrusive thoughts or memories of the event, suffer "flashbacks," feel emotionally detached and blunted, startle easily, and have trouble sleeping and difficulty concentrating while awake. *DSM-IV* provides a specific list of symptoms to assist in making the diagnosis. By definition, the symptoms of PTSD last for more than one month and cause significant distress and/or impaired functioning.

PTSD can be further specified by duration or by onset as follows:

Duration:
   Acute (less than three months)
   Chronic (three months or longer)
   Onset, specify if: With delayed onset (six or more months after the stressor)

ACUTE STRESS DISORDER (308.3)

(*DSM-IV*, pp. 429–432)

Acute Stress Disorder is a new category introduced into *DSM-IV* to describe acute short-term reactions to severe stress. The authors of *DSM-IV* added Acute Stress Disorder to the manual to maintain compatibility with *ICD-10* and to foster early identification of cases. The presence of acute stress disorder may predict the later development of a posttraumatic stress disorder.

The symptoms of acute stress disorder are similar to those of PTSD. The individual has experienced a traumatic event that involves the threat of "death or serious injury, or a threat to the physical integrity of oneself or others" and has reacted with feelings of horror, extreme fright, or helplessness. During or immediately after the traumatic event, the individual experiences at least three of five dissociative symptoms, including depersonalization, derealization, amnesia, reduced awareness, and/or a sense of detachment, numbing, or unresponsiveness.

The individual also experiences intrusive thoughts, images, or memories of the traumatic event; distress when reminded of the traumatic event; and anxiety and/or increased arousal. As is true with all mental disorders, there must be clinically significant distress or impaired functioning. By definition, the symptoms begin within four weeks of a traumatic event and last for at least two days, but for no more than four weeks. In addition, the symptoms are not due to substance use, to a general medical condition, or to another mental disorder.

Both PTSD and acute stress disorder have in common: (1) exposure to a traumatic event that threatens life or physical integrity, (2) a reaction of fear, horror, or helplessness, (3) recurrent reexperiencing of the trauma, (4) avoidance of evocative stimuli, (5) increased arousal, and (6) significant distress or impaired functioning. Acute stress disorder also requires significant dissociative symptoms that may be but are not necessarily part of PTSD. In addition, the symptoms of acute stress disorder begin within four weeks of the event and last from two days to a maximum of four weeks. By contrast, PTSD can have delayed onset, with symptoms beginning more than six months after the traumatic event.

GENERALIZED ANXIETY DISORDER (INCLUDING OVERANXIOUS DISORDER OF CHILDHOOD) (GAD) (300.02)

(*DSM-IV*, pp. 432–436)
Some people are chronically nervous. They feel anxious, apprehensive, and worried about a variety of situations most of the time

and are unable to control their excessive fearfulness. They do not meet criteria for any of the other specific anxiety disorders. To categorize the generalized, persistent anxiety of such individuals, *DSM-III* introduced the diagnosis of Generalized Anxiety Disorder (GAD) in 1980.

According to *DSM-IV*, the diagnosis of GAD requires "excessive anxiety and worry" about several situations, as well as difficulty controlling the worry. (*DSM-IV* has dropped the old *DSM-III-R* criterion that the worry be unrealistic.) The anxiety and worry must be present for at least six months for "more days than not." In addition, *DSM-IV* requires the presence of at least three out of six anxiety symptoms (there were eighteen items in *DSM-III-R*), including such items as feeling restless, fatigued, or irritable, or having muscle tension, poor concentration, or trouble sleeping. The anxiety must not be the result of substance use or of a general medical condition. As with other disorders, the symptoms must cause significant distress or impairment. Finally, the anxiety must not be characteristic of another Axis I disorder or specific anxiety disorder, such as social phobia, specific phobia, panic disorder, agoraphobia, PTSD, acute stress disorder, hypochondriasis, and so on.

The following two categories, which are defined by etiology (i.e., due to a general medical condition, or substance induced), are included in the Anxiety Disorders section of *DSM-IV* to facilitate differential diagnosis.

ANXIETY DISORDER DUE TO A GENERAL MEDICAL CONDITION (293.89)

(*DSM-IV*, pp. 436–439)
   Specify if:

   −With generalized anxiety
   −With panic attacks
   −With obsessive-compulsive symptoms

As the name implies, this condition refers to an anxiety disorder that is due to a general medical condition (excluding delirium and dementia) as evidenced by the medical history, laboratory tests, or physical examination. The prominent symptoms may be feelings of anxiety, panic attacks, and/or obsessive-compulsive features not occurring exclusively during the course of a delirium or a dementia. As with all mental disorders, there must be significant distress or impaired functioning. In addition, the symptoms must not be better accounted for by another mental disorder such as an adjustment disorder with anxiety in response to a general medical condition.

Substance-Induced Anxiety Disorder

(DSM-IV, pp. 439–444)
   (Refer to specific substances for codes.)
   Specify if:

   —With generalized anxiety
   —With panic attacks
   —With obsessive-compulsive symptoms
   —With phobic symptoms

   Specify if:

   —With onset during intoxication
   —With onset during withdrawal

Many substances (including medications) can induce symptoms such as anxiety, panic, obsessions, or compulsions. In some cases these symptoms occur during intoxication and in other cases during withdrawal. Researchers sometimes take advantage of substance-induced symptoms to study the anxiety disorders. Sodium lactate, for example, can induce panic attacks when given to experimental subjects. Clinicians should be aware that some of the drugs used to treat psychiatric disorders may cause anxiety as a side effect.

According to *DSM-IV,* the diagnosis of Substance-Induced Anxiety Disorder can be made when significant anxiety, panic, obsessions, or compulsions occur within a month of substance intoxication or withdrawal and are not better accounted for by another specific anxiety disorder. *DSM-IV* requires that the anxiety symptoms not occur solely during the course of delirium or dementia and that they cause significant distress or impaired functioning.

The Substance-Induced Anxiety Disorder is coded according to the specific substance involved, as follows:

Alcohol (291.8)
Amphetamine or related substance (292.89)
Caffeine (292.89)
Cannabis (292.89)
Cocaine (292.89)
Hallucinogen (292.89)
Inhalant (292.89)
Phencyclidine or related substance (292.89)
Sedative, Hypnotic, or Anxiolytic (292.89)
Other or Unknown Substance (292.89)

ANXIETY DISORDER NOT OTHERWISE SPECIFIED (NOS) (300.00)

(*DSM-IV*, p. 444)

This is a residual category for disorders that are characterized by anxiety or phobic avoidance, but that do not meet criteria for any of the specific anxiety disorders, nor for an adjustment disorder with either anxiety or with mixed anxiety and depressed mood.

Appendix B of *DSM-IV* includes criteria for a *Mixed Anxiety-Depressive Disorder* (*DSM-IV*, pp. 723–725), which could be coded in this NOS category.

19

Somatoform Disorders

"Anyone who takes up psycho-analytic work will quickly discover that a symptom has more than one meaning and serves to represent several unconscious mental processes simultaneously."

Sigmund Freud, *Fragment of an Analysis of a Case of Hysteria,*
Standard Edition, Vol, VII (1905), p. 47

THE SOMATOFORM DISORDERS:

300.81   Somatization Disorder (Briquet's Syndrome)
300.81   Undifferentiated Somatoform Disorder
300.11   Conversion Disorder
             Specify type of symptom or deficit:
                With motor symptom or deficit
                With sensory symptom or deficit
                With seizures or convulsions
                With mixed presentation
307.80   Pain Disorder Associated with Psychological Factors
             Specify duration.
                Acute (less than six months)
                Chronic (six months or longer)
307.89   Pain Disorder Associated with Both Psychological Factors
             and a General Medical Condition
                Acute (less than six months)
                Chronic (six months or longer)
             For Pain Disorder Associated with a General Medical
             Condition (without psychological factors, this is not a
             mental disorder), code the Anatomical Site on Axis III:
789.0   Abdominal
724.5   Back
611.71   Breast

786.50	Chest
388.70	Ear
379.91	Eye
784.0	Headache
719.40	Joint
729.5	Limb
625.9	Pelvic
788.0	Renal Colic
719.41	Shoulder
784.1	Throat
529.6	Tongue
525.9	Tooth
788.0	Urinary
300.7	Hypochondriasis
	Specify if: with poor insight (client has minimal recognition of the unreasonableness or excessive nature of the symptoms)
300.7	Body Dysmorphic Disorder
300.81	Somatoform Disorder Not Otherwise Specified (NOS)

The term *somatoform* derives from the Greek *soma*, meaning "body." The essential feature of somatoform disorders is the presence of bodily complaints in the absence of explanatory physical pathology. Individuals with somatoform disorders are often said to "somatize"—that is, to experience emotional conflict or distress in the form of a physical ailment. *DSM-IV* provides seven broad groups of somatoform disorders: Somatization, Conversion, Hypochondriasis, Body Dysmorphic, Pain, and Undifferentiated Somatoform Disorders, and a Not Otherwise Specified category. We will review each disorder in more detail.

SOMATIZATION DISORDER (BRIQUET'S SYNDROME) (300.81)

(*DSM-IV*, pp. 446–450)

In the older literature, somatization disorder was known as *hysteria*, a term derived from the Greek for uterus. In fact, the ancient Greeks reportedly attributed the cause of the dramatic and multiple bodily symptoms affecting certain women to the wanderings of the uterus. Based on this theory of etiology, the Greek doctors apparently placed fragrant substances near the vagina to attract the uterus back to its proper place. Modern psychiatric nosology has dropped the term *hysteria* because of its misleading implication that somatization is a disorder of the uterus rather than of the mind.

Hysteria played a major role in the development of psychoanalysis. Sigmund Freud attended Jean Martin Charcot's neurology clinic in Paris to study the disorder and later developed many of the techniques of psychoanalysis in his efforts to treat patients with hysterical symptoms. Freud believed that his female patients with hysteria suffered from "reminiscences"—that is, from emotionally laden, conflictual memories that had been repressed (rendered unconscious) and then had emerged under disguise in the form of physical ailments or loss of functioning.

Much like the term *borderline personality* in modern psychiatry, the label *hysterical* came to have a pejorative connotation. Doctors used the label *hysteria* to refer to impossible-to-treat, difficult, demanding women with numerous unfounded physical complaints. In an effort to bring scientific enlightenment to the diagnosis of hysteria, researchers in 1962 proposed "Briquet's checklist" of signs and symptoms, after the French physician Paul Briquet, who redefined hysteria in 1859 as a disorder of multiple physical symptoms (i.e., a polysymptomatic disorder). Briquet's checklist became the basis of the diagnosis of hysteria (Somatization Disorder) in *DSM-III* and *DSM-III-R*.

Diagnosing Briquet's Syndrome in *DSM-III* and *DSM-III-R*, however, was an onerous task. The clinician had to sift through a list of thirty-five diagnostic items in Briquet's checklist and could make the diagnosis if the patient suffered thirteen out of the thirty-five unexplained symptoms. *DSM-IV* has greatly simplified the diagnosis of Somatization Disorder by condensing the thirty-five somatization items into four broad groupings: pain (e.g., headache, backache), gastrointestinal (e.g., nausea, diarrhea), sexual (e.g., anorgasmia, menstrual problems), and pseudoneurological (e.g., paralysis, globus hystericus, double vision, anesthesia) symptoms.

According to *DSM-IV*, Somatization Disorder is characterized by multiple physical complaints that begin before age 30 and continue for several years. These physical complaints either have no medical or substance-related etiology or the intensity of the complaints cannot be explained by an existing medical condition. The physical complaints cause the patient to seek medical treatment or bring about significantly impaired functioning. *DSM-IV* has reduced the thirty-five-item Briquet's checklist, now requiring that the patient have four pain symptoms, two gastrointestinal symptoms, one sexual symptom, and one pseudoneurological symptom. In *DSM-V*, we may code such individuals as 4P2G1S1P.

Somatization disorder appears to run in families and is more common among women. Interestingly, the male relatives of women with this disorder have a significant incidence of antisocial personality disorder and substance-related disorders. Problems associated with somatization disorder include repeated surgeries and unnecessary medical workups, marital difficulties, substance abuse, major depressive episodes, suicide attempts, panic disorder, and personality disorders, especially the Cluster B dramatic personality disorders.

UNDIFFERENTIATED SOMATOFORM DISORDER (300.81)

(*DSM-IV*, pp. 450–452)

Undifferentiated Somatoform Disorder is a residual category for individuals who do not meet full criteria for Somatization Disorder (300.81) or for another somatoform disorder, but who have one or more unexplained physical complaints of at least six months duration. As with most *DSM-IV* disorders, the physical symptoms that cannot be fully explained by a general medical condition or by substance use must cause significant distress or impairment. In addition, the physical complaints must not be intentionally feigned, as happens in malingering and in factitious disorder.

The four most common complaints seen in undifferentiated somatoform disorder are unexplained fatigue, decreased appetite, gastrointestinal upset, and genitourinary symptoms. If the patient meets all but the six-month duration criterion for this disorder, a diagnosis of Somatoform Disorder NOS should be given. Undifferentiated somatoform disorder also needs to be distinguished from disorders that also may present unexplained physical symptoms including major depressive episode, schizophrenia, anxiety disorders, and adjustment disorders.

CONVERSION DISORDER (300.11)

(*DSM-IV*, pp. 452–457):
Specify type of symptom or deficit (adapted from *ICD-10*):

−With motor symptom or deficit
−With seizures or convulsions
−With sensory symptom or deficit
−With mixed presentation

Freud's patient Dora lost her voice when the man she loved went away on a business trip. There was no medical or neurological explanation for her aphonia. Freud concluded that Dora suffered from conversion hysteria and made the following symbolic interpretation: "When the man she loved was away she gave up speaking; speech had lost its value since she could not speak to *him*" (Freud, *Standard Edition*, vol. VII, p. 40). The idea of a psychological impulse or conflict being expressed through physical symptoms became a key psychoanalytic explanation of conversion.

The definition of Conversion Disorder has changed in *DSM-IV*. The older *DSM-III-R* concept of conversion included the loss or alteration of physical functioning suggestive of a physical disorder. The *DSM-IV* definition of Conversion Disorder now requires the presenting problem to be a symptom or deficit that affects either voluntary motor or sensory functioning and mimics a neurological or medical disorder. Whereas *DSM-III-R* required the clinician to judge whether psychological factors are "etiologically related" to the conversion symptom, *DSM-IV* only requires that psychological factors are judged to "be associated" with the conversion symptom or deficit.

DSM-IV now puts the older *DSM-III-R* disorders that involve alterations in functioning (e.g., false pregnancy) into the Somatoform Disorder Not Otherwise Specified category. To be compatible with *ICD-10*, *DSM-IV* has also added motor, seizure, sensory, and mixed subtypes to specify the symptoms or deficits seen in the conversion disorder.

According to *DSM-IV*, the diagnosis of Conversion Disorder requires the presence of one or more physical symptoms or deficits "associated with" psychological factors that affect voluntary motor or sensory bodily functions. The conversion symptoms or deficits, which by definition cause significant distress or impairment, are suggestive of medical or neurological disorder in the absence of a fully explanatory medical, neurological, or substance-related etiology. The symptoms are not feigned, as occurs in malingering and in factitious disorder. If the unexplained symptoms are limited to pain or to sexual problems, a diagnosis of Pain Disorder or of Sexual Dysfunction is given instead.

Conversion symptoms or deficits often conform to the patient's concept of disease or human anatomy rather than to a scientific understanding of the human body. For example, conversion anesthesia may occur on the entire hands and feet (stocking and glove anesthesia) rather than following the course of the actual distribution of the nerves of the skin. Nonetheless, the diagnosis of conversion can be difficult to make because many times (in some studies, up to a third of cases) the patient is later diagnosed with a medical illness that could have accounted for the presumed conversion symptom. Clinicians should read the classic paper by E.T.O. Slater and E. Glithero (1965) entitled "A Follow-Up of Patients Diagnosed as Suffering from 'Hysteria.' "

The literature seems to support a subtype (not included in *DSM-IV*) of good prognosis conversion disorder. Favorable prognostic factors include acute onset, presence of a definite precipitating stressor, good premorbid functioning, and the absence of a general medical condition or of another major psychiatric disorder. Interestingly, some of these factors resemble the good prognostic features of schizophreniform disorder.

Conversion disorder not uncommonly occurs with a major depressive episode, dissociative disorder, schizophrenia, somatization disorder, and personality disorders. There are reports in the literature of associated suicide. In addition, the conversion symptoms or deficits themselves can be severely disabling.

PAIN DISORDERS

(DSM-IV, pp. 458–462)
Pain Disorder Associated with Psychological Factors (307.80):
Specify duration:

−Acute (less than six months)
−Chronic (six months or longer)

Pain Disorder Associated with Both Psychological Factors and a General Medical Condition (307.89):
Specify duration:

—Acute (less than six months)
—Chronic (six months or longer)

For Pain Disorder Associated with a General Medical Condition (without psychological factors; not a mental disorder), code Axis III for the anatomical site (see list at beginning of this chapter).

The essential feature of the pain disorders is the presence of clinically significant pain related to psychological factors that clearly affect the onset, intensity, persistence, or worsening of the pain. There may or may not be a coexisting medical illness. If organic pathology exists, the pain of pain disorder far exceeds what is customary for the medical disorder.

DSM-IV simplified the name from *DSM-III-R*'s Somatoform Pain Disorder to Pain Disorder in the new manual. *DSM-IV* also expanded the definition of Pain Disorder to include pain associated with psychological factors as well as pain associated with both psychological factors and a general medical condition. The clinician is asked to subtype each pain disorder by course, that is, as either acute (less than six months duration) or chronic (more than six months duration).

For the diagnosis of Pain Disorder, *DSM-IV* requires that psychological factors play an important role in the pain symptoms. As with most *DSM-IV* disorders, the predominant symptom of pain must cause significant distress or impairment. In addition, the pain or presumed pain must not be better explained as part of a factious disorder or malingering (feigned self-induced pain), a mood disorder, an anxiety disorder, or a psychotic disorder.

If the pain occurs with sexual intercourse and the client meets criteria for Dyspareunia (302.76), a diagnosis of Pain Disorder cannot be made.

If the pain is associated only with a general medical condition and psychological factors play a minimal or no role in the onset, exacerbation, intensity, or persistence of the pain, then the *ICD-9-CM* diagnosis of Pain Disorder Associated with a General Medical Condition can be coded on Axis III. A pain disorder without psychological factors is not considered a mental disorder in *DSM-IV*.

HYPOCHONDRIASIS (300.7)

(*DSM-IV*, pp. 462–465)

Specify if: With poor insight (client has minimal recognition of the unreasonableness or excessive nature of the symptoms). This "poor insight" specifier is new in *DSM-IV*.

Individuals with hypochondriasis blow minor bodily symptoms out of proportion. A slight ache, pain, or spot on the skin leads to an intense anxious preoccupation with having a serious medical illness. Usually the hypochondriacal individual seeks medical attention, but is not reassured by negative findings or the doctor's reassurance.

For example, a young man with well-controlled bipolar disorder went with some friends to a striptease show in a sleazy part of New York City. After the performance, the dancers mixed with the men in the audience. The patient made a lewd remark to one of the female dancers, provoking her to spit at him. The woman's saliva struck the patient in the eye. Shortly thereafter, the young man became preoccupied with the fear that he would get AIDS from the dancer's saliva because "all those women are prostitutes and probably carry the AIDS virus." His anxious worry about having contracted AIDS persisted for almost a year despite repeated reassurance by his internist and several negative blood tests for the HIV virus. Only when a year had passed with repeatedly negative HIV testing did his hypochondriacal preoccupation subside and eventually disappear.

For the diagnosis of Hypochondriasis, *DSM-IV* requires the presence of at least six months of non-delusional preoccupation with the fear or idea of having a serious medical illness based on a misinterpretation of one's physical symptoms. The hypochondriacal preoccupation persists despite a negative medical work-up and the doctor's reassurance. As is true with most *DSM-IV* disorders, the hypochondriacal concern causes significant distress or impairment. If the somatic preoccupation deals solely with an imagined defect in bodily appearance, a Body Dysmorphic Disorder is diagnosed instead. In addition, the somatic concern is not better explained as part of another *DSM-IV* disorder, such as Generalized Anxiety Disorder, Obsessive-Compulsive Disorder, Panic Disorder, Major Depressive Episode, Separation Anxiety Disorder, or Somatoform Disorder.

Hypochondriacal concerns can be of delusional proportions. In such cases the clinician should consider a Psychotic Disorder diagnosis. As with conversion disorder, it is important to rule out the possibility of an underlying, occult medical or neurological condition.

BODY DYSMORPHIC DISORDER (300.7)

(*DSM-IV*, pp. 466–468)

The essential feature of body dysmorphic disorder is an inordinate preoccupation with an imagined or minor defect in one's physical appearance. By definition, this preoccupation causes markedly distress or impairment and must not be better explained by another mental disorder. For example, the unrealistic appraisal of one's obesity seen in anorexia nervosa does not qualify for the diagnosis of Body Dysmorphic Disorder.

Individuals with body dysmorphic disorder often feel ugly. They report being embarrassed or tormented by their imagined defects of appearance, and they may withdraw from social contacts to avoid being observed by others. In addition, body dysmorphic disorder may coexist with mood disorders, delusional disorders, schizophrenia, social phobia, and obsessive-compulsive disorder.

For example, an 18-year-old man had been preoccupied with some slight excess breast tissue in his mid-teens. He would not remove his shirt in public and avoided going to the beach and other activities where his breasts might be seen. He visited numerous plastic surgeons, who all refused an operation to alter the appearance of his breasts. At age 18 he developed a profound retarded major depressive episode. He was placed on antidepressant medication and within several days suffered a full-blown manic episode.

In *DSM-III-R* one could not diagnose Body Dysmorphic Disorder if the imagined body defect were of delusional proportions as occurs in delusional disorder, somatic type. *DSM-IV* now allows delusional somatic preoccupations in the new definition of Body Dysmorphic Disorder. In other words, one can now suffer from both a body dysmorphic disorder and a delusional disorder at the same time.

In *Koro*, a culture-bound syndrome of Southeast Asia, a man develops a fear of death connected to an anxious concern that his penis is shrinking and disappearing into his abdominal cavity.

SOMATOFORM DISORDER NOT OTHERWISE SPECIFIED (300.81)

(*DSM-IV*, pp. 468–469):

As usual, *DSM-IV* provides another residual category for disorders that do not meet criteria for any of the specific somatoform disorders above, including undifferentiated somatoform disorder. For example, an individual who meets all but the six-month duration criteria for one of the specific somatoform disorders could be coded as having a Somatoform Disorder NOS. *DSM-IV* also places pseudocyesis (false pregnancy) in this NOS category.

20

Factitious Disorders

"There's a sucker born every minute."
Saying attributed to Phineas T. Barnum (1810–1891)

CODES FOR FACTITIOUS DISORDERS (*DSM-IV*, pp. 471–475):
300.16   Factitious Disorder with Predominantly Psychological
          Signs and Symptoms
300.19   Factitious Disorder with Predominantly Physical Signs
          and Symptoms (Munchausen's Syndrome)
300.19   Factitious Disorder with Combined Psychological and
          Physical Signs and Symptoms
300.19   Factitious Disorder Not Otherwise Specified (NOS)

The word *factitious* comes from the Latin verb *facere*, meaning to act or to do. Anything factitious is made up or artificial, as opposed to being natural, genuine, or spontaneous. The essence of the factitious disorders is that they are intentionally made up by patients who are seeking to assume the sick role and who have no external incentives for deliberately feigning the signs and symptoms of a physical or mental illness. The absence of ulterior motives for faking illness distinguishes Factitious Disorder from Malingering (V65.2).

Patients with factitious disorder sometimes make hospitalization a way of life, the so-called "hospital hoboes." A colorful synonym for Factitious Disorder with physical symptoms is *Munchausen's syndrome*, a term coined by Richard Asher (1951) after the German cavalry officer Karl Friedrich Hieronymus, Freiherr von Münchhausen (1720–1797), who was known for his exaggerated renderings of his adventures. A compulsive need to assume the sick role is a proposed mechanism for the generation of this disorder. According to some estimates, as many as 10 percent of hospital admissions may be for factitious disorders.

In recent years there have been a number of reports of parents feigning illness in their children rather than in themselves, a kind of factitious disorder by proxy. The parent may either falsely report symptoms about the child or actually induce the child to become ill. As a result, the child suffers repeated, unnecessary hospitalizations to satisfy the parent's needs.

Appendix B of *DSM-IV* contains a criteria set for Factitious Disorder by Proxy (DSM-IV, pp. 725–727). The essential feature of this research diagnosis is the assumption of the sick role by proxy through deliberately faking or producing illness in another person who is under the diagnosed individual's care.

The extent to which Munchausen patients will go to simulate illness is remarkable and often quite inventive. Most commonly, the patient will try to fake physical rather than mental illness. In addition to supplying the doctor with false medical information, patients may heat thermometers or tamper with other medical instruments. They may ingest toxins, put blood in feces or urine, take insulin to lower blood sugar, or inject themselves with feces or other contaminants to make themselves ill. Some patients secretly take medications or deliberately injure themselves. For example, one man repeatedly ate broken glass and then presented himself to the emergency room of a city hospital for admission; he seemed to like the care and attention he received from the hospital staff. In another case, a woman was hospitalized for excessive urination and abnormal electrolytes; she had been secretly taking diuretics ("water pills") while denying any use of medications.

Munchausen's syndrome appears to be a chronic disorder with onset in early adulthood, often beginning after the patient or a significant other is hospitalized for a genuine medical illness. Many of those who develop factitious disorder are well versed in medical terminology because of their employment in health-related occupations, such as nursing or laboratory medicine. Because of their medical knowledge, these Munchausen's syndrome patients are able to knowingly fake medical illness. Such patients may exhibit textbook perfect presentations of medical disorders and tend to make specific demands for the kinds of medication or therapy they desire. There is usually a long and complicated medical history, including several surgeries. When hospitalized, the Munchausen patient rarely receives visits from family or friends.

Some patients intentionally feign psychiatric illness rather than medical symptoms. They can present with convincing stories of hallucinations, delusions, depression, suicidal ideation, bizarre behavior, and so on. They sometimes invent histories of major life crises as precipitants for their distress. In one instance, a woman seeking admission presented herself as hallucinating, depressed, and suicidal. She attributed the acute onset of her symptoms to the recent diagnosis of a fatal form of cancer in one of her children, who, she claimed, was receiving chemotherapy at a major cancer treatment hospital in New York City. When the hospital staff investigated her story, it turned out that she had no children and had made up the entire history and symptomatology to get herself admitted to a psychiatric unit.

Two interesting phenomena that may be seen with factitious disorders are *pseudologia fantastica* and impostorship. In pseudologia fantastica, patients simply invent stories about their lives and their medical histories. Patients appear to believe these exaggerated renderings of their history and will often elaborate to play on the sympathy of the interviewer. The woman who falsely claimed to have a child dying of cancer is an example of pseudologia fantastica. Impostorship is closely related to pseudologia fantastica and involves claiming a different identity, often of an important or prestigious person.

Several psychodynamic factors may play a role in the production of factitious disorder. There is sometimes a history of serious illness or of deprivation in childhood. The future patient's mother may have been rejecting and the patient's father absent. The comfort the child received from caregivers outside the home far outweighed any love within the family. As a result, the patient developed an early positive institutional transference to the hospital as the good parent. The suffering involved in repeated surgeries and invasive medical tests may satisfy masochistic needs to atone for imagined wrongs. In some cases, assuming the sick role is a way of identifying with an actually ill significant other. The patient with factitious disorder is aware of knowingly feigning illness, but is unaware of the motive for doing so. Psychological testing on individuals with factitious disorders generally reveals a poor sense of identity with sexual identity confusion, inadequate sexual adjustment, narcissism, dependency, low frustration tolerance, and the absence of a formal thought disorder.

DIFFERENTIAL DIAGNOSIS

Factitious disorder is difficult to detect. The following conditions should be considered in the differential diagnosis.

Actual Medical Illness

Since the most common types of symptoms feigned by patients with factitious disorder are medical, it is important to rule out the existence of a genuine medical illness. Some clues to the possible presence of Munchausen's disorder include:

1. The patient's manner of presentation.
2. History of multiple hospitalizations.
3. Multiple surgical scars ("gridiron abdomen").
4. Extensive medical knowledge.
5. Absence of visits from family or friends.
6. Absence of distress in the face of complaints.
7. Drug seeking, especially for pain relievers.
8. History of extensive travel.
9. Noncompliance with hospital rules.
10. Frequent arguments with hospital staff.
11. Disruptive behavior on the hospital ward.
12. A dramatic presentation.
13. Pseudologia fantastica.
14. History of vagrancy.
15. History of time in jail for minor offenses.
16. Dramatic stories that play on the listener's sympathy.
17. Narcissism and strong dependency needs.
18. Low frustration tolerance.
19. History of poor sexual adjustment.
20. Lying and manipulative behavior.

Somatoform Disorders

Unlike the deliberate feigning of symptoms in factitious disorders, patients with somatoform disorders do not intentionally produce their physical symptoms. Patients with Hypochondriasis (300.7) are preoccupied with physical illness but do not voluntarily produce symptoms and tend to avoid surgery and invasive medical tests. In Conversion Disorder (300.11) the physical symptoms are not produced voluntarily and are often obviously symbolic of an unconscious conflict.

Personality Disorders

Unlike patients with factitious disorder, patients with Antisocial Personality Disorder (301.7) do not voluntarily undergo surgeries and painful invasive diagnostic testing as a way of life. The patient with Munchausen's syndrome, however, does display several antisocial traits, such as lying, manipulation of others, lack of close relationships, drug abuse, and criminal behavior. In addition, antisocial personality disorder has an earlier age of onset. Because of their dramatic, attention-seeking behavior, some factitious disorder patients may show traits of Histrionic Personality Disorder (301.50). Others may meet criteria for Borderline Personality Disorder (301.83) because of their identity disturbance, disturbed interpersonal relationships, self-mutilation, inappropriate anger, and affective lability.

Schizophrenia and Delusional Disorders

Patients with psychotic disorders may have somatic delusions and firmly believe they need hospital treatment when no documented medical disorder exists.

Malingering (V65.2)

Like factitious disorder, malingering involves the feigning or intentional production of symptoms. Unlike factitious disorder, malingering involves the presence of an external incentive like monetary gain, avoidance of responsibility, evasion of prosecution, and so on. Malingerers have specific goals other than assuming the sick role.

Substance Abuse

Many patients with factitious disorder surreptitiously abuse drugs or medications to feign illness. Abuse of pain relievers, especially opioids, is common with factitious disorders.

Ganser's Syndrome (300.15)

Sometimes called the syndrome of "approximate answers," Ganser's syndrome is commonly seen in prison inmates who give astonishingly inaccurate answers to simple questions. For example, the client might say that 2 plus 2 is 5 rather than 4. Some believe that Ganser's syndrome is a type of malingering to avoid taking responsibility. In *DSM-IV* Ganser's syndrome is classified under Dissociative Disorder NOS (300.15) because of its association with dissociative amnesia or fugue.

Compensation or Accident Neurosis

This is not an official *DSM-IV* category. Compensation neurosis refers to the development of symptoms after an accident or injury in which there is a pending unsettled claim for monetary compensation. The prospect of getting large amounts of money for prolonged symptomatology may be a strong unconscious determinant in maintaining the symptoms. The clinician cannot determine whether the patient is feigning illness for an external incentive, is unconsciously maintaining symptoms, or is genuinely suffering a prolonged physical disorder.

21

Dissociative Disorders

"The horror of that moment," the King went on, "I shall never, never forget!" "You will, though," the Queen said, "unless you make a memorandum of it."

Lewis Carroll, (1832–1898) *Through the Looking-Glass*

THE DISSOCIATIVE DISORDERS:

300.12	Dissociative Amnesia
300.13	Dissociative Fugue
300.14	Dissociative Identity Disorder (Multiple Personality Disorder, or MPD)
300.6	Depersonalization Disorder
300.15	Dissociative Disorder Not Otherwise Specified (NOS)

In naming these disorders, *DSM-IV* has replaced the adjective "psychogenic" from *DSM-III-R* with the adjective "dissociative" to be more descriptive and to be compatible with *ICD-10*. The distinguishing feature of the dissociative disorders is a disturbance of one's sense of personal continuity due to a disruption of the normally integrative functions of memory, consciousness, or sense of personal identity. During the heyday of psychoanalysis, these disorders were termed hysterical neurosis, dissociative type.

Dissociation refers to the ability to separate off certain mental contents from the usual flow of consciousness. In the nineteenth century, the French physician Pierre Janet viewed dissociation as a sign of neurosis and regarded it as a defect in mental integration that underlay hysterical symptomatology, including dissociative states and conversion symptoms. Other psychologists and theoreticians saw dissociation as a universal and fundamental adaptive ability of the healthy human mind—an ability that, when taken to extremes, could lead to disordered states of consciousness.

Altered states of consciousness frequently have a dissociative basis. Individuals often mobilize dissociation to protect themselves from being overwhelmed by intense pain and trauma by splitting off clusters of distressing thoughts, feelings, and memories from conscious awareness. As a result, the individual feels detached from or remains unaware of certain painful memories or emotional states.

Dissociative phenomena are ubiquitous and can occur in many of the *DSM-IV* mental disorders as well as in healthy individuals under stress. Many individuals, for example, have experienced the trance-like state of "highway hypnosis" during long, tedious travel by automobile. It is also not uncommon to find dissociative phenomena as part of the symptom picture of schizophrenia, mood disorders, anxiety disorders, eating disorders, substance-related disorders, posttraumatic stress disorder, borderline personality disorder, and adjustment disorders. Individuals who suddenly find themselves in life-threatening situations frequently feel numb or detached from their bodies. Fatigue, stress, sleep deprivation, and alcohol or drug use often cause a feeling of unreality or unfamiliarity.

The Structured Clinical Interview for *DSM-IV* Dissociative Disorders (SCID-D) is a semi-structured interview that clinicians may find useful in making the diagnosis of dissociative disorders. The SCID-D (1993), published by the American Psychiatric Press, was developed by Marlene Steinberg, M.D., an authority on dissociative disorders. The SCID-D rates the severity of five essential dissociative symptoms, namely:

1. *Amnesia:* the loss of memory (inability to recall) personal information or events of a specific time period.

2. *Depersonalization:* the feeling of detachment from oneself (e.g., feeling invisible, experiencing one's body or thoughts as foreign or not one's own, viewing oneself as from a distance, or feeling numb or unreal).

3. *Derealization:* the feeling of detachment from one's surroundings, including people in one's environment (e.g., experiencing one's family members or home as unfamiliar or unreal).

4. *Identity confusion:* a feeling of puzzlement, confusion, or inner conflict about one's sense of identity (e.g., "I don't know who I am").

5. *Identity alteration:* an organized shift in the characteristic way in which one perceives, thinks about, and relates to others and the world at large. Identity alteration often involves an alteration in fundamental personality traits, tastes, and fund of information. The actress Linda Blair portrayed identity alteration in the movie *The Exorcist.* With severe identity alteration, there may be amnesia for behavior and events that occur during the altered identity state. Individuals suffering identity alteration may use different names and talk to or about themselves in the third person singular ("he" or "she"), or as "we" or "they," or may use no pronoun at all for self-reference. The most severe identity alteration occurs with multiple personality disorder, which may be confused with schizophrenia when patients report voices talking back and forth inside of themselves.

Another useful clinical tool is the Dissociative Experiences Scale (DES), developed by Eve Bernstein Carlson, Ph.D., and Frank W. Putnam, M.D. The DES is a self-administered questionnaire consisting of twenty-eight items describing a diverse dissociative experiences ranging from ordinary to unusual. Patients are asked to rate on a scale from 0 to 100 percent the degree to which each experience applies to them when they are not under the influence of drugs or alcohol. Questions range from ordinary daydreaming or becoming very absorbed in a movie to losing track of time, hearing voices inside oneself, or finding oneself in a place without any idea of how one got there.

DISSOCIATIVE AMNESIA (FORMERLY PSYCHOGENIC AMNESIA) (300.12)

(DSM-IV, pp. 478–481)
Amnesia is the loss of memory or inability to recall previously known information. Dissociative Amnesia was called Psychogenic Amnesia in *DSM-III-R.* The primary feature of dissociative amnesia is amnesia (loss of memory) for significant personal information, typically of a traumatic or distressing nature. Such loss of memory is more than simple forgetfulness and is not due to multiple personality

disorder, the use of substances, dementia, or a general medical condition.

In dissociative fugue a person suffers amnesia and suddenly travels away from home. In dissociative identity disorder a person has amnesia for a customary identity and assumes a new one.

The differential diagnosis of dissociative amnesia includes general medical and neurological conditions that affect brain function (e.g., brain tumors, head trauma, concussion, seizure disorders, delirium, dementia), other dissociative disorders, substance-induced disorders, catatonic stupor, factitious disorders, and malingering. In dissociative fugue there is not only amnesia, but also purposeful travel and the partial or complete assumption of a different identity. In dissociative identity disorder (MPD), there are repeated alterations of identity. Clinicians should also be alert to the possibility of transient global amnesia, a neurological condition usually seen in older individuals with underlying vascular disease.

DISSOCIATIVE FUGUE (FORMERLY PSYCHOGENIC FUGUE) (300.13)

(*DSM-IV*, pp. 481–484)

Dissociative Fugue was called Psychogenic Fugue in *DSM-III-R*. The term *fugue* derives from the Latin *fuga*, meaning flight. The principal feature of dissociative fugue is the sudden, unexpected flight or travel away from one's customary residence or workplace, accompanied by an amnesia for one's past. The person in a fugue state partially or completely takes on a new identity, but does not meet criteria for multiple personality disorder. *DSM-IV* has dropped the *DSM-III-R* requirement of the assumption of a new identity because the field trials and literature review found that confusion about personal identity is the predominant symptom. The amnesia, identity disturbance, and flight seen in dissociate fugue are not due to substance use or a general medical or neurological condition. Psychologically, fugues appear to be attempts to flee from severe stress. They are usually brief, but may last for several months.

The differential diagnosis of Dissociative Fugue is similar to that of Dissociative Amnesia.

DISSOCIATIVE IDENTITY DISORDER (FORMERLY MULTIPLE PERSONALITY DISORDER) (300.14)

(*DSM-IV*, pp. 484–487)

DSM-IV conceives of personality as one's enduring pattern of thinking, perceiving, and relating to oneself and the world. Dissociative identity disorder (multiple personality disorder) presumes the existence of two or more distinct personality states or personal identities that recurrently take charge of the individual's behavior. In dissociative identity disorder, there is an amnesia for significant personal information that goes beyond mere forgetfulness or childhood fantasy and is not due to substance use or a general medical or neurological condition. Multiple personality disorder appears to be most common in women who have suffered severe abuse in childhood. Some clinicians believe that MPD results from self-hypnosis in which one dissociates oneself from intolerable and inescapable abuse.

Because of its dramatic quality and the interest shown by Hollywood in multiple personality disorder, many clinicians doubt the validity of this diagnosis. Writing in *The Harvard Mental Health Letter*, Professor Paul R. McHugh (1993) of Johns Hopkins argued that therapists have created multiple personality disorder in highly suggestible clients. In other words, MPD may be an iatrogenic disorder (from the Greek *iatros* for physician), created by the therapist's persuasion, interest, encouragement, and countertransferential delight in the dramatic presentation. McHugh likened MPD to the hystero-epilepsy that Charcot induced in his suggestible patients during the 1880s. It seems that therapists who believe in MPD make the diagnosis with regularity, while therapists who are not true believers simply do not see cases of this disorder. For those who have faith, no explanation is necessary; for those who do not have faith, no explanation is possible.

Writing in rebuttal to Dr. McHugh, clinical professor Richard P. Kluft (1993) maintains that skeptics offer strongly held opinions that are not supported by research or clinical experience. Kluft argues that MPD has a similar presentation in different cultures and that the disorder follows an established natural history suggestive of a true disorder. Kluft also feels that critics too readily and selectively discount the observations of the many competent clinicians who work with patients suffering from MPD.

The differential diagnosis of Dissociative Identity Disorder includes other dissociative disorders, schizophrenia, delusional disorders, other psychotic disorders, mood disorders with psychotic features, factitious disorder, malingering, and general medical and neurological conditions that affect brain function (e.g., epilepsy and brain tumor). Clients with MPD often meet criteria for other *DSM-IV* disorders, such as Somatization Disorder, Borderline Personality Disorder, and Major Depressive Episode (Chu 1993).

DEPERSONALIZATION DISORDER (300.6)

(*DSM-IV*, pp. 488–490)

The essential feature of depersonalization disorder is a clinically significant feeling of detachment from one's own body or mind. Such feelings of detachment tend to recur or persist and cause marked distress or dysfunction. Psychodynamic clinicians regard depersonalization as a defense mechanism by which the individual can disavow unacceptable impulses through a feeling of unreality. Although individuals suffering depersonalization disorder may feel mechanical or as if living in a dream, their reality testing remains intact. The sense of detachment in depersonalization disorder is not due to another *DSM-IV* disorder (e.g., Schizophrenia, Multiple Personality Disorder, Posttraumatic Stress Disorder), substance use, or a general medical or neurological condition. Symptoms of depersonalization may be seen with schizophrenia, major depressive episodes, panic and anxiety disorders, phobias, substance-induced disorders, sleep deprivation, fatigue, stress, complex partial seizures, and migraine.

For example, Paulo, a 20-year-old man who lived at home with his staunchly religious Italian-American parents, was afraid to tell them that he had recently gotten his girlfriend pregnant. While driving by himself to work, Paulo began to feel like someone else was doing the driving. He felt like he was living in a dream. Even his usual route to work seemed somewhat unfamiliar. His feeling of unreality and his fear that he might have an accident in this dreamlike state led Paulo to seek psychiatric treatment. After a brief series of family sessions that addressed the issue of his girlfriend's pregnancy with his parents, Paulo's feelings of unreality about himself and his surroundings completely disappeared.

DISSOCIATIVE DISORDER NOT OTHERWISE SPECIFIED (300.15)

(*DSM-IV*, pp. 491–492)

According to *DSM-IV*, the Not Otherwise Specified Dissociative Disorders are those disorders that do not meet criteria for any of the specific Dissociative Disorders, but whose chief symptom is dissociation—that is, a disturbance in the normal integrative functions of memory, identity, and consciousness. Some patients may have disorders closely resembling one of the specific dissociative disorders, but not fulfilling all the criteria for the disorder. Other examples of NOS dissociative disorders include, but are not limited to, the following:

1. Ganser's syndrome of "approximate answers." This syndrome was first described in 1898 by the German psychiatrist S. J. M. Ganser. Patients with Ganser's syndrome typically "talk past the point" by giving responses that are slightly off target. They remain in the ballpark, but do not hit a home run. For example, individuals with Ganser's syndrome might reply that 2 plus 2 equals 5, indicating that they understood the question and voluntarily chose a slightly incorrect response. Ganser's syndrome is associated with amnesia, fugue, conversion symptoms, and perceptual disturbances. It appears to be more common in men and in prisoners.

2. Loss of consciousness that is apparently psychologically based and is not due to physical trauma or a general medical or neurological condition.

3. Dissociative states that occur in the context of brainwashing and other coercive methods of persuasion.

4. Derealization without depersonalization in adults. Sometimes individuals may feel detached from their surroundings without feeling detached from themselves. Derealization refers to the sense of unreality or unfamiliarity about people or locations that should be

familiar. For example, people undergoing derealization may experience their parents or their homes as not being their own. Significant derealization is often associated with a history of a trauma. Mild derealization can occur with stress, fatigue, or intoxication. It can also occur with other major mental disorders and with neurological conditions, such as brain tumors and seizure disorders.

For example, a young man with chronic schizophrenia, paranoid type, experiences the city where he lives as foreign. For him the sun now looks different from when he was a child. He believes that all the people on the street act differently, more childishly and less mature, than in previous years. He is convinced that he was abducted and transported to a different planet in a parallel universe as part of a government plot to rid the real world of "defective people like me." He also believes that the people who appear to be his parents on this parallel planet are really look-alike impostors who are impersonating his real parents who are back on earth (Capgras's syndrome).

Capgras's syndrome refers to the delusional belief that other people in the environment are not their real selves, but are doubles or impostors. This syndrome was first described in 1923 by the French psychiatrist Jean Marie Capgras as the *illusion des sosies*. Capgras felt that this condition required a psychotic loss of reality testing, paranoid distrust, and a sense of strangeness or unreality about one's environment.

5. Culture-bound dissociative syndromes (dissociative trance disorders). The psychiatric literature documents syndromes in a variety of cultures that are characterized by abnormal behavior during a trance. Such syndromes usually involve grossly disordered speech and behavior and often have a component of danger to self and others. Dissociative trance disorders are not the trancelike states that accompany many culturally accepted religious practices (e.g., talking in tongues).

Some examples of culture-bound dissociative syndromes (dissociative trance disorders) include:

    a. *Amok* of Indonesia.

        Amok, a Malaysian term which means "to engage furiously in battle," typically occurs in males confronted by extreme stress or frustrating circumstances. The syndrome of *Amok* begins with a period of brooding followed by a rage attack consisting of wild, aggressive, and violent behavior (running *Amok*) in a dissociated state. The episode sometimes ends in suicide. (See *DSM-IV*, p. 845.)

b. *Ataques de nervios* (attacks of nerves) of the Caribbean and Latin America. (See Chapter 11 of this text and *DSM-IV*, p. 845.)

c. *Bebainan* of Indonesia.

Bebainan is a dissociative trance state involving narrowed awareness of one's surroundings and stereotyped movements felt to be beyond the individual's control. (See *DSM-IV*, p. 490.)

d. *Latah* of Malaysia, Indonesia, Southeast Asia, Bantu of Africa, and Ainu of Japan.

Latah, a characteristically female response, is a startle reaction involving hypersensitivity to sudden frightening stimuli (loud noises, sudden movements, upsetting words). The episode of *Latah* is usually brief (minutes to an hour or two) and may include automatic obedience, echolalia, echopraxia, coprolalia, and copropraxia, which often amuse the individual's associates. (See *DSM-IV*, p. 846, Kaplan 1994, p. 190 and Peck 1974, p. 544.)

e. *Piblokto (Arctic hysteria, Pibloktoq)* of the Arctic.

Piblokto is an acute, dissociative episode (Arctic hysteria) seen primarily among Eskimo women residing in Arctic and subarctic regions, including the Eskimos of northern Greenland. The attack, which may be preceded by a period of social withdrawal and irritability, consists of such behaviors as screaming, cursing, running wildly, breaking things, tearing off one's clothing, and throwing oneself naked in the snow in subzero temperatures. Believing that the attack is due to the influence of an evil spirit, other Eskimos generally will not touch the afflicted individual. After several minutes of wild behavior, the affected individual may appear to convulse and lapse into an apparent comatose state that may last for several hours. (See *DSM-IV*, p. 847, and Kaplan 1994, p. 494.)

f. *Possession states.*

Possession trance involves the experience of feeling taken over or possessed by a spirit or external force so that one loses one's sense of personal identity and personal control as one assumes the identity of the controlling spirit or external agent. Actress Linda Blair, in the movie *The Exorcist*, brought this dissociative disorder to public attention. (See *DSM-IV*, p. 490.)

6. Appendix B of *DSM-IV* contains research criteria for Dissociative Trance Disorder (*DSM-IV*, pp. 727–729). The essential feature of dissociative trance disorder is an involuntary trance state that is not culturally (or religiously) sanctioned. This involuntary trance must cause significant distress or impairment and must not be more appropriately accounted for by another mental disorder.

22

Sexual and Gender Identity Disorders

"And most of all would I flee from the cruel madness
of love—
The honey of poison-flowers and all the measureless
ill."

Alfred, Lord Tennyson (1809–1892), *Maud*, Pt. I.iv.10 (1855)

This section of *DSM-IV* deals with three broad classes of disorders:
the sexual dysfunctions, the paraphilias (sexual perversions), and the
gender identity disorders.

SEXUAL DYSFUNCTIONS (GENERAL SPECIFIERS):
The following types apply to all sexual dysfunctions:
Specify type:
  Due to psychological factors, or
  Due to combined factors (psychological and a generalized
  medical condition)
  Lifelong (during the sexual life) or acquired
  Generalized or situational

THE SEXUAL DYSFUNCTIONS:
Sexual Desire Disorders:
302.71   Hypoactive Sexual Desire Disorder
302.79   Sexual Aversion Disorder
Sexual Arousal Disorders:
302.72   Female Sexual Arousal Disorder

302.72   Male Erectile Disorder
Orgasmic Disorders:
302.73   Female Orgasmic Disorder
          (Inhibited Female Orgasm)
302.74   Male Orgasmic Disorder
          (Inhibited Male Orgasm)
302.75   Premature Ejaculation
Sexual Pain Disorders:
302.76   Dyspareunia (not due to a general medical condition)
306.51   Vaginismus (not due to a general medical condition)
Sexual Dysfunctions Due to a General Medical Condition:
625.8   Female Hypoactive Sexual Desire Disorder Due to a
          General Medical Condition
608.89   Male Hypoactive Sexual Desire Disorder Due to a
          General Medical Condition
607.84   Male Erectile Disorder Due to a General Medical
          Condition
625.0   Female Dyspareunia Due to a General Medical Condition
608.89   Male Dyspareunia Due to a General Medical Condition
625.8   Other Female Sexual Dysfunction Due to a General
          Medical Condition
608.89   Other Male Sexual Dysfunction Due to a General
          Medical Condition
———.——   Substance-Induced Sexual Dysfunction
          (refer to specific substance for codes)
          Specify if:
              With impaired desire
              With impaired arousal
              With impaired orgasm
              With sexual pain
          Specify if:
              With onset during intoxication
302.70   Sexual Dysfunction Not Otherwise Specified (NOS)

PARAPHILIAS:
302.4   Exhibitionism
302.81   Fetishism
302.89   Frotteurism
302.2   Pedophilia

Specify if:
    Sexually attracted to males
    Sexually attracted to females
    Sexually attracted to both males and females
Specify if: limited to incest
Specify type:
    Exclusive type (attracted only to children)
    Nonexclusive type
302.83   Sexual Masochism
302.84   Sexual Sadism
302.3   Transvestic Fetishism
         Specify if: With gender dysphoria (persistent discomfort
         with gender role or identity)
302.82   Voyeurism
302.9   Paraphilia Not Otherwise Specified (NOS)

GENDER IDENTITY DISORDERS (302.xx):
302.6   Gender Identity Disorder in Children
302.85   Gender Identity Disorder in Adolescents and Adults
         For sexually mature persons, specify if:
             Sexually attracted to males
             Sexually attracted to females
             Sexually attracted to both males and females
             Sexually attracted to neither males nor females
302.6   Gender Identity Disorder Not Otherwise Specified
         (NOS)
302.9   Sexual Disorder Not Otherwide Specified

THE SEXUAL DYSFUNCTION DISORDERS

(*DSM-IV, pp.* 493–496)
    The sexual dysfunction disorders are subdivided into four major
types: the sexual desire disorders, the sexual arousal disorders, the
orgasm disorders, and the sexual pain disorders. As described below,
the division of sexual dysfunction disorders into types follows closely
the description of the normal human sexual response cycle originally
researched by Masters and Johnson (1966). *DSM-IV* breaks the human

sexual response cycle into four stages: (1) appetitive, (2) excitement, (3) orgasm, and (4) resolution. Sexual dysfunctions may be "lifelong" or "acquired," and they may be "generalized" or "situational." Some may be "due to psychological factors" and others may be "due to combined psychological factors and a general medical condition."

Because sexual dysfunctions often have a medical or substance-related etiology, *DSM-IV* has added categories to the chapter on Sexual Disorders for Sexual Dysfunction Due to a General Medical Condition and for Substance-induced Sexual Dysfunction. As usual, there is also a Sexual Dysfunction Not Otherwise Specified category (302.70) for sexual dysfunctions that do not meet criteria for any of the specific sexual dysfunctions.

The Sexual Desire Disorders

(*DSM-IV*, pp. 496-511)

The idea of diagnosing specific sexual disorders to provide therapy is fairly recent in the history of modern medicine. With the pioneering work of Masters and Johnson in the 1960s, sexual problems came out of the closet. Unfortunately the story of the treatment of sexual disorders in Western civilization is replete with hushed tones, super-stitions, taboos, old wives' tales, and the meddling influence of religious zealots (Krohne 1982).

The religious influence on sexual behavior dates back thousands of years. In the story of Onan in the Old Testament (Genesis 38: 8–10), Onan spilled his semen on the ground rather than impregnate his deceased brother's wife. The Hebrew God looked askance at Onan's contraceptive efforts and struck him dead for choosing to spill his valuable seed. Five thousand years later many boys still feel guilty for spilling their seed in masturbation. Some modern authorities have speculated that Onan may have suffered from premature ejaculation (*DSM-IV* code 302.75), which rendered him unable to voluntarily control his orgasms prior to penetrating the vagina. If so, Onan received a death sentence for committing a 302.75, now a treatable sexual dysfunction.

Since the time of Christ, the Church has had a major influence on Western attitudes toward sexuality. In the thirteenth century the brilliant Roman Catholic thinker, Saint Thomas Aquinas, espoused the classical theory of Natural Law. According to this theory, the goal of sexual activity in the natural order is to impregnate a woman so that she can bear children to love and serve God. Any of the pleasurable aspects of sex are strictly secondary to its primary purpose of procreation. To engage in sex solely as recreation is to pervert its natural and true purpose of procreation.

As recently as a century ago there was still little enlightenment about sexual matters. In the mid-nineteenth century the medical profession believed that overindulgence in sexual intercourse could cause barrenness and that masturbation ("self-pollution") could cause a host of maladies.

A book entitled *Light and Life*, published in the 1800s by C.H. Robinson and Company of Charlotte, North Carolina, advised its readers about the typical appearance of a "self-polluter" as someone who has "hot, dry skin with something of a hectic appearance" (p. 457). Other symptoms believed to be caused by masturbation included poor sleep, restlessness, night sweats, disturbing dreams, discharge from the urethra, headache, giddiness, ringing in the ears, stiff neck, darting pains in the forehead, and poor vision. Treatment for the nineteenth-century self-polluter consisted of sleeping on a hard bed and rising early to take a sponge bath in cold water every morning. Additional measures included eating only light suppers, emptying the bladder thoroughly before bedtime, avoiding spicy foods as well as caffeine and alcohol, vigorous exercise, taking iron tonic, and reading good wholesome books. Above all else, the pathological masturbator was advised, "never sleep lying on your back."

An 1866 American medical textbook by W. Paine, M.D., grouped masturbation, spermatorrhoea, nymphomania, and satyriasis together with gonorrhea, balanitis, and syphilis as sexual pathologies needing treatment. Dr. Paine believed that spermatorrhoea (involuntary loss of semen) was most often caused by "self-abuse," or self-pollution. According to Dr. Paine, the pernicious habit of self-abuse could lead to insanity, "besides so enfeebling the general forces of the body as to predispose the sufferer to many other maladies" (p. 920). In women masturbation could lead to nymphomania, "a disease of females, consisting of an irresistible desire for sexual intercourse" (p. 921). Dr. Paine reports that he cured many cases of nymphomania with a combination of two grains of Senecin to one-tenth of a grain of

Gelsemine two or three times a day. In cases where masturbation was driving the nymphomania, he recommended cauterizing the clitoris with *argentinitras*. Being a man himself, Dr. Paine did not see any need for cauterizing the penis of male self-polluters.

Such was the state of enlightenment about sexuality into which Freud was born in 1856. Freud trained in neurology, but he turned to psychology and psychiatry, partly to earn a living and partly because he realized that many of the symptoms his patients exhibited were rooted in sexual conflict and sexual repression. Through his clinical work Freud came to realize that sexual drives have a developmental history beginning in infancy. Sexual interest does not spring forth fully blown at puberty like Venus on a half-shell.

Freud described the oral, anal, phallic, latent, and genital stages of sexual development. He argued that sexual interest can be arrested at any stage of development due to psychological conflict or trauma. Freud felt that what was repressed at an early age lives on in the unconscious and continues to affect adult behavior in the formation of symptoms. In Freud's theory, repressed sexual desires can also be sublimated into productive aspects of personality function.

William Masters and Virginia Johnson (1966), the twentieth century pioneers of sexual research, made sex therapy into a modern health care specialty. They considered sexual dysfunctions that occurred without a medical cause to be learned behaviors fostered by ignorance, performance anxiety, and poor communication. Masters and Johnson developed a system to treat sexual problems through directive psychotherapy, improved communication skills, education about sexual functioning, and desensitization through sensate focus or pleasuring exercises. In sensate focus therapy the therapist asks the couple to set aside time to give each other physical pleasure without engaging in coitus and orgasm. In doing so, the couple learns to enjoy each other's bodies in an accepting manner without the pressure and anxiety of having to engage in sexual intercourse.

One of Masters and Johnson's prime achievements was the documentation of the physiology of the human sexual response cycle. They divided sexual response into four stages: 1) excitement, 2) plateau, 3) orgasm, and 4) resolution.

Phase I, *excitement*, begins with sexual fantasy and/or the presence of the love object. During the excitement phase the vagina lubricates and the penis hardens. The nipples of both partners become erect.

The clitoris becomes firm and turgid, and the labia minora thickens as its veins become engorged. Excitement may last minutes to hours and is followed by a plateau stage.

During phase II, *plateau*, there is a 50 percent enlargement and elevation of the man's testes and, in the woman, constriction along the outer third of the vagina, the so-called "orgasmic platform." The woman's breasts enlarge by 25 percent. The clitoris elevates and retracts. Both the penis and vagina change color, large muscle groups begin to contract, the heart rate and respirations increase, and blood pressure rises. The plateau phase lasts from about 30 seconds to several minutes and culminates in the third stage of orgasm.

Phase III, *orgasm*, lasts from 3 to 15 seconds and is accompanied by a mild clouding of consciousness. In men there is a sense of ejaculatory inevitability followed by the forceful ejection of about a teaspoon of semen containing 120 million sperm cells. In women, orgasm consists of three to fifteen contractions of the lower third of the vagina and powerful sustained contractions of the uterus. Orgasm leads to a sense of well-being. After orgasm, men undergo a refractory period that can last from minutes to several hours during which they are physiologically incapable of achieving another orgasm. Women have no refractory stage and may have multiple successive orgasms.

During phase IV, *resolution*, there is a detumescence or disgorgement of blood from the genitals, and the body returns to its resting or pre-excitement state. The resolution stage is brief following an orgasm, but if no orgasm occurs, resolution can take several hours, during which the person feels irritable and uncomfortable. There are no sexual dysfunctions associated with phase IV.

DSM-IV has modified the four stages of sexual response described by Masters and Johnson and defines seven primary syndromes of sexual dysfunction based on its revision. *DSM-IV* inserts an appetitive phase before the Masters and Johnson excitement and plateau phases. *DSM-IV* further combines the excitement and plateau phases of Masters and Johnson into a single excitement phase. The orgasm and resolution phases are identical in both systems.

HYPOACTIVE SEXUAL DESIRE DISORDER (302.71)
(*DSM-IV*, pp. 496–498)
SEXUAL AVERSION DISORDER (302.79):
(*DSM-IV*, pp. 499–500)

The *DSM-IV* Appetitive Phase I refers to sexual fantasies and the desire for sex based on inner motivations, drives, and personality factors. The sexual desire disorders of the *DSM-IV* appetitive phase include Hypoactive Sexual Desire Disorder (302.71) and Sexual Aversion Disorder (302.79).

In Hypoactive Sexual Desire Disorder (302.71), there is a clinically significant diminution of sexual fantasy and desire that causes distress and/or problems in a relationship. Such lack of sexual interest is not due to another mental disorder like major depression, nor is it due to substance use or a general medical condition.

In Sexual Aversion Disorder (302.79), there is a clinically significant dislike or avoidance of genital sexual activity with a partner that is not due to another Axis I mental disorder, such as major depression, hypochondriasis, or obsessive compulsive disorder. To meet criteria for being a disorder, such aversion to genital sexuality must cause marked distress or problems in a relationship.

Among couples presenting to sex therapy clinics, lack of sexual desire is the most common complaint. Proposed causes of such lack of interest include unconscious fears about sex, depression, stress, medical illness, anxiety, drug or alcohol use, and marital disharmony. Sometimes suppressed homosexual wishes in a marriage partner cause decreased heterosexual desire in the marriage. Often the withholding of sex is an expression of hostility between partners.

Freud attributed diminished sexual desire to inhibitions arising during the phallic phase of sexual development as a result of castration anxiety. Some men experience vagina dentata fantasies of the woman's genitals possessing teeth that can bite off the penis during intercourse. One college student who sought psychiatric consultation had a bad trip after ingesting LSD in which he hallucinated a vagina with sharp teeth and became flooded with panic. Following this horrifying experience, he ceased dating women and began to wonder if he might be homosexual.

In one study of the reasons young married couples ceased having sexual intercourse for a significant period of time, there was a difference found between men and women. Men lost interest in sex under social pressures like job stress, immigration, religious factors, and their wives' employment status. Women cited factors like dominance in the relationship, the amount of affection they received from their husbands, the decision-making process in the marriage, and threats by the husband to leave home. Both partners felt that lack of privacy inhibited their desire for sexual activity.

Sexual Arousal Disorders

FEMALE SEXUAL AROUSAL DISORDER (302.72):
(DSM-IV, pp. 500–502)
MALE ERECTILE DISORDER (302.72)
(DSM-IV, pp. 502–504)

DSM-IV Excitement Phase II consists of all the physiological changes of the Masters and Johnson excitement and plateau phases plus the subjective sense of sexual pleasure. The disorders of this phase are the Female Sexual Arousal Disorder (302.72) and Male Erectile Disorder, or impotence (302.72). Such disorders may be caused by medical problems, drug or alcohol abuse, or psychological factors, as described under Phase I (Appetitive Disorder), or by a combination of all three. Many patients placed on the newer serotonin-reuptake inhibiting antidepressants (e.g., Prozac, Zoloft, and Paxil) experience drug-induced problems with sexual arousal and orgasm. Some clients will not volunteer such information unless asked directly by the clinician. *DSM-IV* has dropped the *DSM-III-R* statement that these excitement phase disorders can be diagnosed on the basis of subjective complaints alone, and now requires the presence of difficulties with physiologic arousal.

In Female Sexual Arousal Disorder (302.72), the woman has difficulty with the lubrication and swelling responses of the phase of sexual excitement and that leads to marked distress or problems in the relationship. Such difficulties are not due to other Axis I disorders nor to drug usage or a general medical condition.

In Male Erectile Disorder (302.72), the man cannot get or keep an erection for the duration of the sexual activity. In interviews, men commonly complain, "I can't get it up" or "I'm impotent." The impotence is not due to another Axis I disorder nor to drug usage or a general medical condition. The impotence also causes significant distress or interpersonal problems.

For example, one client became distressed to learn that his father, who was approaching retirement age, was laid off unexpectedly by his factory after thirty years of service. Shortly thereafter, the client's own boss at his job was suddenly transferred to another department because of the company's dissatisfaction with his performance. The client became preoccupied that his own job security might be in jeopardy. The very day his boss was transferred, the client was unable to achieve an erection with his wife. "My wife doesn't understand why this is happening," he said. "It has to do with being a man." His situational impotence lasted three weeks until he came to terms with his worries about his job.

Clinicians should keep in mind, however, that impotence in men frequently has a medical basis, perhaps as often as in 75 percent of cases. Some common medical conditions associated with impotence include heart disease, kidney disease, liver disease, diabetes mellitus, prostate surgery, multiple sclerosis, spinal cord injury, and medical complications of substance abuse.

Orgasm Disorders

FEMALE ORGASMIC DISORDER (formerly Inhibited Female Orgasm) (302.73)
(DSM-IV, p. 505–507)
MALE ORGASMIC DISORDER (formerly Inhibited Male Orgasm) (302.74)
(DSM-IV, pp. 507–509)

The *DSM-IV* Orgasm Phase III consists of a peak of sexual pleasure and the release of sexual tension accompanied by rhythmic contractions of the perineal musculature and the pelvic reproductive organs. The disorders of orgasm include Female Orgasmic Disorder (302.73; Inhibited Female Orgasm, anorgasmia), Male Orgasmic Disorder (302.74; Inhibited Male Orgasm, retarded ejaculation), and Premature Ejaculation (302.75).

In Female Orgasmic Disorder (302.73), orgasm is either delayed or does not occur at all following a normal excitement phase. The disorder is not due to another Axis I condition nor to substance use or to a general medical condition. It also causes marked distress or problems in the relationship. Psychological factors are usually associated with inhibited female orgasm. Often there is a fear of damage to the vagina, a concern about getting pregnant, or a fear of rejection by the partner. The woman may experience orgasm as a loss of control or may view sexual intercourse as a violent or brutal victimization. Cultural and religious precepts may also play a role. In addition, the overall nature of the relationship between the partners will affect the orgiastic phase of sexual activity.

In Male Orgasmic Disorder (302.74), orgasm is either delayed or does not occur at all following a normal excitement phase. The disorder is not due to another Axis I condition nor to substance use or to a general medical condition. It also causes marked distress or problems in the relationship. Inhibited male orgasm that is not caused by a medical problem usually indicates significant psychological difficulties. Such men have often grown up in strict puritanical families that regard sex as filthy and sinful. They tend to have problems getting close in any kind of interpersonal relationship.

In Premature Ejaculation (302.75) (*DSM-IV*, pp. 509–511), the man reaches orgasm and ejaculation before he wants to and is unable to keep his penis inside the vagina long enough to satisfy his female partner during sexual intercourse. This condition causes marked distress or problems in the relationship. It is more common among better educated men and may be related to anxiety about being able to satisfy the partner. Stress in the marriage tends to worsen the problem. The same conflicts that underlie male impotence often play a role in premature ejaculation.

Sexual Pain Disorders

(*DSM-IV* pp. 511–515)

Not surprisingly, the sexual pain disorders are characterized by genital pain associated with sexual activity. The *DSM-IV* distinguishes two types of sexual pain syndromes: Dyspareunia (302.76) and Vaginismus (306.51).

DYSPAREUNIA (not due to a general medical condition) (302.76)
(*DSM-IV*, pp. 511–513)

In choosing the term *dyspareunia* for this disorder of distressing genital pain connected with sexual intercourse, the authors of *DSM-*

III and *DSM-IV* lost sight of their commitment to keep psychiatric terminology simple and descriptive. Using *dyspareunia* is almost as obscure as using the phrase *body dysmorphic disorder* to describe those who don't like their physical appearance. This pedantic term derives from the Greek *dys* meaning "bad" or "ill" and *páreun* meaning "bedfellow." Both men and women may suffer from dyspareunia. One medical student, who was trying to learn this odd term, quipped, "Dys-pareunia is better than no pareunia at all." The diagnosis does not apply in cases where the pain is due exclusively to lack of lubrication, or to substance use, a general medical condition, or another Axis I condition, like somatization disorder.

VAGINISMUS (not due to a general medical condition) (306.51)
(*DSM-IV*, pp. 513–515)

Vaginismus refers to painful involuntary spasms of the muscles of the outer third of the vagina that interfere with sexual intercourse. As with dyspareunia, the diagnosis of vaginismus does not apply in cases where the disorder is due to substance use, a general medical condition, or another Axis I condition, like somatization disorder.

Sexual Dysfunctions Due To a General Medical Condition

(*DSM-IV*, pp. 515–518)

Certain medical conditions may cause sexual dysfunctions that are clinically significant. Typically there is evidence from the medical history, laboratory tests, or physical examination that a medical condition exists that the clinician judges to be etiologically related to the sexual disorder. *DSM-IV* distinguishes the following sexual dysfunctions due to medical conditions:

625.8 Female Hypoactive Sexual Desire Disorder Due to a General Medical Condition

608.89 Male Hypoactive Sexual Desire Disorder Due to a General Medical Condition

607.84 Male Erectile Disorder Due to a General Medical Condition

625.0	Female Dyspareunia Due to a General Medical Condition
608.89	Male Dyspareunia Due to a General Medical Condition
625.8	Other Female Sexual Dysfunction Due to a General Medical Condition
608.89	Other Male Sexual Dysfunction Due to a General Medical Condition

The clinician should include the name of the medical condition on Axis I after the phrase "due to" and should also code the medical condition on Axis III.

Substance-Induced Sexual Dysfunctions

(*DSM-IV*, pp. 519–522)

Substance use or abuse frequently results in sexual dysfunction. Typically there is evidence from the medical history, laboratory tests, physical examination, or clinical course of substance intoxication or withdrawal that the sexual dysfunction developed within a month of significant substance abuse or withdrawal. In addition, the sexual problems are not due to a sexual disorder unrelated to the substance use. The clinician should code the specific substance that causes the sexual dysfunction. In addition, the clinician should code if a specific substance intoxication or withdrawal is present.

———.—— Substance-Induced Sexual Dysfunction
(refer to specific substance for codes)

Specify if:

—With impaired desire
—With impaired arousal
—With impaired orgasm
—With sexual pain

Specify if:

—With onset during intoxication

Sexual Dysfunction Not Otherwise Specified (302.70)

(*DSM-IV*, p. 522)

Sexual Dysfunction Not Otherwise Specified (NOS) is a residual category for sexual dysfunctions that do not meet criteria for any of the specific sexual dysfunction disorders. The clinician can also use this category to express uncertainty about whether the sexual dysfunction is primary, substance induced, or due to a general medical condition.

PARAPHILIAS (SEXUAL DEVIATIONS)

(*DSM-IV*, pp. 522–532)

The term *paraphilia* derives from the Greek *para*, meaning "beside, at the side of," and *phílos*, meaning "loving." In days of yore, when psychiatrists spoke understandable English, these disorders were called sexual deviations. The authors of *DSM-IV* chose the term *paraphilia* to emphasize that the deviation (para) has to do with what sexually arouses (philia) the person. The characteristic features of the paraphilias are powerful sexual urges or fantasies that involve unusual stimuli or practices, such as: (1) things rather than people; (2) children, animals, or nonconsenting adults; or (3) the inflicting of pain, suffering, and humiliation on oneself or one's sexual partner. The diagnosis requires that the person act on these desires or be significantly distressed by them. The nature of the preferred deviant sexually arousing stimulus determines the particular diagnosis. By definition, *DSM-IV* requires all the paraphilias to have a duration of at least six months of recurring intense sexual urges, behaviors, or sexually arousing fantasies involving the preferred stimulus.

The typical patient with a paraphilia is a heterosexual man who masturbates to orgasm while focusing on the bizarre object of his desire. Paraphilias are commonly associated with personality disorders, other sexual disorders, mood disorders, substance abuse, and other psychiatric disorders.

Until 1973 homosexuality was diagnosed as a sexual deviation in the *Diagnostic and Statistical Manual* of the American Psychiatric

Association. Despite pervasive anti-homosexual bias in the United States, the APA now officially considers homosexuality to be a normal variant of the human sexual response. If the winds of politics shift further to the right, homosexuality may again become a disease in the United States at some future date. Clients who are currently chronically distressed by their homosexuality can still receive a diagnosis of "ego-dystonic homosexuality" under the rubric of Sexual Disorder Not Otherwise Specified (302.9).

DSM-IV provides criteria for the following eight specific paraphilias.

Exhibitionism (302.4)

(*DSM-IV*, pp. 525–526)
The person with exhibitionism, typically a heterosexual man, becomes sexually aroused by exposing his genitals to an unsuspecting stranger, usually a woman or a girl. About a third of sexual offenders who are referred for treatment are exhibitionists. The more timid individual with exhibitionism will expose his flaccid penis. The more aggressive exhibitionist may masturbate his erect penis and delight in shocking the unwary female. There is an apocryphal story of a female psychoanalyst who was confronted by an exhibitionist in New York's Central Park. She looked directly at the man's penis, shook her head calmly, and said with deep concern in her Viennese accent, "You poor man, it's so tiny." The man then apparently fled.

Fetishism (302.81)

(*DSM-IV*, p. 526)
The individual with fetishism becomes sexually aroused by inanimate objects like shoes or women's clothing. Vibrators and other equipment used for tactile genital stimulation don't count in the criteria.

Frotteurism (302.89)

(*DSM-IV*, p. 527)

" . . . ay, there's the rub . . . "

Shakespeare, *Hamlet*, Act III, scene i

Frotteurism is supposed to be another of those simple descriptive words that the *DSM-III* and *DSM-IV* are committed to using in psychiatric diagnosis. The term derives from the French *frott(er)* meaning "to rub." A "frotteur" is one who practices "frottage"—that is, one who gets sexual stimulation by rubbing against a nonconsenting person. The touching and rubbing, rather than any coercion, is the sexually arousing aspect of the act.

Pedophilia (302.2)

DSM-IV, pp. 527–528)
Most individuals with pedophilia are shy, interpersonally inadequate men who are sexually aroused by prepubescent children. Pedophiles are often attracted to both prepubescent boys and girls. The person with pedophilia commonly knows the child and wishes to touch, fondle, masturbate, or have intercourse with the child. The involved children are usually less than 14 years old. By definition, the pedophile is at least 16 years old and is five or more years older than the involved child. Thus, a 17-year-old who is having a sexual relationship with a 13-year-old would not receive the diagnosis of Pedophilia.

Pedophiles sometimes pursue positions of trust in society that allow them access to young children. All too often we read newspaper accounts of priests, teachers, and scout leaders who have taken sexual advantage of the children under their care. For example, Paul, a 19-year-old college student, sought psychotherapy because he was distressed about sexual concerns. He recounted the tremendous guilt he felt, as a Roman Catholic, because he "gave in" to urges to masturbate. Paul also admitted that he was harboring a "horrible secret." He recalled discussing masturbation at age 13 with his parish priest, who invited him back to the rectory for a private conversation. The priest asked Paul to masturbate in front of him so that he could better understand what Paul was talking about. To Paul's dismay, this trusted advisor began to assist him in the act and appeared to become sexually aroused by touching Paul's genitals. Paul remained troubled by the experience and kept it a secret until he finally discussed the matter in psychotherapy six years later.

DSM-IV allows the clinician to specify if the sexual attraction is to males, females, or both. The clinician can also code whether the pedophilia is "limited to incest" and whether it is "exclusive" (attraction only to children) or "nonexclusive" (attraction to both children and adults).

Sexual activity with children does not necessarily warrant the diagnosis of Pedophilia. Inappropriate sexual behavior may be a symptom of another disorder in which judgment is impaired. For example, sexual experiences with children may occur during a manic or a schizophrenic episode, as part of a dementing illness, during intoxication, or in mental retardation.

Sexual Masochism (302.83)

(*DSM-IV*, p. 529)

Sexual masochism involves getting sexual pleasure from being beaten, bound, raped, asphyxiated, cut, pierced, humiliated, or otherwise made to suffer. There have been deaths from practices such as hanging from a noose around the neck to achieve masochistic sexual pleasure through oxygen deprivation ("hypoxyphilia").

Sexual Sadism (302.84)

(*DSM-IV*, p. 530)

Sexual sadism refers to becoming sexually aroused by the suffering of another. This disorder may be associated with antisocial personality disorder. When the sadistic urges are strong, there is danger of serious harm or death to the victim. Sexual sadism, however, only infrequently leads to rape.

Transvestic Fetishism (302.3)

(*DSM-IV*, pp. 530–531)

This disorder occurs only in males who become sexually aroused by dressing in women's clothing. Often it begins at puberty. The individual may get an erection and masturbate when cross-dressing. Transvestic fetishism may occur with "gender dysphoria"—that is, with discomfort with one's gender role or identity. Transvestic fetishism is not diagnosed if it occurs solely during the course of a gender identity disorder.

Voyeurism (302.82)

(*DSM-IV*, p. 532)

The term *voyeurism* derives from the French *voi(r)* meaning "to see." Common English refers to voyeurs as *Peeping Toms*. The voyeur becomes sexually aroused by watching unsuspecting individuals getting undressed, being naked, or having sex. The Peeping Tom may masturbate to orgasm during the act of spying or later to the memory of the sight. The object of the voyeur's excitement is an unsuspecting person, so that seeing one's consenting lover naked or watching sex scenes in a movie do not meet criteria for the disorder.

Paraphilia Not Otherwise Specified (302.9)

(*DSM-IV*, p. 532)

This residual category is for paraphilias that do not meet criteria for any of the eight specific paraphilias above. When making the diagnosis, note the preferred sexual stimulus. Some possibilities include sexual arousal by:

Animals (Zoophilia)
Body parts (Partialism)
Dead bodies (Necrophilia)
Enemas (Klismaphilia)
Feces (Coprophilia)
Hair (Trichophilia)
Talking dirty on the telephone (Telephone Scatologia)
Urine (Urophilia)

The authors of this section of *DSM-IV* may actually suffer from a rare paraphilia NOS (i.e., *neologophilia:* the obtaining of perverse sexual pleasure from coining obscure words of Greek etymology for *DSM-IV* disorders).

GENDER IDENTITY DISORDERS

(DSM-IV, pp. 532–538)

GENDER IDENTITY DISORDER IN CHILDREN (302.6)
GENDER IDENTITY DISORDER IN ADOLESCENTS OR ADULTS
(302.85)

In *DSM-IV*, Gender Identity Disorder refers to a persistent and powerful identification with the opposite sex, accompanied by a discomfort with one's gender role or identity. Individuals with gender identity disorder are uncomfortable with their actual sex and its gender roles and have a fervent desire to be a member of the opposite sex. The disorder is not concurrent with an actual physical intersex condition, such as congenital adrenal hyperplasia. To qualify for the diagnosis in childhood, *DSM-IV* requires that children meet four of the following five criteria:

1. A wish to be of the opposite sex.
2. A preference for clothing of the opposite sex.
3. Fantasies of being of the opposite sex, or a preference for roles of the opposite sex.
4. Wishes to engage in opposite sex play.
5. Preference for opposite sex playmates.

Adults with the disorder will state that they feel like they are of the opposite sex or were born as the wrong sex. They wish to be and to be treated as members of the opposite sex. They may request medical treatment or surgery to become more like the opposite sex. Children may express disgust at their genitalia and may engage in gender-specific behaviors of the opposite sex. A feeling of self-loathing is one of the symptoms that may bring the child in for treatment.

DSM-IV allows the clinician to specify whether a sexually mature individual with gender identity disorder is sexually attracted to males, females, neither, or both.

Individuals with disorder of gender identity that do not meet full criteria for Gender Identity Disorder may be classified as Gender Identity Disorder Not Otherwise Specified (302.6) *(DSM-IV,* p. 538).

The first four years of life appear to be the crucial period for gender identity formation, and gender identity disorder can begin as early as age 2. Fantasies about being a member of the opposite sex are common and considered normal among 3-year-olds. In one study (Goleman 1994) of preschool-age children, Dr. Linda Linday found that about half the girls had fantasies of having a penis or being a boy, and about half the boys had fantasies about being pregnant. A certain amount of experimentation with the clothing or gender roles of the opposite sex is part of the normal exploration of early childhood. Around age 4, children begin to realize that not everything is possible, and they start to face the limits of their actual gender. Only then does the child begin to develop the intellectual capacity to contemplate the notion that "anatomy is destiny."

Gender identity disorder is rare and appears to be related to certain types of family dynamics. Boys with gender identity disorder often have a distant father and a mother who is overtly hostile and devaluing toward men. Other boys with the disorder have mothers who are suddenly traumatized and distressed so that they become emotionally inaccessible to the boy, often around ages 2 or 3; the boy may then seek to be like an emotionally nurturing female.

Girls with gender identity disorder also seem to develop in difficult family situations. In one study (Goleman) about half the girls with gender identity problems had violent or abusive fathers. In addition, about 80 percent of these girls had mothers who became profoundly depressed or otherwise emotionally inaccessible when the girls were between 1 1/2 and 4 years of age.

A NOTE ON HOMOSEXUALITY AND DSM-IV

Homosexual individuals, as a rule, do not suffer from a gender identity disorder. The vast majority of homosexual men and women do report, however, having engaged in some form of cross-gender activity during childhood. In the New York Times of March 23, 1994, Daniel Goleman reported the results of a study by Zucker and Bailey that included 5,734 gay men, 1,729 gay women, and several thousand straight men and women. According to Zucker and Bailey's study:

> 89 percent of gay men had a history as children of frequently engaging in cross-dressing, playing girls' games and preferring to play with girls.

Only 2 percent of heterosexual men reported that they had engaged in these activities frequently. For lesbians, 81 percent recalled such cross-gender activities in childhood, as compared with 12 percent of heterosexual women. [Goleman, *New York Times*, 3/22/94]

Other studies in the scientific literature suggest a genetic predisposition toward homosexuality. For instance, identical male twins are both more likely to be gay than are non-twin brothers. Scientists at the National Cancer Institute published in the journal *Science* their hypothesis that a small region of the X chromosome contributes to a homosexual orientation in males. In this study of 114 gay males (Hamer et al. 1993), the incidence of male homosexuality appeared to travel genetically in an X chromosome pattern—that is, in the maternal rather than the paternal side of the family. Analysis of 40 pairs of gay, non-twin brothers revealed that 33 of the 40 pairs had identical segments of DNA on one tip of their X chromosomes.

The issue of the origins and nature of homosexuality has become a matter of both politics and scientific investigation. Under pressure from the gay community, the American Psychiatric Association removed homosexuality from *DSM-II* in 1973, citing evidence that homosexuality did not meet criteria for a mental disorder. To acknowledge those individuals who were troubled by and who sought therapy to alter their homosexuality, the APA maintained the diagnosis of Ego-Dystonic Homosexuality in *DSM-III*.

Gay activists campaigned hard to eliminate ego-dystonic homosexuality from psychiatric nosology because of the implication that homosexuality itself was a psychiatric disorder. Bowing to pressure from the gay community and citing the lack of evidence that ego-dystonic homosexuality constituted a genuine mental disorder, the APA eliminated this diagnosis from the *DSM-III-R*. By the mid-1980s it became politically incorrect to utter the words "homosexuality" and "mental disorder" in the same sentence. Even those treatment programs aimed at helping bisexual men become heterosexual did not use the ego-dystonic homosexuality diagnosis.

Now only a small group of therapists remain who offer psychiatric treatment to change sexual orientation in those bisexual individuals who are sufficiently troubled by the homosexual part of their personality. Such therapists usually make a distinction between being "homosexual" (attracted sexually to members of the same sex) and being "gay" (being homosexual and adopting a non-heterosexual life-style and value system). While acknowledging a likely biological component to homosexual orientation, these clinicians attempt to work with the familial and social influences that influence homosexual attraction and behavior.

Early in 1994 the APA trustees approved a "Position Statement on Psychiatric Treatment Designed to Change Sexual Orientation" to be sent for approval by the Assembly at the May 1994 annual APA meeting in Philadelphia. The position statement would essentially make it unethical for a psychiatrist to intend to change a person's sexual orientation. According to the APA trustees:

> The Board of Trustees of the American Psychiatric Association removed homosexuality from *DSM-II* in 1973 after reviewing evidence that it did not meet criteria for a mental disorder. In 1987 ego-dystonic homosexuality was removed from *DSM-III-R* based on similar evidence. The APA does not endorse any psychiatric treatment that is based either upon a psychiatrist's assumption that homosexuality is a mental disorder or a psychiatrist's intent to change a person's sexual orientation. A psychiatrist should remain nonjudgmental and respectful of a patient's sexual orientation and the patient's objective for treatment. [reported in *Psychiatric News*, April 15, 1994, p. 18]

Armed with this new APA position statement on homosexuality, spokespersons for the gay community were quick to warn psychiatrists of the potential for lawsuits should they engage in so-called "reparative" therapy with gay adolescents. According to the *Mental Health Reporter* (June 1994), psychiatrist William Womack "noted that adolescents could file suit over homophobic counseling when they become adults" (p. 42). Nonetheless, psychiatrists and other mental health professionals can still practice reparative therapy, billing insurance companies under the *DSM-IV* rubric of Sexual Disorder Not Otherwise Specified (302.9).

23

Eating Disorders

"Der Mensch ist, was er isst."
(Man is what he eats.)

Ludwig Feuerback (1804–1872),
from an advertisement for Moleschott,
Lehre der Nahrungsmittel: Für das Volk (1850)

"Dis-moi ce que tu manges, je te dirai ce que tu es."
(Tell me what you eat, I will tell you what you are.)

Anthelme Brillat-Savarin (1755–1826),
Physiologie du Goût (1825)

THE THREE *DSM-IV* EATING DISORDERS:
307.1   Anorexia Nervosa
         Specify type:
         Restricting type (does not regularly binge or purge)
         Binge eating/purging type (self-induced vomiting,
         laxatives, diuretics)
307.51   Bulimia Nervosa
         Specify type:
         Purging type
         Nonpurging type
307.50   Eating Disorder Not Otherwise Specified (NOS)

ANOREXIA NERVOSA (307.1)

(*DSM-IV*, pp. 539–545)
     In 1868 the English physician William Gull described a condition in
which patients starved themselves in a relentless effort to become and

stay thin. The premium that American culture places on thinness as a sign of beauty probably contributes to the prevalence of this disorder in modern times. The majority of sufferers of anorexia nervosa in the United States are white females between the ages of 10 and 30, often from the higher socioeconomic classes. Anorexia nervosa is uncommon in underdeveloped countries and among blacks in the United States. Although anorexia nervosa manifests in individuals, it may be a reflection of a disordered value system of white upper-middle-class American society. Such values focus on appearances and externals.

Women who become anorexic frequently grow up in competitive upper-middle-class families that place a premium on achievement. The parents are often demanding and controlling so that the young woman feels little sense of personal autonomy. For example, during a family evaluation of a college student with anorexia nervosa, the young woman's father chided the male therapist for not having his shoes polished to a high sheen. The father seemed more concerned with superficial appearances than with the substantive psychological issues being discussed.

To meet criteria for the diagnosis of anorexia nervosa in *DSM-IV*, patients must satisfy four conditions. Specifically, patients with anorexia nervosa: 1) keep their body weight at less than 85 percent of their minimal normal weight for their height and age, 2) live in dread of fatness or weight gain, 3) have a disordered body image, and 4) in women, miss three consecutive menstrual periods.

Patients with anorexia go to extremes to avoid fatness and delight in their excessive thinness. The restricting type of anorexia nervosa is characterized by avoidance of food and by strenuous exercise to lose weight. Eating disorders are not uncommon among fashion models, female athletes (e.g., runners, body builders), ballet dancers, and male wrestlers whose avocations require them to rigorously control their weight. The binge eating/purging type of anorexia nervosa involves the use of diuretics (water pills), laxatives, and self-induced vomiting to keep the weight off. Patients with anorexia nervosa suffer numerous health complications and risk death from starvation in about 7 percent of cases. The singer Karen Carpenter appears to have died as a consequence of anorexia nervosa.

The differential diagnosis of anorexia nervosa includes other psychiatric disorders in which weight loss and changes in appetite occur. In a major depressive episode there is often significant weight loss, but there is not the relentless pursuit of thinness, the distorted body image, or the fear of fatness seen in anorexia nervosa. It is not uncommon, however, for patients with anorexia nervosa to also suffer from a major depressive episode. Schizophrenia can present with bizarre dietary habits and weight loss as part of the psychotic picture. It is possible to meet criteria for both anorexia nervosa and schizophrenia. In obsessive-compulsive disorder there may be rituals around food and eating that lead to weight loss, but the distorted body image and fear of fatness are absent. Anorexic patients may also meet criteria for personality disorders, substance abuse (e.g., stimulants), or bulimia nervosa. In *DSM-IV*, however, binge eating and purging that occur exclusively during anorexia nervosa do not require a separate diagnosis of Bulimia Nervosa, as was the case in *DSM-III-R*.

BULIMIA NERVOSA (307.51)

(*DSM-IV*, pp. 545–550)

Like the Sybarites of ancient Rome, patients with bulimia nervosa regularly eat like gluttons and then purge or vomit to compensate for the enormous amount of food they have just devoured. Bulimic patients share with anorexic patients an immoderate preoccupation with their body's size, shape, and weight. Unlike anorexic patients, those suffering from bulimia nervosa often have normal body weight and usually manage to keep their bingeing and purging a secret. For example, the actress and exercise enthusiast Jane Fonda has publicly admitted to suffering from bulimia for many years.

DSM-IV characterizes Bulimia Nervosa as consisting of recurrent episodes (averaging twice weekly for at least three months) of both binge eating and inappropriate compensatory behavior aimed at preventing weight gain in a person whose self-evaluation is overly dependent on body image. To meet criteria for Bulimia Nervosa in *DSM-IV*, the disturbed eating behavior must not occur exclusively during episodes of anorexia nervosa.

DSM-IV subdivides Bulimia Nervosa into purging and nonpurging types. The purging type abuses laxatives, diuretics, or self-induced vomiting to avoid gaining weight. The nonpurging type becomes obsessed with exercise, fasting, or dieting to control body weight.

The differential diagnosis of bulimia nervosa is similar to that of anorexia nervosa. It is not uncommon for bulimic patients to shoplift food from stores; such behavior may be confused with kleptomania. Major depressive episodes commonly accompany bulimia nervosa.

EATING DISORDER NOT OTHERWISE SPECIFIED (307.50)

(*DSM-IV*, p. 550)

Many people engage in abnormal eating behaviors, such as binge eating, excessive fasting, or self-induced vomiting without meeting criteria for anorexia nervosa or bulimia nervosa. When such eating behaviors cause clinically significant distress or impairment, the diagnosis of Eating Disorder NOS applies.

For example, some women with regular menstrual cycles will meet the other criteria for anorexia nervosa. Other patients may meet all the criteria for bulimia nervosa, except that the binge eating and compensatory behaviors occur on average less than twice weekly or for less than three months. Certain individuals may purge regularly after eating normal amounts of food. In addition, *DSM-IV* suggests the term *Binge Eating Disorder* for a condition in which individuals binge without engaging in inappropriate compensatory behaviors. One clinician suggested that Jeffrey Dahmer, the mass murderer who killed and ate his victims, met criteria for Eating Disorder Not Otherwise Specified.

Appendix B of *DSM-IV* contains research criteria for Binge-Eating Disorder (*DSM-IV*, pp. 729–731). This disorder consists of repeated bouts of binge eating without the inappropriate compensatory behaviors seen in bulimia nervosa.

24

Sleep Disorders

"Thou hast been call'd, O Sleep! the friend of Woe,
But 'tis the happy who have called thee so."
Robert Southey (1774–1843), *The Curse of Kehama*, XV.12 (1810)

PRIMARY SLEEP DISORDERS:
DYSSOMNIAS:
307.42   Primary Insomnia
307.44   Primary Hypersomnia
          Specify if: recurrent (periods of at least three days of
          excessive sleepiness several times a year for at least two
          years)
347   Narcolepsy
780.59   Breathing-Related Sleep Disorder
307.45   Circadian Rhythm Sleep Disorder (Sleep-Wake Schedule
          Disorder)
          Specify type:
            Delayed sleep phase type
            Jet lag type
            Shift work type
            Unspecified
307.47   Dyssomnia Not Otherwise Specified (NOS)

PARASOMNIAS:
307.47   Nightmare Disorder (Dream Anxiety Disorder)
307.46   Sleep Terror Disorder
307.46   Sleepwalking Disorder
307.47   Parasomnia Not Otherwise Specified (NOS)

SLEEP DISORDERS RELATED TO ANOTHER MENTAL DISORDER:
307.42   Insomnia related to an Axis I or Axis II Disorder
307.44   Hypersomnia related to an Axis I or Axis II Disorder

OTHER SLEEP DISORDERS:
Sleep Disorder Due to a General Medical Condition:
780.52   Insomnia Type
780.54   Hypersomnia Type
780.59   Parasomnia Type
780.59   Mixed Type
Substance-Induced Sleep Disorder:
---.--   Substance-Induced Sleep Disorder (refer to specific
           substances for codes)
           Specify if:
              With onset during intoxication
              With onset during withdrawal
              (Code for substance-specific intoxication or withdrawal
           if criteria are met.)
           Specify type:
              Insomnia type
              Hypersomnia type
              Parasomnia type
              Mixed type
           (Note: The same *DSM-IV* code (292.89) applies to
           Specific Substance Sleep Disorders in the following
           categories: Alcohol; Amphetamine or related substances;
           Caffeine; Cocaine; Opioids; Sedatives, Hypnotics, or
           Anxiolytics; Other or Unknown Substances.)

Occasional problems with sleep are part of the human condition. Almost everyone will have trouble sleeping during times of extreme stress. According to a 1980 survey by the National Institute of Mental Health, during the course of a year about one-third of the population have difficulty sleeping and one-sixth suffer from insomnia that disrupts their lives. In addition, disturbances of sleep are often symptoms of other *DSM-IV* disorders, such as affective disorders and psychotic disorders. Medical disorders and substance use can also affect the quality or amount of sleep.

The types of sleep disorders described in *DSM-IV* are the chronic rather than the transient disturbances of sleep. The diagnostic manual divides the primary sleep disorders into two types: the *dyssomnias* and the *parasomnias*. Dyssomnias involve problems with the amount, quality, or time course of sleep (insomnia, hypersomnia, narcolepsy, breathing-related disorders, and circadian rhythm disorders). Parasomnias refer to unusual events (nightmares, sleepwalking, sleep terrors) that disrupt the normal sleep cycle.

Normal sleep is an active cyclical process. Each cycle consists of a period of non-rapid-eye-movement (NREM) sleep, followed by rapid-eye-movement (REM) sleep. A period of REM sleep occurs about every 90 to 100 minutes. During a full night's sleep, an individual goes through four or five cycles. Each cycle involves a progression through the various stages of sleep, classified as stages 1, 2, 3, and 4. These stages can be measured by polysomnography, which records the brain's electrical activity, eye movements, and muscle tone simultaneously. Each sleep stage has a characteristic appearance on the EEG or electroencephalogram.

During wakefulness, the EEG shows random, low-voltage, very fast waves. As we become drowsy, the EEG begins to display random, fast alpha waves of 8 to 12 cycles per second (CPS). Drowsiness gives way to Stage 1 sleep, the lightest stage of sleep, during which the EEG shows low-voltage, regular 3 to 7 CPS theta waves. The sleeping person descends in a stepwise fashion over about 30 minutes from Stage 1 to Stage 4 sleep.

Stage 2 occurs after several seconds or minutes and marks the onset of "true sleep." Stage 2 consists of 12 to 14 CPS sleep spindles and high-spike triphasic K complexes on the EEG. Stage 3 is characterized by some EEG high-voltage, slow 0.5 to 2.5 CPS delta waves. The individual is said to enter Stage 4 when the delta waves occupy more than 50 percent of the EEG. Most Stage 4 sleep occurs during the first third of the night.

Stage 4 is a deep, dreamless sleep. Stages 3 and 4, the deepest portions of non-REM sleep, are sometimes referred to as "delta" sleep. A person who is awakened between 30 minutes and an hour into the sleep cycle will be in the midst of deep delta sleep. Such a person will be confused and disoriented and will probably have amnesia for any events that occur during a brief arousal. Stages 3 and 4 NREM delta sleep is also associated with unusual arousal patterns, such as bed wetting, sleep walking, sleep talking, and night terrors (fearful screaming episodes that interrupt NREM Stage 4 sleep). Most dreaming occurs during REM and Stage 3 NREM sleep. Nightmares are particularly frightening dreams that occur during REM sleep.

Following a descent from Stage 1 to Stage 4 sleep, the individual remains in Stage 4 for several minutes and then ascends to lighter stages (1 or 2) of sleep before entering REM sleep about 90 to 100 minutes after falling asleep. Individuals spend about 25 percent of their total sleep in REM sleep. The first REM period of the night is the shortest, often less than 10 minutes. Most REM sleep takes place during the final third of the night, and the later REM periods may extend to about 40 minutes.

During REM sleep, the EEG shows sawtooth waves similar to those of drowsy sleep. Dreaming is common during REM sleep, which has a depth similar to Stage 2 sleep. During REM sleep there occur rapid synchronous eye movements, inhibition of muscle tone, changes in heart rate, respiration and blood pressure, and penile erections in men. As the night progresses, the REM periods become longer, and Stage 4 sleep disappears as the sleep becomes lighter. After each period of REM sleep, the cycle repeats. People normally pass through four or five such cycles during a single night's sleep.

The amount of time it takes to enter the first REM period is called the *REM latency*. Normal REM latency is about 90 minutes. Patients suffering from a major depressive episode commonly display a short REM latency and diminished delta sleep. Some researchers consider shortened REM latency to be a "biological marker" for major depressive disorder. Individuals with narcolepsy may have a REM latency of 10 minutes or less. In addition, children with attention-deficit/ hyperactivity disorder frequently have trouble falling asleep and about 20 percent of such children show decreased REM latency and increased delta sleep latency on sleep EEGs.

Being deprived of sleep can lead to uncomfortable symptoms. Prolonged sleep deprivation may provoke a disorganized hallucinatory or delusional state. People who are deprived of REM sleep will experience *REM rebound*—that is, increased REM sleep when allowed to sleep undisturbed. Lack of sufficient REM sleep is also associated with daytime irritability and listlessness.

The Association of Sleep Disorders Centers has suggested two mnemonics for disorders of sleep and arousal, namely, *DIMS* and

DOES. It is useful for the clinician to be familiar with these mnemonics that appear in the sleep literature. The DIMS are Disorders of Initiating and Maintaining Sleep. The DOES are the Disorders of Excessive Somnolence.

THE PRIMARY SLEEP DISORDERS

The Dyssomnias

Primary Insomnia (307.42)

(*DSM-IV*, pp. 553–557)

Primary insomnia is a disorder of initiating or maintaining sleep or of not feeling rested after a night's sleep (daytime fatigue), for a period of a month or longer. To meet criteria, the insomnia must cause significant distress or impairment. In addition, the insomnia must not be due to another mental or sleep disorder, to substance use, or to a general medical condition.

People with insomnia complain that they do not get enough sleep, that their sleep is disturbed, or that they do not feel rested even after a night's sleep. About 9 percent of Americans complain of chronic problems with insomnia. The daytime consequences of insomnia include lethargy, headaches, dysphoria, decreased concentration, and psychomotor impairment, which may contribute to accident proneness.

Insomnia may be primary or may be secondary to medical illness, psychiatric disorders, or substance use. Any disease that causes breathing difficulties, discomfort, or pain during the night may lead to insomnia. Alcohol, stimulant drugs, steroids, decongestants, some of the newer antidepressants, and many medications used for cardiac and lung disease may cause insomnia as a side effect. A certain amount of insomnia is a behaviorally conditioned response; the anxiety and worry about not being able to sleep becomes a self-fulfilling prophecy. In assessing insomnia, the clinician should also consider circadian rhythm disturbances, erratic sleep-wake schedules, restless legs syndrome, sleep apnea, and other breathing disorders.

Primary Hypersomnia (307.44)

(*DSM-IV*, pp. 557–562)

Primary hypersomnia is a disorder of excessive sleepiness. Individuals complain of sleeping too many hours at night or of sleeping during the day as well (daytime somnolence). To meet criteria, the excessive sleepiness must cause clinically significant distress or impairment. In addition, the hypersomnia is not due to substance use, to a general medical condition, to another mental disorder, or to insufficient sleep, nor does it occur exclusively during another sleep disorder, like narcolepsy or sleep apnea. If the hypersomnia occurs for periods of at least three days several times a year for two or more years, the clinician can code the disorder as "Recurrent." *Kleine-Levin syndrome* is a rare form of episodic primary hypersomnia and hyperphagia that affects adolescent boys.

Narcolepsy (347)

(*DSM-IV*, pp. 562–567)

Narcolepsy is a disorder of sleep attacks, cataplexy, and abnormal manifestations of REM sleep, such as sleep paralysis or hypnogogic/hypnopompic hallucinations. The word *narcolepsy* derives from the Greek *narke*, meaning "numbness" or "stupor," and *lepsia*, meaning "fit" or "attack." To meet criteria for the disorder, the affected individual must not be able to avoid or resist the attacks of sleep that are refreshing and occur daily for at least three months.

The term *cataplexy* comes from the Greek *kata*, meaning "down, downward," and *plessein*, meaning "to strike." Narcoleptic patients are "stricken down" by loss of muscle tone, often brought on by laughing, anger, or other intense emotional reactions.

The abnormalities of REM sleep seen in narcolepsy consist of intrusions of aspects of REM sleep into the twilight zone between sleep and wakefulness. Some people with narcolepsy experience vivid, dreamlike auditory or visual hallucinations while falling asleep (hypnogogic) or while waking up (hypnopompic). The narcoleptic individual may also have sleep paralysis, the experience of feeling awake, but being unable to voluntarily move a muscle at the beginning or end of a period of sleep. These attacks of flaccid paralysis can be quite frightening. Sudden attacks of sleep can also lead to accidents.

Narcolepsy usually begins in adolescence or young adulthood. The cause seems to be a genetic abnormality of the sleep mechanisms of the central nervous system. A particular antigen called HLA-DR2 occurs in more than 95 percent of narcoleptic patients, as opposed to only 25 percent of the general population and up to 40 percent of patients with other sleep disorders. Thus, the HLA-DR2 antigen may be a necessary but not sufficient marker of narcolepsy. Research also shows that the narcoleptic brain's caudate nucleus binds more dopamine than in controls. Narcoleptics also have more dopamine D2 receptors. Cases of narcolepsy have been documented in dogs as well as humans. The neurophysiological defect of narcolepsy leads to a disinhibition of REM sleep with patients entering REM sleep almost immediately.

Breathing-Related Sleep Disorder (780.59)

(*DSM-IV*, pp. 567-573)
Some individuals have problems with breathing during sleep. The breathing difficulty may disrupt the sleep sufficiently to cause clinically significant insomnia or hypersomnia. Typical breathing disorders that affect sleep are sleep apnea syndrome and central alveolar hypoventilation syndrome. This diagnosis is not made if the sleep disruption is due to substance use, to a non-breathing-related general medical condition or to another mental disorder.

The *sleep apnea syndromes* are a group of potentially deadly disorders in which breathing repeatedly stops during sleep (apneic pauses) long enough to cause deoxygenation of the blood or in which breathing stops more than 30 times per night for periods of 10 seconds or longer. Sleep apnea can be obstructive (due to blockage of the airway), central (due to an abnormality in the brain's respiratory center), or mixed. Airway obstruction, the most frequent cause of sleep apnea, occurs most often in obese persons (Pickwickian syndrome, named after the character created by Charles Dickens).

Patients with obstructive sleep apnea may complain of daytime drowsiness. They are often irritable and display impaired performance. Clinical depression is commonly associated with sleep apnea. The medical literature suggests that obstructive sleep apnea may also be linked with several physical illnesses, including high blood pressure, cardiac arrhythmias, strokes, heart attacks, and sudden death during sleep.

Central alveolar hypoventilation syndrome is a disorder of impaired ventilation of the lungs that occurs or markedly worsens only while the person sleeps. Individuals with central alveolar hypoventilation syndrome do not have significant apneic pauses as seen in sleep apnea; rather, they simply do not take enough air into their lungs during sleep. The condition can be so severe that the patient must stay awake to stay alive. *Ondine's curse* refers to death brought on by falling asleep and being unable to inhale enough oxygen to maintain life.

Circadian Rhythm Sleep Disorder (Formerly Sleep-Wake Schedule Disorder) (307.45)

(*DSM-IV*, pp. 573–578)

Circadian rhythms occur in most living organisms (Hauri 1992). The human circadian clock completes one cycle approximately every 24 hours during preadolescence and middle age. The clock slows down during the mid-teens and remains slow through young adulthood, allowing members of these age groups to become "night owls."

Humans actually have two body clocks: a circadian clock and a chemical clock. These two body clocks keep time separately and need to be reset daily to remain coordinated. One's wake-up time is the most potent time setter for both clocks.

The center for the circadian clock is in the suprachiasmatic nucleus of the brain. Among its important functions, this nucleus regulates daytime alertness, REM sleep, body temperature, and the daily pattern of cortisol release. Daylight is a potent setter of the suprachiasmatic clock. In *seasonal affective disorder*, the individual's moods are apparently influenced by the amount and intensity of daylight, which affects the sleep–wake cycle through the mediation of the melatonin system of the pineal gland (Erush 1994).

The body's chemical clock consists of chemicals that accumulate in the body during the day and are metabolized during the night. One's activity level will help reset the chemical clock.

Sleep is one of the many body functions that follows a circadian rhythm. Thus, sleep during the daytime differs qualitatively from sleep during the nighttime. For example, in a normal nighttime sleeper, a nap before noon will contain significantly more REM sleep than a nap later in the day.

Some individuals keep schedules in which they need to be awake at a time their body would normally sleep and vice versa. A Circadian Rhythm Sleep Disorder is diagnosed when the mismatch between the required sleep–wake schedule and the circadian sleep–wake cycle causes clinically significant disruption of sleep, with consequent insomnia or hypersomnia. The disorder is not due to substance use, a general medical condition, or another sleep or mental disorder.

Clinicians should specify the type of phase shift in the disorder. *DSM-IV* offers four options:

Delayed sleep phase type: Individuals go to sleep and wake up later than desired. They are unable to fall asleep or wake up as early as they would like to.

Jet lag type: This usually occurs after traveling across several time zones. Individuals feel sleepy and alert at inappropriate times of day relative to the local time zone. In jet lag, one's activity level resets the body's chemical clock while the change in the hours of daylight resets the suprachiasmatic clock.

Shift work type: This usually occurs among shift workers who either work all night or frequently vary their schedules from day to evening to night work. They may be unable to sleep when they want to or feel excessively drowsy when they should be awake and alert.

Unspecified type: None of the above.

Circadian rhythms are not present at birth.

Dyssomnia Not Otherwise Specified (307.47)

(DSM-IV, p. 579)

The Not Otherwise Specified category allows the clinician to diagnose disorders of insomnia, hypersomnia, or circadian rhythm disturbances that do not meet criteria for the specific dyssomnias. In addition, the clinician can code here those dyssomnias whose etiology is uncertain. For example, a dyssomnia may be present, but it may be unclear if the disorder is substance induced, medically caused, or a primary insomnia.

Nocturnal Myoclonus: *DSM-IV* also suggests using this NOS category to code nocturnal myoclonus or "restless legs syndrome." Nocturnal myoclonus consists of repeated jerks of the limb muscles, especially of the legs, during sleep. These abrupt muscle contractions cause brief periods of arousal and interfere with sleep.

The Parasomnias

Sleep researchers humorously refer to the parasomnias as "things that go bump in the night." Technically, the parasomnias are disturbing events or behaviors that occur during sleep or in the twilight zone between sleep and wakefulness. Patients with parasomnias complain about the event itself, whereas patients with dyssomnias complain about the problem with their sleep. For example, individuals with the dyssomnia of sleep apnea report daytime drowsiness rather than repeated cessation of breathing during the night.

Nightmare (Formerly Dream Anxiety) Disorder (307.47)

(DSM-IV, pp. 580–583)

Most people have had a nightmare at some time in their lives. Individuals with nightmare disorder repeatedly awaken frightened from terrifying vivid dreams, usually occurring in REM sleep during the second half of the night. In contrast with the confusion and disorientation seen upon arousal from sleep terror disorder, the person who awakens from a nightmare is able to quickly regain orientation and alertness. The anxiety-provoking dreams of nightmare disorder cause significant distress or impairment and are not the result of substance use or of a general medical condition.

Nightmares seem to occur commonly after alcohol ingestion, during fevers, and with excessive fatigue. They are also a feature of Separation Anxiety Disorder of Childhood (309.21). Frequent nightmares have been linked to artistic talent as well as to vulnerability to schizophrenia.

Sleep Terror Disorder (307.46)

(DSM-IV, p. 583–587)

Night terrors (pavor nocturnus) consist of fearful episodes of flailing and screaming that interrupt Stage 4 NREM sleep. Affected individuals are commonly children who have a panicky dream that abruptly awakens them in terror during the first third of the night. The awakened individual is disoriented and confused and will have amnesia for the episode. Upon awakening from a night terror, the person feels intense anxiety and autonomic arousal (the "fight or flight" response: rapid heart rate, fast breathing, sweating, elevated blood pressure, etc.). Those who try to comfort the panicky individual are generally unable to do so.

Night terrors may be the result of a minor neurological abnormality. When the onset of sleep terror disorder occurs in adolescence or young adulthood, it may be the first sign of temporal lobe epilepsy. Sleep terror is also associated with sleepwalking and bed wetting.

At one time, night terrors were attributed to an incubus, a spirit who had sexual intercourse with women during sleep, or to a succubus, a female demon who had sexual intercourse with sleeping men. Those were the days!

Sleepwalking Disorder (307.46)

DSM-IV, pp. 587–591)
Sleepwalking (somnambulism) usually occurs during Stage 4 NREM sleep of the first third of the night. The individual gets out of bed and walks about with eyes open and a blank facial stare. Those who try to communicate with or awaken the sleepwalking individual are usually unable to do so. If the person is awakened from the episode, there may be a brief period of confusion or disorientation followed by normal cognitive functioning within several minutes. Upon awakening in the morning, the individual has no recollection of the event. The sleepwalking episodes are not due to substance use or to a general medical condition.

In addition to sleepwalking, somnambulism may include sitting up, talking, screaming, dressing, going to the bathroom, and on occasion even driving a car! The disorder usually begins between ages 6 and 12 and tends to run in families. It occurs more frequently in boys than in girls. Most likely a minor neurological abnormality underlies the disorder.

Parasomnia Not Otherwise Specified (307.47)

(DSM-IV, p. 592)
This Not Otherwise Specified category can be used to code distressing abnormal events that occur during sleep, but that do not

meet criteria for other specific parasomnias. For example, some medical disorders tend to occur or be exacerbated during sleep. Such disorders include nocturnal angina pectoris (chest pain), sleep-related cluster headaches, asthma, bruxism (teeth grinding), head banging (*Jactatio Capitis Nocturnus*), familial sleep paralysis, sleep epilepsy, painful erections, abnormal swallowing, esophageal reflux, and paroxysmal nocturnal hemoglobinuria. In addition, the clinician can use this code to express uncertainty about whether a parasomnia is primary or due to substance use or to a general medical condition.

REM sleep behavior disorder consists of attacks of agitated or violent behavior during REM sleep. This disorder is most commonly seen in older men who may injure themselves as they appear to be acting out their dreams. The underlying mechanism may be a failure of inhibition of the voluntary muscles that normally occurs during REM sleep. About one-third of cases of this disorder have an associated neurological condition.

THE SLEEP DISORDERS RELATED
TO ANOTHER MENTAL DISORDER

Sometimes sleep disorders are clearly part of another mental disorder. For example, psychotic and affective disorders may have sleep disturbances as a feature of their clinical picture. Persons with anxiety disorders or adjustment disorders may lie awake worrying much of the night. Individuals with personality disorders (Axis II) may have abnormal sleep patterns because of chronic maladaptive character styles.

For cases in which the sleep disorder is part of an Axis I or an Axis II condition, but in which the clinician judges that the dyssomnia warrants independent clinical attention, *DSM-IV* provides the following two categories to code the problem.

Insomnia Related to [Axis I or Axis II] Disorder (307.42)

(*DSM-IV*, pp. 592–597)

Insomnia refers to at least a month of difficulty initiating/ maintaining sleep, or non-restful sleep that causes excessive daytime fatigue or impaired functioning. The insomnia is part of another Axis

I or Axis II disorder other than substance use or a general medical condition.

Hypersomnia Related to [Axis I or Axis II] Disorder (307.44)

(*DSM-IV*, pp. 592–597)

Hypersomnia refers to at least a month of excessive drowsiness, as evidenced by an almost daily need for extra hours of sleep at night or for naps during the day. The hypersomnia causes clinically significant distress or impairment and is part of another Axis I or Axis II disorder other than substance use or a general medical condition.

OTHER SLEEP DISORDERS

Because sleep disorders may be substance induced or secondary to a general medical condition, *DSM-IV* includes the following two categories in its chapter on disorders of sleep.

Sleep Disorder Due to a General Medical Condition (780.5x)

(*DSM-IV*, pp. 597–601)

In addition to narcolepsy and breathing disorders that disrupt sleep, many other medical conditions can cause sleep problems that produce significant distress or impairment and therefore warrant independent clinical attention. To meet criteria for this diagnosis, there must be evidence in the medical history, physical examination, or diagnostic tests of a medical or neurological illness that is causing the sleep disorder. In addition, *DSM-IV* requires that the sleep disturbance not occur solely as part of a delirium.

The clinician can use the fifth digit to code the type of sleep disorder, as follows:

Sleep Disorder Due to a General Medical Condition
780.52   Insomnia Type
780.54   Hypersomnia Type

780.59   Parasomnia Type
780.59   Mixed Type

The clinician should code the name of the medical condition on Axis I after the phrase "due to" and should also code the medical condition on Axis III.

Substance-Induced Sleep Disorder

(*DSM-IV*, pp. 601–607)

Many drugs and medications can induce sleep disorders. To meet criteria for this diagnosis in *DSM-IV*, the following conditions must be met:

1. There is a clinically significant problem with sleep that causes marked distress or impairment.
2. There is medical evidence of substance intoxication and withdrawal, and the sleep disturbance started during or within a month of the intoxication or withdrawal.
3. The sleep problem is not better accounted for by a separate sleep disorder that is unrelated to substance use.

Some common substance-related sleep disorders include:
291.8   Alcohol-induced Sleep Disorder
292.89   Amphetamine-induced Sleep Disorder
292.89   Caffeine-induced Sleep Disorder
292.89   Cocaine-induced Sleep Disorder
292.89   Opioid-induced Sleep Disorder
292.89   Sedative/Hypnotic/Anxiolytic-induced Sleep Disorder
292.89   Other/Unknown Substance-induced Sleep Disorder

The clinician should also code the substance-specific intoxication or withdrawal if one exists.

In addition, the following specifiers apply to substance-induced sleep disorders:

Specify if Substance-Induced Sleep Disorder occurs:

−With onset during intoxication
−With onset during withdrawal

Specify type of Substance-Induced Sleep Disorder:

−Insomnia type
−Hypersomnia type
−Parasomnia type
−Mixed type

25

Impulse Control Disorders Not Elsewhere Classified (312.3x)

"I can resist everything except temptation."

Oscar Wilde (1845–1900),
Lady Windermere's Fan, Act I (1891)

THE IMPULSE CONTROL DISORDERS NOS:

312.34	Intermittent Explosive Disorder
312.32	Kleptomania
312.33	Pyromania
312.31	Pathological Gambling
312.39	Trichotillomania
312.30	Impulse Control Disorder Not Otherwise Specified

Many disorders of impulse control are classified elsewhere in the manual. For example, substance abusers may feel impelled to consume psychoactive substances. Children with attention deficit/hyperactivity disorder may impulsively blurt out answers to questions in class or have difficulty waiting their turn in a group activity. Persons with paraphilias feel compelled to act on intense sexual urges that society considers deviant. This chapter deals with five specific disorders of impulse control that are not treated elsewhere in the manual, namely, intermittent explosive disorder, kleptomania, pyromania, pathological gambling, and trichotillomania. As usual, *DSM-IV* provides an Impulse Control Disorder NOS category.

According to *DSM-IV,* three essential features characterize the impulse control disorders:

1. Giving in to an urge or impulse to perform a harmful act.
2. An inner sense of tension or arousal prior to performing the harmful act.
3. A sense of relief, gratification, or pleasure while committing the harmful act.

INTERMITTENT EXPLOSIVE DISORDER (312.34)

(DSM-IV, pp. 609–612)

Many clinicians and researchers doubt the existence of a disorder of episodic dyscontrol of aggressive impulses that is not accounted for by some other *DSM-IV* diagnosis. Nonetheless, the *DSM-IV* has included Intermittent Explosive Disorder for cases characterized by several distinct episodes of loss of control of aggressive impulses that is out of proportion to any stressors and that leads to assaults on other people or to destruction of property.

To make this diagnosis according to *DSM-IV,* the episodic dyscontrol must not be better accounted for by one of the following *DSM-IV* conditions: Antisocial or Borderline Personality Disorder, a Psychotic Disorder, a Manic Episode, Conduct Disorder, Attention Deficit/ Hyperactivity Disorder, a Substance-Induced condition, or a General Medical condition. Other *DSM-IV* conditions that may present with explosive outbursts include Major Depression, which can present with irritability and angry outbursts; Adult Antisocial Behavior (V71.01); Factitious Disorder; and Malingering.

KLEPTOMANIA (312.32)

(*DSM-IV,* pp. 612–613)

The term *kleptomania* comes from the Greek work *kleptes,* meaning thief. People with kleptomania repeatedly give in to urges to steal items that they do not need for personal use or for monetary value. There is a period of rising tension before the theft and a sense of relief or pleasure during the act of stealing. Other reasons for the theft (such as anger, delusions, or command hallucinations) are absent. In addition, *DSM-IV* requires that the stealing not be part of another *DSM-IV* syndrome, such as Conduct Disorder, a Manic Episode, or Antisocial Personality Disorder. Other *DSM-IV* conditions that may present with stealing include Dementia, Delirium, Mental Retardation, Dissociative Disorder, and some neurological disorders.

For example, injury to both temporal lobes, as may occur with head trauma and encephalitis, can produce the so-called Klüver-Bucy syndrome. In 1937 Drs. Heinrich Klüver and Paul C. Bucy described a dramatic behavioral syndrome in monkeys who suffered bilateral temporal lobectomies. The monkeys developed "psychic blindness" (visual agnosia), hypersexuality, hyperorality (taking and placing all objects of interest in their mouths), placidity, and amnesia. It is not uncommon for humans to develop Klüver-Bucy syndrome following herpes simplex encephalitis. One post-encephalitic woman in a nursing home regularly took objects from other residents' rooms and hoarded them in her clothing and among her possessions. She denied any recollection of her repeated "thefts," had no insight into her behavior, and her apparent "stealing" did not respond to counseling or behavioral intervention. Her repeated taking of others' possessions appeared to be a neurological consequence of her brain injury and was not evidence of kleptomania.

PYROMANIA (312.33)

(*DSM-IV*, pp. 614–615)

People with pyromania are fascinated by anything having to do with fire. They often set off false fire alarms. They also deliberately set fires and enjoy watching the professional firefighters fight the blaze. As with the other impulse disorders, there is a sense of rising tension before setting the fire and a sense of relief or pleasure during and after the act.

Pyromania appears to be more common in men than in women. Some studies have found among fire setters an increased incidence of below average intelligence, alcohol abuse, antisocial traits, petty stealing, resentment of authority, sexual dysfunction, and a history of cruelty to animals. Female fire setters may have a history of promiscuity.

Pyromania involves the failure to resist an impulse. It must be distinguished from arson, social protest, criminal behavior, lack of judgment during a manic episode, response to command hallucinations or delusions, and carelessness due to delirium or dementia.

PATHOLOGICAL GAMBLING (312.31)

(*DSM-IV*, pp. 615–618)

People who are pathological gamblers get hooked on gambling as if it were a substance of abuse. They engage in a prolonged chronic course of maladaptive gambling activity. Preoccupied with gambling, they may experience discomfort or irritability when they try to stop or reduce their habit, as they often do repeatedly and without success. They may wager ever increasing amounts of money as they "chase" their losses. Often they will resort to lying, stealing, and cheating to obtain money for their habit. Not uncommonly, by gambling they eventually harm themselves, their families, and their careers.

DSM-IV gives a polythetic criteria set for diagnosing Pathological Gambling. To receive the diagnosis, the client must meet any combination of five out of ten possible symptoms. In addition, the gambling must not be better explained by a manic episode, which often involves risky, impulsive behavior. Pathological gambling may be associated with antisocial personality disorder and with substance-related disorders.

TRICHOTILLOMANIA (312.39)

(*DSM-IV*, pp. 618–621)

The prefix *trichotillo* comes from the Greek *tricho*, meaning hair, and *tillein*, meaning to pluck or pull out. The person with trichotillomania has a passion for pulling out so much hair that other people begin to notice. Trichotillomania is typically a disorder of childhood, but onset can be at any age. The most common site of hair pulling is the scalp, but any area of the body may be affected. Many patients put the hair in their mouths after they pluck it (trichophagy). As with the other impulse disorders, there is rising tension before pulling out the hair and a sense of relief or gratification during the act. In addition, the hair loss is not the result of a medical or dermatological condition, nor is the pulling out of hair better explained by another *DSM-IV* disorder, such as a Delusional or Psychotic Disorder.

The medical term for hair loss or baldness is alopecia. Male-pattern baldness runs in families and is quite common. Female-pattern alopecia is not uncommon and involves a thinning of the hair. Several medical illnesses and some medications can cause a toxic alopecia. In *alopecia areata*, there is a circumscribed hair loss in persons with no obvious skin disorder or systemic disease. Alopecia areata may be difficult to distinguish from trichotillomania. A biopsy of the scalp may be necessary to differentiate the various forms of alopecia.

Hair pulling may also be seen in Obsessive-Compulsive Disorder (300.3), Factitious Disorders (300.19), and Stereotypic Movement Disorder (307.3). Sometimes psychological factors can aggravate a dermatological condition that causes hair loss, and the diagnosis of Psychological Factors Affecting Medical Condition (316) may apply.

IMPULSE CONTROL DISORDER NOT OTHERWISE SPECIFIED (312.30)

(*DSM-IV*, p. 621)

This NOS category allows the clinician to record disorders of impulse control that do not meet criteria for any of the specific impulse control disorders described above.

26

Adjustment Disorders

"These are the times that try men's souls."
Tom Paine (1737–1809), *The Crisis*,
Introduction (1776)

DSM-IV CODES FOR THE ADJUSTMENT DISORDERS:
(*DSM-IV* pp. 623–627)
309.0   Adjustment Disorder with Depressed Mood
309.24   Adjustment Disorder with Anxiety
309.28   Adjustment Disorder with Mixed Anxiety and Depressed
             Mood
309.3   Adjustment Disorder with Disturbance of Conduct
309.4   Adjustment Disorder with Mixed Disturbance of
             Emotions and Conduct
309.9   Unspecified Adjustment Disorder
             For each of the above Adjustment Disorders, specify if:
             Acute: Symptoms have lasted for less than six months,
             or
             Chronic: Symptoms have lasted more than six months.

The essential feature of an adjustment disorder is the presence of clinically significant distress or impairment due to an emotional or behavioral reaction to a recent (within three months) identifiable stressor. The level of distress exceeds the distress that would normally be expected in reaction to the stressor. By definition, the emotional or behavioral disturbance seen in adjustment disorders is not the result of another Axis I or Axis II disorder or of a normal grief reaction (bereavement). According to *DSM-IV*, the symptoms of an Adjustment Disorder should clear up within six months of the removal of the stressor or of the alleviation of the consequences of the stressor.

The codes for Adjustment Disorders are based on predominant symptoms—that is, whether the disorder occurs with anxiety, depressed mood, disturbed conduct, or a combination of these features. A modifier specifying the duration as chronic or acute indicates whether the disorder has persisted for more or less than six months.

The distinction between acute and chronic Adjustment Disorders did not exist in *DSM-III-R*. The addition of the "chronic" modifier for Adjustment Disorders is clinically sound. Many otherwise mentally healthy clients suffer ongoing stressors that prompt maladaptive reactions lasting more than six months. For example, a person going through a difficult divorce or someone dealing with the terminal illness of a loved one may meet criteria for Adjustment Disorder lasting a year or longer.

The reader should be aware, however, that one psychiatrist was admonished by a managed care company not to use the "chronic" specifier for an adjustment disorder because it would prompt a stringent audit of the case. The not-too-veiled implication was that the managed care company might then deny payment for treatment of a chronic disorder.

The *DSM-III* introduced the term *Adjustment Disorder* to describe maladaptive reactions to stressful events that did not meet criteria for other psychiatric disorders. In prior editions of the manual, Adjustment Disorders were classified as "transient situational personality disorders" in *DSM-I* and as "transient situational disturbances" in *DSM-II*.

The *DSM-IV* has simplified the category of Adjustment Disorder by eliminating three of the types described in *DSM-III-R*. Specifically, *DSM-IV* no longer contains criteria for Adjustment Disorder with Physical Complaints (*DSM-III-R* 309.82), with Withdrawal (*DSM-III-R* 309.83), or with Work or Academic Inhibition (*DSM-III-R* 309.23).

Andreasen and Wasek (1980) studied the types of stressors that commonly provoke adjustment disorders in individuals. As one might expect, the nature of the stressor varied with the age and social milieu of the individual. Adolescents rated school problems as the most common stressor. Other common precipitants of adjustment reactions among adolescents included parental rejection, alcohol/drug problems, parental separation or divorce, boyfriend/girlfriend problems, marital problems in the parents, change of residence, legal difficulties, and work-related problems. Among adults, marital problems, separation, and divorce were the most common stressors triggering adjustment reactions. Other stressors endorsed by adults in the study included change of residence, financial problems, school and work problems, alcohol/drug problems, illness, and legal difficulties.

Adjustment disorders can occur at any age. By definition, the disturbance begins within three months of the stressor and clears up within six months of the resolution of the stressful situation. Adults with adjustment disorders generally have a good prognosis. Adolescents with adjustment disorders, however, frequently exhibit signs of a major psychiatric disorder, such as schizophrenia, affective disorder, substance abuse, or antisocial personality disorder. Adjustment disorders have also been associated with an increased risk of suicide.

DIFFERENTIAL DIAGNOSIS
OF ADJUSTMENT DISORDER

Adjustment disorders must be distinguished from other disorders in which reaction to stress plays a significant role. Such disorders include:

Affective disorders.

Anxiety disorders.

Disruptive behavior disorders of childhood and adolescence.

Other conditions not attributable to a mental disorder that may be a focus of clinical attention (V codes).

Personality disorders that can be exacerbated by stress.

Psychological Factors Affecting Medical Condition (316).

Schizophrenia and schizoaffective disorders whose prodromal phases may resemble an adjustment disorder.

Posttraumatic Stress Disorder (309.81): Here the person has experienced a severe trauma accompanied by feelings of profound fear, helplessness, or horror. A characteristic pattern of reactions follows the trauma, including reexperiencing the traumatic event, avoiding associated stimuli, emotional numbing, and persistent arousal.

Acute Stress Disorder (308.3): This is similar to a Posttraumatic Stress Disorder, but lasts for a minimum of two days and a maximum of four weeks, with onset within four weeks of the trauma.

Brief Psychotic Disorder (298.8) in which an individual develops psychotic symptoms in response to a stressful event.

Case Example

A woman whose husband was diagnosed with Parkinson's disease in his early 40s developed symptoms of tearfulness, poor concentration, distractibility, sadness, depressed mood, anxiety, and inefficiency at work. Her symptoms caused significant distress and functional impairment and occurred in response to an identifiable stressor. She did not meet criteria for a Mood Disorder. Her symptoms lasted much longer than six months. Her depression and anxiety improved when her husband was doing better medically and worsened whenever her husband's condition deteriorated. She was diagnosed to have a Chronic Adjustment Disorder with Mixed Anxiety and Depressed Mood.

27

Personality Disorders

"It is more important to know what sort of person has a disease than to know what sort of disease a person has."

Hippocrates

"We don't like Axis II diagnoses; they take too long to treat."

Representative of a national managed care company

CLUSTER A: ("Eccentric")
301.0 Paranoid Personality Disorder
301.20 Schizoid Personality Disorder
301.22 Schizotypal Personality Disorder
(Note: For Cluster A Personality Disorders, if the client meets criteria before the onset of Schizophrenia, add the modifier "pre-morbid" to the Personality Disorder diagnosis.)

CLUSTER B: ("Dramatic, Acting-out")
301.7 Antisocial Personality Disorder
301.83 Borderline Personality Disorder
301.50 Histrionic Personality Disorder
301.81 Narcissistic Personality Disorder

CLUSTER C: ("Anxious")
301.82 Avoidant Personality Disorder
301.6 Dependent Personality Disorder
301.4 Obsessive-Compulsive Personality Disorder
301.9 Personality Disorder Not Otherwise Specified

DSM-IV's *Appendix B* contains criteria for two proposed personality disorders, namely:

Depressive Personality Disorder (*DSM-IV*, pp. 732–733), and
Passive-Aggressive (Negativistic) Personality Disorder (*DSM-IV*, pp. 733–734).

THE CONCEPT OF A PERSONALITY DISORDER

Certain characteristics of a person remain stable over time and in different situations. We refer to such enduring attributes of an individual's thinking, feeling, perceiving, and relating as personality traits or personality style. Personality styles consist of a cluster of traits that include basic assumptions about oneself and the world, characteristic modes of perception, habitual behaviors, and patterned ways of relating to others.

Each personality style has its advantages and disadvantages. Healthy individuals are capable of being flexible and of adapting their assumptions, feelings, and behaviors to meet the needs of changing situations. Rigid, unyielding personality styles tend to be maladaptive and to cause distress and functional impairment. When long-standing personality styles are sufficiently inflexible and maladaptive to cause significant distress and/or impaired social or job functioning, we make the diagnosis of a Personality Disorder. Individuals with personality disorders exhibit personality attributes that are enduring but not endearing.

DSM-IV uses a polythetic diagnostic schema to diagnose personality disorders. In *DSM-IV*, the presence of a combination of three, four, or five personality characteristics out of a list of seven, eight, or nine possibilities will trigger a specific Personality Disorder diagnosis. Each personality disorder criteria set covers the areas of interpersonal relationships, cognition, and self-concept.

The diagnostic manual groups Personality Disorders into three clusters that have clinical similarity. Thus, Cluster A, the "eccentric" or "odd" disorders, contains Paranoid, Schizoid, and Schizotypal Personality Disorders. Cluster B, the "dramatic" or "acting-out" disorders, includes Antisocial, Borderline, Histrionic, and Narcissistic Personality Disorders. Cluster C, the "anxious" disorders, contains the Avoidant, Dependent, and Obsessive-Compulsive Personality Disorders.

The maladaptive traits that characterize the personality disorders are generally evident in adolescence or early adulthood and remain typical of the individual's long-standing and recent functioning. Many of the major Axis I *DSM-IV* disorders present with maladaptive behaviors similar to those seen in the personality disorders. However, if the dysfunctional personality trait is limited to episodes of an Axis I mental disorder (state) and is not present during remissions, then the diagnosis of Personality Disorder cannot be made. For example, a person may exhibit dependent, avoidant, or obsessive-compulsive traits during an episode of major depression, but not demonstrate these traits when the depression is in remission. In contrast, personality disorders are stable and enduring trait-like phenomena.

Personality disorders are coded on Axis II to separate them from major Axis I mental disorders and to ensure that they get due consideration in treatment planning. Some clinicians believe that the personality disorders lie on a continuum with their corresponding Axis I disorders. It is possible that certain Axis I and Axis II disorders are biogenetically similar and that Axis II personality disorders represent trait-like, temperamental variants of Axis I disorders.

For example, avoidant personality disorder appears to fall in the spectrum of the anxiety disorders. Borderline personality disorder with its affective instability resembles the mood disorders. Schizotypal personality disorder seems to belong to the spectrum of schizophrenic disorders, and paranoid personality is akin to the schizophrenic and delusional disorders. A notable exception is obsessive-compulsive personality disorder, which, according to research, does not form a continuum with obsessive-compulsive disorder.

The development of the Personality Disorders section of *DSM-IV* was not without controversy. After much debate, the *DSM-IV* task force decided to omit the proposal for a Self-Defeating Personality Disorder (SDPD) category. Although the concept of unconsciously motivated self-defeating behavior is useful in psychotherapy, the authors of *DSM-IV* could not find a way to operationalize this psychodynamic formulation. The notion that people may defeat their own purposes in an attempt to resolve inner conflicts is highly subjective and inferential on the part of the clinician. Behavior that is self-defeating for one person may be highly adaptive for another. The task force concluded that the SDPD diagnosis had limited descriptive validity in the field trials. Some members of the *DSM-IV* committee also worried that a Self-Defeating Personality Disorder diagnosis might carry an inherent bias against women. The concern was that inclusion of a Self-Defeating Personality Disorder category could allow victimizers to blame their victims.

CLUSTER A ("ECCENTRIC")

Note: For Cluster A Personality Disorders, if the client meets criteria before the onset of schizophrenia, one should add the modifier "pre-morbid" to the personality disorder diagnosis.

301.0 Paranoid Personality Disorder

(*DSM-IV*, pp. 634–638)

The term *paranoid* comes from the Greek *para*, meaning beside, and *nous*, meaning the mind. People with paranoid traits are unduly suspicious and untrusting. With little justification, they often feel slighted, deceived, exploited, threatened, demeaned, disparaged, taken advantage of, insulted, and used by others. They may hold a grudge and react hostilely to imagined slights. They find it difficult to confide in or trust others and may suspect associates of malicious backstabbing. In close relationships they tend to suspect significant others of infidelity.

DSM-IV provides a list of seven such traits. To meet criteria, the individual must display at least four paranoid attributes from the list. The paranoid view of others' motives as malevolent must have begun by early adulthood and must be exhibited in a variety of situations. The paranoid symptoms must not occur elusively during an episode of schizophrenia or other psychotic disorder, major depression with psychotic features, or as a result of substance use (e.g., cocaine) or a general medical condition.

Because of their general distrust of everyone, paranoid individuals rarely seek treatment. Some individuals who are diagnosed with Schizophrenia or Delusional Disorder may meet criteria for a premorbid Paranoid Personality Disorder; in such cases the clinician should add the modifier "pre-morbid" to the diagnosis. Psychoanalysis has linked paranoid traits with anal character and with unresolved homosexual conflicts in both men and women. Behaviorists regard paranoid suspiciousness and mistrust as learned behaviors that are reinforced.

Clinical Vignette

One woman with a paranoid personality disorder constantly felt demeaned by her office mates. One particularly cold winter morning a male co-worker commented as he entered the office, "Boy, it's frigid today." The paranoid woman immediately assumed that her co-worker was referring to her sexual performance and filed a complaint against him for sexual harassment.

Clinical Vignette

A middle-aged woman with a paranoid personality disorder had just completed a training program in word processing and was thinking of applying for jobs. Her husband commented, "You've worked really hard in your studies, why don't you take a little vacation before applying for a job?" The woman became enraged with her husband. "See how he torments me!" she complained. "He knows I really want to find work—why else would I have studied so hard and he's just saying that to aggravate me!"

301.20 Schizoid Personality Disorder

(*DSM-IV*, pp. 638–641)

Schizoid personality disorder was originally conceived of as a precursor to full-blown schizophrenia. Clinicians had observed that, pre-morbidly, individuals who went on to develop schizophrenia were often emotionally detached and constricted, eccentric, and afraid of rejection or criticism. *DSM-III* made three categories out of the original schizoid personality diagnosis: Schizoid (detached), Schizotypal (odd, eccentric), and Avoidant (fearful of criticism) Personality Disorders.

The essential feature of *DSM-IV* Schizoid Personality Disorder is a pervasive emotional constriction and detachment in interpersonal relationships. Schizoid individuals lead a relatively unemotional existence devoid of friendships and close interpersonal or sexual relationships. They come across as detached, solitary, objective, uninvolved, emotionally cold, devoid of passion, colorless, and indifferent to praise or criticism. They tend to stay quietly by themselves in the role of passive observers. In popular jargon, they might be described as "all head and no heart."

DSM-IV requires the presence of at least four out of seven schizoid attributes to meet criteria for the diagnosis. The schizoid detachment and emotional restriction must have begun by early adulthood and must be exhibited in a variety of situations. The schizoid symptoms must not occur exclusively as part of schizophrenia or other psychotic disorder, pervasive developmental disorder, mood disorder with psychotic symptoms, substance abuse, or a general medical condition.

Some individuals with schizophrenia will have met criteria for pre-morbid schizoid personality disorder prior to the onset of the schizophrenia. In such cases the clinician should add the modifier "pre-morbid" to the Schizoid Personality Disorder diagnosis. Because of their aversion to intimate situations, schizoid individuals rarely seek psychotherapy.

301.22 Schizotypal Personality Disorder

(*DSM-IV*, pp. 641–645)

Both Kraepelin and Bleuler noticed that the relatives of their schizophrenic patients exhibited odd and eccentric but nonpsychotic behavior. *DSM-III* created the Schizotypal Personality Disorder diagnosis to classify individuals displaying such weird behavior. According to *DSM-IV*, people with this diagnosis exhibit three types of symptoms: deficits in social and interpersonal relationships, distortions of cognition and perception, and strange or bizarre behavior. In describing such patients, the early psychiatric literature used to speak of "latent," "ambulatory," or "borderline" schizophrenia. Schizotypal personality disorder is one of the more common personality disorders.

People with schizotypal personality disorder exhibit traits that lie along the spectrum of symptoms seen in schizophrenia. They may feel alienated and uncomfortable in interpersonal relationships and may avoid friendships because of distrust or paranoid ideas about the motives of others. Their affect may be flat, constricted, or inappropriate. They may dress, act, and speak in an odd, peculiar, or socially inept manner. Their thinking is often unusual and may be marked by non-delusional ideas of reference, suspiciousness, mild paranoid ideation, odd superstitious beliefs, magical thinking, or overly abstract and metaphorical preoccupations.

DSM-IV requires the presence of at least five out of nine schizotypal attributes to meet criteria for the diagnosis. The odd interpersonal, cognitive, perceptual, and behavior traits must have begun by early adulthood and must be exhibited in a variety of situations. The schizotypal symptoms must not occur exclusively as part of schizophrenia or other psychotic disorder, pervasive developmental disorder, mood disorder with psychotic symptoms, substance abuse, or a general medical condition.

Some individuals with schizophrenia will have met criteria for pre-morbid schizotypal personality disorder prior to the onset of the schizophrenia. In such cases the clinician should add the modifier "pre-morbid" to the Schizotypal Personality Disorder diagnosis.

CLUSTER B ("DRAMATIC, ACTING-OUT")

301.7 Antisocial Personality Disorder

(DSM-IV, pp. 645–650)

In the nineteenth century, antisocial personality disorder was referred to as "moral insanity" because of its characteristic guiltless exploitative immoral behavior in the absence of psychosis or otherwise impaired reasoning. The older literature also refers to individuals with this disorder as "sociopaths" or "psychopathic deviates." Hervey Cleckley's classic 1938 text, *The Mask of Sanity*, differentiated the psychopathic personality from mere criminal behavior and from social deviance. Cleckley portrayed the antisocial individual as self-centered, devoid of guilt or remorse, incapable of love or genuine concern for others, lacking in conscience, and unable to learn from experience. Such a person's motivation appears to be, "I want what I want when I want it regardless of what I do to get it."

DSM-III and DSM-III-R criteria for Antisocial Personality Disorder consisted of an elaborate smorgasbord of conduct disturbances and antisocial behaviors that were difficult to use in clinical practice and that did not include many of the psychological traits that clinicians believed to be characteristic of the disorder. DSM-IV has greatly simplified and condensed the diagnostic criteria to make them clearer and more clinically useful.

According to DSM-IV, Antisocial Personality is a disorder that is diagnosed in adults age 18 and older, but that begins by age 15. Individuals with this disorder meet criteria for conduct disorder of childhood with onset before age 15 and show a pattern of unconcern for the rights of others since the age of 15. The antisocial behavior is not solely part of a schizophrenic or a manic episode. Such individuals repeatedly disregard and violate the rights of others. To meet criteria for the diagnosis, the individual must show a pattern of violating others' rights in at least three out of seven ways specified in the manual. For example, antisocial individuals typically lie, cheat, steal, fight, assault others, violate the law, act on impulse, behave irresponsibly, endanger the safety of others, feel no remorse, do not accept responsibility for their harmful actions, and blame others for their behavior. Substance-related disorders commonly coexist with antisocial personality disorders.

301.83 Borderline Personality Disorder (BPD)

(DSM-IV, pp. 650–654)

DSM-III introduced the diagnosis Borderline Personality Disorder to describe individuals who have "stably unstable" character pathology. In DSM-II such individuals were labeled "emotionally unstable personalities." What used to be called "borderline" schizophrenia is now diagnosed as Schizotypal Personality Disorder in DSM-IV.

Characteristically, people with borderline personality disorder display an enduring instability in their self-identity, interpersonal relationships, emotional regulation, and impulse control. They often engage in self-mutilation in an attempt to regulate painful affect; for example, self-cutting may be the only method that such individuals have to calm themselves. Borderline patients also tend to use suicidal threats or gestures to maintain contact with significant others (Sherman 1993). They frequently use defensive splitting as they alternately idealize and then devalue other people.

Psychologist Marsha M. Linehan (1993), who has developed a highly effective cognitive-behavioral treatment for BPD, believes that the inability to regulate affect is the core problem of the borderline personality disorder. There is frequently a history of early abuse, trauma, family chaos, and invalidation of the borderline individual's thoughts and feelings. Linehan suggests that clinicians treating these individuals bear in mind that borderlines live in a nightmare.

To meet criteria for *DSM-IV* Borderline Personality Disorder, the individual must display from early adulthood a persistent pattern of unstable interpersonal relationships, self-image, affective regulation, and impulse control by demonstrating at least five out of nine possible types of "borderline" attributes. Their affective life may be typified by feelings of emptiness, rage attacks, marked emotional instability, and a dread of abandonment. They may become paranoid or dissociative under stress. They tend to be impulsive, self-endangering, self-injurious, and prone to suicidal threats, gestures, or attempts. They typically engage in intense relationships with others, characterized by extremes of idealization alternating with devaluation.

Because of the essential affective instability of the borderline individual, some researchers regard BPD as a variant of an affective disorder. Borderline personality disorder is common in the first-degree relatives of an identified individual. Borderline individuals also tend to display several biological markers of depressive disorders, namely, a shortened REM latency, an abnormal dexamethasone suppression test, and an abnormal thyrotropin-releasing hormone test.

Psychopharmacologist Donald Klein regards borderline personality disorder as a heterogeneous group and has subdivided such patients according to their clinical presentation and response to medication. Klein (1977) describes a phobic anxious type, an emotionally unstable character type, and a hysteroid (rejection sensitive) dysphoric type. Klein's hysteroid dysphoric patients are typically women who are exquisitely sensitive to rejection and who fall into depressions when they are jilted in a relationship. Hysteroid dys-phoria is not uncommon in gay men who present suicidally to hospital emergency rooms after a breakup with their lovers. Klein found that the monoamine oxidase inhibiting (MAOI) antidepres-sants (e.g., phenelzine) are especially helpful in rejection-sensitive dysphoria. Klein also believes that minor tranquilizers may help the chronically anxious borderline patient and that low-dose antipsy-chotic medication like thioridazine, as well as the anti-manic medica-tion lithium carbonate, help to control the emotional lability of the borderline patient. Klein found that markedly histrionic patients (see Histrionic Personality Disorder) generally do not respond well to medication. The reader should note that Klein's work (1977) was done prior to the introduction of many newer psychotropic medications. Today the selective serotonin reuptake inhibiting (SSRI) antidepres-sants, like Prozac, are rapidly replacing the MAOIs in the treatment of hysteroid disphoria and other atypical depressions.

Because of the intense anger, devaluing attacks, emotional hostage-taking, and self-destructive behavior of the borderline patient, the BPD diagnosis often carries a negative connotation. The borderline patient is at times likened to the little girl of the limerick that goes: "When she was good, she was very, very good; but when she was bad, she was horrid!" Some mental health professionals live in dread of treating borderline individuals and use the BPD diagnosis as a kind of waste basket term for patients they do not like and would rather avoid.

The research of John Gunderson (1983, 1985, 1993) led to an additional criterion for BPD in *DSM-IV*, namely, the occurrence of "transient, stress-related paranoid ideation or severe dissociative symptoms" (*DSM-IV*, p. 654).

301.50 Histrionic Personality Disorder

(*DSM-IV*, p. 655–658)

Histrionic personality disorder had been called Hysterical Person-ality in *DSM-II*. The authors of *DSM-III* changed the name from *hysterical* (from the Greek for "wandering uterus") to *histrionic* (from the Latin for "actor") for several reasons. They made the change to provide a more descriptive label, to avoid the implied female sex-bias in the term *hysterical*, and to separate the Axis II personality disorder from Axis I hysteria, which itself was renamed Somatization Disorder in *DSM-III*. Some critics regard histrionic personality disorder as a stereotyped caricature of feminine behavior. Interestingly, clinicians have noted that caricatured, gaudy, histrionic women are often drawn to stereotyped, macho, tattooed, antisocial men.

The dictionary defines *histrionic* as overacted, theatrical, artificial, or melodramatic. Individuals with histrionic traits are typically dramatic, attention-seeking, highly emotive, vain, seductive, provocative, emotionally shallow, flashy, exhibitionistic, superficially charming, overly concerned with their appearance, and fond of being the center of attention. They frequently feel bored in the absence of constant excitement and stimulation. Their cognitive style is global, diffuse, and impressionistic, lacking in factual detail and in sharp definition. Often they have a naively romantic world view ("some day my prince will come") that leads them to see intimacy where none exists and to become repeatedly disappointed in love. David Shapiro (1965) describes the emotional experience of these individuals as "explosive and vivid but ephemeral and not 'deeply' experienced" (p. 132).

To meet *DSM-IV* criteria for Histrionic Personality Disorder, the individual must display an enduring pattern from early adulthood of "excessive emotionality and attention seeking" (*DSM-IV*, p. 657), as indicated by at least five out of eight histrionic attributes.

The histrionic traits mentioned in *DSM-IV* include discomfort at not being the center of attention, emotional shallowness, seductive or provocative behavior, impressionistic speech, excessive emotionality, suggestibility, and an exaggerated sense of intimacy in relationships.

Studies of the families of histrionic personalities reveal a higher than expected incidence of somatization disorder and of antisocial personality disorder among blood relatives. Some researchers believe that histrionic personality disorder in women and antisocial personality disorder in men are gender-related expressions of the same underlying genetically transmitted tendency, perhaps shaped by culture, hormones, and upbringing. In clinical work we often find a mutual attraction between histrionic women and antisocial men.

301.81 Narcissistic Personality Disorder

(*DSM-IV*, pp. 658–661)
Narcissus was the beautiful young man of Greek mythology whom

the nymph Echo adored. Narcissus felt little or nothing for Echo, and, when Narcissus did not requite her love, Echo died of a broken heart. No doubt Echo suffered from Klein's hysteroid dysphoria and might have survived had she been given a monoamine oxidase inhibitor or Prozac by one of the gods. To punish Narcissus for Echo's demise, Nemesis caused Narcissus to fall in love with his own reflection in a pool of water. Consumed by passion for his gorgeous self-image, Narcissus himself pined away and became the flower that bears his name. The term narcissism has come to mean inflated self-love.

Like Narcissus, people with Narcissistic Personality Disorder have an exaggerated sense of self-importance. They are extremely self-absorbed and have little empathy for others whom they view mainly as potential admirers. They wish to feel superior, and their excessive need for praise and admiration reflects a fragile sense of self-esteem. Their narcissistic vulnerability manifests as exquisite sensitivity to evaluation or criticism and as intense envy of others. They often behave in a grandiose or entitled manner, acting as if they were especially important and demanding special treatment. They tend to engage in a grandiose fantasy life and usually believe that others are envious of their many talents and accomplishments. Others may view them as arrogant, condescending, haughty, exploitative, and/or patronizing.

To qualify for the diagnosis, *DSM-IV* requires the presence since early adulthood of "grandiosity (in fantasy or behavior), need for admiration, and lack of empathy" (*DSM-IV* p. 661) as indicated by at least five out of nine *DSM-IV* criteria for narcissism. Some therapists feel that the diagnosis can only be made on the basis of the emergence of a characteristic narcissistic transference in an ongoing psychoanalytic therapy.

CLUSTER C ("ANXIOUS")

301.82 Avoidant Personality Disorder

(*DSM-IV*, pp. 662–665)

Prior to *DSM-III*, individuals who were excessively self-conscious, sensitive to criticism, awkward, timid, anxious, socially inept and inhibited, and avoidant of interpersonal contact were labeled "schizoid" or "inadequate" personalities. *DSM-III* did away with the old "inadequate personality" category and restricted "schizoid personality" to those individuals who were extremely interpersonally detached and emotionally constricted.

According to *DSM-IV*, people with Avoidant Personality Disorder exhibit from early adulthood a pattern of "social inhibition, feelings of inadequacy, and hypersensitivity to negative evaluation" (*DSM-IV*, p. 664) as indicated by at least four out of seven listed avoidant traits. As the name implies, such individuals typically avoid interpersonal contact. They tend to be shy, inhibited, nervous, uneasy, tentative, restrained, introverted, socially apprehensive and uncomfortable, self-conscious, and easily embarrassed. They overvalue acceptance by others to such an extent that any rejection, disapproval, or criticism is experienced as a terrible event. They tend to lack friends and pull away from potentially intimate relationships. Often they see themselves as unattractive or inferior to others.

301.6 Dependent Personality Disorder

(*DSM-IV*, pp. 665–669)

Freud located dependency traits in fixation at the oral (cannibalistic pregenital) stage of psychosexual development in which sexual activity has not yet been separated from the ingestion of food. The *DSM-I* classified dependent personality "trait disturbance" as a subtype of passive-aggressive personality trait disturbance. The *DSM-II* omitted Dependent Personality Disorder altogether. The *DSM-III* returned this diagnosis to the manual.

Dependent individuals make a basic assumption that they are unable to care for themselves and therefore must rely on dominant others for support. They tend to take a passive, submissive role in relationships and to shy away from competition. To avoid alienating others on whom they feel they must rely, they may hide their hostile or aggressive feelings. Because they tend to express their aggression indirectly, the *DSM-I* classified dependent personalities with the passive-aggressive disorders. Such individuals lack confidence in their ability to manage independently and often come across as congenial but wishy-washy because they avoid taking a firm stand on any issue. Low self-esteem is a common accompaniment of their chronic belief in being unable to function independently.

DSM-IV characterizes the Dependent Personality Disorder as "a pervasive and excessive need to be taken care of, leading to submissive and clinging behavior and fears of separation" (*DSM-IV*, p. 668). To qualify for the diagnosis, the individual must satisfy five out of eight criteria of dependent behavior. Because this disorder appears to be diagnosed more frequently in women, critics have raised the possibility of a sex-bias in the *DSM-IV* criteria for the disorder.

301.4 Obsessive-Compulsive Personality Disorder

(*DSM-IV*, pp. 669–673)

Psychoanalysis located obsessive-compulsive traits at the anal-sadistic stage of psychosexual development. Freud described the anal triad of obstinacy, parsimony, and orderliness in such anal-erotic individuals. His anal patients shared a history of requiring a long time to be bowel-trained. According to Freud,

> as infants, they seem to have belonged to the class who refuse to empty their bowels when they are put on the pot because they derive a subsidiary pleasure from defaecating; for they tell us that even in somewhat later years they enjoyed holding back their stool, and they remember—though more readily about their brothers and sisters than about themselves—doing all sorts of unseemly things with the faeces that had been passed. [Freud, "Character and Anal Eroticism," *Standard Edition*, vol. IX, p. 170]

Obsessive-compulsive personalities value perfection and fear making mistakes. They believe in mottos such as "a place for everything and everything in its place," "time is money," "you can't be too careful," and "it's my way or the highway." Their excessive conscientiousness is accompanied by emotional rigidity and a constricted affect. Their manner of relating is generally stilted, formal, and proper, somewhat like Mr. Spock in the television series *Star Trek*. Wilhelm Reich (1950) described compulsive personalities as "living machines," rigid in body and in mind. Their anal sadism is evident in the coexistence of submissiveness to those who hold power over them with a tendency to dominate, control, and demean those beneath them. They want to control everything just as they used to control their feces. Obsessive individuals are often miserly with their money and with their time.

Compulsive traits often lead to success in medical and technical fields. Such individuals are dutiful and conscientious, acutely aware of what they "should" be doing. They excel at making lists, attending to details, and organizing large masses of information. Workaholics, they spend long hours at tasks that many people would find tedious or objectionable. In many ways the obsessive-compulsive style lies at the polar extreme from the histrionic personality style.

DSM-IV characterizes the Obsessive-Compulsive Personality Disorder as evidencing "preoccupation with orderliness, perfectionism, and mental and interpersonal control, at the expense of flexibility, openness, and efficiency" (*DSM-IV*, p. 672). To meet criteria for the disorder, individuals must exhibit at least four out of the eight obsessive-compulsive character traits listed in *DSM-IV*.

301.9 Personality Disorder Not Otherwise Specified

(*DSM-IV*, p. 673)

This residual category allows the clinician to code the presence of a personality disorder that does not meet criteria for any of the specifically defined Personality Disorders in *DSM-IV*. In addition the clinician may wish to code the proposed but not yet official disorders such as Passive-Aggressive and Depressive Personality Disorders.

APPENDIX B CRITERIA FOR TWO PROPOSED PERSONALITY DISORDERS

Depressive Personality Disorder (DPD)

(*DSM-IV*, pp. 732–733):

Kraepelin described the depressive personality in 1921, and European psychiatry has included the diagnosis of Depressive Personality Disorder in the *ICD-9*. The DPD has not yet made it into American psychiatry but will appear in the Appendix of *DSM-IV* for further study.

An extensive clinical literature on DPD describes such individuals as temperamentally melancholic (full of black bile). They come across as gloomy, joyless, pessimistic, brooding, worrying, complaining, self-critical, passive, and unable to have fun. They habitually see the glass as half-empty. Often they feel inadequate, guilty, self-blaming, and powerless to affect their fate. They are frequently critical and judgmental toward others. The pervasive depressive cognitive and behavior style of DPD is not more appropriately attributed to a Dysthymic Disorder and does not occur solely as part of a Major Depressive Disorder.

Passive-Aggressive Personality Disorder (PAPD) (Negativistic Personality Disorder)

(*DSM-IV*, pp. 733–734)

Although *DSM-III-R* included Passive-Aggressive Personality Disorder (301.84) in the body of the text, *DSM-IV* has moved this disorder to the Appendix because of questions raised about the validity of the *DSM-III-R* Passive-Aggressive Personality Disorder diagnosis. Critics argued that the *DSM-III-R* PAPD diagnosis may represent a single trait rather than a true personality disorder. The PAPD diagnosis was introduced into American psychiatry by the U.S. War Department in 1945 to label military personnel who opposed authority in an indirect, "subverting" manner. The *DSM-IV* work group suggested expanding the diagnosis from its narrow military origins to include negativistic and oppositional traits and their cognitive, affective, and behavioral features. To indicate the broader scope of the diagnosis, the *DSM-IV* committee suggested changing the name of PAPD to Negativistic Personality Disorder. Because it represents a "new" diagnosis, it will go into the Appendix of *DSM-IV* for further research.

Individuals with Negativistic Personality Disorder may express aggression in indirect, resistant, and subverting ways. They are chronically dissatisfied, malcontent, and complain of being victimized and unappreciated. One gets the impression that they never felt properly nurtured as children and are now making the whole world pay the price of their early parental maltreatment and neglect. Others often view them as whiny, irritable, complaining, and subtly accusatory, as if they had a chip on their shoulders. They passively resist the demands of authority through procrastination, obstructionism, delay, dawdling, "forgetting," losing things, and behaving inefficiently in secret defiance. They are frequently cynical, pessimistic, negativistic, sullen, envious, and resentful. The *DSM-I* definition implied a conflict within these individuals between strong dependency needs and resentment of the more powerful individuals upon whom they must depend. They "bite the hand that feeds them."

28

Other Conditions That May Be a Focus of Clinical Attention

"There are more things in heaven and earth, Horatio,
Than are dreamt of in your philosophy."

Shakespeare, *Hamlet*, Act I, scene v

ADDITIONAL CONDITIONS THAT MAY BE A FOCUS OF CLINICAL ATTENTION:

316   PSYCHOLOGICAL FACTORS AFFECTING MEDICAL CONDITION:
(*DSM-IV*, pp. 675–678)
(Choose a psychological factor from the list below, based on the clinical presentation)
Mental Disorder Affecting Medical Condition
Psychological Symptoms Affecting Medical Condition
Personality Traits or Coping Style Affecting Medical Condition
Maladaptive Health Behaviors Affecting Medical Condition
Stress-Related Physiological Response Affecting Medical Condition
Other or Unspecified Psychological Factors Affecting Medical Condition

MEDICATION-INDUCED MOVEMENT DISORDERS:
(*DSM-IV* pp. 678–680) (These are coded on Axis I.)
332.1   Neuroleptic-Induced Parkinsonism
333.92   Neuroleptic Malignant Syndrome

333.7	Neuroleptic-Induced Acute Dystonia
333.99	Neuroleptic-Induced Acute Akathisia
333.82	Neuroleptic-Induced Tardive Dyskinesia
333.1	Medication-Induced Postural Tremor
333.90	Medication-Induced Movement Disorder Not Otherwise Specified (NOS)
995.2	Adverse Effects of Medication Not Otherwise Specified (NOS)

RELATIONAL PROBLEMS (*DSM-IV*, pp. 680–681):

V61.9	Relational Problem Related to a Mental Disorder or General Medical Condition
V61.20	Parent–Child Relational Problem
V61.1	Partner Relational Problem
V61.8	Sibling Relational Problem
V62.81	Relational Problem Not Otherwise Specified (NOS)

PROBLEMS RELATED TO ABUSE OR NEGLECT (*DSM-IV*, p. 682):

V61.21	Physical Abuse of Child
V61.21	Sexual Abuse of Child
V61.21	Neglect of Child *(for V61.21, code 995.5 if the focus of attention is on the victim)*
V61.1	Physical Abuse of Adult
V61.1	Sexual Abuse of Adult *(for V61.1, code 995.81 if the focus of attention is on the victim)*

ADDITIONAL CONDITIONS THAT MAY BE A FOCUS OF CLINICAL ATTENTION:
(*DSM-IV*, pp. 683–684)

V15.81	Noncompliance with Treatment for a Mental Disorder
V65.2	Malingering
V71.01	Adult Antisocial Behavior
V71.02	Childhood or Adolescent Antisocial Behavior
V62.89	Borderline Intellectual Functioning *(code this on Axis II)*
780.9	Age-Associated Cognitive Decline
V62.82	Bereavement
V62.3	Academic Problem
V62.2	Occupational Problem

313.82   Identity Problem
V62.89   Religious or Spiritual Problem
V62.4   Acculturation Problem
V62.89   Phase of Life Problem

ADDITIONAL CODES (*DSM-IV*, p. 687):
300.9   Unspecified Mental Disorder (Nonpsychotic)
V71.09   No Diagnosis or Condition on Axis I
799.9   Diagnosis or Condition Deferred on Axis I
V71.09   No Diagnosis on Axis II
799.9   Diagnosis Deferred on Axis II

This seventeenth and final section of *DSM-IV* deals with Other Conditions That May Be a Focus of Clinical Attention. Except for Borderline Intellectual Functioning (V62.89, Axis II), the other conditions described below are coded on Axis I. In general, the conditions in this section may relate to the *DSM-IV* mental disorders in one of three ways:

1. The Other Condition, which is the focus of clinical attention, exists in the absence of any mental disorder. For example, a boy presented with worsening grades, an Academic Problem (V62.3). Physical examination revealed that the child needed eyeglasses, but that neither the boy nor his parents were aware of the problem. Once the child's vision was corrected, his grades improved considerably.
2. The person presenting with the Other Condition that is a focus of clinical attention also suffers from a mental disorder that is unrelated to the Other Condition. For example, a man in treatment for Social Phobia (300.23) suffered the loss of his spouse in a car accident. He presented with symptoms of waves of grief, sadness, tearfulness, insomnia, distress, preoccupation, loss of appetite, and decreased energy. Within several weeks his symptoms gradually subsided but did not disappear entirely. He met criteria for Bereavement (V62.82) independent of his social phobia.
3. The Other Condition is related to a client's mental disorder, but the Other Condition is sufficiently severe to warrant consideration in its own right. For example, it is not uncommon for partners of chronically depressed clients to get into a pattern of negative interactions in the relationship. Such a Partner Relational Problem (V61.1)

is related to the recurrent Major Depressive Disorder (296.3x), but may require independent attention, such as couples therapy.

PSYCHOLOGICAL FACTORS AFFECTING MEDICAL CONDITION (316)

(*DSM-IV*, pp. 675–678)

This code (316) is used when the patient has a general medical condition, which is coded on Axis III, and when psychological factors are negatively affecting that medical condition. Such psychological factors may affect the course or the treatment of the medical problem, or they may pose other health risks or cause additional undesirable stress. For example, a middle-aged man was hospitalized following a heart attack. He had a troubled marriage (V61.1, Partner Relational Problem). Every time his wife visited him in the coronary care unit, he suffered dangerous arrhythmias.

DSM-IV gives the clinician six choices of types of psychological factors affecting medical condition. The clinician should choose one of the six names below based on the nature of the problem. If more than one factor applies, the clinician should indicate which factor is the most prominent. The six types for code 316, Psychological Factors Affecting Medical Condition, are:

1. Mental Disorder Affecting Medical Condition.
2. Psychological Symptoms Affecting Medical Condition.
3. Personality Traits or Coping Style Affecting Medical Condition.
4. Maladaptive Health Behaviors Affecting Medical Condition.
5. Stress-Related Physiological Response Affecting Medical Condition.
6. Other or Unspecified Psychological Factors Affecting Medical Condition.

MEDICATION-INDUCED MOVEMENT DISORDERS

(*DSM-IV*, pp. 678–680 and pp. 735–751)

Patients taking psychotropic medications frequently suffer movement disorders that may or may not be induced by medication. For example, clients on lithium carbonate for bipolar disorder often display a fine tremor in the upper extremities. Clients on antipsychotic drugs may exhibit motor restlessness, rigidity, muscle stiffness, dystonic reactions, and so on. Because the antipsychotic agents typically block dopamine receptors in the brain and these dopamine receptors affect the extrapyramidal nerve pathways, the side effects of neuroleptic medications are sometimes called the "extrapyramidal syndromes," or EPS. Blockade of dopamine receptors may produce acute dystonias (muscle spasms), Parkinson's symptoms, or akathisia (motor restlessness).

In addition, some Axis I disorders present with motor symptoms. For example, extremely anxious patients can appear to have a motor akathisia. This section of *DSM-IV* defines the six commonly seen movement disorders among psychiatric patients and allows for a seventh NOS category. Some of these disorders are genuinely induced by medication; others may appear even in the absence of exposure to medication.

DSM-IV uses the term *neuroleptic medication* to refer to drugs that antagonize the neurotransmitter dopamine. Traditional antipsychotic drugs are thought to work by blocking dopamine receptors in the brain.

Neuroleptic-Induced Parkinsonism (332.1)

(*DSM-IV*, pp. 679 and 736–739))

Antipsychotic (neuroleptic) medications commonly induce symptoms identical to those of idiopathic Parkinson's disease, a hypokinetic movement disorder. Parkinsonism (also called paralysis agitans or shaking palsy) is a progressive degenerative disease of the central nervous system that affects about 1 percent of the elderly population. It has four characteristic symptoms: slow impoverished movements, muscle rigidity, resting tremor, and postural instability. The resting tremor, often seen in one of the hands, is of the "pill-rolling" three cycles per second type. Parkinsonian tremor worsens with stress and fatigue, but diminishes during movement and disappears during sleep. Attempts to passively move the limbs of the Parkinsonian patient are met with "cogwheel rigidity," a combination of "lead pipe" rigidity with superimposed bursts of tremor that create a ratchet-like sensation. Parkinsonian patients also exhibit extreme slowing and poverty of movement (bradykinesia) or difficulty initiating movement (akinesia) followed by a "festinating gait." They may show stone-like "masked facies," which must be distinguished from the poverty of facial expression of flattened affect. Drooling is not uncommon.

Neuroleptic Malignant Syndrome (NMS) (333.92)

(*DSM-IV*, pp. 679 and 739–742)

Neuroleptic malignant syndrome (NMS) is an uncommon but potentially fatal complication of treatment with antipsychotic medications. Patients with NMS characteristically display a clouding of consciousness, confusion, severe muscle rigidity, profuse sweating, a high temperature, elevated or fluctuating blood pressure, rapid heartbeat, rapid breathing, drooling, and other signs of autonomic dysfunction. Extreme muscle tone can lead to muscle tissue damage with elevated blood levels of muscle enzymes (creatinine phosphokinase, or CPK), an elevated white blood cell count, and possible kidney damage from the degenerative byproducts of muscle tissue breakdown (myoglobiuric renal failure). In cases of NMS it is essential to discontinue antipsychotic medications and to initiate supportive treatment. NMS is most likely to occur early in treatment with high-potency neuroleptics, but it can occur at any time with any antipsychotic agent. The estimated mortality rate is about 10 percent.

Neuroleptic-Induced Acute Dystonia (333.7)

(*DSM-IV*, pp. 679 and 742–744)

Dystonia refers to acute muscle spasms due to sudden and persistent increased muscle tone (tonic spasms). Neuroleptic-induced acute dystonias are most common among young male patients during the first five days after starting treatment with an antipsychotic medication (*Merck Manual* 1992). Dystonia can also follow an increase in dosage of neuroleptic medication or a decrease in dosage of anti-Parkinsonian medication. Compazine, often given by suppository to vomiting patients, commonly causes dystonias. The muscle spasms of dystonia can affect any voluntary muscle group in the body. Commonly, the tongue, eyes, jaw, and/or neck go into sudden spasm. If unexpected by the patient, sudden dystonias are extremely frightening. Dystonias may be relieved by anti-Parkinsonian agents, such as benztropine (Cogentin) or diphenhydramine (Benadryl).

Neuroleptic-Induced Acute Akathisia (333.99)

(*DSM-IV*, pp. 679 and 744–746)

Akathisia refers to a feeling of motor restlessness often accompanied by anxiety and a sense of inner disquiet. Patients with akathisia feel compelled to pace about, rock back and forth, tap their feet, and keep moving. They often cannot sit or lie still without discomfort. Akathisia may follow an increase in neuroleptic drug dosage or a decrease in medication used to treat extrapyramidal side effects. Akathisia is often unresponsive to anti-Parkinsonian drugs, but many patients find relief from propranolol (Inderal) or benzodiazepines.

Neuroleptic-Induced Tardive Dyskinesia (TD) (333.82)

(*DSM-IV*, pp. 679–680 and 747–749)

Tardive dyskinesia (TD) is a late occurring movement disorder that follows prolonged blockade of dopamine receptors in the brain. TD usually occurs only after months to years of treatment with neuroleptic medication. The symptoms of TD include involuntary choreiform (brief, purposeless), athetoid (writhing, serpentine), or rhythmic movements of the tongue, jaw, face, trunk, or extremities. Movements of the mouth, tongue, lips, and jaw are most common, but any muscle group can be affected. Because the movements of TD may become permanent, tardive dyskinesia has become a cause of malpractice lawsuits. Patients need to understand the risks and benefits of neuroleptic medications and should give informed consent to their treatment with such agents. On a single examination, it may be difficult to distinguish tardive dyskinesia from acute extrapyramidal symptoms. In addition, both tardive dystonia and tardive akathisia have been described in the psychiatric literature; these would be coded as 333.90 (Medication-Induced Movement Disorder NOS).

Medication-Induced Postural Tremor (333.1)

(*DSM-IV*, pp. 680 and 749–751)

Several psychoactive medications can induce a fine tremor as a side effect. Tremors are commonly seen during treatment with lithium carbonate, tricyclic antidepressants, and valproate. Tremor refers to rhythmic, oscillating, alternating movements caused by a repeated pattern of muscle contractions and relaxations. While a fine tremor often accompanies therapeutic levels of lithium carbonate, a coarse or gross tremor may be a sign of lithium toxicity.

Medication-Induced Movement Disorder Not Otherwise Specified (NOS) (333.90)

(*DSM-IV*, pp. 680 and 751)

As usual, *DSM-IV* provides an "other" category for medication-induced movement disorders not described in one of the six classes above. For example, it is possible that a non-neuroleptic medication might induce Parkinsonism, a malignant syndrome, an acute dystonia, acute akathisia, or tardive dyskinesia. In addition, a patient may suffer from tardive dystonia or tardive akathisia.

ADVERSE EFFECTS OF MEDICATION NOT OTHERWISE SPECIFIED (NOS) (995.2)

(*DSM-IV*, p. 680)

At times the side effects of a medication (other than the medication-induced movement symptoms) become a focus of clinical concern. For example, the newer serotonin-reuptake inhibiting antidepressants like Prozac may cause sexual dysfunction, which patients find distressing. The antidepressant trazodone can cause priapism, a painful persistent erection of the penis which can lead to permanent damage of penile structure. The antipsychotic drug thioridazine (Mellaril) can cause retrograde ejaculation, which sexually active young men find frightening. Women on antipsychotic medication may begin to lactate or to miss their menstrual periods. Elderly patients may suffer hypotension, with the risk of losing consciousness.

RELATIONAL PROBLEMS

(*DSM-IV*, pp. 681–682):
   Relational problems, as the name implies, occur in the context of an ongoing relationship. Parents may have difficulties communicating with or disciplining their children, who, in turn, may feel overprotected or smothered by their parents. Siblings may experience extreme rivalry or animosity toward one another. Spouses or partners may be enmeshed or overly distant. Interactions between individuals may be dysfunctional and marked by hostility, negativism, overinvolvement, poor communication, and so on. *DSM-IV* offers the following five V codes for relational problems:

V61.9   Relational Problem Related to a Mental Disorder or
            General Medical Condition.
V61.20   Parent–Child Relational Problem.
V61.1   Partner Relational Problem.
V61.8   Sibling Relational Problem.
V62.81   Relational Problem Not Otherwise Specified (NOS)

PROBLEMS RELATED TO ABUSE OR NEGLECT

(*DSM-IV*, p. 682):
   These all too common problems of abuse and neglect are self-explanatory.

V61.21   Physical Abuse of Child
V61.21   Sexual Abuse of Child
V61.21   Neglect of Child

(For V61.21, *DSM-IV* specifies code 995.5 if the focus of clinical attention is on the child victim.)

V61.1   Physical Abuse of Adult.

V61.1   Sexual Abuse of Adult.

(For V61.1, *DSM-IV* specifies code 995.81 if the focus of clinical attention is on the adult victim.)

ADDITIONAL CONDITIONS THAT MAY BE A FOCUS OF CLINICAL ATTENTION

(*DSM-IV*, pp. 683–686)

Noncompliance with Treatment for a Mental Disorder (V15.81)

(*DSM-IV*, p. 683)

There are clients who do not comply with recommended treatment for a mental disorder. Such noncompliance may be the result of ignorance, lack of understanding, cultural differences, lack of money for medication or travel to doctors, medical illness, fear, distrust, denial, delusional beliefs, alternate value systems, oppositional behavior, religious convictions, prior bad experiences with mental health providers, considered judgment of the risks and benefits of the treatment, and so on. This V Code (V15.81) is used when the focus of treatment is the client's noncompliance with treatment for a mental disorder.

Malingering (V65.2)

(*DSM-IV*, p. 683):

Malingering refers to the deliberate feigning of mental or physical illness to achieve an external incentive such as financial gain or the avoidance of responsibility. For example, during the Vietnam War some men falsely claimed to be homosexual to avoid being drafted into the army. At that time in American history, homosexuality was considered a mental disorder that made men unfit to serve in the armed forces. Today many substance abusers present at emergency rooms and falsely claim to be suicidal to secure a bed on a psychiatric ward.

Malingering differs from factitious disorder in that the malingerer is seeking to gain an external incentive, whereas the client with factitious disorder is seeking to maintain the sick role. In both malingering and factitious disorder, however, there is a feigning of illness and often an intentional production of symptoms.

Patients with somatoform disorders do not intentionally fake their symptoms and do not have obvious external motives for feigning illness. Furthermore, the somatoform disorders often occur in the context of underlying emotional conflict. Unlike conversion disorder symptoms, the symptoms in malingering are usually unresponsive to hypnosis or sodium amobarbital.

Some factors that should raise the suspicion of malingering include the following:

1. Obvious external incentives.
2. A pending lawsuit (i.e., a medicolegal context).
3. The client's apparent desire to escape a difficult situation.
4. Lack of cooperation with evaluation or treatment.
5. Antisocial personality disorder.
6. Discrepancy between symptoms and objective findings.
7. Some clinicians regard the presence of tattoos as warning signs of potential antisocial traits, including malingering.

Adult Antisocial Behavior (V71.01)

(*DSM-IV*, pp. 683–684)

Childhood or Adolescent Antisocial Behavior (V71.02)

(*DSM-IV*, p. 684)

Some individuals engage in criminal activity that is not due to a mental disorder. Children may perform isolated antisocial acts that are not a pattern of antisocial activity. Individuals of any age may behave in antisocial ways that are not part of a conduct disorder, an impulse control disorder, or an antisocial personality disorder. In some cases criminal behavior is an acceptable part of family or subcultural expectations.

Borderline Intellectual Functioning (V62.89)
(*This is coded on Axis II.*)

(*DSM-IV*, p. 684):
    An IQ from 71 to 84 is considered in the range of borderline intellectual functioning. The clinician may have difficulty differentiating borderline intellectual functioning from mental retardation (IQ below 71). Clients suffering simultaneously from a major psychiatric disorder and borderline intellectual functioning may appear to be mentally retarded during an evaluation.

Age-Related Cognitive Decline (780.9)

(*DSM-IV*, p. 684):
    Some individuals will seek clinical attention because of a decline in memory that is within normal limits for the person's age and is not due to a medical or neurological disorder. The clinician should use this V code only if a dementing illness or disorder has been ruled out.

Bereavement (V62.82)

(*DSM-IV*, pp. 684–685):
    Grief (mourning, bereavement) is a normal experience after a significant loss. Bereavement involves painful feelings of sadness following a loss. The loss may that be of a person, a pet, a job, a valued object, or a position. Such painful feelings often come in waves and are often accompanied by lack of energy, loss of interest, decreased libido, preoccupation with the lost person (or thing), social withdrawal, and problems with sleep and appetite. Uncomplicated bereavement does not involve profound hopelessness, suicidal ideation, or a sense of utter worthlessness.

Perhaps the most clinically astute description of normal grief was given by Lindemann (1944) in his classic report about the bereaved friends and relatives of those who died in the Coconut Grove fire in Boston. Lindemann identified five reactions that he felt were pathognomonic for grief:

1. Somatic distress
2. Preoccupation with the image of the deceased
3. Guilt
4. Hostile reactions
5. Loss of patterns of conduct

Lindemann also noted the appearance of traits of the deceased in the behavior of the bereaved. He described the syndrome of acute grief as follows:

The picture shown by persons in acute grief is remarkably uniform. Common to all is the following syndrome: sensations of somatic distress occurring in waves lasting from twenty minutes to an hour at a time, a feeling of tightness in the throat, choking with shortness of breath, need for sighing, an empty feeling in the abdomen, lack of muscular power, and an intense subjective distress described as tension or mental pain. The patient soon learns that these waves of discomfort can be precipitated by visits, by mentioning the deceased, and by receiving sympathy. There is a tendency to avoid the syndrome at any cost—to refuse visits lest they should precipitate the reaction, and to keep deliberately from thought all references to the deceased. [p. 143]

Lindemann also described among grieving persons the following common symptoms: a slight sense of unreality, intense preoccupation with the image of the deceased, self-accusations and guilt, loss of warmth in relationships, irritability, hostility, withdrawal from others, lack of zest, and exhaustion.

A significant loss may precipitate a major depressive episode in certain individuals. It is important, therefore, to distinguish bereavement from a major depressive episode. A review of the literature suggests that bereavement tends to be overly diagnosed. A person who meets criteria for a major depressive episode two months after a significant loss will most likely be suffering from major depression a year after the loss, if the depression goes untreated.

Depressive syndromes are common after the death of a spouse (Boschert 1994). In a lecture in 1994, Stephen R. Shuchter, M.D., professor of clinical psychiatry at the University of California, San Diego, School of Medicine, reported that 15 percent of people who have a major depressive episode after the death of a spouse continue to suffer from depression two years later. In a 1991 study of 350 widows and widowers, Sidney Zisook and Shuchter found that 24 percent met *DSM-III-R* criteria for a depressive episode two months after the loss, 23 percent at seven months, and 16 percent at thirteen months after the death of their spouse. By contrast, the prevalence of depressive episodes in the control group was 4 percent among 126 subjects living with their spouses.

DSM-IV diagnoses a Major Depressive Episode (*DSM-IV*, p. 327) rather than bereavement if, after a significant loss, the depressive symptoms persist for more than two months or are exceptionally severe. For example, if the symptoms accompanying bereavement include extreme feelings of worthlessness, marked impairment, suicidal preoccupation, psychosis, and severe psychomotor retardation, then *DSM-IV* would diagnose a Major Depressive Episode.

Academic Problem (V62.3)

(*DSM-IV*, p. 685):

Clinicians may treat individuals who exhibit poor academic performance that is not due to a mental disorder. In addition, clients with mental disorders may have academic problems that warrant attention in their own right. If the academic difficulty is a response to an identifiable stressor, an Adjustment Disorder is the likely diagnosis.

Occupational Problem (V62.2)

(*DSM-IV*, p. 685)

Clinicians may treat individuals with occupational difficulties that are not due to a mental disorder. In addition, clients with mental disorders may have occupational problems that warrant attention in their own right. In today's troubled economic times, many individuals experience job burnout or are forced to change careers in mid-life. If the occupational problem is a response to an identifiable stressor, an Adjustment Disorder is the likely diagnosis.

Identity Problem (313.82)

(*DSM-IV*, p. 685)

This code is used when the focus of clinical attention is a problem with one's sense of personal identity. Typical identity problems include distressful uncertainty about one's sexual orientation, personal goals, value system, moral standards, career path, choice of friends, and so on. Identity disturbances are a common feature of many *DSM-IV* disorders, such as Dissociative Disorders, Psychotic Disorders, Gender Identity Disorders, and Borderline Personality Disorder.

Religious or Spiritual Problem (V62.89)

(*DSM-IV*, p. 685)

American psychiatrists traditionally have treated religious concerns as evidence of immaturity, dependency, neuroticism, or psychosis. Many clients, however, seek counseling because of religious or spiritual experiences. They may be questioning their faith or spiritual values. They may have religious experiences that are puzzling or frightening. For example, many people report "near-death" or "after-death" experiences during a cardiac arrest or a near-fatal accident. Some people experience mystical or ecstatic states during prayer. In the past, American psychiatry, with its solar mythological perspective, has tended to regard most spiritual experiences as evidence of mental illness. Sigmund Freud considered religion to be an illusion that the mature individual would outgrow. The intent of adding this new category to *DSM-IV* is to avoid the previous stereotyping of religious and spiritual experiences as necessarily psychopathological. *DSM-IV*'s treatment of religious issues reflects its growing sensitivity to issues of cultural diversity.

Acculturation Problem (V62.4)

(*DSM-IV*, p. 685)

Many individuals have difficulty adjusting to a new culture. Immigrants may have to learn a new language as well as new customs and different modes of social interaction. Immigrants to the United States must deal with the discrimination, racial prejudice, chauvinism, and jingoism that are part of North American culture. Even those born and raised in America may experience cultural difficulties when moving from one part of the country to another. For example, Northerners may be uncomfortable with Southern culture and vice versa.

Phase of Life Problem (V62.89)

(*DSM-IV*, pp. 685–686):

Some individuals will experience difficulties coping with the transition from one phase of development to another. Examples of such developmental phases include leaving home, entering college, embarking on a career, getting married, having children, the mid-life crisis, divorce, retirement, and so on. This V code is used for phase of life difficulties that are not due to a mental disorder, or if they are due to a mental disorder, they nonetheless require their own clinical attention. When the difficulties arise in reaction to a specific stressor, the diagnosis of Adjustment Disorder should be considered.

ADDITIONAL CODES

(*DSM-IV*, p. 687)

Unspecified Mental Disorder (Nonpsychotic) (300.9)

The clinician can use this category when a nonpsychotic mental disorder is present, but there is not yet sufficient information to make a more definitive *DSM-IV* diagnosis. Once more information becomes available, the diagnosis can be changed to a more specific *DSM-IV* disorder. In addition, the clinician can use this code (300.9) when the mental disorder exists, but does not appear in *DSM-IV* or when none of the NOS categories adequately describes the mental disorder.

No Diagnosis or Condition on Axis I (V71.09)

The clinician should indicate when no Axis I condition or diagnosis is present. It is still possible to have an Axis II Personality Disorder or Mental Retardation diagnosis.

Diagnosis or Condition Deferred on Axis I (799.9)

The clinician defers the diagnosis on Axis I (799.9) when there is not enough information to make an Axis I diagnosis.

No Diagnosis on Axis II (V71.09)

The clinician should indicate when no Axis II Personality Disorder or Mental Retardation diagnosis is present. It is still possible to have an Axis I condition or diagnosis.

Diagnosis Deferred on Axis II (799.9)

The clinician defers the diagnosis on Axis II (799.9) when there is not enough information to make an Axis II diagnosis.

REFERENCES

Abad, V., and Boyce, E. (1979). Issues in the psychiatric evaluations of Puerto Ricans. *Journal of Operational Psychiatry* 10:28–39.

Administration officials explain mental health benefit, rationale. *Mental Health Report*, October 21, 1993; 17:161–162.

AIDS Primer (1990). Washington, DC: American Psychiatric Association (AIDS Education Project).

Akiskal, H. S., and McKinney, W. T. (1973). Psychiatry and pseudopsychiatry. *Archives of General Psychiatry* 28:367–373.

Alonso, L., and Jeffrey, W. D. (1988). Mental illness complicated by the Santeria belief in spirit possession. *Hospital and Community Psychiatry* 39:1188–1191.

American Heritage Dictionary (1980). Boston: Houghton Mifflin.

American Psychiatric Association's Psychiatric Glossary (1984). Washington, DC: American Psychiatric Press.

Andreasen, N. C. (1987). The diagnosis of schizophrenia. *Schizophrenia Bulletin* 13:9–22.

Andreasen, N. C., and Black, D. W. (1991). *Introductory Textbook of Psychiatry*. Washington, DC: American Psychiatric Press.

Andreasen, N. C., and Carpenter, W. T. (1993). Diagnosis and classification of schizophrenia. *Schizophrenia Bulletin* 19:199–214.

Andreasen, N. C., and Wasek, P. (1980). Adjustment disorders in adolescents and adults. *Archives of General Psychiatry* 37:1166–1170.

APA Trustees' Position Statement on Psychiatric Treatment Designed to Change Sexual Orientation. Quoted in: Sexual orientation and treatment. *Psychiatric Times*, April 15, 1993, p. 18.

Ash, P. (1949). The reliability of psychiatric diagnosis. *Journal of Abnormal Social Psychology* 44:272–276.

Asher, R., (1951). Munchausen's syndrome. *Lancet* 1:339.

Attempts to "cure" homosexuality could lead to liability. *Mental Health Law Reporter*, June, 1994, 12(6):42.

Barlett, P., and Low, S. (1980). Nervios in rural Costa Rica. *Medical Anthropology* 4:523–564.

Beck, A. T. (1962). Reliability of psychiatric diagnoses, I: a critique of systematic studies. *American Journal of Psychiatry* 119:210–216.

Bird, H. R., (1982). The cultural dichotomy of colonial people. *Journal of the American Academy of Psychoanalysis* 10:195–209.

Bleuler, E. P., (1950). *Dementia Praecox or the Group of Schizophrenias*. New York: International Universities Press.

——— (1924). *Textbook of Psychiatry*. New York: Macmillan.

Bloombaum, M., Yamamoto, J., and James, Q. (1968). Cultural stereotyping among psychotherapists. *Journal of Counseling and Clinical Psychology* 32(1):99.

Bluestone, H., and Vela, R. M. (1982). Transcultural aspects in the psychotherapy of the Puerto Rican poor in New York City. *Journal of the American Academy of Psychoanalysis* 10(2):269–283.

Bohnen, N., and Jolles, J. (1992). Neurobehavioral aspects of postconcussive symptoms after mild head injury. *Journal of Nervous and Mental Disease* 180:683–692.

Boschert, S. (1994). If grief persists after the death of a spouse, "'Think depression and treatment." *Clinical Psychiatry News*, March, 1994, 22(3):1.

Brenneis, C. B., and Roll, S. (1975). Ego modalities in the manifest dreams of male and female Chicanos. *Psychiatry* 38:172–185.

——— (1976). Dream patterns in Chicano and Anglo young adults. *Psychiatry* 39:280–290.

Brown, L. S., and Ballou, M., eds. (1992). *Personality and Psychopathology, Feminist Reappraisals*. New York: Guilford.

Burns, L. E., and Thorpe, G. L. (1977). The epidemiology of fears and phobias. *Journal of International Medical Research* 5 (suppl 5):1–7.

Burton, R. (1621). *The Anatomy of Melancholy, What It Is. With All Kindes, Causes, Symptomes, Prognostickes, and Severall Cures of It*. Oxford. Printed by John Lichfield and James Short, for Henry Cripps.

Campbell, J. (1964). *The Masks of God: Occidental Mythology*. New York: Penguin Books.

Campbell, J., with Bill Moyers. (1988). *The Power of Myth*. New York: Doubleday.

Canino, I. A., and Spurlock, J. (1994). *Culturally Diverse Children and Adolescents*. New York: Guilford.

Choca, J. (1980). *Manual for Clinical Psychology Practicums*. New York: Brunner/Mazel.

Chu, J. A. (1993). Critical issues committee report: Comorbidity and MPD. *ISSMP&D News*, October, 1993, pp. 3–11.

Clark, M. (1970). *Health in the Mexican-American Culture*. Los Angeles: University of California Press.

Clarkin, J., Widiger, T., Frances, A., et al. (1983). Prototypic typology and the borderline personality disorder. *Journal of Abnormal Psychology* 92:263–275.

Cleckley, H. (1964). *The Mask of Sanity*. St. Louis, MO: C. V. Mosby, 1938.

Cooper, J. E., Kendell, R. E., and Gurland, B. J. (1972). *Psychiatric Diagnosis in New York and London*. Maudsley Monograph, No. 20. London: Oxford University Press.

Crane, G. E. (1970). Use of monamine oxidase inhibiting antidepressants. In *Principles of Psychopharmacology*, editor-in-chief W. G Clark, pp. 643–651. New York: Academic.

Cross, W. L., and Brooke, T., eds. (1993). *The Yale Shakespeare: The Complete Works*. New York: Barnes & Noble.

Crow, T. (1985). The two-syndrome concept: origins and current status. *Schizophrenia Bulletin* 11:471–483.

DeLaCancela, V., Guarnaccia, P., and Carrillo, E. (1986). Psychosocial distress among Latinos: a critical analysis of ataques de nervios. *Humanity and Society* 10:431–447.

Desorden Obsesivo Compulsivo, Preguntas y Respuestas. Pamphlet published by the OC Foundation, Inc., P.O. Box 70, Milford, CT, 06460–0070.

Diagnostic and Statistical Manual of Mental Disorders, Third Edition (DSM-III, 1980). Washington, DC: American Psychiatric Association.

Diagnostic and Statistical Manual of Mental Disorders, Third Edition Revised (DSM-III-R, 1987). Washington, DC: American Psychiatric Association.

Diagnostic and Statistical Manual of Mental Disorders, Fourth Edition Revised (DSM-IV, 1994). Washington, DC: American Psychiatric Association.

Díaz-Guerrero, R. (1975). *Psychology of the Mexican: Culture and Personality*. Austin, TX: University of Texas Press.

Does DNA make some men gay? Science: the biology of destiny. *Newsweek*, July 26, 1993, p. 59.

Dow, J. (1986). *The Shaman's Touch: Otomi Indian Symbolic Healing*. Salt Lake City, UT: University of Utah Press.

DSM-IV Draft Criteria (1993). Task Force on *DSM-IV* (3/1/93). Washington, DC: American Psychiatric Association.

DSM-IV maximizes differential diagnosis, cultural relevance (1994). *Mental Health Report,* June 2, 1994, 18(11):81–84.

DSM-IV Update (January/February 1993). Office of Research. Washington, DC: American Psychiatric Association.

_____ (March 1993). Office of Research. Washington, DC: American Psychiatric Association.

_____ (July 1993). Office of Research. Washington, DC: American Psychiatric Association.

Ellenberger, H. F. (1974). Psychiatry from ancient to modern times. In *American Handbook of Psychiatry, Second Edition*, vol. 1, ed. S. Arieti, pp. 3–27. New York: Basic Books.

Endicott, J., Spitzer, R. L., Fleiss, J. L., et al. (1976). The Global Assessment Scale: a procedure for measuring overall severity of psychiatric disturbance. *Archives of General Psychiatry* 33:766–771.

Enelow, A. J., and Adler, L. M. (1979). Basic interviewing. In *Interviewing & Patient Care, Second Edition*, eds. A. J. Enelow and S. N. Swisher, chapter 3, pp. 35–61. New York: Oxford University Press.

Enelow, A. J. and Swisher, S. N. (1979). *Interviewing & Patient Care, Second Edition*. New York: Oxford University Press.

Engel, G. L. (1977). The need for a new medical model: a challenge to biomedicine. *Science* 196:129–136.

English, H. B., and English, A. C. (1958). *A Comprehensive Dictionary of Psychological and Psychoanalytical Terms*. New York: David McKay.

Frush, S. C. (1991). The use of melatonin in the allowlation of jet lag. *JAT* 19(6):555–561.

Fabrega, H. (1970). On the specificity of folk illnesses. *Southwest Journal of Anthropology* 26:305–314.

Fasnacht, B. (1993a). Child and adolescent disorders get fine-tuning in *DSM-IV*. *Psychiatric News*, September 3, 1993, p. 8.

_____ (1993b). Empirical process guided development of *DSM-IV*. *Psychiatric News*, August 20, 1993, pp. 1 and 6–7.

Feighner, J. P., Robins, E., Guze, S. B., et al. (1972). Diagnostic criteria for use in psychiatric research. *Archives of General Psychiatry* 26:57–63.

Feinstein, A. R. (1967). *Clinical Judgment*. Baltimore: Williams & Wilkins.

Fernández-Marina, R. (1961). The Puerto Rican syndrome. *Psychiatry* 24:79–82.

First, M. B., Frances, A. J., Pincus, H. A., et al. (1994). Changes in substance-related, schizophrenic, and other primarily adult disorders. *Hospital and Community Psychiatry* 45(1):18–20.

First, M. B., Vettorello, N., Frances, A. J., and Pincus, H. A. (1993). Changes in mood, anxiety, and personality disorders. *Hospital and Community Psychiatry* 44(11): 1034–1043.

Flaum, M., and Andreasen, N. C. (1991). Diagnostic criteria for schizophrenia and related disorders: options for *DSM-IV Schizophrenia Bulletin* 17:133–142.

Fleiss, J. L., Spitzer, R. L., Endicott, J., et al. (1972). Quantification of agreement in multiple psychiatric diagnosis. *Archives of General Psychiatry* 26:168–171.

Folstein, M. F., Folstein, S. E., and McHugh, P. R. (1975). Mini-mental state—a practical method for grading the cognitive state of patients for the clinician. *Journal of Psychiatric Research* 12:189–198.

Frances, A. J. (1993). *DSM-IV. Audio Digest Psychiatry* 22(8).

Frances, A. J., Alger, I. E., Andreasen, N. C., et al. (1994). *The Diagnostic Process and DSM-IV Course 33*. Presented at the American Psychiatric Association annual meeting, Philadelphia, PA, May 22.

Frances, A. J., First, M. B., Pincus, H. A., et al. (1994). Changes in child and adolescent disorders, eating disorders, and the multiaxial system. *Hospital and Community Psychiatry* 45(3):212–214.

Frances, A. J., Pincus, H. A., Widiger, T. A., et al. (1990). *DSM-IV*: work in progress. *American Journal of Psychiatry* 147:1439–1448.

Frances, A., Widiger, T. A., and Pincus, H. A. (1989). The development of *DSM-IV Archives of General Psychiatry* 46:373–375.

Frank, J. (1973). *Persuasion and Healing*. New York: Schocken Books.

Freud, S. (1955). *The Standard Edition of the Complete Works of Sigmund Freud*, trans. by James Strachey. London: Hogarth.

García-Preto, N. (1982). Puerto Rican families. In *Ethnicity and Family Therapy*, eds. M. McGoldrick, J. K. Pearce, and J. Giordano, pp. 164–186. New York: Guilford.

Garrison, V. (1977). The Puerto Rican syndrome in psychiatry and espiritismo. In *Case Studies in Spirit Possession*, eds. V. Crapanzano and V. Garrison, pp. 383–449. New York: John Wiley & Sons.

Gay, P. (1988). *Freud, A Life for Our Time*. New York: W. W. Norton.

Glazer, W. (1993). PsychPro will bolster role of psychiatrist. *Connecticut Psychiatrist*: 34:7–8.

Glazer, W., and Gray, G. (1993). A decision support system for psychiatric care in an HMO setting. *Medical Interface*, June, pp. 111–114.

Goldman, E. L. (1993). Visions from the spirit world may complicate diagnosis. *Clinical Psychiatry News*. November, p. 21.

Goldman, H. H., Skodol, A. E., and Tamara, R. L. (1992). Revising Axis V for *DSM-IV*: A review of measures of social functioning. *American Journal of Psychiatry* 149:1148–1156.

Goleman, D. (1994). The "wrong" sex: a new definition of childhood pain. *The New York Times* 3/22/94, pp. C1 and C9.

Good, B., and Good, M. J. D. (1982). Toward a meaning-centered analysis of popular illness categories: "fright illness" and "heart disease" in Iran. In *Cultural Conceptions of Mental Health and Therapy*, eds. A. J. Marsella and A. J. White, pp. 141–166. Dordrecht, Holland: D. Reidel.

Goodwin, J. M., Goodwin, J. S., and Kellner, R. (1979). Psychiatric symptoms in disliked medical patients. *Journal of the American Medical Association* 241:1117.

Guarnaccia, P. J. (1993). *Ataques de nervios* in Puerto Rico: culture-bound syndrome or popular illness? *Medical Anthropology* 15:157–170.

Guarnaccia, P. J., Canino, G., Rubio-Stipec, M., and Bravo, M. (1993). The prevalence of *ataques de nervios* in the Puerto Rico disaster study. *Journal of Nervous and Mental Disease* 181:157–165.

Guarnaccia, P. J., DeLaCancela, V., and Carrillo, E. (1989). The multiple meanings of ataques de nervios in the Latino community. *Medical Anthropology* 11:47–62.

Guarnaccia, P. J., and Farias, P. (1988). The social meanings of nervios: a case study of a Central American woman. *Social Science and Medicine* 26:1223–1231.

Gunderson, J. G. (1983). DSM-III diagnoses of personality disorders. In *Current Perspectives on Personality Disorders*, ed. J. Frosch, pp. 20–39. Washington, DC: American Psychiatric Press.

Gunderson, J. G., and Siever, L. (1985). Relatedness of schizotypal to schizophrenic disorders. *Schizophrenia Bulletin* 11:532–537.

Guze, S. B. (1970). The need for toughmindedness in psychiatric thinking. *Southern Medical Journal* 63:662–671.

Hahn, R. A. (1985). Culture bound syndromes unbound. *Social Science and Medicine* 21:165–171.

Hamer, D. H., Hu, S., Magnuson, V. L., et al. (1993). A linkage between DNA markers on the X chromosome and male sexual orientation. *Science* 261:321–327.

Harwood, A. (1977). *Rx: Spiritist as Needed*. New York: Wiley–Interscience.

Hauri, P. (1992). Circadian rhythms. *Audio Digest Psychiatry*, March 9; 21(5).

Haynes, R. M., Resnick, P. J., Dougherty, K. C., and Althof, S. E. (1993). Proverb familiarity and the mental status examination. *Bulletin of the Menninger Clinic* 57(4):523–528.

Herman, J. (1993). DSM-IV to omit self-defeating personality disorder category. *Psychiatric Times*, April, p. 23.

Hersen, M. and Turner, S. M. (1991). *Adult Psychopathology and Diagnosis*. New York: John Wiley & Sons.

HIV Management Council: AIDS. Dementia Complex (1994). *Clinical Insight* (Guidelines for management of HIV infection newsletter) 4(3):1–8.

Holy Bible, Saint Joseph Edition (1963). New York: Catholic Book Publishing Company.

Hooker, E. (1957). The adjustment of the male overt homosexual. *Journal of Projective Techniques* 21:18–31.

Horowitz, M. J. (1970). *Image Formation and Cognition*. New York: Appleton-Century-Crofts.

———— (1988). *Introduction to Psychodynamics*. New York: Basic Books.

International Classification of Diseases, 9th Revision, Clinical Modification (ICD-9-CM), Third Edition, (March, 1989). U.S. Department of Health and Human Services, HCFA, DHHS. Publication No., (PH.S) 89–1260.

Iqbal, N., Schwartz, B. J., Cecil, A., et al. (1993). Schizophrenia diagnosis. *Psychiatric Annals* 23(3):105–110.

James, W. (1902). *The Varieties of Religious Experience*. New York: Macmillan.

———— (1990). The will to believe. In *The World Treasury of Modern Religious Thought*, ed. J. Pelikan, pp. 93–114. Boston: Little, Brown.

Javier, R. A. (1985). Linguistic considerations in the treatment of bilinguals. Paper presented at the XX International Congress of Psychology, Caracas, Venezuela, July.

Jones, B. N., Teng, E. L., Folstein, M. F., et al. (1993). A new bedside test of cognition for patients with HIV infection. *Annals of Internal Medicine* 119:1001–1004.

Jones, E. (1961). *The Life and Work of Sigmund Freud*. New York: Basic Books.

Kahlbaum, K. L. (1874). *Die Katatonie ode das Spannangsirresein*. Berlin: Hirschwald.

Kaplan, H. S. (1974). *The New Sex Therapy*. New York: Brunner/Mazel.

Kaplan, I. K., Sadock, B. J., and Grebb, J. A., eds. (1994). *Kaplan and Sadock's Synopsis of Psychiatry*, Seventh Edition. Baltimore: Williams & Wilkins.

Karno, M. (1966). The enigma of ethnicity in a psychiatric clinic. *Archives of General Psychiatry* 14:516–520.

Karno, M., and Edgerton, R. B. (1969). Perception of mental illness in a Mexican-American community. *Archives of General Psychiatry* 20:233–238.

Kasanin, J. (1933). The acute schizoaffective psychoses. *American Journal of Psychiatry* 90:97–126.

Kay, S. R. (1991). *Positive and Negative Syndromes in Schizophrenia*. New York: Brunner/Mazel.

Kay, S. R., Fiszbein, A., and Opler, L. A. (1987). The positive and negative syndrome scale (PANSS) for schizophrenia. *Schizophrenia Bulletin* 13:261–267.

Keller, M. B. (1979). The mental status examination. In *Outpatient Psychiatry, Diagnosis and Treatment*, ed. A. Lazare. Baltimore: Williams & Wilkins.

Kendell, R. E., Cooper, J. E., and Gourley, A. J. (1971). Diagnostic criteria of American and British psychiatrists. *Archives of General Psychiatry* 25:123–130.

Kessler, R. C., McGonagle, K. A., et al. (1994). Lifetime and 12-month prevalence of DSM-III-R psychiatric disorders in the United States. *Archives of General Psychiatry* 51:8–19.

Kiev, A. (1968). *Curanderismo: Mexican American Folk Psychiatry*. New York: Free Press.

Kirk, S. A. and Kutchins, H. (1994). Is bad writing a mental disorder? *New York Times*, June 20, Op-Ed page.

Klein, D. (1977). Pharmacological treatment and delineation of borderline disorders. In *Borderline Personality Disorders*, ed. P. Hartocollis, p. 365. New York: International Universities Press.

Kleinman, A. (1988). *Rethinking Psychiatry*. New York: Free Press.

Klerman, G. L. (1986). Historical perspectives on contemporary schools of psychopathology. In *Contemporary Directions in Psychopathology*, eds. T. Millon and G. Klerman, pp. 3–28. New York: Guilford.

Kline, L. (1969). Some factors in the psychiatric treatment of Spanish-Americans. *American Journal of Psychiatry* 125:88–95.

Kline, M., Sydnor-Greenberg, N., Davis, W. W., et al. (1993). Using field trials to evaluate proposed changes in DSM diagnostic criteria. *Hospital and Community Psychiatry* 44(7):621–623.

Kloppenburg, B. (1983). *Fuerzas Ocultas*. Bogota, Colombia: Ediciones Paulinas.

Kluft, R. P. (1993). Multiple personality disorder. *The Harvard Mental Health Letter* 10(4):5–7.

Klüver, H. and Bucy, P. C. (1937). "Psychic blindness" and other symptoms following bilateral lobectomy in rhesus monkeys. *American Journal of Physiology* 119:352.

Kraepelin, E. (1913). *Psychiatre: Ein Lehrbuch* (8th Ed.) Leipzig: Barth.

────── (1919). *Manic Depressive Insanity and Paranoia*. Edinburgh: Livingstone.

────── (1921). *Dementia Praecox and Paraphrenia*. Edinburgh: Livingstone.

Kreisman, J. J. (1975). The curandero's apprentice: a therapeutic integration of folk and medical healing. *American Journal of Psychiatry* 132(1):81–83.

Krippner, S. and Welch, P. (1992). *Spiritual Dimensions of Healing*. New York: Irvington.

Krohne, E. C. (1982). *Sex Therapy Handbook*. Lancaster, England: MTP Press Limited.

LaBruzza, A. L. (1981). Physical illness presenting as psychiatric disorder: guidelines for differential diagnosis. *Journal of Operational Psychiatry* 12:24–31.

_____ (1984). Medical illness as a cause for psychosis. In *Transient Psychosis*, eds. J. P. Tupin, U. Halbreich, and J. J. Pena, pp. 43–60. New York: Brunner/Mazel.

Lewis-Fernández, R. (1993). Dissociation, trauma, and the *ataque de nervios*: a case-control study of Puerto Rican out-patients in Massachusetts. Paper presented at the Annual Meeting of the American Psychiatric Association, San Francisco, CA, May.

Light and Life (1800s). Charlotte, NC:, C. H. Robinson and Co.

Lindemann, E. (1944). Symptomatology and management of acute grief. *American Journal of Psychiatry* 101:141–148.

Linehan, M. M. (1993). *Cognitive Behavioral Treatment of Borderline Personality Disorder.* New York: Guilford.

Louis, A. (1991). *Horary Astrology: The History and Practice of Astro-divination.* St. Paul, MN: Llewellyn.

Low, S. M. (1981). The meaning of *nervios*: a sociocultural analysis of symptom presentation in San Jose, Costa Rica. *Culture, Medicine, and Psychiatry* 5:25–47.

Lowenstein, R. J. (1991). An office mental status examination for complex chronic dissociative symptoms and multiple personality disorder. *Psychiatric Clinics of North America* 14(3):567–604.

Lukoff, D., Lu, F., and Turner, R. (1992). Toward a more culturally sensitive *DSM-IV*, psychoreligious and psychospiritual problems. *Journal of Nervous and Mental Disease* 180:673–682.

MacKinnon, R. A. and Yudofsky, S. C. (1986). *The Psychiatric Evaluation in Clinical Practice.* New York: J. B. Lippincott.

Maldonado-Sierra, E. D., Trent, R. D., and Fernández-Marina, F. R. (1960). Neurosis and traditional family beliefs in Puerto Rico. *International Journal of Social Psychiatry* 6:237–246.

Marcos, L. R., Urcuyo, L., Kesselman, M., and Alpert, M. (1973). The language barrier in evaluating Spanish-American patients. *Archives of General Psychiatry* 29:655–659.

Masters, W. H. and Johnson, V. E. (1966). *Human Sexual Response.* Boston: Little, Brown.

McHugh, P. R. (1993). Multiple personality disorder. *The Harvard Mental Health Letter* 10(3):4–6.

McGoldrick, M. (1982). Ethnicity and family therapy: an overview. In *Ethnicity and Family Therapy*, eds. M. McGoldrick, J. K. Pearce, and J. Giordano, pp. 3–30. New York: Guilford.

Mehlman, K. R. D. (1961). The Puerto Rican syndrome. *American Journal of Psychiatry* 118:328–332.

Menninger, K. (1963). *The Vital Balance.* New York: Viking.

Mental Health Report (1993). Administration officials explain mental health benefit, rationale, October 21, 17:161–162.

_____ (1994). *DSM-IV* maximizes differential diagnosis, cultural relevance, June 2, 18(11):81–84.

Merck Manual of Diagnosis and Therapy. (1992). 16th Edition. Editor-in-Chief: R. Berkow, M.D. Rahway, NJ: Merck & Co.

Millon, T. (1986). On the past and future of the *DSM-III*: personal recollections and projections. In *Contemporary Directions in Psychopathology*, eds. T. Millon and G. Klerman, pp. 29–70. New York: Guilford.

_____ (1993). Negativistic (passive–aggressive) personality disorder. *Journal of Personality Disorders* 7(1):78–85.

Mora, G. (1985). History of psychiatry. In *Comprehensive Textbook of Psychiatry/IV*, eds. H. I. Kaplan and B. J. Sadock, pp. 2034–2054. New York: Williams & Wilkins.

Morel, B. A. (1852–1853). *Etudes Cliniques: Triate Theorique et Pratique des Maladies Mentales*. Paris: Masson.

Morris, C. G. (1992). *Psicología Un Nuevo Enfoque*. Mexico: Prentice-Hall Hispanoamericana.

Nestler, E. J. (1993). From the editor. *Yale Psychiatry*, Fall, 3(1):2.

Oquendo, M., Horwath, E., and Martinez, A. (1992). Ataques de nervios: proposed diagnostic criteria for a culture specific syndrome. *Culture, Medicine and Psychiatry* 16:367–376.

Othmer, E. and Othmer, S. C. (1989). *The Clinical Interview Using DSM-III-R*. Washington, DC: American Psychiatric Press.

Padilla, A. M., ed. (1976). *Psychotherapy with the Spanish-speaking: Issues in Research and Service Delivery*. Los Angeles: Spanish Speaking Mental Health Research Center, Monograph No. 3.

Padilla, A. M. and Ruiz, R. A. (1973). *Latino Mental Health: A Review of the Literature*. Rockville, MD: National Institute of Mental Health.

Paine, W. (1866). *A Treatise on the Principles and Practice of Medicine and Pathology, Diseases of Women and Children, and Surgery*. Philadelphia: Pub. Soc.

Papajohn, J. and Spiegel, J. (1975). *Transition in Families*. San Francisco: Jossey-Bass.

Pasnau, R. O. (1987). The remedicalization of psychiatry. *Hospital and Community Psychiatry* 38:145–151.

Peck, H. B. (1974). Psychiatric approaches to the impoverished and underprivileged. In *American Handbook of Psychiatry*, second edition. Editor-in-Chief, S. Arieti. Volume II, pp. 524–567. New York: Basic Books.

Peñalosa, F. (1968). Mexican family roles. *Journal of Marriage and the Family* 30:680–689.

Pérez Foster, R. M. (1994). Panel: psychoanalytic technique and the bilingual patient—introduction and literature review. Paper presented at the 14th Annual Division 39 Meeting, April, Washington, DC.

Phillips, K. A., Hirschfeld, R. M. A., Shea, M. T., and Gunderson, J. G. (1993). Depressive personality disorder: perspectives for *DSM-IV*. *Journal of Personality Disorders* 7(1):30–42.

Pierce, C. (1993). World psychiatrists still not speaking same Dx language. *Clinical Psychiatry News*, August, p. 14.

Pincus, H. A. (1993). Preview of *DSM-IV Grand Rounds Review*. National Medical Enterprises, 6th Issue, p. 4.

Pincus, H. A., Frances, A., Davis, W. W., et al. (1992). *DSM-IV* and new diagnostic categories: holding the line on proliferation. *American Journal of Psychiatry* 149:113–117.

Professional Staff of the U.S.-U.K. Cross National Project (1974). The diagnosis of psychopathology of schizophrenia in New York and London. *Schizophrenia Bulletin* 1:80–102.

Putnam, F. W. (1989). *Diagnosis and Treatment of Multiple Personality Disorder*. New York: Guilford.

Putnam, F. W., Guroff, J., Silberman, E., et al. (1986). The clinical phenomenology of multiple personality disorder: 100 recent cases. *Journal of Clinical Psychiatry* 47:285–293.

Quick Quotes (1992). WordStar International Corporation. San Rafael, CA: Micropro.

Ramirez, M. (1967). Identification with Mexican family values and authoritarianism. *Journal of Social Psychology* 73:3–11.

Reich, W. (1950). *Character Analysis*. London: Vision.

Reiser, M. (1988). Are psychiatric educators "Losing the mind"? *American Journal of Psychiatry* 145:148–153.

Rendón, M. (1984). Myths and stereotypes in minority groups. *International Journal of Social Psychiatry* 30:297–309.

Renik, O., Spielman, P., and Afterman, J. (1978). Bamboo phobia in an eighteen-month-old boy. *Journal of the American Psychoanalytic Association* 26(2):255–282.

Richmond, C. A. (1992). *Twisted*. Chicago: Noble.

Robert, E. (1937). *Candle in the Sun*. New York: Bobbs-Merrill.

Robins, L. N., Helzer, J. E., Croughnan, J., and Ratcliffe, K. S. (1981). National Institute of Mental Health Diagnostic Interview Schedule. *Archives of General Psychiatry* 38:281–389.

Rogler, L. H., Blumenthal, R., Malgady, R., and Costantino, G. (1985). *Hispanics and Culturally Sensitive Mental Health Services* (Research Bulletin, 8[3–4]). New York: Fordham University, Hispanic Research Center.

Rogler, L. and Hollingshead, A. B. (1961). The Puerto Rican spiritualist as a psychiatrist. *American Journal of Sociology* 67(1):12–22.

_____ (1965). *Trapped: Families and Schizophrenia*. New York: John Wiley & Sons.

Roll, S., Rabold, K., and McArdle, L. (1976). Disclaimed activity in the dreams of Chicanos and Anglos. *Journal of Cross-Cultural Psychology* 7:335–345.

Rosenhan, D. L. (1973). On being sane in insane places. *Science* 179:250–258.

Rothblum, E. D., Solomon, L. J., and Albee, G. W. (1986). A sociopolitical perspective of DSM-III. In *Contemporary Directions in Psychopathology*, eds. T. Millon and G. Klerman, pp. 167–189. New York: Guilford.

Rothenberg, A. (1964). Puerto Rico and aggression. *American Journal of Psychiatry* 20:962–970.

Rubel, A. J. (1964). The epidemiology of a folk illness: *Susto* in Hispanic America. *Ethnology* 3:268–283.

Rubel, A. J., O'Neill, C., and Collado-Ardon, R. (1984). *Susto, A Folk Illness*. Berkeley, California: University of California Press.

Rubio, M., Urdaneta, M., and Doyle, J. L. (1955). Psychopathologic reaction patterns in the Antilles command. *US Armed Forces Medical Journal* 6:1767–1772.

Rubio-Stipec, M., Shrout, P., Bird, H., et al. (1989). Symptom scales of the Diagnostic Interview Schedule: factor results in Hispanic and Anglo samples. *Journal of Consulting and Clinical Psychology* 1:30–34.

Rush, B. (1812). *Medical Inquiries and Observations upon the Diseases of the Mind*. Philadelphia.

Sacks, O. (1993). A neurologist's notebook. *The New Yorker*, December 27, 1993/ January 3, 1994, pp. 106–125.

Salzman, L. (1975). Interpersonal factors in depression. In *The Nature and Treatment of Depression*, eds. F. F. Flach and S. C. Draghi, pp. 43–56. New York: John Wiley & Sons.

Sandoval, M. C. (1977). Afrocuban concepts of disease and its treatment in Miami. *Journal of Operational Psychiatry* 8:52–63.

_____ (1979). Santeria as a mental health care system: a historical overview. *Social Science and Medicine* 13(3):137–157.

Saunders, L. (1954). *Cultural Differences and Medical Care: The Case of the Spanish-Speaking People of the Southwest*. New York: Russell Sage Foundation.

Schacht, T. and Nathan, P. E. (1977). But is it good for the psychologists? Appraisal and status of *DSM-III. American Psychologist*, December, pp. 1017–1025.

Scheck, A. (1993). Hispanics share common traits, but mental health symptomatology is not one of them. *Clinical Psychiatry News*, December.

Schneider, K. (1959). *Clinical Psychopathology*. New York: Grune and Stratton.

Sexual orientation and treatment (1994). *Psychiatric News*, April 15, p. 18.

Shapiro, D. (1965). *Neurotic Styles*. New York: Basic Books.

Shea, M. T. (1993). *DSM-IV* reviews of the personality disorders: introduction to the third part of the special series. *Journal of Personality Disorders* 7(1):28–29.

Sherman, C. (1993). Do you unwittingly reinforce borderline behavior? *Clinical Psychiatry News*, October, p. 5.

_____ (1994). *DSM* kills "organic" and grows subtypes. *Clinical Psychiatry News*, May, pp. 1, 18.

Simons, R., and Hughes C., eds. (1985). *The Culture-Bound Syndromes*. Dordrecht, Holland: Reidel.

Skodol, A. E. (1989). *Problems in Differential Diagnosis*. Washington, DC: American Psychiatric Press.

Slater, E. T. O. and Glithero, E. (1965). A follow-up of patients diagnosed as suffering from "hysteria." *Journal of Psychosomatic Research* 9:9–13.

Spitzer, R. L. and Fleiss, J. L. (1974). A reanalysis of the reliability of psychiatric diagnosis. *British Journal of Psychiatry* 125:341–347.

Spitzer, R. L., Williams, J. B., Kass, F., and Davies, M. (1989). National field trial of the *DSM-III-R* diagnostic criteria for SDPD. *American Journal of Psychiatry*, 146:1561–1567.

Steinberg, M. (1993a). Advances in detecting dissociation. *Psychiatric Times*, April, pp. 21–23.

_____ (1993b). *The Structured Clinical Interview for DSM-IV Dissociative Disorders (SCID-D)*. Washington, DC: American Psychiatric Press.

Stone, A. (1977). Stone sees psychiatry advancing despite criticism. *Psychiatric News*, June 3, p. 24.

Strub, R. L. and Black, W. F. (1977). *The Mental Status Examination in Neurology*. Philadelphia, PA: F. A. Davis.

_____ (1988). *Neurobehavioral Disorders, A Clinical Approach*. Philadelphia, PA: F. A. Davis.

Sullivan, H. S. (1947). *Conceptions of Modern Psychiatry*. Washington, DC: William A. White Psychiatric Foundation.

_____ (1954). *The Psychiatric Interview*. New York: W. W. Norton.

Swiercinsky, D. P., Price, T. L., and Leaf, L. E. (1987). *Traumatic Head Injury*. Shawnee Mission, KS: Kansas Head Injury Association.

Szasz, T. (1961). *The Myth of Mental Illness*. New York: Harper & Row.

Thomas, L. (1983). *The Youngest Science*. New York: Viking.

Tissot. (1795). *Aviso Al Pueblo Acerca De Su Salud*. Madrid: Imprenta de Marín.

Torrey, E. H. (1969). The case for the indigenous therapist. *Archives of General Psychiatry* 20:365–373.

Trautman, E. C. (1961). The suicidal fit. *Archives of General Psychiatry* 5:98–105.

Trotter, R. T. and Chavira, J. A. (1981). *Curanderismo: Mexican American Folk Healing*. Athens, GA: University of Georgia Press.

VanNoppen, B. L., Pato, M. T., and Rasmussen, S. (1993). *Learning to Live with Obsessive Compulsive Disorder*. Milford, CT: OC Foundation.

Vasquez, C. and Javier, R. A. (1991). The problem with interpreters: communicating with Spanish-speaking patients. *Hospital and Community Psychiatry* 42:163–165.

Villa, J. (1993). *Ataques de nervios* at the Greater Bridgeport Community Mental Health Center. Unpublished paper.

Westermeyer, J. (1985). Psychiatric diagnosis across cultural boundaries. *American Journal of Psychiatry* 142:798–805.

Widiger, T. and Frances, A. (1985). The *DSM-III* personality disorders: perspective from psychology. *Archives of General Psychiatry* 42:615–623.

Will, O. (1970). Introduction to *The Psychiatric Interview* by Harry Stack Sullivan (1954), pp. iv–xxiii. New York: W. W. Norton.

Wilson, M. (1993). *DSM-III* and the transformation of American psychiatry: a history. *American Journal of Psychiatry* 150:399–410.

Winkelman, M. (1984). *A Cross-Cultural Study of Magico-Religious Practitioners*. Unpublished doctoral dissertation, University of California at Irvine.

Young, A. (1982). The anthropologies of illness and sickness. *Annual Review of Anthropology* 11:257.

Zisook, S. and Shuchter, S. R. (1991). Depression through the first year after the death of a spouse. *American Journal of Psychiatry* 148(10):1346–1352.

——— (1992). "Depression after the death of a spouse"; Reply. *American Journal of Psychiatry* 149(4):580.

CREDITS

The authors gratefully acknowledge permission to reprint material from the following sources:

From a chapter on human sexuality by Anthony Louis, to be published in a forthcoming book edited by Noel Tyl and published by Llewellyn Publications, St. Paul, Minnesota.

Adaptations from the proverb list in "Proverb Familiarity and the Mental Status Examination" by R. M. Haynes, P. J. Resnick, K. C. Dougherty, and S. E. Althof in *Bulletin of the Menninger Clinic* 57(4)523–528. Copyright © 1993 The Menninger Clinic. Used by permission of the authors and the publisher.

Quotations from *DSM-IV* and the use of the *DSM-IV* trademark are used with the kind permission of the American Psychiatric Association, Washington, DC.

INDEX